156 – Dead child restored
grist mill ?

*The Making of*
# A MORMON APOSTLE

ACEBIC ACERBIC ss

# The Making of
# A MORMON APOSTLE

## The Story of Rudger Clawson

David S. Hoopes
and
Roy Hoopes

MADISON BOOKS
Lanham • New York • London

**Library of Congress Cataloging-in-Publication Data**

Hoopes, David S.
The making of a Mormon apostle : a biography of Rudger Clawson /
David S. Hoopes and Roy H. Hoopes.
p.    cm.
Bibliography: p.
1. Clawson, Rudger.   2. Mormon Church—Apostles—Biography.
3. Church of Jesus Christ of Latter–Day Saints—Apostles—Biography.
I. Hoopes, Roy, 1922–    . II. Title.
BX8695.C32H66    1989    289.3'32'092—dc20    89–31917 CIP
[B]

ISBN 0–8191–7298–7 (alk. paper)

All Madison Books are produced on acid-free paper.
The paper used in this publication meets the minimum requirements of American
National Standard for Information Sciences—Permanence of Paper for Printed Library
Materials, ANSI Z39.48–1984.    ∞

*For Lydia Clawson Hoopes*
*who never wavered in her belief that her*
*father's story should be told*

# CONTENTS

*Thirty-six pages of photographs follow page 156.*

# ACKNOWLEDGMENTS

The principal acknowledgment must go to Lydia Clawson Hoopes, Rudger Clawson's daughter and mother of the authors. Her belief in this project continued unshaken over the years after her father's death. When she passed on, she transferred that belief to her sons as a legacy, along with the Rudger Clawson diaries and other papers.

Thanks go especially to Woodrow and Judy Marriott, who provided a grant to David Hoopes to undertake an initial project to catalogue the materials and prepare a review of Rudger Clawson's life, and to the University of Utah, which was extremely cooperative in several aspects of this project.

We also wish to express our gratitude to our sister Linda Tracy who lent her wholehearted support to the project; to cousins Marian Bond and Betty Turner; to others in the Clawson family who helped along the way; and to Cora Hoopes, who offered encouragement in various aspects of the book's development.

Special appreciation goes to Kathleen Hoopes who provided editorial support and whose contribution to the project has been immeasurable. She read every word of Rudger Clawson's diaries, taking systematic notes that were invaluable when the writing commenced. She researched background materials and critiqued, revised, and copy-edited each chapter as it progressed. Accolades also go to copy editor Linda Busetti, whose attention to detail and sharp eye helped immensely, and to Charles Lean and Jill Bradberry Keeley at Madison Books.

Very sincere thanks to Stewart L. Udall, Elma Udall, and Keith and Gwen Udall for their cordial response to our inquiries about Pearl Udall. We also wish to extend our thanks to Professor D. Michael

Quinn for his willingness to share with us as yet unpublished research on aspects of Rudger Clawson's life and to critique the manuscript.

Finally, we are grateful for the help of two skilled typists, Beverly Unsworth and Frances Ladd, the latter of whom has since become an avid reader of Mormon history.

# PREFACE

Rudger Clawson's rise in the Church of Jesus Christ of Latter-day
Saints (the Mormon Church) began when, as a young man, he
returned to Salt Lake City from Georgia with the body of his missionary companion, Joseph Standing, who had been murdered by a mob
of Georgian anti-Mormons. Later, Clawson's prosecution and trial for
polygamy was a landmark case in the federal government's judicial
crusade against the practice of plural marriage among the Mormons.
His forthright statement to the judge concerning his feelings about
religion, marriage, and the Constitution, as well as his exemplary
conduct during his three years in prison, gained him the respect of
church leaders. His release from jail was followed by his appointment
to the presidency of the Box Elder Stake in Brigham City and later his
elevation to the ruling body of the church, the Quorum of the Twelve
Apostles. Early in the twentieth century, when he headed the Latter-
day Saint mission to Europe, he was attacked and stoned by English
anti-Mormon mobs. Ultimately he became President of the Quorum
of the Twelve. He would have succeeded to the presidency of the
church had he not been outlived by President Heber J. Grant.

At the time of his death in 1943, he left an extensive collection of
his papers—including diaries covering eighteen important years of his
life, memoirs, letters, speeches, blessings, and other papers and
memorabilia—to his daughter, Lydia Clawson Hoopes. In his later
years he had discussed with her frequently his desire for her to write
his biography. Lydia was a professional writer, who, for many years,
was a Washington social correspondent for the *Deseret News* and
subsequently the *Salt Lake Tribune*. She also published a number of
articles and short stories.

Lydia considered writing either a biography of her father or a novel based on his eventful life. However, the project proved to be too large for her and at the time of her death in 1980, the biography was still unwritten. Nevertheless, she had taken voluminous notes which included many valuable autobiographical fragments which shed light on the life of her mother and father.

The Rudger Clawson papers were inherited by Lydia's three children—Roy, David, and her daughter, Linda Hoopes Tracy. In countless conversations prior to her death, Lydia made two things clear— that she wanted her children to use the papers to write her father's biography and that she wished the papers eventually to be placed in a library where they would be readily accessible to scholars and researchers. Immensely proud of her father and aware that he was a significant figure in the history of the American West, she was particularly concerned that the papers not be given to the church archives where access to them might be restricted. Her children agreed.

By 1977, David had become interested in exploring the potential of the Clawson papers. With a grant from the Woodrow Marriott family, he and his wife, Kathleen, undertook to catalogue the collection and prepare a seventy-one page review of Rudger Clawson's life. David then wrote a chapter of a prospective biography and sought (in vain) to find a publisher or obtain funding that would enable him to work further on the book. Later Roy and David decided to share the burden of writing it, but still could not generate the money that would sustain them financially while they did the work. The solution came from the University of Utah, which expressed an interest in buying the papers for its extensive collection of Western Americana (which includes a substantial collection of papers of Hiram Bradley Clawson, Rudger's father).

Rudger's papers are now housed in the University's J. Willard Marriott Library—an appropriate resting place, since J. Willard Marriott and his wife Alice were close friends of the authors' parents in the 1920s, both having come east to Washington at about the same time and having lived, for a while, in the same apartment building in Washington's Foggy Bottom where the U.S. State Department now stands. The University provided the funds needed to get the writing under way.

The book was finally produced by Roy, David, and David's wife, Kathleen. A publisher was found, and the story as drawn from Rudger

Clawson's papers unfolds in the following pages—with one exception. All their lives the children of Rudger and Lydia Clawson believed that their father had had only two wives, one of whom divorced him while he was in the penitentiary. It was Kathleen who first found reference in the diaries to another woman, someone with whom he clearly had an intense relationship later in his life, but whom he did not identify. He also did not reveal the outcome of the relationship. At first called by the authors "the mystery woman," she was ultimately identified by Mormon historian, D. Michael Quinn (an identification later confirmed by members of her own family) as Pearl Udall, daughter of the Arizona pioneer and Mormon leader, David K. Udall. It was also determined that Rudger and Pearl were secretly married in polygamy against both government law and church policy at the time. Thus, the Clawsons of Utah and the Udalls of Arizona, two prominent pioneer families, were united by celestial marriage. It was a marriage kept secret for seventy years and only discovered in the last stages of researching and writing this book.

The process of co-authoring the book was not as easy as had been hoped. David and Kathleen live in Vermont; Roy, near Washington, D.C. Chapters were shuttled back and forth in what seemed like a two-man effort to keep UPS solvent. Trips were made to Georgia, Utah, and England; and research was conducted on a much broader range of subjects than was anticipated. A great deal of effort—far more than had been imagined—went into integrating the writing styles of the two authors.

The resulting work is not a biography in the fullest sense. The story of Rudger Clawson essentially ends here after his return from Europe in 1913 at the age of fifty-six. The last thirty years of his life are covered in the Epilogue.

One reason for this is that most of the more dramatic events in Rudger Clawson's life were over by 1913. There is evidence that in 1935, when he compiled his memoirs, he himself considered his later years as less notable, since his memoirs end with his return from Europe. Another is that Rudger Clawson did not maintain a diary or record the story of his later life. A substantive account could only be told if one had access to the church archives and to the diaries of such men as Heber J. Grant and Joseph F. Smith.

A request was made to the church in December, 1988, for permission to conduct research at the church archives and to be allowed access to the diaries of Rudger Clawson's associates in the church administration. No reply was received until March 1989, and then the authors were told that most of the archival materials they needed would be restricted. Further, some of the diaries they wished to see might be available, but those of a number of church leaders, including Heber J. Grant and Joseph F. Smith, would definitely not be. It was also determined that the church requires that anyone researching restricted materials at the archives must sign an agreement to submit to church authorities for approval that part of any writing which uses a quotation from the archival materials of more than a phrase or line. If the use of the quotation is disapproved and is published anyway the researcher will never be allowed to conduct research in the archives again. The authors found this restriction unacceptable. They also were frustrated in their attempt to pursue research at Brigham Young University's Harold B. Lee Library, where they were informed that the library had no resources not available at the church archives.

It should be noted that the authors were on all occasions treated courteously and with respect by church personnel.

Perhaps an official or definitive biography of Rudger Clawson will someday be written (though we were surprised at how few substantive biographies have been written about major figures in the middle era of church history) and perhaps it will tell in more detail the story of Rudger Clawson's later years. For now, we are happy to be able to recount what happened to him during the years in which, one after another, he was caught up in dramatic events which affected not only his own life but also the history of his people. We do not, however, go extensively into the historical background of Mormonism. For those unfamiliar with its history, *The Mormon Experience: A History of the Latterday Saints* (New York: Random House, 1979) by Leonard Arrington and Davis Bitton, is recommended.

Rudger Clawson was in some ways a quintessential Mormon of his time. It was an era of consolidation in Utah, of defending the faith in the nation, and of spreading the gospel abroad. Rudger was an active, prominent, and effective participant in each of these. More importantly, he was a man of dogged loyalty and unswerving conviction. He was literal-minded in his beliefs and defended them fiercely against the "enemy." He devoted himself to his church selflessly, even to the detriment of his personal life. He was also a man of courage who was called upon time and again to stand on his principles and defend his faith.

The authors do not share that faith, but they do share a feeling with many others that Rudger Clawson's story is one that should be told.

David S. Hoopes, Vershire, Vt.
Roy Hoopes, Bethesda, Md.

# CHRONOLOGY
## of the Life of Rudger Clawson

| | |
|---|---|
| March 12, 1857 | - Born in Salt Lake City to Hiram Bradley and Margaret Gay Clawson |
| October 3, 1868 | - Baptized in Salt Lake City |
| June 23, 1873 | - Received endowments in Salt Lake City |
| April 9, 1879 | - Called to fill a mission to the southern States |
| July 21, 1879 | - Companion, Elder Joseph Standing, murdered by a mob in Georgia |
| August 12, 1882 | - Married Florence Ann Dinwoodey |
| | Children: Rudger Elmo |
| March 29, 1883 | - Married Lydia Elizabeth Spencer |
| | Children: Rudger Remus, Hiram Bradley, Margaret Gay, Daniel Spencer, Vera Mary, Samuel George, Lorenzo Snow, Francis Marion, Lydia |
| November 4, 1884 | - Convicted of polygamy in Federal court |
| December 13, 1887 | - Released from Utah Territorial Penitentiary (term: three years, one month and ten days) |
| February 5, 1888 | - Set apart as President of Box Elder Stake |
| February 12, 1888 | - Ordained a high priest by Lorenzo Snow |
| October 10, 1898 | - Ordained an apostle and member of the Quorum of the Twelve |
| October 6, 1901 | - Sustained as a second counselor in the First Presidency of Lorenzo Snow |
| October 17, 1901 | - Dropped as counselor in the First Presidency |
| August 3, 1904 | - Married Pearl Udall |
| November 18, 1904 | - Death of Rudger Remus |
| April 7, 1910 | - Called to preside over the European Mission |
| November 17, 1912 | - Mobbed in Bristol |
| April 15, 1913 | - Released from duties in Europe |
| November 23, 1918 | - Sustained as acting president of the Council of the Twelve |
| March 10, 1921 | - Sustained as president of the Council of the Twelve and set apart by President Heber J. Grant |
| February 1, 1941 | - Death of Lydia |
| June 21, 1943 | - Death of Rudger |

# CHAPTER 1
# THE MURDER

$E$ arly one morning in May 1879, Rudger Clawson, the twenty-two year-old future hero, polygamist, convict, and Mormon apostle, sat in a small railroad station in Varnell, Georgia, struggling vainly to put on his ill-fitting boots. As he pulled at the stiff leather he remembered the day he had gone down to Z.C.M.I., a department store in Salt Lake City, to buy them. It was only appropriate that someone about to leave on a mission to do the work of the Lord should be sturdily shod.

But how had he gotten the wrong size? And why hadn't he tried them on before leaving? For a few minutes longer he yanked and pulled at them, jamming his feet as far in as he could and then stomping on the floor until the station master glanced up at him in disapproval. One boot was still not fully on when he finally stood and asked the station master to direct him to the road to Ludville in Pickens County.

The man pointed out the window toward a road leading east into the rising morning sun. In a thick southern accent, he also said something about "Holly Creek" and "Ella Jay."

Without further inquiry, Rudger hobbled out and set off on his search for Joseph Standing.

He remembered the day only a few short weeks before in Salt Lake

1

when the train of events that had brought him to this point had been set in motion. He had been attending General Conference, an annual meeting of the Church of Jesus Christ of Latter-day Saints. It included church leaders and as many members as could crowd into the great tabernacle on Temple Square and was used to conduct church business, review the progress they had made in building Zion, and exhort the faithful to greater diligence. Rudger felt comfortable there, very much at home and, indeed, moved. Though he was a lively young man who enjoyed parties, girls, and dancing, he was deeply religious and appreciated the ceremonies in which his religion was embodied.

It was customary at the conference for the president of the church or one of his counselors to read out the names of newly designated missionaries—frequently without having given them notice. When George Q. Cannon, church president John Taylor's first counselor, began to call the roster of new missionaries, Rudger may not have been listening closely. After all, it was April. The sun was shining and spring was in the brisk air. A young man might be forgiven if his thoughts were elsewhere than on the droning recitation of names drifting from the rostrum. Fifty-eight were read before his came up. He was startled when he heard it.

"I remember it now very distinctly," he wrote in his memoirs. "How could I forget it? I was sitting there quietly when I heard my name called out for a mission to the Southern States. You can very well believe that this was like a bolt from a clear sky. It nearly took me off my feet—it *would* have taken me off my feet had I been standing, but fortunately I was sitting."

He also "knew very well that it would not be safe for me to reject a call from the Prophet of God. . . ." Missionary calls came directly from the president of the church who, according to the beliefs of the Latter-day Saints, was a prophet. "So I interpreted this call to mean that it was from the Lord and that I was to go upon the Lord's errand." Besides, the son of Hiram Bradley Clawson could hardly refuse. Hiram was a prominent business man in Utah. He had been one of Brigham Young's closest associates prior to Brigham's death in 1877 and had taken two of Brigham's daughters as wives.

Now, barely a month later, here Rudger was limping down a sandy road under a ferocious Georgia sun on the Lord's errand—to preach the gospel and bring the world to the true faith of the Church of Jesus

Christ of Latter-day Saints. Yet what a sight he was: "I was a cripple hobbling along through the hot sand and the heat, with a knapsack over one shoulder containing literature and a knapsack over the other shoulder containing personal supplies [Actually the knapsacks were saddlebags.] . . . People looked at me as I passed along and wondered, and then at times I looked at myself and wondered too."

He passed corn and wheat fields where pallid green shoots poked up sparsely and erratically from the overworked soil. Here and there someone, man or woman, black or white, walked slowly behind a mule-drawn plow. The farmhouses were small, sometimes little more than shacks, and the people he saw wore ragged clothes and looked poor. When they turned to watch him limp down the road, their faces were expressionless.

He had not seen much of Varnell. It seemed to be little more than a collection of small frame houses clustered around the railroad station. There was nothing particularly forbidding about it, nothing to warn him of the tragedy that lay quietly in wait for him in the piney woods north of the town. A large coaling platform just south of the station indicated that Varnell served as a fueling stop for the trains which plied north and south, one of which had deposited him there an hour or so before.

He had spent long days and nights jolting across the continent in railroad cars. He knew in the stiffness of his joints and the soreness of his rear how vast this country was and how promethean the task that lay before the Lord and his Saints. He was happy that his small "errand" would contribute to its accomplishment.

His friends, other missionaries, had dropped off along the way or gone on to the headquarters of the Southern States Mission in Rome, Georgia. Only he had disembarked at Varnell, the starting point in his quest for his assigned companion, Joseph Standing.

Joseph was a true laborer in the Lord's vineyard—though that may not be just the right image for an abstemious Mormon—and was admired and loved by John Morgan, president of the Southern States Mission. Joseph had worked with Morgan in Illinois and Indiana during his first two-year mission. When he decided to stay in the field for another two years, he followed Morgan south. That had been sixteen months ago, and now he was the presiding elder for all of Georgia.

Currently Joseph was working in Pickens County which lay some seventy miles to the east and south of Varnell. Rudger was not certain just where Joseph would be, but he had been assured that inquiries at Ludville, the Pickens county seat, would bring him quickly to his fated companion.

Finally, he could stand it no longer. Stopping, he sat beside the road on a bank of almost blindingly red clay and, dropping his knapsacks, began to struggle with the boots. When he had them off, he tied them together, threw them over his shoulder and continued on barefoot.

Although the dirt and sand were hot and rough against his tender soles, the relief was so overwhelming that he continued on unshod despite what was happening to his image as the Lord's messenger. "You will readily see that as a minister of the gospel I made a sorry spectacle indeed."

Actually, Rudger, despite his lack of shoes, did not make a sorry spectacle. He was a well-groomed young man of twenty-two years, inclined to stiff white shirts and neat bow ties. Even on his exhausting trek through Georgia back country, he wore a stylish jacket and a neatly buttoned vest. His sandy hair was properly combed and parted and grew at just the right fullness around the sides. He had a high forehead, smooth skin, and a youthful face with a moustache which was already full and which in later years would grow to walrus proportions. He was short, perhaps 5' 7" or 8", but he did not seem small.

Later, during the murder trial, the *Atlanta Constitution* would describe him as

> an intelligent looking blonde, with clean cut rather handsome features, and bright blue eyes. He wore what college girls would call a "lovely" moustache. When he smiled . . . he displayed white and perfectly formed teeth. His hands are small and symmetrically shaped and [the writer went on to note with dubious relevance, but of interest here] he appeared to wear No. 6 boots.

Soon the road, after crossing a rather lazy-looking stream, began to climb gently to a valley leading into the hills. Then it followed the twists of the stream, which flowed toward him and became bubbly as the incline steepened. Rudger sat on a rock and let his feet dangle in the cool, soothing water. He remembered the station master's directions. Was this Holly Creek?

It was, and the road he was traveling was in the heart of Cherokee country, the fertile plains and mountains of northern Georgia from which the Cherokees had been herded in 1838 to make room for land-hungry Georgians and Tennesseans. It was still haunted by Cherokee spirits, however, and superstitious people conducted their lives by the phases of the moon. DeSoto had been here searching for the Fountain of Youth. A few miles up in the hills from where Rudger was walking, he had built a fort—or so the story went—to protect his band against marauding Indians.

The Civil War had devastated the northwest corner of Georgia, where troops marched back and forth through the gaps in Missionary Ridge and Lookout Mountain, south and east of Chattanooga, Tennessee, and engaged in bloody battles, culminating in the Battle of Chickamauga and Sherman's drive from Dalton to Atlanta. The devastation had not reached as far as these hills, though Reconstruction had. The Ku Klux Klan was active throughout the area and, even in 1879, a noose hanging from the thick limb of a black walnut or oak tree in the morning sometimes signalled the meaning of a night's clamor of hoofbeats and voices.

The woods Rudger walked through now were thick with oak, hickory, and black cherry, sweet gum, beech, and chestnut trees. Big willows drooped over the stream while the brush along the road was twined with honeysuckle. In places the trees were draped thickly with vines, while elsewhere the soil was thin and little grew but scrub oak that reminded Rudger of the Wasatch foothills around Salt Lake.

Noontime came and with it hunger. He had had little to eat before getting off the train and nothing since. For some time he had been ignoring the pangs which struck him at midmorning. He knew what lay ahead. Mormon missionaries traveled "without purse or scrip"—a practice on which John Morgan placed great emphasis—so that he would have to approach a house and ask for food. It was an idea he found quite repugnant: "I espied a rather unpretentious home nearby and concluded to present myself at the door and ask for a meal of victuals, something I had never done in all my previous life. I shrank at the idea. I felt embarrassed. I felt humiliated. It seemed to me I would be acting the role of a beggar."

He consoled himself, however, by recalling the scriptual dictum: The laborer is worthy of his hire. "And upon further reflection, I readily perceived that the true gospel of Jesus Christ, involving the principle of salvation, which I was authorized to offer the woman, more than offset the value of the food given a thousand times. Thus reassuring myself, I felt perfectly justified in boldly asking for something to eat."

But he still had the problem of his boots. He felt that his approach would hardly be successful if he had to stand before his benefactor in bare feet. So with a "superhuman effort to get the boots back on," which was only partially successful, he "hobbled up to the door and knocked. A lady answered and said, "Who are you and what do you want?"

"I am a minister of the gospel," he answered, "and would you be kind enough to furnish me with some food?"

Much to his surprise she said, "Yes, come in."

When he had finished eating and was about to leave, Rudger offered his hostess the gospel, but to no avail. "I told her in a few words that I was a 'Mormon' missionary traveling through the country preaching the true gospel of Jesus Christ, which would be of far more worth to her than anything she had to give in return. 'And will you receive it,' " I asked.

She answered, "No, I will not."

So much for Rudger Clawson's first foray into converting northern Georgia to Mormonism. More rebuffs were to come before he was crowned with any successes.

From the woman, he confirmed the fact that he was on Holly Creek Road and that the Ella Jay referred to by the station master was not a woman he might expect to meet along the way (the idea of which rather intrigued him despite the seriousness of his "errand") but was instead the town of Ellijay on the other side of the mountains, approximately fifteen miles away. Ludville and Pickens County were some distance beyond that.

So Rudger started off, refreshed if also somewhat daunted at the long trek ahead under the withering afternoon sun.

In Salt Lake City, May was a beautiful month with the broad valley turning green and blossoming under the cultivation of the Saints. The air during the day was warm, though the breezes coming down from the mountains still blew wintry from time to time. The air was dry and the evenings were cool.

As he trudged along, these memories provided some surcease from the rigors of his journey, but not much. If the heat was unbearable now, what would it be like when summer really came? The sun seemed merciless and the humid air enveloped him in a clammy embrace. His feet were sore and became worse with every step. They were the feet of a city boy, too tender to take much more of this Georgia gravel (no longer was he willing to call it "sand").

He had also, inescapably, become disheveled. His clothes had been loosened to let out the heat or were simply askew, his hair was limp and hanging awry, his trousers were thickly coated with dust. By the time he turned the last bend (having given up hope that this would in fact be the last bend because there had been so many of them) and descended from the mountains, he was shuffling along in a state of utter weariness, his shoulders ached from the knapsacks as much as his feet and legs ached from the road. Arriving in Ellijay, where crowds of people stood casually around a large brick building in the middle of the town square, many staring at him in open curiosity and surprise, he must, at last, have appeared something of a spectacle.

He wondered why so many people were loitering about. They were mostly men, well dressed in suits, clean white shirts and Sunday hats and shoes—obviously not town idlers. Nicely attired women occasionally entered or left the building's entrance.

Ringing the building was a low wall of thick stones where men sat or stood with their legs propped up smoking and talking or simply watching the weary, barefoot stranger walk into town.

Rudger made no attempt to avoid their stares. He could think of nothing but resting his tired body. He could go no further. It was late in the day and he was hungry again. He would need directions and would probably have to find lodging for the night. Spying an open place to sit on one of the stones, he approached and lowered himself with a groan, throwing off his knapsacks and the boots he still had slung over his shoulder. Soon, however, he was surrounded by curious people who gazed at him in wonderment. "They were mystified. It seemed to be a question with them as to whether I had come along the highway or had dropped from the sky."

One of the men finally asked where he was from. They whistled

and looked at each other when he told them he had walked from
Varnell that day. In his weariness he had no thought of preaching the
gospel now, but when they found out he was a Mormon missionary,
they took the decision out of his hands. Gathering closer, they began
peppering him with questions.

He could not be expected to know, of course, that he had ventured
into a land where religious disputation was a way of life. The evangelical Christian sects wrangled continuously with each other over varia-
tions in doctrine and scriptural interpretation. Some years before, the
conflict had come to a head when James Madison Ellis, a fiery,
Primitive Baptist who preached hellfire and damnation, challenged
Charles Jones, an equally fiery minister of the Church of Christ, to a
public debate right there in Ellijay. The debate went on for days before
Ellis was judged the loser and Baptist churches in the area began
closing down right and left.

Arguing religion was a form of entertainment among Ellijayans and
they engaged this young Mormon with relish. It was a heated debate
in which Rudger felt he held his own, matching them argument for
argument, doctrine for doctrine, scriptural quotation for scriptural
quotation.

Later, what he remembered most was a little man sitting on the
wall near him: ". . . if I quoted a passage of scripture, which I did
occasionally, the crowd contradicted me and said, 'No, that is not in
the Bible,' or 'You have not quoted it correctly,' but invariably a small
man in the crowd—smaller than I am, so you must know he was quite
small—stood up and said: 'The gentleman is correct.' That is, if I
quoted the scripture correctly, which I did. Then when I disputed
with them after some of their number had quoted the scriptures
incorrectly, and would say, 'You have quoted the scripture incorrectly,'
. . . the little man would step forward and say, 'The gentleman is
correct.' "

Even when they got to polygamy and the level of belligerency
among the Georgians rose, the man stood by him. Rudger demolished
them on the Old Testament, in which polygamy was more or less
rampant, and even forced them to concede that Jesus himself wasn't
very specific on the issue. But they stood their ground with the Apostle
Paul. "He absolutely condemned it," insisted one of the disputants.

"He did not," Rudger replied.

"He did."

"Quote the passage."

"Paul the Apostle said a bishop shall be the husband of but one wife," said the man.

"You have quoted the passage incorrectly."

"I have not."

"You have."

"Quote the passage," the man said pugnaciously.

"Paul the Apostle said that 'a bishop shall be the husband of one wife,' [meaning] at least one [wife] . . . You have introduced that little word 'but,' " said Rudger. "It is not there."

"It is."

Then Rudger's little friend stood up and said: "It is not there. The gentleman is correct."

When the crowd dispersed, Rudger turned to the man who had defended him and who seemed in such complete agreement with the doctrines of the Latter-day Saints. "How is it you defend me?" he asked. "I am a 'Mormon.' I am unpopular and yet you have stood by me like a man."

"Well," the little man replied, "I like to see fair play. When these men quoted the scriptures correctly I was willing to say so. When they quoted them incorrectly I was willing to say so. That was my attitude in your case."

Rudger grew excited, seeing a convert behind the man's phlegmatic manner. In retrospect he realized that his own behavior was "singular." But at the moment he saw the Lord favoring him with the opportunity to make his first conversion. Eagerly he plunged ahead, not hearing in the little man's voice the note of pride in simply being an impartial judge.

"I was only twenty-two years of age," Rudger wrote later in good-humored self-exculpation, "just like many of these boys that are going [on mission] today, perhaps a little greener."

So he said, "What hinders? Come down to the stream and be baptized." Walking into town he had passed a gentle little stream with a nice shallow pool which even in his weariness he had recognized as a choice spot for a baptism.

The man was puzzled. "What do you mean?" he asked.

"You have been defending a servant of God, you are entitled to the blessing. . . . Come down and I will baptize you."

Now the man was indignant. "But I do not want your baptism. I do not believe in your religion. I do not want it."

Rudger was taken aback.

While he was recovering, the little man left, and Rudger was approached by a man closer to his own size and somewhat more distinguished looking. He introduced himself as Dr. William Young and invited the youthful missionary to his office to rest and chat.

Young was particularly interested in Utah and asked Rudger a series of questions about the territory: how many people were there, what was the climate like and the health conditions, how did the people live, were they prosperous? Finally he got to the point: were there openings for professional men in Utah?

Rudger was annoyed. "He was looking for the dollars. I did not give him much encouragement to come out to Utah for the purpose of making money. That was not my business." Rudger and the other Mormon missionaries of the time were seeking believers to send to Utah to join in the building of Zion. Hungry gentile professionals did not fit into the scheme. Salt Lake already had enough non-Mormons.

Nevertheless they chatted amiably for a long time, the doctor querying him extensively about his beliefs and his missionary aims.

Finally he said grandly, "You are here to preach the gospel then? That is your business is it not? Well, I have an idea, my boy."

His idea was that Rudger speak to an assemblage of ladies and gentlemen in town for court. It seems that Ellijay was the local county seat and Rudger's arrival coincided with a session of the circuit court— which explained why all the people were gathered in the square around what was no doubt the courthouse.

"In the Southern states the people do not go to the court, the court comes to the people," the doctor said somewhat pompously. (It would not be long before Rudger would have his own version of how the courts in northern Georgia worked.)

"If I can get the courtroom for tonight, will you be the speaker?"

Terror struck the young missionary: "This was a moment of great perturbation for me. I trembled in my boots [which was quite a feat in those boots!]. My knees knocked together." Though he could hardly refuse such a chance, his "yes" came out no more than a whisper.

They went in search of the sheriff to get permission. Rudger was delighted to see that the sheriff was a large and courageous-looking man who would certainly be a match for the more diminutive physician. When informed that the doctor wanted to engage the courtroom for a Mormon missionary to preach, the sheriff exploded, "I will be damned if he is."

"I tell you he is," Dr. Young shouted back.

"No, he is not." The sheriff seemed adamant, and Rudger silently cheered him on. "I said (to myself), 'Go it, sheriff, go it.'" Unfortunately, the intrepid physician "spunked up to the sheriff and browbeat him until he 'threw up the sponge' and left the field to the doctor and myself." Rudger was stuck.

At the appointed hour, the judge and the lawyers—and their "ladies"—along with other townspeople filled the room to capacity. "That large audience," wrote Rudger, "was a sight such as would intimidate a 'hardened' preacher. . . ."

Uncertain how to begin, the first thing he did was apologize for not being able to sing. Preaching, singing, and proselytizing were fused together in evangelical America, and Rudger felt himself at a disadvantage. Instead of singing, he awkwardly read a number of hymns and then launched into his sermon, until he was interrupted by a man who called out from the audience.

"Look here young man, that may be very good, what you are saying . . . but it is not altogether what we want to hear."

"Oh," said Rudger, with a kind of naivete he would exhibit all his life, "What do you want to hear?"

"We want to hear something about polygamy."

So there it was, "polygamy," the inescapable issue that would plague the Mormon church and Rudger Clawson down through the years, the practice that Joseph Smith had secretly introduced and that, during the time of Brigham Young and his apostles, had become woven inextricably into the weft of Mormon theology and social life. It was an important belief for the Saints, especially for the hierarchy, its principal practitioners, but it was not the whole of Mormonism. Yet the rest of Christian society found it either so monstrous or so lasciviously fascinating that they could see nothing else. Mormonism meant polygamy. The two were equated and the fury and innuendo which followed prevented the Mormons from being recognized as anything other than strange folk who must be called upon continuously to explain their peculiar practice.

Rudger was caught off guard, though it is hard to explain why since he had surely dealt with the question before and had, in fact, encountered it only an hour or two earlier that day. But he was.

He said that he had grown up in a polygamous family and that his mother was a plural wife.

"I can tell you something about polygamy if you want to hear it," he concluded.

"We do," said the man—whereupon "those grand society ladies who were occupying the first seats, all with one accord rose to their feet and made for the door. . . ."

Poor Rudger. It must have been planned.

He called out: "Ladies, ladies, just a moment. Do not go. . . . I won't say anything to offend the most delicate ear. Whereupon they went faster than ever and fairly swept out of the room, and fairly swept me off the rostrum."

Somewhat shaken and very annoyed Rudger said to the man who had asked the question, "You want to hear something about polygamy, do you?" and proceeded to launch into a long and vigorous theological and moral justification, ending with a peroration—his "testimony"—on plural marriage, which, he said, "if practiced in righteousness, tends to morality and to a good life and a pure one, much more so, perhaps than monogamy."

Little there either to offend female sensibilities or titillate the licentious male mind.

"I am quite sure I did not tell him what he wanted to hear," wrote Rudger of his questioner, "but I did tell him what *I* wanted him to hear." It must be assumed that the congregation left disappointed.

So ended the first day of Rudger Clawson's brief mission to northern Georgia.

Presumably Dr. Young arranged lodging for him; it was the least he could do for the young man he had so obviously set up. (In Ellijay the good Dr. Young was last heard of heading for Texas—no doubt in search of the professional dollar in more fertile territory than he perceived the land of the ardent Saints to be.)

\*   \*   \*

Rudger left Ellijay the next morning and found Joseph Standing working in Pickens County. Joseph was an intense young man, somewhat taller and stockier than Rudger. His nose was a little too large for his face, and thick, pouty lips turned down at the corners, combined with dark, narrow eyes, gave him a perpetually worried look. He too dressed well, except that his clothes were always somewhat baggy. His most handsome feature was a head of thick, wavy brown hair.

Joseph had been in the field a long time. He had been sent from Salt Lake in February 1876, to join John Morgan, a dedicated convert who was working in Indiana and Illinois where he hoped, as part of his mission, to convert his own family. Joseph was also a convert and went to Canada the following summer to try to convert *his* relatives. Both were unsuccessful.

In the fall of that year, Morgan left to undertake the formal organization of the Southern States Mission. Joseph stayed in the north and then returned to Utah until he joined his friend in Georgia in February 1878. The records do not make clear precisely what, other than zeal and dedication, motivated Joseph to return to missionary work. The normal length of a mission was two years. He was personally very close to John Morgan, however, and must have been inspired by the story of an experience Morgan had when he arrived in Georgia. It was an experience which proved to Morgan, as it must have to Joseph, that not only was he doing God's work but that he was, in fact, the direct instrument of God's will.

Morgan, who had been color sergeant in the 123rd Illinois Mounted Infantry Regiment during the Civil War, traveled southward through areas of Kentucky, Tennessee, and Georgia over which northern and southern armies had fought ferociously and through which he had passed as a soldier. The signs of devastation were still apparent: shattered trees, desolate fields, deserted towns where chimneys stood starkly over the charred ruins of Southern homes.

He had stopped in a small community near Rome (inauspiciously called Dirt Town) and had begun to prepare for his work. Shortly thereafter he set out for Rome to call his first meeting of the small group of Saints who lived there, but along the way he became quite distracted by the fact that the very road on which he was walking was one over which he had marched as a Union soldier.

His mind drifted back until suddenly he was brought out of his reverie by a fork in the road, or more precisely by the memory of a dream he had had in Utah ten years before (prior to his conversion) in which he had arrived on foot at this same fork, only in the dream Brigham Young had appeared before him. The prophet had told him that the right fork led to Rome, but that if he took the left fork he would have an experience which would prove conclusively the truth of the gospel as preached by the Latter-day Saints.

John Morgan was no man to miss a message as clear as that. Now, back on the real road in Georgia, he followed the left fork until he came to a small community located in a lovely valley swathed in autumn colors. When he asked the name of the place he was startled to learn it was "Haywood Valley." At the time of the dream in Salt Lake he had been living with the bishop of the Seventeenth Ward, Brother Joseph Heywood!

He stopped at the first house he came to, announced who he was, and was cordially invited to dinner and to remain overnight. He engaged the family in an extensive discussion of the Mormon Gospel and its scriptural basis and at one point, late in the evening, the man of the house brought out his Bible and showed where most of the passages referred to by Morgan had already been marked. He said that about ten days before, another pleasant, nicely dressed young man had visited them, marked the passages and told them that in a short time another man would come to interpret them and "show the way for this life and eternity."

Morgan decided then and there to postpone his visit to Rome and concentrate his efforts on Haywood Valley, where he found that almost every home in the valley had had the same experience.

When Morgan told Joseph Standing about it, he said that he believed the stranger who had visited the homes was one of the Three Nephites who in the Book of Mormon had been blessed by Jesus and protected from death until His second coming. And "they shall minister unto all the scattered tribes of Israel, and unto all nations. . . ." said the Book of Mormon, and "great and marvelous works shall be wrought by them. . . ." It was a sign, Morgan believed, of the kind so often demanded by unbelievers but only manifested to those who had faith.

By the time Joseph arrived in Georgia, Morgan had not only

converted every family in Haywood Valley which had been visited by the stranger but had also organized the emigration of most of them, along with other converts from the Southern states, to Colorado.

It was when Morgan returned from the west—to begin his third two-year stint in the field—that Joseph joined him. Morgan had brought nine new missionaries with him and trunks full of literature. But Joseph was his strong right hand and once again they worked side by side, walking the roads, wading the streams, knocking on doors and organizing meetings. When their literature was exhausted, Morgan, with characteristic energy, decided to write his own tract. The result was the *Plan of Salvation*, a concise twenty-two-page booklet outlining Mormon belief, first published in June 1878.

The *Plan of Salvation*, which eventually was adopted as the standard tract for Mormon missionary work and was distributed in millions of copies throughout the world, galvanized the Southern mission, creating a sense of unity and interdependence which was not always easy to achieve given the distances involved.

The accomplishments of John Morgan were not without their price, especially in intensifying the hostility the local population already felt against the Mormons. The antipathy among Methodist and Baptist preachers was almost fanatical. They preached incessantly against the missionaries from the pulpit and peppered the newspapers with articles and letters "exposing" Mormonism. While the missionaries were helped in some degree by the curiosity stimulated by these diatribes, they were also subjected more frequently to threats of violence, and the number of direct attacks increased. Rowdy mobs gathered to drive elders out of town when they appeared and regularly disrupted their meetings, and the Ku Klux Klan posted notices—a number of which were directed expressly at John Morgan—threatening their lives.

It was into this atmosphere that Rudger Clawson walked on a hot May morning in 1879.

Joseph Standing had not had a companion for some time. Since Mormon missionaries always travel in pairs, Rudger was probably assigned to work with him to meet that requirement. John Morgan was in Utah at the time, having finally left the missionary field to return to his family. Rudger might well have been "set apart" (formally appointed and blessed) by Morgan and no doubt thoroughly briefed on conditions in the Southern States Mission as well. Morgan would also have told Rudger and his seven new fellow appointees to the South what kind of missionary elders he expected them to be—

> Elders who feel the responsibility [Morgan's biographer wrote] of their high and holy calling; Elders who come out not simply to fill a Mission, but to preach the Gospel, and who go as they were commanded to go as of old, without purse or scrip; who will not hesitate to climb mountains, cross rivers, walk wearisome journeys, go hungry and poorly clad; endure scorn and contempt, but who will, in addition, sound the Gospel, trump loud and long, with force, power, and authority, to the convincing of the honest in heart.

Finally, Morgan would have provided them with the *Plan of Salvation*, a supply of "missionary calling cards" (which he himself had introduced into missionary work and which had the elder's name on one side and the Articles of Faith (thirteen fundamental Mormon beliefs) on the other and a specific list of essentials to take with them:

> A large heavy double soled pair of boots or shoes, of the best leather, three colored shirts, same amount of underclothing, half dozen colored linen collars and a pair of old-fashioned saddle pockets to carry the complement in; a copy of the Bible, Book of Mormon, Hymn Book, Voice of Warning, Spencer's Letters, Key to Theology, Answers to Questions and the Pratt-Newman Debate on Plural Marriage. With these and the Spirit of God, he can travel anywhere and answer any and all questions. . . . Stout heavy clothing of our home manufacture would be much better than the ready made clothing imported from the east. All these things are helps that increase our ability to do good.

It is doubtful that Joseph wasted any time in putting the younger man to work. And Rudger was ready, having shown his mettle on his hike from Varnell. Together they plunged into their labors in the northern Georgia counties to which Joseph had been assigned—Pickens, Fannin, Murray, Gilmore, of which Ellijay was the county seat, Whitfield, where Varnell was located, and Catoosa, site of the Battle of Chickamauga. Not only was this area felt to be fertile ground for proselytizing, it was also in the hills of rural Georgia where the missionaries could not easily be reached by "Yellow Jack" fever. This was a debilitating malarial disease which each summer swept the coastal lowlands and urban centers of the deep South and ravaged the poor. Missionaries kept to the high country during the hot weather—

as did Southerners who could afford retreating to resorts like Catoosa Springs, a watering place from which Rudger would later send his message of death back to Salt Lake.

They were up early, on the road or making calls, organizing meetings, or ministering to the needs of converts. They preached, baptized new converts and members' children when, according to the dictates of the Mormon doctrine, they were eight or nine years old, and established branches of the church wherever there were ten or twelve Saints close enough together to enable them to gather easily. They traveled as their mentor insisted, without purse or scrip, depending on the beneficence of Saints and strangers alike for food and lodging. In return they helped with the farmwork or chores, chopped wood or washed dishes, harvested crops, and dispensed the gospel to grateful recipients who had not been visited by an elder for months, sometimes years.

They arranged meetings where and when they could, in schools, in courthouses, in the homes or yards of the faithful, in clearings in the woods or out in the open fields. Occasionally a church was offered, though often as not the offer would be withdrawn by a higher authority and they would have to move outside, no matter what the weather.

They walked everywhere they went and came to know the country well. While this area did not show the physical ravages of the war evident in much of the rest of the Southern States Mission, the economic, social and psychological impact had been just as severe. Farms had been left untended during the war and drought had hindered their recovery. Industry was only beginning to revive, but the economy was depressed. The market for whatever they produced was thin and hard to get to. Wages were twenty-five to fifty cents a day and taxes were high. Personal property taxes were so onerous that people who did own possessions had little of their income left after paying the taxes on them. For many people the hellfire and damnation theologies of the traditional churches did not meet their needs. The Mormons often attracted large crowds of the curious and the desperately poor looking for something more.

Thus, despite the anti-Mormonism they encountered everywhere, the missionaries were struck by the cordiality and hospitality of the people. They were usually poor, but they were willing to share their homes and food with the elders whether they were interested in the gospel or not and often at the risk of the rather vocal displeasure of their fellow Georgians.

"The people are willing," the elders often said to each other. But even so, the number of converts was small. In August 1878, a statistical report on the total membership of the Southern States Mission showed under 550 members, and 261 of those had emigrated in 1877. Many who did convert were struck almost immediately—and for reasons obviously not unrelated to economic and social conditions in the South—with the "spirit of gathering," the desire to emigrate west. The Haywood Valley Saints expressed this desire as a body (though ultimately enough were left behind to maintain a branch of the church). All of which was fine with the church authorities, who encouraged migration of the Saints out to the Rocky Mountain region.

Thus, it was not the average person who caused trouble for the missionaries; it was the Protestant ministers, church deacons and minor church figures. They charged the Mormons with many evils, especially stealing their women and girls to take them off to harems in Utah. While doubtlessly adamantly opposed to Mormonism on theological grounds, their accusations may also have been reflections of a deeper fear—that they might lose not only their women but their men as well and find their diminishing congregations eroding their own social and economic positions. The Mormons, in fact, regularly accused the leaders of other denominations of being more concerned with making money than saving souls. The self-righteous air of superiority which often occurred among Mormons of this time and which contributed to the conflicts they had experienced elsewhere in the country, no doubt aggravated the hostile relations between the two groups.

The most common practice of the anti-Mormons was to rally a host of cohorts to show up at a Mormon meeting and ask provocative questions, make long speeches denouncing Mormonism, and generally confuse and disrupt the proceedings. But the line between this kind of harassment and violence was a thin one.

Morgan, the veteran soldier, generally dealt with the mobs and groups of marauding Klansmen in their own terms, by marshalling the available artillery and facing them down. On one occasion, when word got to him that the Klan was threatening to break up a meeting he was holding in the yard of a convert, Morgan stacked three loaded rifles beside the table from which he was speaking. When the hooded Klansmen rode up, he and the congregation completely ignored them. They got the message, however, and just as quickly rode away.

Catoosa and northern Whitfield (the Varnell area) had become hotbeds of anti-Mormonism, probably because of the relative success Joseph Standing and John Morgan had had there in winning converts, a success jocularly recognized elsewhere in Georgia where the area was referred to as "Utah."

In October of the previous year they had established a branch of the church in Varnell. Catoosa and Varnell, in contrast to the more easterly areas where Joseph and Rudger were presently working, had lain directly in the path of the war. Catoosa Springs was used as headquarters by Union General Oliver Otis Howard, while the little house of Mitchell Varnell, after whom the town of Varnell was named, not only served as headquarters for both Union and Confederate generals, but was at one point used as a hospital as well.

The area had still not recovered and now the people tended to wallow in their poverty and blame the war for all their troubles. As John Morgan wrote for the *Deseret News* in 1877:

> Poverty of the most pinching character stares them in the face and they see only a gloomy future before them. 'Since the war' you hear on every side and 'since the war' appears to be the explanation for all the evils to which they are subject. 'Since the war we can only afford bacon and corn bread,' one constantly hears. The result of this diet is that numerous ills they were not subject to before the war have appeared amongst them—then the constant use of tobacco. . . . has also had its effect. . . .

In this kind of atmosphere, searching for scapegoats was a tempting pastime. Varnell ministers had whipped the local churches into a frenzy and their agitation did not abate when Morgan returned to Utah. The Klan often rode at the mere appearance of the missionaries. On two occasions since Morgan's departure, mobs had driven Mormon elders out of the community. In one case they had broken into the house of a local Saint to find the elders and then threatened to kill their protectors if they ever harbored Mormon preachers again.

When Joseph Standing heard of these incidents, he was outraged and fired off a letter to the Georgia governor, John Colquitt. In the letter, dated June 12, 1879, and posted from "Van Zandt's Store" in

Fannin county northeast of Ellijay, he protested the treatment of the elders, pointing out "that the laws of Georgia are strictly opposed to all lawlessness and extend to her citizens the right of worshipping God according to the dictates of conscience." These laws were obviously not being executed properly. "A word from the Governor," he ended with a kind of naive imperiousness, "would undoubtedly have the desired effect."

The governor's secretary replied promptly, affirming at some length that the laws of Georgia were indeed opposed to lawlessness and in favor of freedom of worship and that the governor would instruct the state prosecutor "to inquire into the matter." There is no evidence, however, of any inquiry having been made.

A district conference in Rome had been called for late in July. Rudger and Joseph discussed at length whether they should go via Varnell to find out what was actually happening and finally decided they should.

They set out on about the tenth of July from Ludville in Pickens County, walking the Old Federal Road and visiting converts along the way.

To their north, rich green hills rose dramatically out of the flat farmland. They constituted the southern spur of the Appalachian mountains which jut gracefully into northern Georgia and then stop suddenly as though the Creator had simply decided to quit making hills at that point.

The Old Federal Road, originally the principal route through Cherokee territory, skirted just south of the mountains and ran through rolling farm land. They wrote to Morgan on July 15 from Spring Place that they would stop in Varnell on the way to Rome and accompany the Saints there to the conference, which was scheduled to start on July 25.

As they continued on their way, Joseph fell quiet, and Rudger could see that something was bothering him. Finally Joseph confessed that he was disturbed by a terrible dream he'd had recently and wondered if Rudger might help him interpret it. In the dream he had gone to Varnell—which had been overhung by a heavy, black cloud—and stopped at the home of one of the Saints. But when he entered, the woman of the house turned deathly white and, without saying why, told him he could not stay—at which point he awoke.

They discussed the dream at some length, but neither could—or were willing—to interpret it.

They arrived July 20 at 10:00 p.m. on a moonless night, stopping as they had planned at the home of Jane Ellege, whom Joseph had baptized into the church only four months earlier, in March 1879.

Jane's mother, Elizabeth, was in a state of agitation and proceeded to act as Joseph's dream had foretold. Rudger and Joseph could not stay there, she said. The family had been threatened with harm if they entertained the elders. The lives of Joseph and Rudger had also been threatened. Her husband was away, and she was frightened for herself and her children. The elders would have to go. Elizabeth, who had been converted the previous November, was related to a Varnell family named Nations, the members of which were rabidly anti-Mormon. It was the wrath of her relatives that Elizabeth apparently feared.

But where could Rudger and Joseph go? They were tired and hungry. It was dark now and they knew they were personally in danger.

Elizabeth provided them with food while they rested and then directed them to the home of Henry Holston two miles down the road. Although Holston was not a Mormon, he had no patience with the mobs that were harassing the missionaries. But unlike others, he openly condemned mob violence.

Leaving their knapsacks, the two young men started out. Of all the miles they had walked—hundreds in their missionary travels—these were the longest. They groped their way through the pitch black, looking hard for the landmarks Elizabeth had given them, guessing, at one fork in the road, the right way. They stopped occasionally to listen for telltale sounds of a party out searching for them, but there were none.

They commented on the irony of being sent from the home of a Latter-day Saint to find haven with a non-Mormon. And Joseph's dream lay heavy on both of them.

They finally reached the Holston house. "From what we could see of it in the dark," Rudger wrote,

> it appeared to be a desolate looking place. It stood like a ghost in the midst of a forest of trees. There was an awful, terrible stillness all about us. The silence of one of those Georgia forests is depressing. . . . We entered the premises, walked along the foot path and up the steps of Mr. Holston's

porch. The porch boards were loose and creaked and rattled under our feet like dead men's bones.

The house was dark so they knocked hard and waited. Finally a firm voice from inside cut through the night, "Who's there?"

"Elders Standing and Clawson," they replied and explained the circumstances under which they had been sent. "We would like the privilege of stopping overnight."

After lighting a lamp, Holston opened the door and welcomed them. He was a big, hearty man with a somewhat gruff but not unkind manner.

"In all likelihood the mob will be out tonight in search for you. . . ." he said. "But if they come into my yard, damn them, I will shoot them down like dogs."

To Rudger, this statement was frightening but somewhat reassuring. They would at least be safe for the night—though Joseph, apparently, did not feel the same. They were shown their room, but as they began to prepare for bed, Joseph became greatly agitated. He had reason to be. He knew from experience what a mob was.

The Klan had come after him and John Morgan in Haywood Valley just after conference in August 1878. They had lain in wait one night in a cornfield, but the elders had escaped. A couple of nights later, hooded and armed, the Klansmen had come again when the missionaries were at the home of Queen Bailey, who warned them of the mob's approach. Old soldier Morgan went into action. The warning gave them "time to bring out the Bailey firearms and prepare to meet the mobsters who were masked and otherwise disguised. When they came we halted and drove them off, so they had another failure."

Rudger, however, was less experienced: "I was perfectly innocent. I had never met a mob." But Joseph also knew how to take precautions. He examined the locks on the windows and doors, looked under the bed, opened the closet door, and then began searching the dark corners of the room. These actions made Rudger nervous. He innocently said to Joseph, "You seem anxious about something."

Joseph might have become a little impatient with his companion at this point, but instead replied, "Brother Clawson, I am looking for some kind of instrument of defense. If the mob comes tonight we shall be under the necessity of defending ourselves." Whereupon he turned and held up before him an iron poker, which he swung lustily several times. He put it under his pillow, "and that seemed to afford him some comfort," said Rudger, "but I do not remember that it comforted me."

They slept fitfully, but the mob did not come and "the spirit of oppression and anxiety of the night" finally left them. The dawn of July 21, 1879 came, "a fateful day in our lives. The morning was bright and beautiful although warm. There was a spirit of tranquility and perfect calmness in the air which pervaded the neighborhood. We felt comforted and reassured and thought perhaps the danger had passed."

They left Holston's early, indicating they would be back to say goodbye after they had retrieved their knapsacks from the Ellege residence. The thick pine and cedar forests surrounded them as they walked but did not seem as ominous as the night before. They did not dally at the Elleges's since Elizabeth was still in a state of extreme nervousness; in fact, the mob was out looking for them.

They later learned that Mrs. Hamline, "a good sister," had seen the mob and "divining their wicked intention," had sent her eighteen-year-old daughter, Mary, to warn the elders. Taking a short cut, Mary hoped to reach them at the fork in the road where the two men had nearly become lost the night before. Unfortunately, she arrived too late. They had already passed the fork and were face to face with their pursuers, "When the mob saw us and we saw them, it was a tense moment. We paused; they paused. They were some little distance away, and then it was they took off their hats and swung them over their heads with an awful yell and came charging down upon us."

There were twelve of them, three on horseback, the rest on foot; a ragged lot, all armed with pistols or rifles. As they drew up, one of the mounted men, apparently the leader, announced, "You are our prisoners." Another jumped from his horse and waved a cocked pistol in Rudger's face shouting profanities.

Joseph, who had faced off with Governor Colquitt over the lawlessness of mobs, was not about to let the mob get away with an illegal arrest.

"By what authority do you arrest us upon the public highway here?" he asked boldly. "If you have a warrant of arrest, we would like to see it."

"There's no law in Georgia for Mormons," the leader yelled. "You must go with us."

"We'll show you by what authority we act," one of them shouted to the laughter of his companions.

The elders, surrounded by the mob, were forced then to turn around and go back the way they had come. There were no houses along the densely forested road so that there was little chance of being seen or helped.

Joseph and Rudger continued to ask why they were being detained and to demand their release. Joseph, his face with a deathly pallor, walked at a rapid pace keeping up with the lead horsemen as he argued and expostulated. They were leaving town anyway, he said, so why bother them. They didn't coerce people into becoming Mormons. People made their own choices.

The ruffians laughed and told them they were going to be whipped so they would never forget it and never bring their Mormonism back to Varnell. "You'll be pretty limber when we finish with you," said one.

Rudger looked at Joseph. Above all other dangers to which the Mormon elders were subject, the threat of whipping most frightened Joseph. Victims were stripped, tied face down on a fallen log, and lashed with willow branches until their backs were bloody. He had spoken of it on several occasions, and when they heard stories of other missionaries being beaten or whipped, Rudger observed Joseph turn pale and begin to shake. Now it must have been terrifying for him to see his fears and nightmares one by one coming true.

The members of the mob asked repeatedly about John Morgan and where he could be found. He had bested Georgia mobs too often and was clearly the object of their particular hatred.

At this point Joseph suddenly developed an overwhelming thirst and began to badger the gang leader. "I am thirsty. I want a drink of water," he said over and over again, sounding as if he would die any moment if he didn't get it.

The men laughed and told him to shut up.

Rudger himself dragged his feet. His instinct was to balk, to slow their progress as much as possible, to delay their arrival at wherever they were going. He quite honestly believed he was walking to his death and was in no hurry to get there. His dilatory tactics were not well received by the "mobocrats," as Rudger called them. An exasperated member, whom the others called Ben (eventually identified as Baptist deacon Ben Clark), who had been ungently urging him along, suddenly struck him viciously from behind, knocking off his hat and throwing him forward so that he had to stop himself with outstretched arms to keep from falling on his face in the dirt.

When he recovered and turned on his assailant, he was angered to find that Ben was the youngest and smallest of the group. "I would have been glad to meet him with my right hand free and my left hand tied behind me." His disdainful look would have earned him another blow had not one of the other men grabbed the arm of the young hothead before he could strike.

They had now progressed back to the fork in the road where Rudger was dismayed to see a girl coming toward them. It was Mary Hamline returning home by the road rather than via the shortcut she had taken in her attempt to warn them. She stopped speechless. A surge of raw courage flowed through Rudger, and he readied himself—if the girl were attacked—to fight "unarmed as we were, no matter what might be the consequences. . . ."

But they allowed her to pass.

A short time later a rider approached. He was the homeliest man Rudger had ever seen and his horse was "a rack of bones" which the mob ridiculed, saying that perhaps the Mormons could heal it by the "laying on of hands" (referring to the Mormon ritual of the laying on of hands for the healing of the sick). The man, Jonathan Owensby, ignored them and rode on, but he was a man of courage and later willingly testified against the gang members at the trial.

Joseph continued to pester them about his thirst, until they finally announced they were taking him to a nearby spring. It was just off the road in an open field, the pool partially shaded by the spreading branches of a huge tree.

Rudger noticed that two of the three horsemen, later identified as Jasper Nations and Andrew Bradley, had left the party.

They sat in a circle around the spring. Joseph was invited to drink but hesitated until the leader assured him they would not hurt him while he did so. He thereupon threw himself to the ground at the poolside and drank—"and drank and drank and drank. It appeared that he would never be able to quench his thirst."

After Joseph had finished and sat down facing Rudger across the pool, one of the older men, later identified as James Fawcett, spoke up: "Gentlemen, I want you to understand that I am captain of this party, and after today, if we ever again find you in this part of the country we will hang you by the neck."

There followed a long period of verbal abuse of the elders and of the Latter-day Saints in general. Accusations of all sorts were made. The elders were also treated to further villification of John Morgan and grilling as to his whereabouts.

Finally Nations and Bradley returned. It became clear that they had been looking for a more secluded spot to carry out the whipping. The mob's spokesman said to Rudger and Joseph: "Follow us." It was then that Joseph seized the moment he had no doubt been waiting for. Wresting a revolver from one of the men—or perhaps grabbing a weapon that had been laid down—he jumped to his feet, pointed the gun with outstretched arms at the two men on horseback, and said "in a commanding voice [according to Rudger], 'Surrender!' "

Joseph Nations, a relative of Jane Ellege, who was right next to Joseph Standing, raised his gun to the elder's head and fired. Joseph spun around several times from the impact of the shot, fell to the ground face down and then with a convulsive movement rolled over on his back. For a moment, Rudger was stunned and just stood staring at the cloud of smoke and dust hanging over his friend's body. He looked around at the hostile men who themselves still sat or stood frozen in positions of surprise and shock and then glanced over his shoulder at the woods some seventy-five yards away. "At this critical juncture . . . , the leading mobocrat pointing at me said, 'Shoot that man.' Every weapon was leveled at my head. I . . . at once realized there was no avenue of escape. My time had come. . . . My turn to follow Joseph Standing was at hand. The command to shoot had been given. I was looking down the gun barrels of the murderous mob. I folded my arms and said, 'Shoot,' and almost persuaded myself that I was shot, so intense were my feelings."

Whether the men, who had all jumped up and raised their weapons, were confused by Rudger's courageous stance or merely jolted into a sudden realization of what they had done—or perhaps one of them had simply decided that it would be harder to get out of charges of shooting two men than one—is hard to say, but someone at that crucial moment yelled, "Don't shoot." And the danger passed.

The moment before, however, Rudger actually thought he had been shot and later believed that he had experienced the real agony of a dying man, "gazing into the muzzles of the deadly weapons . . . the sight went out of my eyes, total blindness followed and I was enveloped in total darkness. The world around me seemed blotted out. When I heard the voice in command say, 'Don't shoot,' it was just then the realization came to me that I had not been shot."

Recovering, Rudger went to his friend and knelt beside him. Gently he lifted his head and placed a hat under it to cushion it. He heard the death rattle in Joseph's throat and knew there was no hope. The bullet had entered the side of his head, ripped his left eye out of its socket, and torn a gaping wound in his forehead above the bridge of his nose.

Though he knew Joseph was beyond help, he rose and looked at the leader, Fawcett, who had come to stand beside him. "It's a burning shame that this man should be left here to die in the woods without any assistance. Either you go for help or let me go."

The members of the group looked at one another uncertainly while Rudger repeated several times, "You must go or you must send me."

He hoped dearly that they would give an impulsive response to his impulsive question before they could reconsider whether or not to shoot him. Finally the leader said, "You go and get help."

Rudger then walked slowly away across an open field. He felt certain that if he displayed any fear or haste it would trigger a fatal response from the murderers. So he walked toward the woods, not turning to look behind, his pace steady, his back to the mob, knowing that at any moment a bullet might tear a hole in his body. The two-mile walk in the dark the night before, as long as it had seemed, was now displaced as the longest walk of his life. The hundred yards he had to cross before he was completely out of sight of Joseph's murderers was virtually endless.

Once on the road, he quickened his pace and went straight to Holston's. He asked Mr. Holston to go to Joseph and build a shade over the body while he went for the coroner. Holston lent Rudger a horse and directed him to the Whitfield coroner, A. L. Sutherland, who lived four miles down the road toward Dalton.

Rudger rode as fast as he could, but found that Sutherland was not there. He was given directions to the coroner of Catoosa County, who lived only a few miles west of Varnell. There was also a telegraph office at Catoosa Springs Resort, he was told, where he could wire Salt Lake.

Disappointed at not finding Sutherland and still somewhat in a state of shock, he rode off retracing his route to Varnell before turning west toward Catoosa. As he drove his horse along one of the dusty country roads, he saw in the distance several horsemen coming his way. He took no notice of them until they got closer and he suddenly realized he was riding directly into the face of three of the murderers. Had they had second thoughts about letting him go? He was the only witness to the murder. Perhaps they had decided to silence him.

As he approached, one of the men gave him an ominous look and shouted, "Where are you going?"

"That way," called out the dauntless Clawson, pointing ahead. Then spurring his horse to its greatest effort dashed past them and galloped westward, looking, he hoped, like he would not stop until he reached the Utah border.

Catoosa Springs Resort was a summer resort for wealthy Southerners and Northerners. From the South they came to escape yellow fever and from the North to avoid spending a summer in the torrid cities. Located in the cool Catoosa hills, just south of the Chickamauga battleground, it offered both a pleasant retreat and a healthful access to the resort's fifty-two mineral springs, consisting of "red, white, and black mineral springs—many of them combined with iron and magnesia . . . [and] an inexhaustible well of the purest freestone." These mineral waters, which were also bottled and sold as "Buffalo Water," were renowned for their "medicinal virtues."

The resort was set amid shaded but grassy rolling grounds elaborately maintained with duck ponds and a grand roadway canopied by high, carefully trimmed evergreens. The hotel itself, flanked by cottages for families, was a large four-storied structure, with tall narrow windows and high ceilings. A railed balcony wrapped itself entirely around the building at the second floor and slender columns rose from the ground all the way to the dormered roof.

As Rudger hurried up a wide stairway that led from the ground to the main entrance, he could hear music coming from inside, played by what the hotel's handbill called "an excellent brass and string band of superior musicians." As he entered he passed a ballroom where well-dressed men and women danced gaily. Fatigued and begrimed as he was and deeply shaken and sorrowful over the events of the morning, he found the merrymaking a repugnant sight.

In the telegraph office he wired John Morgan: "Joseph Standing shot and killed today near Varnell's by a mob of ten or twelve men. Will leave with the body for home at once. Notify his family."

He also fired off a telegram to Governor Colquitt. The governor should know the consequences of his failure to act.

It took him another hour or so to roust out the Catoosa coroner and an assistant. When they arrived back in Varnell it was nearly 6:00 p.m.; he had left Joseph before noon.

A. L. Sutherland had already arrived and was in the process of organizing an inquest and selecting a jury from the crowd that had gathered at the spring as word about the shooting spread. The Catoosa coroner returned home. Rudger also found, to his horror, that there were more wounds in Joseph's head and neck. The murderers had apparently decided there was safety in numbers—or the one who fired the first shot insisted that the others join him in ritual complicity.

The verdict of the coroner's jury, based on statements from Rudger, Henry Holston, Mary Hamline, and others was simple and explicit:

> We, the Jury sitting on the inquest over the dead body of Joseph Standing, having heard all the evidence in the premises, and having made examination of the dead body, find that the deceased came to his death by gun and pistol shots, or both, inflicted upon the head and neck of deceased, said wounds consisting of twenty shots or more from guns or pistols in the hands of David D. Nations, Jasper N. Nations, A. S. Smith, David Smith, Benjamin Clark, William Nations, Andrew Bradley, James Fawcett, Hugh Blair, Joseph Nations, Jefferson Hunter and Mack McClure; and in view of the above stated facts, we the Jury, do hereby recommend that the Coroner of said county do issue a warrant for the arrest of the above named parties forthwith.

It was after dark when the body was carried on a plank to Holston's house. On the way, Rudger announced his intention to transport the body to Utah—which Sutherland said would be quite impossible because the railroad would throw it off the train when it became rank. He suggested Joseph be buried in Georgia and exhumed and taken elsewhere at a later date. Rudger remained firm, however; burying Joseph in the soil on which he had been murdered was unthinkable.

The job of cleaning the body, of course, fell to Rudger. That night, with a crowd of curious onlookers standing ghoulishly around him in the eerie, flickering candlelight, he carefully wiped the blood from Joseph's wounds and washed and dressed the body. At about midnight, just as he finished and was spreading one of Holston's white sheets over his dead companion, the Whitfield county sheriff, Fred Cox, and a posse of men rode in from Dalton, twelve miles south. Cox, a tall, wiry man with leathery skin, assured Rudger in vigorous words that every effort would be made to bring to justice the men who had committed cold-blooded murder in "*my* county."

Told that seven of the murderers had been seen heading at some speed toward the Tennessee border, the posse galloped off in a clatter of hoofbeats.

The next day, Rudger went to Dalton and purchased an expensive metal casket which the undertaker assured him was airtight and would seal in the odors of decomposition. A group of townspeople, who had heard of the murder and gathered round when they learned who Rudger was, warned him not to accompany the casket back to Varnell. But he insisted on going, along with a jumpy undertaker's assistant who sealed Joseph's body into the casket as quickly as possible and hurried back to Dalton.

Despite the assurance of the undertaker and his assistant that the casket would not leak, the next day odors emanating from it clearly proved them wrong. Rudger had no alternative than to hire a wagon, take the body and casket back to Dalton, and confront the undertaker.

He now took warm leave of Mr. Holston, thanking him for his aid and support and assuring him that he, Rudger, would return to Georgia to testify at the trial should any of the murderers be caught.

By the time he set out, however, he had become rather jittery. So, borrowing from the driver a little pistol about the size of a toy gun (which gave him "a feeling of confidence and courage that had no foundation in fact"), he dismounted at the outskirts of the village, circled around through the woods, and met the wagon on the other side.

In Dalton, the undertaker was chagrined and puzzled by the leak and at first had no solution. Finally he suggested that they put the defective casket in a larger outer box and fill in around it with cinders, charcoal, and ashes from the Dalton railroad yard (Dalton was a burgeoning rail center for northwest Georgia). After a great deal of scurrying about, this feat was accomplished, and the leak was stopped—except that now Rudger had a box on his hands so heavy it could hardly be lifted! He thought surely the railroad would refuse it, but they put it on an express car with no comment. "I bought two tickets, one for myself and one for Elder Standing. I rode in the passenger coach; he rode in the express car. And thus we came some three thousand miles from Dalton, Georgia, to Salt Lake City."

# CHAPTER 2
# POLYGAMY

*I*n 1841, at the age of fifteen, Hiram Bradley Clawson and his widowed mother joined the Mormon settlement in Nauvoo, Illinois. He was a precocious and talented lad who, encouraged by Joseph Smith, became a prominent member of Thomas Lyne's theater company and acted in plays in Nauvoo (with, among others, Brigham Young) and achieved a certain renown performing with the troupe up and down the Mississippi. In 1847, at the age of twenty-one, he drove his mother and sisters across the plains in the second wave of pioneers headed for the Great Salt Lake valley.

Brigham Young had put him to work virtually from the day of his arrival, first as a supervisor on early construction projects, then as clerk, and ultimately as manager of all the prophet's personal business affairs. In a household that soon numbered seventy people this was no small task. Brigham also frequently sent him back East on business and diplomatic missions. In addition, Hiram was an officer in the territorial militia and a delegate to the territorial legislature. Finally, as a result of his interest in drama, he was the driving force—along with John T. Caine (and, of course, Brigham Young)—in bringing theater to the Salt Lake Valley. It was in the theater that he met and fell in love with Margaret Gay Judd, Rudger's mother.

Margaret, who later became known as the "Mother of the Drama in Utah," was a vibrant young woman, moon-faced and, according to Hiram, "very handsome, lively and full of fun." She had a sharp wit and a great love of the theater. A number of fellow actors were pursuing her, but it was Hiram who prevailed. As Rudger wrote with his usual charm:

> He wooed her not before the curtain on the mimic stage but behind the scenes and won her—won her over and above and in spite of the impetuous attentions of other loves. On the stage the love scenes were simply make-believe. Off the stage his lovemaking was in dead earnest and had he been less insistent, less determined, less attentive, less romantic in his courtship, he would have lost the prize, and in the last analysis where would I have been.

And Hiram won her despite the fact that he already had a wife—or possibly because of it, at least to the degree that it reinforced his image as a man with a future in Mormon Utah. In any event, Hiram Clawson was now a polygamist.

Joseph Smith had been commanded by God to introduce plural marriage. There is evidence that he began to do so in the 1830s; but it is certain that it was being practiced in secret by him and a few trusted followers by at least 1843. From that time on he, and particularly his successor, Brigham Young, urged it on the apostles and other church members who were able to support large families. In 1847 Young transplanted it to the Salt Lake Valley and three years later announced it publicly.

The idea of plural marriage was integrated into the religious framework of Mormonism. The Mormon concept of heaven is complex and expansive. There are different degrees or kingdoms, the highest of which, the celestial, is inherited by those who, either in life or after death, have accepted the gospel and followed its precepts. Within this kingdom, the highest level, called exaltation, is for those who have followed "the fullness" of the gospel by being married, or sealed, celestially in the temple for "time and eternity,"* and by having

---

*There are three forms of marriage in Mormon doctrine: (1) for *time only*; this is the ordinary Christian or secular marriage which ends at death, (2) for *time and eternity*, which all Mormons are encouraged to enter and which involves being "sealed" by those who hold the divine priesthood, and (3) for *eternity* only, a special provision for people whose spouses predeceased them without having been properly sealed to them.

remained faithful. They would be reunited with their families in their heavenly kingdom. Now understood as simple temple marriage to one spouse, the principle of celestial marriage [often referred to then as "The Principle") was, from 1852 to the early 1900s, defined by the church leaders as requiring the taking of plural wives.

By the time Rudger was born, on a blustery 12th of March in 1857, plural marriage had become embedded in Mormon theology and was being more and more widely practiced by the religious and economic leadership of the Mormon community. At that time the Clawson family, at Brigham Young's invitation, was living in a white house on Brigham's estate where Hiram could be close to his employer. Most of the adobe houses in the valley took on a dull blue-grey cast over time. Brigham had this one whitewashed so that it stood out prominently on the hillside above the city. It was a comfortable house, though strange in appearance, looking something like a Spanish villa with Greek and Palladian elements grafted on. But it was too small after Hiram had taken his third wife, Alice Young, one of Brigham's numerous daughters.

As in many, if not all, polygamous households, the advent of a new wife brought stress and uncertainty. Ellen, Hiram's first wife, wrote to her friend Ellen Pratt McGary in November 1856:

> Just ten days ago *Hiram* brought home a new wife, no more or less than Miss Alice Young, the governor's daughter. Our house is all in confusion, being remodelled to make room for her, and it also being my week to superintend the housework. . . . I never thought I could care again if Hiram got a dozen wives, but it seems as though my affections return with double force, now that I feel as if I had lost him but I expect he thinks as much of me as ever, only in a different way . . . you know a new wife is a new thing, and I know it is impossible for him to feel any different towards her just at present. . . . I think perhaps Margaret feels worse than I do for she was the last, and I suppose thought he would never get another. . . .

Indeed, Margaret probably did feel worse. She was four months pregnant with Rudger when Alice joined the family.

Hiram's marriage to Alice was coincidental with the Reformation, a revivalist frenzy which struck the Mormon community in the fall of 1856. Concerned with the degree to which the faithful seemed to be backsliding, the Mormon leadership mounted a furious campaign to call the members back to the true path in both belief and behavior. Harangued and harassed, Mormons of every rank were called upon to admit their sins in public confessions and to be rebaptized into the faith. Among the leadership, pressure on monogamous brethern was increased to take additional wives.

As Ellen Clawson put it in another letter, "I think if Hiram hadn't got Alice before the reformation he would have been called upon, by this time to take one or two more."

The Reformation was also having its impact across the country in Washington where President Buchanan, already responsive to the anti-Mormonism which was rampant in the country, was spurred on in the formulation of his plan to depose Brigham Young as governor of the Utah Territory.

Six months later, prodded by his secretary of war, John B. Floyd, Buchanan secretly launched an army of 2,500 men from Fort Leavenworth, Kansas, to remove Brigham Young from power and restore the authority of the United States government in Utah. Young, who was governor of the Utah Territory as well as president of the Mormon church, had at least from the perspective of Washington, ruled Utah imperiously, creating an environment in which gentiles (the term Mormons use for all non-Mormons) and federal officials, appointed in Washington as often as not from the bottom of the political patronage barrel, were made to feel distinctly unwelcome. When polygamy had been openly acknowledged in 1852, outrage swept the country and calls for the crushing of the Mormons were heard across the land. Though Floyd, a Virginian, was accused of launching his military campaign to siphon off troops that could be used in the impending conflict between the states, he needed little more than the anti-Mormon temper of the times to justify his actions. So began the "Utah War."

After a year of fruitless negotiation, bombastic oratory and sporadic guerilla warfare, Brigham adopted a scorched earth policy. He ordered the evacuation of Salt Lake City and threatened to burn it down if the approaching federal troops, now commanded by Colonel Albert Johnston, marched hostilely into the valley. So, on a cool day in April 1858, 30,000 Mormons began moving south from Salt Lake, walking or driving wagons loaded with their most precious belongings. Hiram was given responsibility for moving and protecting Brigham Young's large family.*

"I can never forget that eventful move south," Margaret wrote in her "Rambling Reminiscences" many years later. "President Young made arrangements for his family to move to Provo and had some board shanties put up for their use. Hiram Clawson, to whom I [was] married, being in his employ, was given two little rooms and a covered wagon. . . . Well, after packing all of our household belongings, the loads were sent down a day ahead of the family. Ellen, who was my husband's first wife, and her four children, myself and my three children were loaded into a three-seated spring wagon and arrived in Provo one spring day, after sundown."

Rudger was just over a year old. "By the time we reached Provo," wrote Margaret, "my son, Rudger, had just begun to walk, but creeping seemed so much easier that he preferred that way. Every day after I would get him cleaned up he would get down and creep right out on the ground and revel in dirt. In fact, it seemed to be his principal diet. It agreed with him alright, for he got fat on it."

There were thirteen in the family, including a new baby born to Ellen after their arrival in Provo and Alice with her own first child.

The conflict was settled in June. Brigham agreed to the appointment of a new governor, and the army marched through but did not occupy Salt Lake. Instead, a base was established some distance to the south, and the Saints returned to their homes, the Clawson family reoccupying the white house.

In 1860 Hiram acquired a large, handsome home on the corner of Third East and Brigham streets. The name of the latter was actually South Temple, but it was called "Brigham Street" because on it were Brigham's own residences, those of many of his relatives, and those of a large number of his close associates in the religious and economic hierarchy of the city. This house had been built in 1852 by Mormon apostle Lorenzo Snow, who would later play a crucial role in Rudger Clawson's life. It was here that Margaret made her home for the next thirty-three years. Standing on an ample plot of ground, Georgian in

---

*During this time, Hiram carried a small double-barreled derringer with a pearl handle. In passing it on to his daughter many years later, Rudger wrote: *Do not use with violence, but hang on to it.* (see plate)

style, with several wings fitting symmetrically together, it was a large, rather graceful near-mansion. A tree-lined walk led to a small, attractive portico topped by a railed balcony. Peach, apple, and plum trees stood among scattered flower gardens. Hiram undertook extensive renovations, adding and enlarging rooms to meet the needs of Margaret, Ellen, and their families. His renovations also made the house ideal as a gathering place for the lively theatrical and social circles in which the Clawsons moved. Alice had her own small cottage behind the larger house and lived there somewhat aloof from the others.

It was a good place to raise a boy. "It is hard to believe," his mother wrote, "the serious, sedate Rudger was a mischievous little urchin, but he generally managed to slip out of deserved punishment. There was a bright, young lady who was very intimate at our home. One day when visiting there, she remarked . . . . 'That little rascal needs a good drubbing.' I said, 'Sarah, if you can catch him, you are at liberty to give him a sound thrashing, with my full consent.' So off and on all day long, she tried to catch and hold him, but he slipped through her fingers every time."

On another occasion, he was sent to bring a stick with which to be whipped for some misdemeanor—and returned with a twig! "And so it has been in his after life," said his mother. "He has escaped from greater calamities."

In the big house, Ellen's and Margaret's twenty children,* Rudger among them, played and romped. There were parties and "sleeping over," musical activities, and masquerades.

Much of the life of the Clawsons revolved around the theater. Margaret continued acting for a number of years between pregnancies and despite her growing brood. Alice performed, as did Emily, Hiram's fourth and last wife (who was also a daughter of Brigham Young). All the children appeared on stage at one time or another, first as elves and fairies (or babes in arms), then as child characters, and later in more substantial roles. Rudger's sister, Teresa (Birdie), achieved fame locally as an actress in later years. Another, Edith, one of Ellen's children, was invited by Edwin Booth to join his company, but refused because she preferred to stay home, marry, and raise a family.

---

*The number in 1866.

Rudger recounted his own experiences:

I myself made two appearances on the stage, although I was not then and am not now gifted with histrionic talent. My first appearance was in the Social Hall at the age of three, when I rushed on the stage crying for my mother, who was greatly startled and for a few moments was unable to proceed with her lines. . . . It is perhaps sufficient to say that my appearance before and withdrawal from the footlights were greeted with vociferous applause.

My next appearance was some ten years later. I took the part of a robber in . . . *The Robbers of the Rocky Mountains*. It was said that I made a 'first class robber.'

The golden age of the theater in Utah began in earnest in 1862 with the completion of the Salt Lake Theater. It was a massive structure covering nearly half a block at the corner of First South and State streets. Five doors sandwiched between flat, two-story Doric columns gave entrance. Though called the "Cathedral of the Desert," it was not a handsome building; but by comparison, the small frame and adobe structures around it looked like shanties, and it symbolized Brigham's commitment to culture and wholesome entertainment. Hiram, who had been instrumental in convincing Brigham to build it, supervised the construction and, with John T. Caine, was appointed co-manager.

The theater seated 7,500 people, and the proscenium and boxes were garlanded with paintings and gilt mouldings. The decorations, fretwork, and hangings were ornate. Brigham liked to inform startled visitors from the East that he had constructed the gilt chandelier from the wheels and hitching chains of ox carts.

Now Salt Lake could attract the great acting companies that toured the American hinterlands, especially after 1869, when the railroad reached Utah. Famous actors and actresses thus passed through the home of Hiram B. Clawson and were encountered by Rudger and the other children, all of whom attended plays frequently.

The theater building stood out because Salt Lake City in 1862 was still a small town with a population of around 15,000 people. The city  consisted principally of square, one- and two-story frame or grey-hued adobe buildings staring at each other across broad, dusty streets where wagons, horses, oxen, and stage coaches bustled by. The exception was Temple Square and adjoining blocks, where, on the high ground below Arsenal Hill and Ensign Peak, the Beehive and Lion houses, the Tithing Office, and others of Brigham's personal and official structures stood out above the city.

Eagle Gate, designed by Hiram, presided over the entrance to the Young estate.* The great tabernacle had not yet been started, and the temple was still only a hole in the ground.

But the streets were no longer barren. Brigham had seen to the planting of trees—lombardy poplar, locust, acacia, box elder, cottonwood, and elm—and throughout the city irrigation canals ran at the sides of the streets watering the trees and other vegetation. The Clawson children played in the irrigation ditches on South Temple Street.

Ensign Peak, a nubby prominence above Brigham's estate, bulged out from the slopes of the Wasatch Mountains. Overlooking the entire valley, Ensign Peak had been used for religious services in the early days of the settlement before church buildings were erected. Now hikers climbed the trails through the brush and dry, sandy soil, and it was a favorite spot for picnickers—and for lovers.

Just below Ensign Peak, City Creek flowed out of its densely shrouded canyon onto the once arid plain, now covered with green farmland. When the first settlers arrived, they climbed the hill (noting that it would be an ideal place to plant a flag or an "ensign") and surveyed the valley. The Great Salt Lake shimmered in the sunlight. The mountains, purple, brown, and grey, with snow capping the highest peaks, surrounded the valley with awesome majesty. The Clawson family went for walks in City Creek Canyon and on the hillside below Ensign Peak, which was called the "Upper Gardens" because of the flowers—columbine, foxglove, bluebells, and wild roses—that blossomed there in the spring and summer. The children played in the creek, and the family would climb the hill to picnic above the valley. City Creek Canyon and Ensign Peak were special places for Rudger Clawson and figured prominently in at least two of his courtships. The lake was also a favorite place for outings and

---

*The eagle still spreads its wings over Main Street in downtown Salt Lake City, though the supporting structure, the "gate," has been rebuilt over the years as the street was widened and widened again.

picnics. They bathed often in the buoyant waters of the lake at Black Rock Beach.

The city, though still small, was growing rapidly. The broad streets Brigham had laid out stretched south into the plain. Other communities could be seen sprouting up around the valley. Ogden and Brigham City to the north, Provo to the south, and a little community, Pleasant Green, west across the valley.

In the years that followed, the rise of the great tabernacle, completed in 1867, must have been fascinating for Rudger to watch. First the maze of low wooden pillars standing in regimented rows, which were then surmounted by great struts to make the dome, the whole massive hood finally covered over with thousands of wooden shingles. It rose humping up above the right angles and pointed gables of the rest of the city as if it were some turtle-shaped prehistoric creature which had lumbered into town from a yet undiscovered, primeval canyon and decided to stay. In it Rudger would spend many hours enjoying the sounds and feelings of his religion.

The temple, under construction since 1853, rose half-finished beside the tabernacle in Temple Square. As work advanced, Rudger watched great blocks of granite from Little Cottonwood Canyon being hauled in by wagon teams of oxen and scattered on the temple grounds like giant cakes fallen from God's dining table. He also enjoyed the parades, picnics, and parties which took place each year on July 24 when the Mormons celebrated Pioneer Day, the anniversary of the arrival of the first pioneers in the valley.

All indications are that Hiram was a caring father, but with four wives and, ultimately, forty-four children, he had to spread himself thin. He also traveled a great deal. According to Rudger, "He crossed the plains forty-two times before the advent of the railroad." He went on diplomatic and business missions for Brigham Young, buying excursions for the Salt Lake Theater, and business trips for his own dry goods firm, Eldredge and Clawson.

While on the road, he wrote his wives faithfully and brought back— or had shipped back—presents for each of his children. The gifts tended to be somewhat standardized. In a package sent in 1868, which he asked Ellen to distribute, "Ruddy" received three handkerchiefs and a pair of suspenders—and so did each of his brothers and half-brothers. His sisters all got three handkerchiefs and an apron. But at least Hiram remembered them and referred to them by name.

Hiram had a fancy phaeton pulled by a sorrel horse in which he and his wives took their families for rides (by turns no doubt). From time to time Rudger also accompanied his father to the Beehive House where Hiram oversaw the management and distribution of supplies to Brigham's copious household. The goods were dispersed by a clerk from a storeroom at the back of the house, and Rudger no doubt begged or pinched bittersweet hoarhound candy which was kept there for Brigham's children.

In his memoirs Rudger does not tell us much about his religious training or how his faith developed. He was never able to express on paper his deeper personal feelings or emotions, but he does give us glimpses:

> Early in life I became deeply interested in the Book of Mormon, which I read and re-read and drew from its divine pages inspiration and hope. Faith sprang in my heart. By a careful study of that glorious book, well-defined ideas of right and wrong were firmly fixed in my youthful mind, and I was thus measurably able to withstand the temptations that assailed me and succeeded in escaping many of the sins and follies to which some of the younger people are addicted. . . .
>
> I remember the interest I felt as a boy in the Sunday meetings at the old Tabernacle and later in the large new Tabernacle on the Temple Block. The sermons of Presidents Brigham Young, Heber C. Kimball, George A. Smith, Daniel Wells and the Apostles and Elders made a profound impression on my 'mind.'

Rudger was baptized on October 3, 1868, attended Sunday school faithfully, was ordained into the priesthood, and on June 23, 1873, at the age of sixteen, received his endowments at the Endowment House in Salt Lake City. The endowment ceremony was an important event in Rudger's life—as it is in the lives of all Mormons who go through it. Wearing special outer- and undergarments and washed and anointed with oil, he was taken through a series of rituals—including handclasps, passwords, and special names—in which the truth of the gospel was impressed upon him. Temptations of the earthly world were acted out and vows of secrecy and of obedience to the priesthood were taken.

But nowhere in his writings about his early years does Rudger explain the depth of commitment he ultimately made to his religious vocation.

His *practical* vocation is easier to trace. It seems clearly to have developed out of his father's and his own experience in business and from his instinctive fascination with the processes of bookkeeping and accounting—which was so great that he devoted approximately twice as much space in his memoirs to describing how he learned bookkeeping as he did to describing his religious training.

His secular education began in one of the private schools that sprang up in the early years in Salt Lake and were often conducted in the home of the teacher.* Rudger started out with a Mrs. Watmough in her home in the Nineteenth Ward and then later shifted to "academic studies" offered at the Social Hall by the Misses Cook. In the early 1870s at about age fourteen he entered the University of Deseret (later to become the University of Utah) which was situated in the Council House across the street from Temple Block. The Council House, a solid square stone and adobe two-story building, was one of the first public buildings erected in Salt Lake, the construction of which was supervised by Hiram Bradley Clawson.

At about the same time Rudger matriculated, John Morgan, who had already founded the Morgan Commercial College and Normal School, was invited by the new principal, John R. Park (a major figure in the development of higher education in Utah) to organize a commercial department in the University—which not long afterward was merged with the academic department. Thus the academic department, in which Rudger studied, apparently had a strong business orientation. It may also have been here that Morgan observed the qualities in Rudger Clawson that caused him to single out the young man later for what he, Morgan, considered a crucial missionary assignment.

While the university at that time was little more than a glorified high school, it did spur the intellectual development of the sons of Utah's elite. One result was the formation of the Wasatch Literary

---

*For example, in 1852, Eli Kelsey—later to become a prominent educator, intellectual and, ultimately, excommunicant—charged $5 for reading, writing, spelling and arithmetic and an additional fifty cents if grammar and geography were included!

Association in February 1874. Most of the male members, like Rudger, were in their teens and twenties and either students at or recent graduates of the university. A significant number of both the men and women were Clawsons or Youngs. The leader was Orson F. Whitney, "Ort" to his friends, a witty, dynamic young man and a lifelong friend of Rudger's.

The association met weekly in the home of its members and was designed to serve both as an outlet for the artistic and literary interests of a core group of Salt Lake blue bloods and as a forum for more social pursuits.

Readings, musical performances, dramatic sketches, and the like were staple fare, but the irresistible youthful impulses of the group and the inevitable realization that real artistic talent was in short supply* inclined members toward fun, satire, and parody. They criticized, ridiculed and played jokes on each other in more and more elaborate ways. Stan Clawson "butchered" a violin piece and Rudger acted in a skit called *Waiting for the Verdict*, described as a "fowl" tragedy which parodied one of the group's current romances.

The activities of the association give us a view into the social life of teenagers and young adults of the time. The members went on weekend outings up City Creek Canyon and to the farms owned by their families. They swam at Black Rock in the summer and went sledding in winter. At Nibley Park they skated or went boating depending on the season.

But dancing seems to have been the principal social pleasure of young and old alike in Salt Lake. As one early resident, Pearl Park Nielsen, reminisced later in life:

> The pioneers had to make their own amusements. In the winter when the nights were long, it was the custom to go bobsleighing and then to someone's home for a dance. Each lady would take some food, pies, tarts, molasses or honey cookies and sometimes boiled ham sandwiches and plenty of popcorn. Sam McNutt usually was the fiddler for our dances and he could swing a lively tune.

---

*A number of the members, including Rudger's sister Birdie did, in fact, later became prominent in the Salt Lake Theater and Will Clawson, Rudger's half-brother, became a rather well-known painter.

Dancing was sanctioned by the church and held under church auspices at the ward houses. But it was subject to strict rules. Dances had to be opened and closed (by midnight) with prayer. Liquor was taboo as were waltzes, round dances and dancing out of turn. "Swinging with one arm around the ladies' [sic] waist shall not be permitted.  To swing a lady more than once against her will shall be considered ungentlemanly; to swing more than twice under any condition shall be disorderly and [the gentleman will be] requested to retire."

"At the dances in those days," Pearl Nielsen noted, "the gentlemen would bow and the ladies would curtsy—a lost art today."

Brigham Young approved of square dancing. He himself "was a graceful dancer and appeared to advantage in the old-fashioned quadrille, Sir Roger-de-Coverly, the Scotch Reel and kindred dances which were in vogue those days." But young people were drawn to the newer round dances, the waltz, the mazurka and the "gallop" which did not find favor with the church hierarchy—"not," Rudger wrote, "because of any evil in itself but by reason of the fact that evil might easily come of it if an improper position were taken and maintained during the dance. It needs no argument to prove said assertion."

One day in 1881 or 1882 when Rudger was a person of some renown and was serving as a home missionary (and probably as role model for younger brethren), Angus M. Cannon, president of the Salt Lake Stake, approached him on behalf of President John Taylor. After confirming that Rudger was "tremendously fond" of round dancing and would, indeed, "prefer to engage in the round dance rather than sit down to an elaborate and sumptuous banquet," Cannon said: "The church authorities are of the opinion that in many instances serious evils grow out of it and therefore counsel against this form of recreation. Brother Clawson, inasmuch as you are a home missionary in the Salt Lake Stake, you will be expected to set a proper example in this matter. As president of the stake, I kindly ask you to give up round dancing. . . . Will you do it?"

The loyal Rudger agreed, even though it was a "real sacrifice," and faithfully kept his promise.

It was a fruitless sacrifice. Later Taylor himself would give permission for one or two round dances to be scheduled during an evening. "But," says Rudger, "the rule was not always observed, so there never were less than two and in many instances there were three or four, and finally the time came when all the dances were round dances."

Rudger was involved in the Wasatch Literary Association, but only at its beginning and near its end, which came in May 1878. In the middle years, his employment with John W. Young kept him in the East much of the time. Though it only lasted four years, the Wasatch Literary Association played its small role in Mormon history. These young people were distinctly up-to-date. They had all been born in Salt Lake, or at least did not share the pioneer experience. Salt Lake was *home* more than it was the Promised Land. They did not burn with the fire of the pioneers. Many of them strongly opposed polygamy and were shocked when one of the women became the fifth wife of John W. Young, Rudger's employer. A few did leave the church; a few others married outside it, and most of them readily discussed ideas which did not square with Mormon doctrine. The Wasatch Literary Association represented the advent of new youthful perspectives and needs not provided for in the Mormon social structure.

These needs did not long go unmet by the church. As early as 1869, under the strong leadership of poet, Eliza R. Snow, the church had established "retrenchment societies" to spur young women to resist Eastern fashions and cut down on the purchase of clothing manufactured outside of Utah (which was expected to flood the territory with the arrival of the railroad). These evolved into organizations designed to keep women from straying from the faith and from proper behavior. In 1875 the societies were revitalized and transformed into the Young Ladies Mutual Improvement Association. A men's association was also established. MIAs or Mutuals, as they were called, were organized in every stake and ward* and provided a church-approved social milieu similar to that found in the Wasatch Literary Association. A "primary" MIA was also established in order to reach the children before they reached the dangerous teenage years.

The members of the Literary Association were not rebels. One of its members, Heber J. Grant, became the seventh president of the church. Another, Orson Whitney, went on a mission, and returned

---

*A ward is the smallest unit of the church organizational structure and is comparable to a parish in the Catholic church. A stake is comprised of a group of wards.

somewhat sobered and more serious about his religion. By July 1879 Whitney was secretary of the Young Men's Mutual.

And, of course, Rudger Clawson was no rebel either. He delighted in the tomfoolery that went on and enjoyed the literary, or quasi-literary, pursuits of the group. But the minor chord of iconoclasm struck by the activities of the association may have reverberated more within the bosom of the church than in Rudger Clawson's.

Rudger's first job after graduating from the University of Deseret was secretary to John W. Young, one of Brigham's many sons and a railroad financier. The prospect of working with Young stirred Rudger's memories of the coming of the railroad to Salt Lake City. "In 1869, my twelfth year," he wrote:

> a thrilling event occurred in Salt Lake City that proved to be of immense importance to the growing community. It was the arrival of the railroad. As a child I viewed the first passenger train that steamed into the city with feelings of awe and regarded the engine as a mysterious and dangerous monster.

Actually the Utah Central's mysterious monster didn't pull into Salt Lake until January 10, 1870. Fifteen thousand people gathered for the occasion and cheered as the engine chugged into sight. Ever since May 1869 when the Golden Spike joining the Union Pacific and Central Pacific railroads had been driven at Promontory Summit, Brigham Young had been pushing the builders to complete the Utah Central to Ogden to connect with them. To the surprise of officials in Washington and gentiles everywhere, Young had supported the coming of the transcontinental railroad. The Mormons knew that it would bring more gentiles to the Salt Lake valley; but it would also make it easier for Mormon converts from Europe and the eastern United States to reach Deseret. And, anyway, as Brigham Young said: Mormonism would "indeed be a . . . poor religion, if it cannot stand one railroad."

Now he was given the honor of driving in the last ceremonial spike of the Salt Lake-Ogden line. As he raised the equally ceremonial mallet (with inscriptions to the railroad, the beehive territory, and God carved on it), the sun, which had been hidden by clouds, "burst forth as in joy to witness the event," (according to historian Edward Tullidge).

John W. Young had also been a driving force behind the Utah

Central Railroad. In earlier years he had been a soldier, a missionary, and president of the Salt Lake Stake. But his principal interest was in finance, particularly the financing of the rail system that burgeoned in the Utah territory after the completion of the transcontinental railroad.

Just how Rudger, in 1875 at eighteen years of age, became his secretary is not recorded. It probably had to do with his father's close relationship with the Brigham Young clan, but may have been directly connected to Hiram's involvement with John W. in the Salt Lake City Street Railroad (a trolley system) of which Young was general manager.

In any event the job took Rudger East with his boss principally to New York, where Young was seeking funds from Eastern financial interests for the floundering Utah Western Railroad. The Utah Western ran twenty miles west and south along the shores of the Great Salt Lake, serving the resort at Black Rock, but aimed ultimately at the lucrative silver mining region around Tooele and further west in Nevada territory.

Rudger felt his time with Young in New York well spent.

> To reside, temporarily though it be, in a great city, the metropolis of the nation, to make the acquaintance of successful businessmen, to enter somewhat into the social life of the city was a rare privilege that comes to but few young people. It gave to me a wider outlook on life in many respects, enlarged my understanding, corrected my judgment and strengthened my sympathies for those living outside and beyond the circle of my people, the Latter-day Saints.

While in New York, Rudger attended the Scott-Browne College of Phonography to learn shorthand. Throughout his life he was known for the fine hand in which he wrote, an attractive quality in a personal secretary. But he also had to transcribe rapidly, particularly since Young apparently gave him dictation whenever and wherever the impulse struck him. In a "Biographical Sketch of Rudger Clawson of Salt Lake City" appearing in *Browne's Phonographic Monthly* in June 1884, Rudger is described as having attended Scott Browne's in 1877 (though it may have been earlier, since he also left John Young's employ and worked for Brigham Young during the first half of that year). "He was at the time," says the article, "serving as Private Secretary to . . . [John W.] Young who was a railroad magnate, operating largely in this city. Upon learning the art, it was not an unfrequent occurrence to see Mr. Clawson standing upon some street corner, note-book in hand, taking down a dictation from Mr. Young of some important matter that had occurred to [him] as they were walking down Broadway."

The article also commended Mr. Clawson not only for his intelligence and congeniality as a student but as "by far the most liberal, wise, earnest believer in the doctrines of the Mormon creed whom we have ever met, and that entirely without bigotry. He often spoke of his three mothers with the greatest respect, and showed, by his fine appreciation and true gentlemanly spirit, that his home training was all that could have been desired, and was even more happy than that of most monogamic homes."

Sometime in late 1876 or early 1877 Rudger followed in his father's footsteps and went to work for Brigham Young as a clerk. Brigham employed a battery of young men to help him keep track of his vast affairs. They sat in rows of desks in the church offices located in a wing of the Beehive House. Rudger's desk was one of a number lined back-to-back in the center of the room under a bright skylight. Nearby, whoever supervised the clerks sat at a huge desk made from hardwood packing boxes. Hardwoods were in short supply in Utah in the early days. Brigham therefore specifically requested that goods being shipped from the East be packed in hardwood boxes so that they could be recycled into furniture and house interiors.

Rudger was overawed by Brigham. He recalled the day the leader stood over him watching him copy and said, "Young man, you write a good hand." Rudger was struck dumb and could not reply. "I was transfixed with astonishment," he wrote. "I was amazed to think that Brigham Young, the President and Prophet, would deign to notice me in such complimentary terms."

Rudger was present when Brigham died in August 1877. "Not knowing just how it came about, it fell to my lot to be near his bedside at the moment he breathed his last. I then knew, as I now know, that a great spirit had passed from mortality to immortality." It may have come about because he was asked to represent Brigham's trusted aide, Hiram, who spent much of his time traveling during these years and may have been out of town. Or perhaps John W. Young, who was there, requested Rudger's presence. In any event, Brigham was in great pain, dying of what in recent times has been diagnosed as a ruptured appendix. He had been under opiates for some days but was restless and was moved to a bed in front of an open window where Rudger and Brigham's relatives could gather round. As they did so, he opened his eyes and called "Joseph! Joseph! Joseph!" and died. The group knelt in prayer.

The funeral services in Temple Square were jammed. Twelve thousand people packed into the tabernacle. Afterward the cortege, Rudger included, marched on foot to a little cemetery by the white house on the hill where Rudger had lived as a baby. Here, as Brigham had instructed, the Mormon leader was buried in a large redwood casket.

When Wilford Woodruff, then an apostle, later president, stepped forward to offer the dedicatory prayer, someone suddenly realized that the church reporter, who was supposed to take it down in shorthand, was not there. After a moment of panic, someone else said, 'Brother Rudger can take it.' This duty was then given to me. Remembering that President* Woodruff was a very rapid speaker, in fact the most rapid in all the Church, I undertook the task with fear and trembling. The words came tumbling out of his mouth one after another in quick succession and with an almighty effort I struggled to catch them."

When the services were over, Rudger was seen hurrying away with perhaps unseemly haste. He knew that the entire funeral service was to be published as a pamphlet and that the appearance of Woodruff's dedication depended on his ability to get it on paper. "I rushed down to the office hurriedly, and feverishly, with the perspiration streaming down my face, transcribed my notes. . . . When the job was finished, I found to my great relief that I had succeeded in getting the prayer, although it must be confessed I had to substitute a word or two here and there and now and then a phrase."

In 1877, probably in the fall or winter, Rudger was employed by the Zion Co-operative Mercantile Institution, or Z.C.M.I. as it has been called since the day of its creation. Considered America's first department store, Z.C.M.I. was founded in 1868 by Brigham Young as part of his effort to counteract the rise of non-Mormon economic

---

*Mormon leaders are referred to as "President" if they hold any of the many presidential positions which exist within the church organizational structure.

influence in the Utah Territory. The advent of the railroad presented a major threat to Mormon hegemony. Anti-Mormon politicians, preachers, and editors confidently predicted the end of Mormonism, or at least its decline into insignificance, once the railroad had opened the territory to access by the rest of America.

The Mormons, especially the church hierarchy, were not unaware of this danger. Eastern suppliers, combined with gentile merchants and the threat of a mining rush to the territory, boded calamity for Mormon rule. The Mormons therefore began systematic efforts to consolidate their control over the economy and business affairs of the territory. In 1868 the church leadership launched a general boycott of gentile businesses, and Brigham initiated a plan to establish a cooperative system of merchandising goods among the faithful. At the heart of the system was Z.C.M.I., which would buy for itself and for mini-Z.C.M.I.s in communities throughout the territory. It would be church-owned and church-run, would offer low prices, and would contribute to the church by paying a tithe. But for it to work, existing Mormon businesses had to join the cooperative, especially since they were the only immediate source of stock to supply the shelves of the new store.

Many Mormon merchants dragged their feet, and Rudger's father found himself in the middle of the conflict which ensued. In the spring of 1865, Hiram had bought half of a dry goods business owned by W. H. Hooper and Horace Eldredge. The firm, thereafter known as Eldredge and Clawson, prospered, with Hiram handling the purchasing back East. By 1868 theirs was one of the three largest and most profitable businesses in Salt Lake. Whatever Hiram felt about Z.C.M.I., he and Eldredge did ultimately agree to join. In 1869 closed their doors and exchanged their inventory for cash and stock in Z.C.M.I. and the impending arrival of the railroad provided an inducement softened the blow considerably. Once rail transportation was available, goods freighted from the East would be dramatically cheaper than those presently on their shelves, goods which had been brought overland by wagon. The price they got from Z.C.M.I. was quite attractive under the circumstances.

There were other inducements as well, at least for Eldredge and Clawson. Eldredge was made a director of Z.C.M.I., and Hiram was appointed general superintendent. Z.C.M.I. was extremely successful under Hiram and by 1873 had paid stock dividends of a half-million dollars. It had also, or so Hiram claimed, saved Mormons $3,000,000 by charging lower prices.

By 1875 Z.C.M.I. was so large the directors decided to spin off the agricultural, wool, and hide divisions in an effort to consolidate. Hiram bought them and went back into business on his own.

Thus when Rudger joined Z.C.M.I. in 1877 as corresponding secretary, his father, who had played a major role in its creation, was no longer there. It was housed in a large, three-story building facing west on Main Street. Each floor was lined with huge floor-to-ceiling windows that in the afternoon were overhung with heavy striped awnings to block the sun burning down from the western sky. William Jennings, a millionaire and one of Utah's true merchant princes, now ran Z.C.M.I. with a strong hand.

Some time after going to work for Z.C.M.I., Rudger, realizing that he needed to expand his practical skills if he were going to get on in the world, took a course in double-entry bookkeeping and ultimately became an excellent bookkeeper and accountant. He was particularly struck by the economics of his "education" in bookkeeping. The class cost $45, expensive then, but, later, in his memoirs, Rudger gleefully recorded how much he had earned—"mostly on the side, so to speak"—from his $45 investment. It totaled $12,890, made by keeping the accounts of various companies and teaching bookkeeping to others.

Then, in the spring of 1879, came his call to the mission in Georgia. Missionary work had from the beginning been one of the foundation blocks of the Mormon church. As a new millenialist religion, it was the responsibility of its believers to bring the gospel to the rest of the world. From the outset, church leaders gave years of their lives to missionary work as preachers, proselytizers, organizers, and managers of missionary operations in this country and abroad. Young men growing up in the faith were expected to follow suit and to do so when called, even though it might disrupt lives or interrupt careers—and possibly even end in tragedy, as in the case of Rudger's missionary companion, Joseph Standing.

\*    \*    \*

It was late July 1879, when Rudger reached Utah with Joseph's body. Sitting on the hard, stuffed straw bench and listening to the steady clack of the wheels and the complaining screech of the cars as they were wrenched around the canyon curves, Rudger stared out the window at the ragged hills through which the Union Pacific had cut its line. He hardly noticed the 1,000-mile-tree, the scraggly conifer that stood approximately 1,000 miles west of Omaha and which had symbolized the progress of the railroad in its early days. The tree stood in Weber Canyon not far from Ogden where Rudger, with Standing's body, would have to disembark and transfer to the Utah Central for the last leg of the journey to Salt Lake.

A solemn crowd composed largely of members of the Young Men's Mutual Improvement Association, of which Joseph had been president before going on his mission, met him at Ogden's Union Station. The casket was lifted to a bier and was accompanied by the Ogden Brass Band playing a dirge as the procession formed and marched down Wall Street to the Utah Central Station.

When they reached Salt Lake, the Utah Central depot was also crowded. On Sunday, August 3, the tabernacle was filled to capacity for the funeral service. Rudger sat quietly and solemnly on the black-draped stand while George Q. Cannon and the president of the church, John Taylor, gave their eulogies.

But Standing's funeral did not end the matter. In October 1879, the attorney general of Georgia wrote Rudger that three of the twelve murderers had been caught and would be tried. Since Rudger was the star witness, he was asked to return and testify. Rudger talked it over extensively with his family and then sought out John Taylor for advice. He felt he had to go because otherwise the men would be set free. "I do not feel like carrying such a heavy responsibility," he said. "I think the State of Georgia should be given the opportunity to vindicate itself. Therefore, I deem it highly important that I should return and attend the trial."

Taylor warned him that it would be dangerous, but approved, though adding, "You must not be alone in Georgia."

John Morgan had been sent back to the Southern states to forestall retaliation by angry Saints. Missionary activity was suspended in the northern part of the state, where the phrase "There is no law in Georgia for the Mormons" had become a watchword among the local populace. Taylor asked Morgan to accompany Rudger during the trial.

After the long train ride across the country he was met in Dalton by

Morgan. "It was not long," Rudger wrote," before we discovered that there was a very bitter feeling against me in Dalton. I could feel it in the air, and could see it in the faces of the people it was so apparent. All the sympathy seemed to go to these three murderers."

They went to visit Rudger's benefactor, Henry Holston, who was happy to see him and glad that he had kept his word. Holston had bet one of his horses against $50 that the young Mormon would return. With Rudger, Holston, Mary Hamline, and Jonathan Owensby testifying against them, the three captives were indicted on two counts of murder and one of riot—much to the surprise and anger of the community. On several occasions during this time, Rudger encountered the murderers themselves in the streets of Dalton. Needless to say, these meetings did nothing to increase his feelings of security.

Morgan hired a lawyer to assist the attorney general in the prosecution. "The man whom we employed was Colonel [W.R.] Moore. It may interest you to know that at that time about every man you met in the Southern States was a colonel. That was a very common title. We notice it on every side—'Colonel' this and 'Colonel' the other. Of course they were not actually colonels at all in the strictest sense of the word." As an incentive they offered "Colonel" Moore an escalating fee, from $100 if the men were convicted of riot up to $500 for first-degree murder.

The trial was heard by Judge Cicero Decatur McCutcheon, a somber man with a snow-white beard, deepset eyes, and a stern mouth. The court, at the request of the defense, agreed to separate trials for the defendants, so that Jasper Nations was tried first, on the charge of first-degree murder.

The *Atlanta Constitution* wrote,

> . . . the famous trial began in earnest. Friends and relations of the prisoner crowded around that portion of the bar set apart to him and his counsel, and the Mormon preachers and their sympathizers ranged near the counsel for the prosecution. It was plain that the legal battle was imminent, and the expectant crowd were eagerly awaiting developments. Presently the sound of the first gun was heard—solicitor Hackett having called the companion of the deceased Standing, Rudger Clawson, to the witness stand. The courtroom was hushed to complete silence. Circuit Reporter Kiker's pencil vibrated nervously as he prepared to record the exact language of the witness as it fell from his lips.

On the stand, Rudger seemed out of place in this upcountry Georgia courtroom. "He was dressed in genteel taste," said the *Constitution*, "and would pass for one of our popular society young men. His language was accurate and concise, his enunciation clear and distinct, and his manner graceful and self-possessed. He certainly evinces education and culture training. No wonder the quiet quaint old-fashioned country folks of the region around about where the homicide was committed thought him dangerous."

At one point during his testimony he was asked about the statements made to him and Joseph prior to the shooting. Rudger repeated the "no law in Georgia for Mormons" boast of one of the gang and then said, "Judging from the manner in which this trial is being conducted I see no reason to question the correctness of his assertion."

The courtroom erupted and McCutcheon had to call a recess.

About the gun which Joseph may or may not have picked up, he waffled. "From the position he assumed," Rudger said of Joseph, "I concluded he had a pistol in his hands, although I did not see it."

Joseph Nations was acquitted, whereupon the murder charges against Andrew Bradley and Hugh Blair were dismissed. Blair and Bradley were then tried for riot in hopes the lesser charge would make a conviction more palatable to the jury, but to no avail.

McCutcheon helped scuttle the prosecution in his charge to the jury by saying that if the group had assembled without intending to do wrong (which each insisted was the case, though clearly they were lying), then only individuals could be convicted of wrongdoing, i.e., murder, not the group as a whole. Since not even Rudger could identify the person who actually fired the fatal shot, the jury was given an easy way out.

Rudger was also furious at McCutcheon for letting one of the defense attorneys attack him personally for the travel and witness fees he could claim. The attorney concluded: "If this man succeeds in getting out of this town alive, he may thank his lucky stars."

"The honorable (?) judge, Judge McCutcheon, sat there like a statue. . . . It was clearly an invitation for somebody, or anyone present, to put me out of the way and thus forestall the payment of my witness fees and mileage."

During the break when the jury was deliberating the Standing murder, Rudger noted the severity with which McCutcheon dispatched the case of a poor black man dragged (literally) into court for stealing a gallon of whiskey. McCutcheon gave him a year at hard labor. Joseph Standing's murderers went free.

But Rudger had little time to dwell on this irony. After the verdict, "The jury in the Standing case was discharged as were also the prisoners at the bar. I felt it was high time I should be discharged too, for one man, a stranger, stepped up to me after the trial and said, 'Mr. Clawson, you do not know me and I am not personally acquainted with you, but if you have any regard for your life, permit me to say you had better get out of here just as quickly as you can.' " He had also heard that there was a movement afoot to have him arrested on perjury charges.

So Rudger departed in haste, leaving the collecting of his fees and mileage to Colonel Moore and feeling once again at the mercy of a Georgia mob. Moore later sent him $500, which was less than he had spent and probably less, Rudger believed, than the colonel had actually collected.

In his memoirs Rudger included without comment the following document written by George Albert Smith, eighth president of the church, who as a youth served in the Southern States Mission:

> While acting as secretary of the Southern States Mission in 1892 I met a man who informed me that he had information as to what had happened to the men who murdered Joseph Standing and that on his return to his home he would write me a letter giving the information, which he did.
>
> Ben Clark resides in Georgia, and is poverty-stricken.
>
> John Fossett [James Fawcett] died a short time after the murder was committed.
>
> James [Hugh] Blair resides in Tennessee and is poverty-stricken.
>
> Newton Nation[s] lives in Arkansas; he has had all kinds of family trouble, and about the same trouble applies to his three brothers, Tom, William and Joe, except the latter, who has paid a small portion of his penalty by losing his eyesight. Joe Nation[s] is supposed to be the one who did the fatal shooting. *
>
> Mack McClure and Jeff Hunter, after absolutely failing to make a living

*The coroner's inquest identified Jasper, David, William and Joseph Nations as gang members. Thomas was apparently a brother to David, William, and Joseph. Newton's identity is uncertain, though he may have been Jasper, who was referred to in the inquest report as Jasper N. Nations.

at their once happy homes, were compelled to ride the 'blind baggage' to ⁊
the West.

Andrew Bradley and Jud [A.S.] and Dave Smith are living in Georgia.
They are all homeless and make a living by doing odd jobs.

This completes the twelve murderers.

George Albert Smith

Rudger went back to work at Z.C.M.I. in November 1879, after
returning from Georgia. It was during this time that he learned
bookkeeping and moved to the bookkeeping department. He also
started moonlighting as a bookkeeper for his half-brother, Spencer
Clawson, a stout, rather sober young man who apparently did not
share the liveliness that seems to have characterized many of his
brothers and sisters. He was fond of and even admired the younger
Rudger, however, and the two were quite close.

Sometime in 1881 or 1882, Spencer, then manager of the Z.C.M.I.
dry goods department, confided in Rudger that he was unhappy with
the salary he was receiving ($150 per month). But instead of asking for
a raise, he decided to wait for the superintendent, William Jennings,
to give it to him without being asked. Jennings was one of Utah's most
active businessmen and community leaders and was mayor of Salt
Lake in addition. It is not difficult to understand why he might forget
to give an employee a deserved raise. Finally Spencer handed in his
resignation and a surprised Jennings immediately offered to increase
his salary to $250. But Spencer turned it down and established his own
dry goods business. (Competing Mormon businesses were now, in
general, tolerated by the church.)

In the summer of 1882 he asked Rudger to assist him in closing his
books, which Rudger accomplished, though he was annoyed when
Spencer insisted that he force a balance with $14 still unaccounted
for. From then on Rudger, working after hours, kept Spencer's books
until he was summarily discharged by Jennings.

It seems that Spencer had taken with him his top salesman at
Z.C.M.I., Orson Rogers. In the ensuing months, Rogers, probably
because of his knowledge of both Z.C.M.I. and the "territory,"
managed to "steal" substantial amounts of business from the larger
firm. Jennings was furious and accused Rudger of supplying Spencer
with inside information which gave Rogers an advantage. He also

charged young Clawson with improper conduct in working for Spencer in his off hours.

Rudger asked for a letter of good character which Jennings refused. Rudger then fired off a missive to John Taylor, who chaired the board of directors of Z.C.M.I., demanding the letter. "I also called attention to the fact that Brother Jennings claimed my full time during, before and after office hours, saying it belonged to Z.C.M.I. and that I had no right, without his permission, to work for Spencer. I told them that I took issue with the General Superintendent on that point, and added that if Brother Jennings' contention is correct then he, being mayor of Salt Lake City, had no right to give attention to city affairs as his whole time belonged to Z.C.M.I." Rudger received his letter from Jennings the day after the next board meeting. A short time later, in January 1883, he went to work full-time for Spencer.

Sometime after his return from Georgia with Joseph Standing's body, Rudger began courting Florence Ann Dinwoodey, daughter of a prominent and increasingly wealthy Salt Lake merchant, Henry Dinwoodey. By 1882 they were engaged to be married.

At eighteen, Florence was a rather large, round-faced young woman, neither plain nor pretty, who wore her dark hair piled on top of her head. There is no record of how she and Rudger met or what the courtship was like, but their engagement was not likely to have surprised anyone. They represented two of the leading families in the Mormon community. Not only was Henry Dinwoodey a rugged entrepreneur who had built a carpenter shop into a large furniture manufacturing and retailing business, but he was also active in church and civic affairs, was a member of the board of a number of businesses, and was a captain in the territorial militia. Earlier, in the Utah War, Dinwoodey had served in a troop of lancers under the command of Hiram Clawson harassing the U.S. army in the mountains between Salt Lake and Fort Bridger.

On a mild spring evening in 1882, Rudger sat in the rather plushly furnished Dinwoodey parlour trying to fathom his fiance's puzzling mood. The course of their relationship had apparently progressed to the point of engagement with little turbulence. Now, however, Florence asked a question which presaged not only immediate trouble but a conflict which would reverberate down through Rudger's life.

"One evening," Rudger recorded in his memoirs, "Florence rather abruptly asked me a significant question, 'If we marry, is it your intention to take another wife during my lifetime?'

"In answer I said, 'Your inquiry surprises me beyond measure. I've never given a single thought to that phase of the subject. However, it is fitting that you should know that being a son of my father's second wife, I am the product of plural marriage. I was born and nurtured and grew to manhood in the atmosphere of plural marriage. I have always believed the doctrine to be a true doctrine. And since you put the question unequivocally and emphatically, I will say frankly, Yes, if conditions arise in the future that make the step appear to be right and proper for me. I will undoubtedly take a plural wife.' "

That Rudger had never thought of becoming a polygamist is very unlikely. As a missionary he had defended plural marriage over and over again. In addition, at that very moment he was courting another woman, one for whom he felt emotions of a kind never inspired by Florence Dinwoodey. Her name was Lydia Spencer.

In the spring of 1880 Rudger had been called to a home mission rather than being sent back into the mission field outside Utah. One of the places he visited was Pleasant Green, a village some fifteen miles west across the valley at Millstone Point. Pleasant Green lay at the northern tip of the Oquirrh Mountains and had been settled by ranchers (mining would come later).

On a Sunday evening, after preaching at the Pleasant Green ward house, Rudger was invited to dinner by Mary Jane and Ulrich Auer. Lydia was one of Mary Jane's daughters by a previous marriage. It was apparently on this evening that love sealed Lydia and Rudger's fate.

"Sam," Lydia said afterward to her younger brother, "if I ever marry, that Brother Clawson will be my husband."

"Why, Lydia, maybe he is a married man," Sam teased.

"I don't care if he has a dozen wives, I'd marry him anyway!"

Sam reminded her that her sister, Alvira, had already invited Lydia to join her in a polygamous marriage with her husband, John Hirst— to which Lydia had replied, "I would rather lie down and die than marry John in polygamy."

Now she said coyly, "Well, it makes a difference who the man is."

Lydia's father, Daniel Spencer, had been a Mormon convert from Massachusetts who became a prosperous farmer and was mayor of Nauvoo at the time the Mormons were driven out. In the exodus he was captain of the first company of Saints to arrive in the Salt Lake valley after Brigham's pioneer band (and earned a footnote in history by bringing with him the first mail to be delivered in the valley). In Utah he "engaged in farming and various industries," including "a ranch in Rush Valley, from which we were unjustly ousted by Johnston's army, at a loss to us of many thousand dollars." The ranching operation was reestablished in Pleasant Green. He also owned a farm southeast of the city. He was the third and most important of the early presidents of the Salt Lake Stake, presiding over the laying out of the streets, the establishment of schools (including the University of Deseret, of which his brother Orson, became chancellor), the establishment of the General Tithing Office and Perpetual Immigration Fund, and the "move south" during the Utah War. He also served as chief justice of the church court (which functioned for some time as the only court of justice in Utah; Brigham Young once called Spencer "the wisest man in Salt Lake"), and was a member of the territorial legislature.

In 1853 he went on a mission to England where he met and fell in love with a recent convert, Mary Jane Cutcliffe. Daniel encouraged her to emigrate and she did, arriving in Utah in December 1856. A week later they were married and she joined his three other wives, two of whom he had just married earlier that year, at his home on Third Avenue South and State Street.

Daniel Spencer was a lean, tough-looking man with the appearance of having been hardened, though not embittered, by his experiences in life. His square-jawed face seemed to have been etched in stone.

Mary Jane had four children in the next ten years and lived comfortably at the home on Third Avenue with occasional periods spent at the ranch in Pleasant Green. But when Daniel died, things changed. As Amelia, Lydia's younger sister, describes it: "My father left considerable property and made provision for all of his children to have a good education, but due to poor management of his estate the property was mostly lost, so that mother was forced to work to support her children." She did retain the house on Third Avenue, however, and apparently some property in Pleasant Green.

Lydia was eight years old when her father died in 1868, and it was this time of relative poverty that she remembered most vividly in later years. Her mother turned to dressmaking which she had learned in

England. Lydia, unable to attend school, earned money taking care of children with her sister Alvira. They also got up early and gathered scraps of material that had been swept from milliners' shops. These sweepings were prized by Mary Jane and Lydia, to be used as trim on the dresses they made. Lydia borrowed a sewing machine and got odd jobs hemming tablecloths and sewing flour sacks at a penny a piece. At first a potential employer laughed at her "because I was very small for my age but I begged of her to give me a trial and she did and I satisfied her." Soon she was hiring out as a seamstress at a dollar a day.

She and Sam also had responsibility for feeding "Bluey," a lone cow they kept. To do so they raided the garbage cans of the city's restaurants and saloons to collect "swill" suitable for the beast. They peddled butter made from the cow's milk, and also kept chickens and sold the eggs.

Sam says that Lydia "was a very pretty girl," hounded by suitors, "but our mother was not in a hurry to let our Lydia slip away," at least not until Alvira was safely sealed to John Hirst. Then came the inevitable first love—a young man with the unlikely name of Nephi McClean, who unfortunately got into a squabble with his stepfather over some horses he, Nephi, believed he owned. He was charged with horse stealing and the newspapers wrote that he "was betrothed to a beautiful innocent girl living at Pleasant Green. Maybe you can just picture the drama. . . ." says Sam. In any event, that ended it. Lydia was heartbroken and threatened to run away to California, but she never did.

Then came Rudger. Soon after their meeting, Lydia persuaded her mother to move back to the Third Avenue house in Salt Lake so that she could pursue her new love, an occupation in which she was certainly engaged in 1882 and to which, judging from what happened later, Rudger was obviously receptive. He saw her often, taking her dancing and to the theater. They took walks in City Creek Canyon and climbed Ensign Peak together. Thus Rudger's disavowal of ever having given a single thought to plural marriage was less than straightforward if not an out-and-out falsehood.

Indeed Lydia believed that Rudger's mother, Margaret Clawson, was distressed that her son would become serious with a girl who, not having been able to go to school, was semiliterate. She had, therefore, cooked up the romance between Rudger and Florence. In her "Small Sketch of Lydia Spencer Clawson", written in the 1930s, Lydia wrote, "After a wile his mother desided she wanted Rud to marie a rich girl and not a Poor sewing girl so we got seperated . . . and after a while he maried Floson Danwoode." Brother Sam agreed: "Margaret saw Lydia as a 'country cousin' kind of girl and not of the popular 'blue blood' City Bug kind. . . ."

But Margaret's machinations, if such they were, received a sudden jolt the night of the lovers' skirmish over the plural wife issue.

"Removing our engagement ring deliberately from her finger," Rudger wrote of Florence, "she returned it to me with this remark, 'If that is your intention, we must part company.' And we parted company, the engagement being broken. A little later I left her home thinking that so far as Florence Ann Dinwoodey and I were concerned, the broken engagement was the closing episode of our lives. Not so, however. In some mysterious manner, I know not how it happened, we came together again some months later, the engagement was renewed and in the fall of the year (August 1882) we were sealed in marriage in the Endowment House, Temple Block, Salt Lake City.

The course of events may not have been anywhere near so mysterious as he thought or said he thought. It is not at all improbable that Margaret not only engineered the romance with Florence in the first place (conspiring perhaps with Anne Dinwoodey, fellow thespian and Florence's mother), but put the engagement back together again as well.

Lydia was shattered. Sam wrote, "Poor sister Lydia heard about it, read about it—and cried about it—but it was too late. It was done. Her Hero love was given to another! So back to the country home came mother and sister Lydia."

One wonders if Rudger's acquiescence in marriage to Florence was somewhat calculated, designed really just to satisfy his mother. Calculated or not, Rudger was quick to patch things up with Lydia, and soon they were courting again.

Early in 1883 he told Florence he was going to marry Lydia. "My words greatly agitated her," he wrote with some understatement. Florence admits she was not deceived, but "I am somewhat surprised at the suddenness of the blow." She had "fondly hoped" he would not take another wife for at least ten years. Rudger recognized that his real mistake was in not marrying them both at the same time. "You would then have had less reason for jealousy and sorrow," he argued with dubious logic.

In the Endowment House, which was the setting for the sacred rites of the church until the temple could be made ready for use, Rudger Clawson, with Florence by his side, knelt before Joseph F. Smith and was sealed to Lydia Spencer for time and all eternity.

It was March 29, 1883.

One year before, almost to the day, President Chester A. Arthur had signed the Edmunds Act of 1882 into law. The Edmunds Act, which put teeth into earlier but ineffective anti-polygamy legislation, was the turning point in the stormy history of Mormon relations with the rest of American society. It also changed Rudger Clawson's life.

# CHAPTER 3
# THE
# TRIAL

C ontroversy had raged over the Edmunds Act in the Utah Territory from the moment it was introduced into Congress early in 1892; newspapers were filled with argumentation about it, and Rudger had discussed it over and over with family and friends.

Senator George Edmunds was the most recent in a long line of Vermont Republicans who, since the time of Justin Morrill, had mounted an almost obsessive legislative attack on the Mormons and polygamy. There was more than a little irony in this fact, since Vermont had been the birthplace of both Joseph Smith and Brigham Young, and it hinted of motives more complex than moral indignation.

But indignation there was. By the early 1880s, editors, preachers, and reformers had aroused the country against polygamy. Congress and federal officialdom were furious at the way Mormons flouted the earlier antibigamy law, the Morrill Act, and manipulated the territorial court system to neutralize it. Control of the Utah judiciary was restored to the federal government by the Poland Law of 1874, but juries could still be packed with Mormons who would not convict polygamists.

In response, Senator Edmunds, a doughty Reconstructionist and a respected constitutional lawyer with presidential ambitions (backed by Theodore Roosevelt he would give Blaine a brief run for the Republican nomination in 1884), drew up the needed legislation and guided it through a flurry of assaults from unreconstructed southern Democrats.

The Democrats, of course, argued that antipolygamy legislation was simply Republican politics as usual. Edmunds and his Republican cohorts, they charged, had no expectation that the law would eradicate polygamy. Their principal aim, now that slavery had at least formally been stamped out, was to keep alive the fervent commitment of those who had originally flocked to the banner of the Republican party in its sacred war against the "twin relics of barbarism."*

Indeed the acerbic, anti-Mormon *Salt Lake Tribune* was already calling the Edmunds Act a failure. The editors ranted at the way the Mormons were outwitting the government. The law had provided for the exclusion of polygamists from public office and from the voter lists, but when carried out, these provisions had had little effect because *believers* in polygamy had not been excluded, only the polygamists themselves. This, said the *Tribune*, left the bulk of the Mormons enfranchised and able to perpetuate the political and moral abuses which the gentiles had hoped the Edmunds Act would curb. The decline in the pro-Mormon vote had been insignificant. The Mormons, charged the gentile opposition, was therefore just as arrogantly in control as before and had been highly effective in thwarting efforts to make the law work.

Implementation of the provisions of the Edmunds Act had been delayed to give the territorial legislature time to pass legislation to bring territorial law into line with federal statutes—as was customary. The Mormon-dominated legislature, however, refused to do so—or to take any other action, real or symbolic, against polygamy. Even the Utah Commission, a group of sober and conservative lawyers sent to oversee the administration of the law had grown weary of the impediments they encountered and was now recommending to Washington more severe measures.

There were two critical—critical at least to Rudger Clawson— provisions of the Edmunds Act. To the $500 fine and five years imprisonment for polygamy already called for in the Morrill Act,

---

*In its first platform in 1856 the newly organized Republican party called on Congress "to prohibit in the Territories those twin relics of barbarism—Polygamy and Slavery."

Congress had added a $300 fine and six months' imprisonment for "unlawful cohabitation." The latter was less severe for the queasy juror and gave the courts an easier charge to prove. More important, the Edmunds Act provided for the exclusion of both polygamists *and* believers in polygamy from juries.

When he married Lydia, Rudger had been counseled to be circumspect. Once the government *did* start prosecuting polygamists, those who had taken plural wives since the passage of the act would be particularly vulnerable.

At least one observer, however, Rudger's friend, Orson Whitney, thought that the precautions taken by Clawson were more or less deliberately inadequate. Rudger, he wrote later in his four-volume *History of Utah*, took "little or no pains to conceal the fact [that he was married to Lydia]. With his usual disregard of danger, he had allowed himself to be seen with her quite often, not only at her home, but upon the streets and in other public places. He did not propose to plead guilty, however, and lose the opportunity of defending in court not only his own case, but the general causes of which circumstances had made him champion."

Rudger and Florence had lived with her family for some months after they were married. Then in March 1883, just before he married Lydia, they had moved to a house on North Temple Street across from Temple Square. It was not a large house, but there was ample room for Lydia.

Yet she did not move in. Caution apparently got the better of the young polygamist. She remained living at her mother's house, though Rudger visited her openly as he had before their marriage. He was often seen taking the little horse-drawn trolley that ran down State Street to Third South to her home. Here he dined with her, made love to her, and socialized with old friends, especially John M. Young, who lived nearby. They attended the theater, went to church together, and visited his father's house.

At some point, Spencer, Rudger's half-brother and employer, hired Lydia as a seamstress. Though she worked at home on the sewing, she came frequently to the store to drop off her work, to shop, or simply to chat with Rudger, sitting with him beside his desk behind a low, dignified oak railing that set his "office" off from the rest of the store.

Whenever she came in, the store began to buzz and the men's eyes followed her, not only because she was a beautiful young woman, but because almost before the final vows were spoken rumors had begun to fly. Orson Rogers, a cousin of Rudger's and the salesman who had taken the measure of the mighty Z.C.M.I., kidded him about having taken another wife, but Rudger never rose to the bait and always responded with good-natured mock surprise that Orson could believe such a thing.

James E. Caine was another matter. Caine, an on-again off-again salesman for Spencer (who, along with most of the other employees, referred to him somewhat derogatorily as a "drummer"), was the son of John T. Caine, a close and long-time associate of Hiram Clawson's in the Salt Lake theater world, and the brother of Rudger's friend and fellow Wasatcher, John T. Caine, Jr. Unfortunately James lacked the charm and capabilities of his father and brother. He had an irritating air of self-importance, a stream of wise-guy patter, and an almost unerring instinct for saying the wrong thing—at least that was Rudger's experience. He was also exasperatingly thick-headed—as he would prove soon enough. When approached by Caine, Rudger had gotten into the habit of responding to him with bored, offhand remarks intended to keep him at bay.

The inevitable moment arrived about a month after his marriage to Lydia, when Caine approached him with a smirk on his face and a snide "Well, Rud, I hear you've taken a second wife." Rudger, not raising his hand from his ledgers, replied with restrained sarcasm, "Mm, yes, so they say." Caine did not persist. But standing nearby, Waldemar Lund, a young Scandinavian immigrant who worked for Spencer, smiled at seeing Caine get his comeuppance.

Not long after Lydia and Rudger were married, Florence announced she was pregnant. Rudger was overjoyed, but not simply out of parental instinct. Florence's pregnancy would give him a way to justify moving Lydia into his house without revealing that she was his plural wife. Ellen, Hiram Clawson's first wife, was the daughter of Daniel Spencer's brother and thus a cousin to Lydia. This made Rudger and Lydia distantly related by marriage. The two of them often jokingly referred to each other as "cousin."

In the fall of the year, when Florence's pregnancy had reached an advanced stage, Rudger moved Lydia into his house ostensibly to provide "cousinly" assistance to his wife. She lived upstairs where she had a sewing room and a bedroom, but the three of them dined and, sometimes, entertained together.

The baby, named Rudger Elmo, was born in January. During Florence's period of confinement, Rudger and Lydia were socially active, especially in the Mutual Improvement Association (MIA) of the Eighteenth Ward in which their house was situated. On January 31 they decided formally to join the MIA, but when it came to signing a register of proposed members, Rudger whispered to her not to use her real name. He smiled as he watched her scrawl laboriously in the space below his: "Lillie Clawson." This too became a private joke between them and among family and close friends.

Rudger was delighted with his new baby and played with him affectionately. But Lydia and Florence—according to stories told later to her daughters by Lydia—did not apparently live in plural bliss. Florence would lock the door between their respective sections of the house to prevent Rudger from going to Lydia and, on occasion, would venture into Lydia's rooms where she would destroy furniture or Lydia's personal belongings. It was clearly a stressful relationship. Florence had been unhappy enough simply at the *idea* of Rudger taking another wife. Now it was not only a reality, but Florence, first restricted by her pregnancy and then confined by childbirth, could only watch helplessly as Rudger escorted Lydia through the Salt Lake winter social season. This situation was almost certainly the spawning ground for the antipathy the two women later displayed toward each other.

But the calm before the storm was about to end. In March 1884 a new U.S. attorney, William H. Dickson, arrived in Salt Lake, and the crusade against polygamy finally got under way. Dickson, an Easterner, came to Utah via Nevada, where he had established a reputation as an able lawyer. With him he brought his partner, Charles S. Varian, who became Assistant U.S. attorney. Varian had been a U.S. attorney in Nevada as well as a member of the state legislature. They knew why they had been appointed and what they had to do and set about the task with a zeal that soon had polygamists throughout Utah on the defensive.

In mid-April Rudger was arrested and brought before a grand jury on charges of polygamy and unlawful cohabitation. During the empaneling of the jury Dickson and Varian rigorously invoked the sections of the Edmunds Act providing for the exclusion of believers in polygamy and engaged in bitter legal brawls with defense attorneys. With the virtual exclusion of Mormons, it took 238 tries before they were finally able to put together a 15-man jury composed solely of jurors who did *not* believe in polygamy. Thirty-eight people were called in open venire* which harked back to Judge James McKean, a fire-eating anti-Mormon (and Vermonter), whose efforts in the early 1870s to bring the Saints to heel by packing juries with anti-Mormons selected through an illegal open venire were struck down by the U. S. Supreme Court. The attorneys also fought over whether the jury selection provisions of the Edmunds Act applied to grand juries at all, the defense maintaining that it was limited to petit juries.

On April 24, Rudger was formally indicted for polygamy and unlawful cohabitation. He was immediately arrested and then released on a $3,000 bond. Franklin Richards, arguing the open venire and jury selection issues, attempted to have the indictment quashed, but was unsuccessful.

It may be that this concentration on legal issues related to jury selection distracted the defense attorneys from the substance of the hearing. Witnesses called before the grand jury were allowed to say things about Rudger and Lydia which were substantially incriminating and which called for an almost ludicrous collective loss of memory by virtually everyone who testified at the subsequent trial.

The last piece in the antipolygamy puzzle fell into place when, in July 1884, Charles S. Zane arrived in Salt Lake to replace Judge John A. Hunter as chief justice of the Third (Salt Lake) District Court. Despite rulings on polygamists, Hunter was considered by Utah radicals to be both incompetent and soft on Mormons.

Zane, on the other hand, was an able and respected judge, no second-rate product of political patronage as were so many of the federal appointees in the Utah Territory. From Illinois, he had known and admired Abraham Lincoln and had replaced him as William Herndon's law partner when Lincoln went to Washington. He had been in positions of some prominence in the circuit courts of Illinois

---

*Jurors are empaneled in "open venire" when they are selected from any source available (frequently off the street) rather than through a systematic, preestablished procedure.

and had surprised many of his friends when he accepted the appointment in Utah. By the time he ascended the bench in September at
the opening of the new term, his strong antipolygamy views were well
known.

The stage was set. The trial of Rudger Clawson, in Utah's Third
District Court in Salt Lake, began on October 5, 1884. It was an
unseasonably warm day, and the courtroom was packed. Despite the
warmth, a large wood stove stood burning just behind the reporters'
bench, causing the journalists to strip to their shirtsleeves.

At the defense table Rudger sat calmly watching the proceedings.
His lawyers were lined up beside him. Franklin S. Richards, tall and
handsome, sat erect and distinguished, despite his youth. He was
attorney for the church and one of the numerous young Mormons
who had started to carve out careers in the law. In the past, the church
court system had stunted the growth of Mormon legal talent capable
of defending the Saints in the courts with skills comparable to those of
the gentiles.

Seeing how vulnerable that had left the church, Brigham Young
began to encourage youthful Mormons to enter the legal profession.
Richards was one of them. Without formal law school training, he
had nevertheless brought to the law an innate brilliance and legal
intuition that made him the match of anyone at the bar. Before a
jury, however, he became stiff and formal.

The proceedings would, therefore, be handled by the dapper, white-
haired non-Mormon, C. W. Bennett, a former judge and a masterful
and eloquent trial lawyer, who had spent most of his adult life in a
courtroom, and by his partner, John Harkness.

Rudger, realizing that he had been thrust into the center of an
impending maelstrom, remembered John Taylor's initial response to
the Edmunds Act:

"We shall abide all constitutional law," Taylor had thundered at
Conference in April 1882, "but . . . we are no craven serfs, and have
not learned to lick the feet of oppressors, nor to bow in base submission
to unreasoning clamor. We will contend inch by inch, legally and
constitutionally, for our rights as American citizens and plant ourselves
firmly on the sacred guarantees of the Constitution."

They were inspiring words and Rudger believed his freedom constituted one of the "inches" over which Taylor promised to contend. On

the bench, Judge Zane, one of the principal contenders, opened the trial. Zane was small of stature, but had an impressive Lincolnesque sobriety and angularity to his face. It was a countenance reflecting sternness and determination. His hair rose to one side in a shock of white, and a neatly-trimmed beard rimmed his strong jaw and chin.

Jury selection, as expected, was a battleground, and once again the government bested the Mormons, although by the end of the first day, they had exhausted their thirty-eight-member panel with only ten jurors selected.

The next day Varian moved an open venire. Zane agreed over Harkness's objection.

The U.S. marshal, Edwin Ireland, stepped forward. Ireland was a tall man with a strong set to his lips and long, unkempt sideburns that sprouted like accidental undergrowth from his youthful cheeks. In the years ahead, he would track down polygamists with relentless determination.

How many people did the judge want?

"A half a dozen names I suppose will suffice. How long will it take you?"

"Fifteen or twenty minutes." While the court recessed, the clerk gave Ireland some slips of paper and he hurried out to the street. There he surveyed the passersby and began accosting non-Mormons until he had six who couldn't think up ways to excuse themselves quickly enough.

Half an hour later the jury was complete, accompanied by a rash of last-minute challenges by Harkness. They had particularly wanted to get rid of Charles Gilmore who, every day, had sported a copy of the *Tribune* and was reported to be "death on Mormons and polygamy." But Zane ruled that they had waited too long.

It was a "straight gentile" jury, the pro-Mormon *Herald* observed.

U.S. Attorney Dickson now came forward to carry the burden of the trial for the prosecution. Dickson was a pale man with smooth, childlike skin and a great growth of carefully trimmed and combed beard hanging from his lower face like some thick wig pasted there in a bizarre disguise. His dark, deep-set eyes evidenced intelligence and determination.

The prosecution began by calling Henry Dinwoodey, Florence's father, and Florence's sister Alice, principally to establish Rudger's first marriage, though bits of information about Lydia's and Rudger's movements were also ferreted out.

The next witness, James E. Caine, was more important. From his encounter with Rudger over the second wife question, Caine had concluded that Rudger had answered in the affirmative. When subpoenas were served on him and others of Spencer's employees to appear at the trial as prosecution witnesses, Rudger had gone to him to help him clarify his memory, but Caine swore that all he had heard was the "yes" in Rudger's reply and not the "so they say." Caine had been extremely stubborn and had blustered about perjury and not going to jail to protect Rudger Clawson's right to marry two wives. Rudger was annoyed and tried to convince Caine that he had misheard, but the drummer would not change his mind, even though he became very confused at one point and said, "By Jove, I don't know what you did say!"—a comment overheard by Orson Rogers and R. V. Decker. If there was doubt, Rudger argued sensibly, then all he had to do was say he wasn't sure. But Caine stiffened and said he *was* sure.

Now, on the stand, Caine was led by Dickson through a description of his relation to Rudger at the store, Lydia's appearances there, and the incident in question. In the end Caine said simply: "I asked him if she was his second wife, and he answered, 'Yes.' "

Caine also described the argument he had had with Rudger after receiving the subpoena. "He declared that he did not say 'yes,' or if he did that it was qualified as 'Yes, that's what they say,' or something to that effect. I replied that I did not hear him say anything but 'Yes.' 'Well, you admit there is a doubt,' he said. I answered, 'Yes, there is a doubt, but not in my mind,' I meant that the doubt was in his mind."

A series of Clawsons followed Caine on the witness stand. Dickson picked at Spencer for a long time, trying to find something incriminating in Lydia's visits to his store. It was not easy since she was in his employ. Did she charge things to Rudger's name? No. What about the parcel incident?

Spencer had almost let the cat out of the bag when, one day, a parcel for Lydia was left at the store. R. V. Decker, the shipping clerk, found it and asked Spencer, "Whose is this?"

"Rud's wife's," Spencer replied.

"Which one?"

Spencer, realizing that Lydia's status had been openly revealed, laughed. "That's a good piece of evidence," he had said.

Now Dickson asked, "Did you say, 'That's a good piece of evidence?' " Spencer thought for a moment, but couldn't recall having said it. Dickson asked how often Rudger had been absent from work. A series of questions along this line succeeded only in portraying Rudger as a man of striking dependability and diligence. He was virtually never absent.

The prosecution would try in subsequent testimony to establish that plural marriages could take place only in the Endowment House in Salt Lake and the temples at Logan and St. George, each of which was some distance away. If they could prove Rudger had not been absent long enough to go to either of the temples, then the marriage would have had to have taken place in Salt Lake, that is, within the jurisdiction of Zane's court. Their efforts along this line, however, were more or less fruitless.

So ended the second day of the trial.

✳   ✳   ✳

The trial reconvened the next day, with Sidney and then Stanley Clawson taking the stand. The questioning shifted to Rudger and Lydia's appearances at the Eighteenth Ward MIA. Varian produced the MIA membership records showing the mysterious "Lillie Clawson" listed just below Rudger's name. Try as they might, however, neither Varian nor Dickson was able to unearth the truth about Lillie. It was hardly surprising since they had to rely on the testimony of a series of witnesses, two of whom were Rudger's brothers and one (Orson Rogers) a second cousin. These men, like Spencer and father Hiram later, all suffered from lapses of memory so incredible that one might have wondered if it were a congenital defect.

Sidney Clawson, Rudger's younger full brother, had actually testified before the grand jury that Lydia had been called "Lillie" at MIA, but now he could not remember having done so. Dickson showed him the minutes of the grand jury hearings and asked again if he remembered, but Sidney stood firm. He went on denying and evading until he finally said flatly: "I know of no member of the Clawson family who is a member of the Eighteenth Ward Society named Lillie Clawson. I do have a sister named Lulu," he added helpfully.

Dickson waved him to the defense in disgust. The defense as usual declined to cross-examine. Dickson was doing their job beautifully.

Stanley Clawson's memory was worse than brother Sidney's. Dapper and articulate, Stanley (Rudger's *older* full brother) nevertheless could not remember testifying that he had seen Lydia and Rudger together the previous Christmas at his mother's house—he might have, but thought not. He also did not remember testifying that he saw them frequently on the Third South Street trolley. "I am not in the habit of traveling that way. These things pass from my mind. I can't remember everything. My memory is not very good at best." After a few more minutes of not remembering much, Stanley was dismissed and Dickson conferred with Varian.

The formidable Hiram Bradley Clawson was next on their list. Having nearly been made fools of by two of his sons, they could hardly have relished a confrontation with the father. But they called him anyway.

Hiram Bradley Clawson was not a big man, but he was sturdily built and somewhat imposing. A high forehead was squared off by the line of his neatly combed hair. His cheeks were full and round, and he wore a large moustache of long, coarse hair. Thick eyebrows shadowed deep-set eyes giving them a slightly fearsome look as if he might at any moment growl through the thicket of hair covering his mouth.

Hiram's examination focused on his testimony at the grand jury hearing where he had said that his son Rudger "had expressed a belief in plural marriage." Why he had said it is hard to explain, but now Dickson bore down on it.

Had he so testified?

Well, he could not remember. Hiram had been coached about how to handle this question without committing perjury, but he was nevertheless treading on thin ice.

Dickson asked if he would deny he had so testified.

No, only that he had no recollection.

The U.S. attorney was furious. His voice rose as he repeated: "Will you say that you did not testify before the grand jury that Rudger Clawson accepted the law of plural marriage as a divine law?"

Bennett objected.

"He testified and he knows it," Dickson said angrily.

"You can't force him to know a thing," Bennett replied.

After a few more frustrating tries, Dickson raised a notebook he had been holding and began. "These grand jury minutes. . . ."

But Bennett interrupted: "What are those minutes? They may have been made on the street. I think they were."

"Why?" Dickson asked, a little flustered.

"Because everybody denies them," Bennett replied to a titter in the courtroom.

From Rudger's father they moved to Lydia's mother, Mary Jane Auer. She too was hostile, "Somewhat of a Tartar," the *Herald* called her. She had remarkably little information about Lydia, including her present whereabouts. "Do you know where your daughter is now?"

"I couldn't say," she replied, bristling underneath.

"When you last saw her, where was she?"

"Traveling westward," Mrs. Auer said to smiles in the courtroom.

Then came church president John Taylor. At the call of his name, Taylor stood up and began to move down the aisle. As he strode toward the witness stand, voices buzzed and the spectators stretched to see. Taylor had been with Joseph Smith at the time of the prophet's martyrdom in Carthage and had been shot five times. He still carried one of the bullets in his leg and sometimes limped on standing.

As he took the witness stand, a hush fell. Seating himself, he filled the chair with his large frame. He had been a journeyman turner and builder when missionary Parley Pratt had chanced upon him in Toronto. His hands were still those of a carpenter. His face was square and handsome, with eyes ready to spark.

Dickson, moving toward him, began in a low tone, respectfully inquiring if Taylor heard well, then verifying that he was president of the church. Moments later he was chasing the elusive Taylor as he would chase him for the rest of his long testimony.

"How long have you occupied the office of president?"

"Well, I cannot say precisely. The records will show." Virtually everyone else in the courtroom could have told him to the day.

"You are familiar with the laws and revelations that have been given to the church?"

"Not as familiar as I might be, perhaps," Taylor replied modestly, "but I know a number of them."

Dickson then turned to the Mormon marriage sacrament. Patiently fighting his way through a thicket of objections thrown up by the defense attorney, Bennett, Dickson sought to establish that plural marriages were required by the church to be performed at the Endowment House and that John Taylor, as president of the church, either performed the ceremony or appointed those who did.

The Endowment House was central to the case. Until this point in time, plural marriages could only be performed in the Endowment House in Salt Lake or in one of the two temples located elsewhere in the territory. Further, the ceremony could only be performed by persons authorized to do so by the president of the church. If these facts could be established before the court and the marriage records subpoenaed, the government would have a stranglehold on the church.

But Taylor was not to be outmaneuvered. As Dickson picked his way through the defense objections toward the admissible question about Endowment House marriages, Taylor retreated, treading carefully the fine line between truth and perjury. Taylor was fully aware that he was laying the foundation for the defense of plural marriage in the time of persecution that clearly lay ahead.

When Dickson was finally able to ask him if the church required marriages in the Endowment House, Taylor's answer was "No."

Surprised, Dickson asked where else they were performed.

But Taylor was off and running again. "I cannot say," he replied.

Dickson, in pursuit, could only get disconnected fragments of information from Taylor, whose loss of memory was Promethean. What slowly emerged, however, was that the authority to perform plural marriages, heretofore concentrated in the hands of a few church leaders, had been granted to others and that the ceremony which from the beginning was carefully guarded and restricted in practice to certain sanctified settings, could now be performed in many different places.

The implications of what Taylor was doing were far-reaching, but were not obvious to Attorney Dickson, who doggedly pursued the names of the people authorized to perform plural marriages—while Taylor just as persistently denied that he had anything to do with such "details."

If Taylor didn't know, could he find out who is authorized, Dickson wondered.

"I might by asking the parties."

"But if you don't know who to ask?"

"Then I wouldn't know who to ask."

When Dickson, a few moments later, wanted Taylor to confirm that with his "unaided recollection" he could not say who is authorized, Taylor replied with a straight face, "My recollection would tell me of hundreds if I could remember their names!"

In frustration Dickson turned to the marriage records, perhaps feeling more comfortable with something concrete. But these were also "details," with which Taylor had nothing to do. Could he find out who did have charge of the records, Dickson asked. Taylor presumed he could.

Dickson, politely: "Will you be good enough to do so?"

Taylor, blandly, "Well, I am not good enough to do so." (Laughter in the courtroom.)

The encounter with Taylor was turning into a fiasco.

"Who is the custodian of the records?" Dickson asked bluntly.

"I cannot tell you."

"Did you ever know who the custodian of the records was?"

"I do not know that I ever did."

"Do you know that you don't know?"

"Yes, I know that I don't."

"You know that you have never known who the custodian was? Have you ever inquired of anyone where the record was?"

"I could not say positively whether I have or not."

"What is your best recollection?"

"I don't know."

"You don't know as to whether you have inquired as to the custodian of the record?"

"I do not think I have."

"Have you ever been told who the custodian of the record was?"

"Not to my recollection."

It was hopeless. Dickson finally launched into the nature of plural marriage itself.

"Is it not a fact, Mr. Taylor, that plural marriage is a secret rite, a secret ceremony?"

"It is secret to some and not to others," Taylor replied obscurely. Dickson tried to clarify. Others could be present, Taylor said. But wouldn't they have to be members of the priesthood or persons in authority, Dickson asked. No, others could be recommended. Aren't the parties who are married enjoined to secrecy? Not that Taylor was aware of.

Dickson turned away and then spun and asked: "What is the ceremony of plural marriage?"

Abruptly motion ceased in the courtroom, fans came to a standstill, arms which had been raised to wipe away sweat or scratch a cheek froze.

"I do not propose to state it."

"Do you decline to answer?"

"I do."

"We object, your honor," this from Bennett who had been caught unaware. The question was withdrawn. The government was not yet ready for the showdown which forcing Taylor into contempt would bring about.

The rest of the prosecution's presentation was pretty much downhill, though Angus Cannon, a member of the Quorum of the Twelve Apostles and president of the Salt Lake Stake provided some light moments as the prosecution sought the same information it had failed to obtain from Taylor. He was a friendly man, rather stout, with a round happy face and a receding hair line.

"How is the record of marriages in your church perpetuated?" Varian asked him brusquely.

"I suppose everyone keeps his own," Cannon replied impishly. "I do mine."

Varian went on, tired of the charade into which the trial had degenerated. "Is there any kind, shape or manner of record written, cut, carved, movable or immovable, or anything else from which these marriages can be learned?"

"I know of none."

"You never saw the record?"

"Never."

"Never heard of it?"

"Never."

"Then you could never get records from the church archives?"

"I don't know," Cannon replied to the delight of the onlookers. "I never had the occasion to find out."

Did he write the names of the parties on a slip of paper when he was officiating? Varian asked. Yes. And did what with them? Burned them.

And what about divorces? Varian almost shouted. How can you separate people if there's no record of having joined them?

But Bennett, hardly able to hide his amusement, stepped in then— though a little reluctantly. "We object. This is not a divorce suit; we are on the other branch of the business."

It was a banner day for the spectators.

In conclusion a few minor character actors were paraded across the stage. The most interesting was Waldemar Lund, the young Norwegian boy who worked for Spencer. On the stand he repeatedly brushed bright blonde hair out of his eyes with a nervous stroke and spoke with a charming accent. Lund had little to add to the testimony. Indeed, he testified that he had never heard Rudger say anything about his relationship with Lydia Spencer, despite the fact that Rudger knew Lund had overheard his exchange with Caine and had agreed to say so in court.

He was apparently frightened and confused, so much so that he started anticipating Dickson's questions, causing the attorney to yell: "Don't say 'no' to my questions until you have heard them!"—after which Lund whispered his answers very slowly, which, given his accent, made them difficult to understand.

On the fourth day of the trial Dickson and Varian valiantly reentered the arena of combat, though they had few weapons left at their disposal. George Q. Cannon, first counselor to President Taylor and Angus's brother, was the most renowned of the day's witnesses, but all they could do was badger him as they had the others about the marriage records and the little slips of paper on which he wrote the names of the marrying parties. It was familiar ground and equally arid. After that, for the rest of the morning and part of the afternoon, came a miscellany of witnesses, most of little help—friends and relatives of Rudger's and landlords and landladies describing how often they saw Rudger with Lydia Spencer. They tried to get someone to identify Lillie as Lydia. They brought Mrs. Auer back to ask if she had heard from her daughter. All for nought.

Their last witness was George Reynolds, who entered to a hush of anticipation. In 1875, after years of more or less ignoring the Morrill Anti-Bigamy Law, Brigham Young and the church authorities had decided to cooperate in testing it. Confident that the law was unconstitutional and would be found so by the Supreme Court, they offered as guinea pig Brigham's private secretary, the two-wived George Reynolds. But contrary to expectations the Supreme Court conclusively affirmed the act's constitutionality and sent Reynolds to the penitentiary for two years. For the church it was a blunder of alarming proportions. It removed the constitutional argument from their arsenal of weapons and greatly strengthened the antipolygamists.

Reynolds' testimony was inconsequential, but Rudger watched him closely as he gave his terse replies to the questions asked. Rudger knew him well, because Reynolds had been with Brigham during the time Rudger had been a clerk in Brigham's office. More important, Rudger felt that the Supreme Court had failed the Mormons in the *Reynolds* case. Many lawyers and politicians had challenged the constitutionality of the antibigamy law under which he was convicted. Rudger agreed with them and with those who felt the Edmunds Act was unconstitutional as well. All the lies, or near lies, that had been spoken here on his behalf, all the evasions, covering of tracks, the blanking out of the church's memory were justified because the law was unconstitutional. If it were not, how could he go on revering the Constitution? His marriages and his wives were his religion. They were part of the gospel for which he had almost died in Georgia—for which Joseph Standing *had* died.

In ending for the prosecution Dickson pointed out that subpoenas had been issued for Lydia Spencer and Margaret Clawson, neither of whom had been found. (Not only had Lydia disappeared, but Rudger's mother, Margaret, and Florence's mother, Anne, had gone into hiding as well.) He simply wanted the court to know that their absence had not occurred for want of trying.

Harkness, in opening for the defense, swept the statement aside by reminding the court that the jury would have to decide on the evidence presented to it, not on prejudicial suppositions about the absence of witnesses.

The defense felt the need to call only a few witnesses. The prosecution hardly had a case. Waldemar Lund, under kindly questioning, admitted to having heard Rudger reply to Caine's question with the phrase, "So they say." On cross-examination Dickson wondered why Lund was now saying that he had heard the conversation, having denied it the day before. Because, Lund replied, he had not understood the question. Then Dickson scuttled himself by asking: "Are you a Mormon?" To which Lund answered, "No, sir." As Dickson did a double-take, there was general astonishment in the courtroom. Everyone, including Dickson, must have assumed that this young man was from one of the hundreds of immigrant families that had come over from Scandinavia as Mormon converts in recent years.

Orson Rogers and R. V. Decker both had heard the argument between Caine and Rudger over what Rudger had said and testified that Caine had indeed exclaimed, "By Jove, I don't know what you did say!"

The final witness was Marshal Ireland who was asked about the arrival and departure times of trains in 1883. The prosecution had spent a great deal of time trying to establish that Rudger could not have been away long enough to get married in some other jurisdiction. Bennett thought it would be nice to throw a little doubt into that just in case any of the jurors were convinced.

Ireland answered as best he could about the trains, though he was obviously somewhat bewildered. Then he was suddenly left speechless when Harkness asked: "Do you know how long it takes to celebrate a plural marriage?"

The marshal finally mumbled, "No, sir," and was dismissed.

As court adjourned the collective sigh of relief was almost audible. It was Saturday. The testimony had come to a nicely timed conclusion. The hiatus over Sunday would build suspense for the summations on Monday.

On Monday the courtroom was jammed. In his summation for the prosecution, Varian opened bluntly, making sure no one would miss the significance of the trial. "Once more," he said, "after a lapse of many years, the government of the United States is brought face to face with the Mormon Church."

He noted the church's defiance of the Congress and the courts and ridiculed the Mormons as "faint-hearted martyrs" who should stand up like men and face the consequences of placing themselves above the law. Instead they tried to cover their tracks by "evasion . . .

equivocation and fraud!" The prosecution, he said, had put all those hostile and useless witnesses on the stand to demonstrate "that there was an effort afoot to frustrate and defeat the administration of justice." He referred scornfully to the missing Lydia Spencer.

> Of all the people who should be interested in this trial, Lydia Spencer should be the most interested, yet where is she? Gone! No one knows where, not even her mother who bore her; she has dropped out of existence, dissipated into air, gone where the woodbine twineth, no more to be resurrected until this jury is discharged. Mrs. Henry Dinwoodey, the mother of Florence, has also vanished into air just as completely. . . . Mrs. Margaret Clawson, she too has taken the underground railway.

By this time he had the spectators warmed up and they burst into laughter as he finished—"and she also has gone into etherealness." He concluded by doing his best to make a case out of the paltry evidence.

Bennett, wearing a bright bow tie and sparkling studs in his shirt, rose to speak for the defense. He knew his first job was to make it clear that it was not the Mormon church on trial. Taylor and the others representing the church had made a shambles of the prosecution's case. But it was still Rudger Clawson who would go to jail if convicted. Bennett had a strong sense of history. He must have known that he stood at the beginning of a great judicial confrontation and relished the moment. He was probably surprised at Judge Zane for letting the defense get away with as much as it had. Zane would have to toughen up if he expected to catch these wily Mormons.

Unpopular churches, he began, had often been the target of tyrannical governments. He didn't have to cite instances; the jury knew its history—though he then went ahead and cited them, touching in the process as many of the sacred tenets of American libertarianism as he could. A climactic plea that "this great government of ours not repeat the crimes of other governments," won him a burst of applause.

Bennett then went on to draw the picture of the cousinly relationship between Lydia and Rudger as it emerged in all its innocence from the evidence of the prosecution. "We find Lydia there [living with Rudger and Florence] just previous to Mrs. Clawson's confinement, occupying a sewing room and a sitting room. She is a cousin of the defendant . . . and yet because she is here ensconced as a sewing woman at a time when Florence was an invalid, you are asked to suspect the defendant to be guilty of—what? An illicit correspondence with the cousin! And yet we have heard of no word of complaint or protest from the first wife."

When he turned to the prosecution, he devastated their case, tearing it apart piece by piece in a brilliant forensic display. It was based entirely on bits and pieces of circumstantial evidence and hearsay. He finished with a ringing peroration on prejudice and seated himself to another round of applause.

Dickson and Richards added their summings-up, but neither contributed much to what had already been said.

In his charge to the jury the next morning, Judge Zane surprised everyone by stating that "admissions and declarations of the defendant hastily made are entitled to but little weight." The prosecution's entire case rested on Rudger's alleged hastily-made admission to James Caine that he had taken a second wife. The Mormons were jubilant and predicted a hung jury. They got it at eight o'clock that evening when the twelve weary men filed back into the courtroom, hopelessly split, eight for conviction, four against.

But as the Clawsons celebrated and the church heaved an ecclesiastical sigh of relief, a critical little drama was taking place back at the apartment where Lydia had been living before going underground. For reasons unknown, she had returned from her hiding place.

When a knock came at the door she hurried to open it, expecting her sister, Millie, who had been keeping her informed on the course of the trial. Instead, there appeared Deputy U.S. Marshal Lindsay Sprague with a subpoena.

Earlier that evening, at about the time Lydia was being served, a deputy had also appeared at Hiram's door looking for Margaret. The imperious Hiram asked if he had a search warrant and, finding that he had not, refused him entry. "Even if I knew the lady you want was forty miles away," he had said in disdain, "I wouldn't let you in without a search warrant." While Hiram was denying the marshal entrance, one of Rudger's brothers, probably Stanley, dressed up in Margaret's clothes and went tearing off in the carriage with half a dozen deputies chasing after. One of them managed to catch hold of the hind straps and hang on for a while until finally, bruised and splattered with mud, he fell off.

Marshal Ireland himself approached Henry Dinwoodey's house in the coordinated assault—but without success. Anne was nowhere about. Lydia was the prize, however, and the marshals must have indulged in an orgy of self-congratulations at having snared her.

The next day, over strenuous objections by the defense (and while Rudger and Lydia exchanged surreptitious glances), Zane, in rapid order, agreed to a new trial, denied a change of venue, and approved an open venire for empaneling a jury.

"If the defendant is guilty," said Zane, "then he should be convicted; if he is innocent he should be acquitted and there is no time like the present for deciding the case."

The trial was then "proceeded" to 2:00 p.m.

Rudger and his cortege gathered at Hiram's while Lydia went back to Mrs. Smith's with Millie and several friends. The young women talked animatedly through the midday meal, then decided to go for a buggy ride. A carriage full of deputies waited behind them ready to follow.

"Let's give them a run," said Lydia, whipping the horse off into a gallop. For the next hour they wound their way through the streets of Salt Lake, laughing as they watched the carriage behind, weighted down with stout male deputies, trying to keep up.

When the court convened that afternoon, Lydia did not answer to her name. Angry, Zane ordered an attachment to issue for her, but a few minutes later she walked briskly in with her friends while the judge glared at her in silence. Still spirited from the chase through the city, she sat and stared back unintimidated.

This time it took them seventy-four tries to select the jury, again "straight gentile."

Zane knew that Rudger's lawyers would carry the open venire issue to the Supreme Court, but he smelled a conviction and would let nothing stand in his way.

The next day after calling only enough witnesses to establish a case, Dickson turned to the clerk and announced in a voice pitched to the drama of the moment: "Call Lydia Spencer."

The courtroom was electric as Lydia rose from the midst of a crowded front bench, made her way to the witness stand, and turned to face the prosecution. She was dressed neatly in black and wore a wide-brimmed straw hat with a white feather in it. Her handsome face was pale but her square jaw was set, her lips in a tight line. She looked straight at Dickson.

The clerk routinely asked her to stand and take the oath.

"I decline to take the oath," she said in a strong, clear voice.

"Will you affirm?" Dickson asked calmly without apparent surprise. Persons declining to take oaths for conscience's sake were given the opportunity to affirm their willingness to testify.

"No, sir."

"What is your reason?"

"Well, I just decline to take it," she said with a simplicity and firmness that made Rudger's heart ache.

Dickson, however, was unmoved. He called for a contempt citation and reminded the court that since this was a federal case Lydia could be jailed for as much as a year rather than the five days called for by territorial law. The defense countered and a long argument ensued.

But the courts had already proven they would imprison women in polygamy cases, and it was expected that Zane would follow suit. Belle Harris had become a heroine when she had been imprisoned for refusing to testify against her husband—even though she was in the process of divorcing him. Pregnant Annie Gallifant's imprisonment had shocked the territory. She was in for only one day, but she had been near term and had delivered shortly after release. Just the preceding spring, Nellie White had served a month and a half in the territorial penitentiary. There was also the threat of being sent to a women's facility back East.

Dickson asked again that a contempt citation be rendered and "if the final decision is not reached now that the criminal be kept in custody." His slight stress on the word "criminal" brought gasps from some of the spectators.

Zane turned to Lydia. "Now, Miss Spencer," he said, in a voice as gentle as circumstances would permit, "Don't you know it is wrong for you not to be sworn or affirm and testify?"

"It may be so," she replied.

"That being so, you don't want to do wrong."

"I decline to testify," she repeated, refusing to respond to the patronizing tone in his voice.

"You know the consequence is that you may have to be imprisoned, for how long I do not wish to say yet."

"No, that depends on you."

"Well, he said, his voice hardening a little, "in view of that, don't you think you ought to answer the truth?"

"Not if I don't feel like it." Her calculated innocence was exquisite.

"Well," said Zane, becoming once again the tough judge, "you take a fearful responsibility in undertaking to defy the government. Remember you become a criminal in the estimation of the law and will have to take the consequence of being a felon as far as the imprisonment is concerned. You will be committed to the custody of the marshal until morning." Adjournment was called.

Most of the spectators stood up but few left as they craned their necks to see what would happen to Lydia, perhaps watching for some kind of exchange between her and Rudger. For a few minutes Ireland observed the mild confusion that resulted and then shouted: "Clear the courtroom," and several deputies began to urge people toward the door.

It was at that point that a young reporter from the *Daily Herald* looked up and saw Lydia more or less unattended. He went over to her and introduced himself. She put out her hand and greeted him warmly.

"Well, Miss Spencer, have you got your courage to the sticking point?" he asked, trying to be cheerful.

"Oh, yes," she replied in a spritely voice. She was not noticeably in need of cheering up. "I made up my mind, and this is no surprise for me."

"Do you think you can stand it if a severe sentence is imposed?"

"I expect nothing but that the judge will go to extremity. I have no hope of anything but a heavy penalty.

"The Marshal says he has not a suitable place about here for me," Lydia said calmly "so I must make up my mind to go out to the penitentiary tonight, I suppose. Well, it won't be anything new to be surrounded by deputy marshals anyway. We have had five of them on duty ever since I was served."

"What do you think of the trial?" the reporter asked. "Were you disturbed by young Caine's testimony?"

"No, he obviously couldn't remember what was said. I don't see why he couldn't just admit it."

"Do you know him well?"

"No, hardly at all. He's a drummer you know. He's on the road most of the time. I'm not sure I would trust him, though."

"Where were you during the first trial?"

She looked at him with a straight face. "Where the woodbine twineth," she said, her eyes sparkling.

"Will spending the night in the penitentiary change your mind about being sworn in?"

"Certainly not."

Ireland came to get her then.

The courtroom crowd had gathered outside to watch her exit. But nothing was said as she was escorted to the police carriage and locked in. No one was allowed to accompany her.

The warden put her in a wing of his house which he reserved for special inmates, where she collapsed on the bed, exhausted and a little nauseous.

That night she wept when Rudger sent a message insisting that she testify. She was pregnant, and the thought of Lydia carrying their baby, possibly in a women's prison a thousand miles away, was too much for Rudger.

The next day the court was so jammed that Ireland had to check the floor supports in the cellar to make sure they would hold. Disappointed spectators who could not get in milled about in the hall until they were chased away, so they waited outside to watch as the prison carriage brought Lydia. She was escorted in by two marshals and seated next to the fractious Utah governor, Eli Murray, who along with the Utah Commission members and other notables filled the front rows.

Lydia was put immediately back on the stand. She had changed dramatically. She looked wan and tired. Her clothes were no longer crisp, her eyes and face without the determination and confidence of the day before. When she spoke, it was in a fainter, slower voice.

Utter stillness fell upon the court as Judge Zane turned to Lydia.

"Are you willing to be sworn this morning, Miss Spencer?" His voice was cold, ready to carry out the requirements of the law.

"Yes, sir, I think I am."

The surprise among the spectators was audible. The clerk swore her in as the court buzzed.

Dickson stood up and moved slowly, almost suspiciously, toward the witness. "Miss Spencer, are you married?"

"Yes, sir, I am."

"To whom?" Again utter stillness.

"Rudger Clawson."

A pandemonium of whispering, so that the judge had to call for silence. It was all over.

"When were you married?"

"In 1883."

"Where?"

"In this city."

"What month was it?"

"I do not remember."

"In 1883?"

"Yes, sir."

Dickson turning in weary triumph to the judge: "That is all."

Lydia, even though having capitulated, left the chair with great dignity. She was greeted by her friends who put their arms around her and made room for her on the bench. A few minutes later Hiram worked his way through the throng and whispered in her ear. She left on his arm.

Arguments were waived and Zane charged the jury almost exactly as he had before. This time it took them only twenty minutes to reach a guilty verdict. Sentencing was set for November 3, eight days later. In the interim, Rudger was allowed to remain free on bail.

On the day of sentencing, Rudger was calm when he entered the courtroom, which was filled, as usual, with his family and friends.

"Mr. Clawson," Zane said in his most judicial manner, "will you stand up, if you please."

Rudger rose as necks craned to see him.

He had been convicted, Zane said, on two counts, of polygamy by marrying Lydia Spencer while his first wife, Florence Ann Clawson, was still living, and on the charge of unlawfully cohabiting with two women, Florence Ann Clawson and Lydia Spencer. He had pleaded not guilty and the jury had found him guilty on both counts.

"Have you a legal cause to show why judgment should not be pronounced upon you?" the judge concluded.

Rudger moved around the table and stepped forward to speak. A rustle and buzz ran around the surprised courtroom and then died out. Beginning deliberately, the words flowing from him in a full and clearly audible voice, he spoke to a courtroom profoundly silent.

"Your Honor, I very much regret that the laws of my country should come in contact with the laws of God; but whenever they do I shall invariably choose the latter. If I did not so express myself I should feel unworthy of the cause I represent. The Constitution of the United States expressly states that Congress shall make no law respecting an establishment of religion or prohibiting the free exercise thereof. It cannot be denied, I think, that marriage, when attended and sanctioned by religious rites and ceremonies, is an establishment of religion. The law of 1862 and the Edmunds Act were expressly designed to operate against marriage as practiced and believed by the Latter-day Saints. They are therefore unconstitutional, and, of course, cannot command the respect that a constitutional law would. That is all I have to say, Your Honor."

Zane had listened intently as Rudger spoke. Now he leaned back in his large chair and meditated for a few moments, his brow furrowed and his sharp features thrown into relief by the shadows of the thoughts he was organizing in his mind. Finally he leaned forward and said:

"The Constitution of the United States, as construed by the Supreme Court, and by the authors of that instrument, does not protect any person in the practice of polygamy. While all men have a right to worship God according to the dictates of their own conscience and to entertain any religious beliefs that their conscience and judgment might reasonably dictate, they have not the right to engage in a practice which the American people, through the laws of their country, declare to be unlawful and injurious to society."

Zane's words were a recitation from the *Reynolds* decision, which would echo down into the twentieth century in the Supreme Court's freedom of religion cases. But they caught American libertarianism at a vulnerable point. Plural marriage had been woven into the texture of Mormon belief and could not be separated out. Nor could it be simplistically compared to such things as ritualistic human sacrifice, which the Court had cited as an example of the kind of practice that, even under the cloak of religion, could not be tolerated in a civilized society. While the constitutional argument was basically sound and politically necessary, it was inescapably a prohibition on the free exercise of religion.

Zane went on to condemn polygamy in the most stringent terms, calling it, among other things, one of those barbarous religious superstitions "whose pathway had been lit with the faggot and reddened with the blood of innocent people."

"I confess," he said in conclusion, "that I should have felt inclined to fix this punishment smaller than I shall, were it not for the fact that you openly declared that you believe it is right to violate the law."

Four years was the sentence, three and a half for polygamy and six months for unlawful cohabitation, plus $800 in fines. It was a severe sentence, which shocked the silent courtroom. With no visible break in his calm exterior, Rudger returned to his seat.

The defense announced that it would appeal and asked for bail for the defendant while the appeal was being heard. A flurry of legal wrangling was followed by a last firm ruling. There would be no bail. "Remand the prisoner," Zane said, "to the custody of the marshal for confinement in the penitentiary."

In the arms of Hiram Clawson, Lydia wept.

# CHAPTER 4
# PRISON

A week after his sentencing and incarceraton, Rudger was brought back to court to hear the decision on his appeal of the bail ruling. It was denied, but in the process he encountered the ever-present *Salt Lake Herald* reporter. They shook hands.

"How do you pass your time out there?" the reporter asked.

"Mostly by reading. I started Milton's *Paradise Lost* just before I went in, and I am now concluding it," Rudger replied with a smile. "The surroundings out there make it somewhat applicable, I can assure you."

The prison stood on a plateau southeast of the city just below the point at which Parley's Canyon cuts into the Wasatch foothills.* In winter, a bitter wind came down from the canyon. From inside the yard only the tips of the tallest mountains could be seen. The yard was an acre square. In addition to the dining hall and the bunkhouse, there were four small structures. Two were covered iron cages just large enough to hold a man standing up or lying down. These were the "sweat boxes" in which refractory prisoners were confined for periods of a few hours to a few months. The two others, also used as solitary confinement cells, were slightly larger structures, each also with an iron cage in it which would hold a man and a cot.

---

 *Sugar House Park is presently on the site where the prison stood.

93

Inside the prison walls, which were twenty feet high and four feet wide with catwalks paced by armed guards and sentry boxes at diagonal corners, the prisoners' bunkhouse was divided into two rooms. Room One was for murderers and other hardened or contentious criminals, many of them fettered with ball and chain. Room Two was for trusties, lesser offenders and well-behaved inmates who were allowed to work outside the walls on the prison farm. On the direct order of Marshal Ireland, Rudger had been assigned to Room One.

As he approached it he heard the raucous voices of the prisoners,

> a strange and fearful noise. . . . which fairly made me shudder. The sound issued from the room where remorseless fate had decreed that I should pass my first night in prison—a night ever to be remembered as long, tedious and full of melancholy apprehension. Before entering, I caught such expressions as 'get the rope,' 'hang him,' 'the blanket—up he goes,' 'make him put on the gloves,' 'we'll fix him,' etc., while the air was rent by profanity and ribald laughter. . . . I paused, bewildered, the lock was turned, the iron door swung on its hinges and a moment later I found myself in a room about 50 by 20 feet, and in the midst of a class of men who compose the lowest stratum of society and who haunt the dens of vice that exist in most of our large cities throughout the country.

The room, ringed on three sides by a triple tier of double bunks, was filled with tobacco smoke. Gasping for air, Rudger looked at the prisoners who glowered back at him "like wild beasts ready to pounce." They surrounded him as soon as he entered and demanded that he put on some kind of performance for them (sing, dance, give a speech, etc.)—which was customary for new arrivals. Some, however, with "malignant and threatening" faces, wanted without delay to "toss him in the blanket"—which was, if not customary, at least a common and rather violent fate for newcomers. "I knew, of course, that they were 'putting me through,' and kept my equanimity, but the profanity and general depravity almost made my blood run cold."

He was saved by a big, more or less friendly convict named "Rocky." Rocky insisted on "fair play"; unfortunately, Rocky's idea of fair play was for Rudger to "put on the gloves," which meant almost certain disaster, since he was smaller and less hardened than virtually any of the criminals he would be expected to fight (in fact, there was a secret plan already in motion—of which Rocky was apparently unaware—to put him "up against a real 'bruiser' who no doubt would have pummeled me to a finish"). But Rudger was saved by the fact that the gloves which the fighters were to use had been left outside the cell and now could not be retrieved until morning. The bout therefore had to be postponed.

His sense of well-being was short-lived, however. The evening "wore away very slowly. The clanking of chains, the profanity, the vulgarity and brutal laughter were a constant source of offence [*sic*] to me." The men also seemed to feel a compulsive need to explain their presence in jail. One after another they "came up during the evening and volunteered statements of their cases, and, according to their representations, they were all innocent. I was astounded to see so many innocent men wearing the convict's garb. . . ."

One of the prisoners simply sat and stared at him with a malignant smile until Rudger suddenly realized his face was familiar. He had stolen some jewelry from Rudger's home several months before and had been caught and convicted. Rudger remembered him from the trial. "I . . . was struck with the novelty of the situation, for whoever heard of a man who had been robbed, and the robber, meeting on equal terms within the walls of a gloomy prison."

"At 9:00 o'clock in the evening, the guard appeared . . . and rapped sharply upon the door—the summons to retire. All loud talking immediately ceased, the prisoners slipped into their bunks and five minutes later, strange to relate, an awful stillness ensued." Rudger had to share a bunk with "a tramp who hailed from Ogden and whose underclothing presented a decidedly unclean appearance. I refrain from going into detail with regard to the filthy condition of his body— but my flesh fairly crawled at the thought of passing the night in that bed." Through the night he had to breathe noxious odors from a poorly ventilated toilet and to listen to the "constant hawking and spitting of the prisoners. . . . My mind was so filled with forebodings concerning the new life, now opening up before me, that I slept only intermittently. The thought of spending four years in a place so undesirable was uppermost in my mind and was oppressive to a degree almost maddening. Yet in this trying hour, I felt the sustaining influence of an invisible power—the power of the Almighty."

Morning finally came, and perhaps the Almighty had intervened: Rudger was assigned to Room Two with the trusties.

If Rudger Clawson, the convict, had the romantic idea that, because he was a martyr for his faith and a man of moral superiority, he would be given some special niche to occupy above and aside from that allotted to the dregs of society with whom he shared his imprisonment, he certainly knew by the end of the night that such would not be the case, even with his transfer to Room Two. Ultimately the Mormons did have a dramatic impact on life in the penitentiary, but for the time being Rudger might as well have been a common criminal. It would be a long time before paradise would be regained. Solitary confinement and a myriad of other indignities loomed ahead.

That morning Rudger was initiated into the routine that would govern his life for the next three and a half years.

The prisoners were awakened at 7:15 a.m. by the guards clanking loudly on the bars of the door and had to rise, dress, make their beds, and wash. The trusties in Room Two were awakened somewhat earlier and marched Indian file out into the fields where they were fed. The others had to be seated in the dining room by eight o'clock. The building used for the dining hall was longer and lower-slung than the bunkhouse and stood across from and parallel to it. It was no more than a wood frame covered with thin boards and a shingle roof with nothing to insulate it from the cold. Stretching around and attached to the inside wall was a two-foot wide plank or "deal board" which served as a table. In the middle of the room were four or five other tables and benches which could be removed. The eating places at the side table were coveted because they were more private and because above the table stretched a small shelf on which the prisoners could keep their eating utensils and other miscellaneous gear. An assignment to a place at the side could be purchased for $3 when it became available.*

Rudger's first breakfast was typical: a piece of tough boiled meat, soggy potatoes, butterless bread and black coffee. Every other day, according to another Mormon prisoner who arrived later, "the meat . . . is omitted, being substituted by a mysterious compound called

*Abraham H. Cannon, a friend and fellow inmate of Rudger's in 1886 (and, subsequently, a fellow apostle), tells us in his diary that in the spring of that year Rudger handled the transaction when Cannon wished to buy one of these favored spots.

hash" (which was frequently rancid), and occasionally a weak, tasteless vegetable soup was served.

It was too much for Rudger. "My appetite suddenly failed, and I could eat nothing." The noise and confusion were also almost overwhelming. "There was chatter, chatter, chatter, intermingled with oaths or vulgar jokes followed by shrieks of laughter," often as not followed by a fight. The leftovers were given to the pigs "which, in their manner of eating, were about as genteel as some of Utah's convicts."

The food was usually rank and sometimes maggoty. Once when the coffee was particularly bad, the warden announced that a bottle of carbolic acid had been accidentally dropped into it.

At noon came the midday meal, "a duplicate," wrote Rudger, "of the morning meal with the single exception that the potatoes . . . were less soggy." The evening meal consisted simply of bread and tea.

Between meals the men were more or less on their own. The movable tables in the dining room were cleared away and some of the men engaged in reading, study, or the pursuit of various crafts—making such things as hair bridles, riding whips, gilt picture frames and gilded horseshoes, fancy wood boxes, wood carvings, ship models and the like, frequently demonstrating a great deal of skill.

On his first day, Rudger encountered Frank Tresedor, a painter of some local note. Tresedor probably found it difficult to make a living as an artist and turned to burglary to supplement his income. Unfortunately, he got caught. But his paintings of the prison were charming and Rudger bought two—an interior view (for $6) and an exterior view (for $4). Later he bought a Tresedor painting of a castle as a present for Lydia.

Much of the time non-Mormon convicts loitered in the yard talking, arguing, and fighting with each other. Because the trusties worked outside the walls, the tone of the yard was set by the toughs. The gloves came out often, and the men stood and slugged it out to the cheers of their fellow prisoners. But they also danced and played music; there were a couple of relatively talented cornetists in prison at one point. In addition, they engaged in sports and other contests.

On the side of the yard where the entry gate stood, a wire was stretched from wall to wall. Appropriately called the "dead line," it could only be crossed by permission of the guard standing on the catwalk with a leveled gun.

Periodically the marshal appeared on an inspection tour or with visitors. At these times, the men were herded into a coi er where they remained until the visit was over.

Periodic surprise searches were called by the warden. Trunks were unlocked and examined and the prisoners were forced to strip while they and their clothes were searched. Rudger found these searches particularly humiliating.

Thursday was visiting day—sometimes each Thursday, at other times, only one Thursday a month. One bell and the call of his name brought a prisoner to the dead line, where he awaited permission to go to the gate. At the gate he was searched; then he entered the guard's dining room where he sat across from his visitor at a long table. A guard was present, and neither whispering nor passing written messages was permitted. These rules, however, were stretched or constricted at the whim of the marshal or the warden.

As Rudger sought to adjust to these dreary routines during his first days there, two important events occurred. The first was the arrival five days after his own imprisonment of Joseph Evans. Evans, a good-natured Englishman, was a personal acquaintance of Rudger. He was a hearty outspoken blacksmith whose plural wife and her mother had testified against him in court. Like Rudger, he'd been convicted of polygamy and gotten almost as heavy a sentence. The support Rudger and Evans gave to each other was invaluable as they plowed the rank soil of prison life to make it more hospitable to the brethren who were to follow.

The other event occurred at the end of November or beginning of December: Florence appeared at the prison with an ultimatum. When Rudger went to jail, Lydia remained living at Mrs. Smith's. It is not certain what Florence did, though it is probable that for some time the two women lived together, Florence moving out of the North Temple house and in with Lydia. Some years later Lydia told one of her daughters that she and Florence had fought bitterly during this time. What is certain is that neither of them was willing or able to make a go of plural wifery while waiting four years for their jailed husband to return.

Florence broke first. One day she appeared at the prison and asked

Rudger what he was going to do when he was released. When Rudger said he did not know what the future would bring, she delivered her ultimatum: choose between her and Lydia. Rudger refused.

There is no record of what Florence did over the next few months. It is possible that she remained with Lydia at least until her (Lydia's) baby was born on March 25, 1885. It was a boy, and they named him Rudger Remus.* Lydia writes in her reminiscences: "I was left alone when [the baby] was two weeks old," but she does not identify who had been staying with her. In an unexplainable gesture of compassion, Marshal Ireland allowed Rudger to visit her for a day.

In early July, Rudger was informed by a prison guard that Florence intended to divorce him and remarry, "having been presented with an engagement ring; also . . . she was at the Lake on the 4th with the scoundrel who is paying his attentions to her."**

In a letter to Lydia in July, Rudger fretted about "the very great dangers which threaten to overwhelm Flo in misery and wretchedness. . . . And when I think of the evil influences to which Elmo will be exposed should she take this course [getting a divorce] it fills my heart with grief and sorrow."

He also maintained his spirits by pinning his hopes on the successful outcome of his appeal on the jury selection (open venire) issue. Franklin Richards was in Washington arguing it before the Supreme Court. It was an important case because a favorable decision would not only free Rudger, it would throw the entire government judicial campaign against the Mormons into disarray. But in April the court ruled against him. Now he had to deal with the certainty of at least three more years in jail.

The arrival of more Mormons during the spring of 1885 brought some relief. They were soon being called "cohabs," because the vast majority who entered prison after Rudger and Joseph Evans were

---

*On Rudger Clawson's Family Group Sheet, the boy's name is listed as Remus Rudger, though he most commonly was called "Rudger Remus," "Rudger," and "Rud."

**Later, in the divorce suit, in August 1885, Florence charged Rudger with adultery and, according to Sam Taylor in his biography of John Taylor, "sacrificed church membership by doing so." If she did, she regained it at a later date. The "scoundrel," according to Taylor, was a local hotel keeper. In 1898 she married Richard P. Morris, a Salt Lake merchant who served as mayor of the city from 1904 to 1906.

convicted on charges of unlawful cohabitation rather than polygamy. Angus M. Cannon, who had testified at Rudger's trial, and four or five others arrived in May or soon after.

During the winter and spring of 1885, Rudger had the opportunity to observe life in the raw as he had never seen it before. The non-Mormons, especially the hardened criminals, were referred to as "toughs," and tough, vulgar, foul-mouthed, vicious, and venal they were. Yet the individuals who populated this rogues' gallery had redeeming qualities of which he took note as he sketched them in his journal.

Jack Bryant was an affable, almost jolly burglar who confided to Rudger in great detail the secret of a successful robbery. Unfortunately, the secret had not worked for him and he had ended up with five years in the penitentiary. But he had managed to bury most of the loot ($750) before he was caught and expected to retrieve it after he had "paid the penalty."

Another prisoner, identified only as Hill, had robbed his wife of $10,000, which Rudger thought was "a deed so base and degrading it seemed almost incredible." It was as if Hill's "conscience had been seared with a hot iron." What galled Rudger almost as much was that with the fruits of his larceny he bought special privileges not allowed other prisoners. Amorality was not a character trait Rudger easily understood.

John Smith's story read like fiction. He had single-handedly robbed a passenger train on the Utah and Northern Railroad (built by Rudger's former employer, John W. Young). When caught, he feigned insanity so successfully that he was confined in a mental institution. There he arranged free access to the room of a female patient and was only caught when he happened to oversleep one morning in her bed. Transferred to the pen, he was a belligerent prisoner who spent a good amount of time in the sweat box. He was so bothersome one winter night that a guard threw a bucket of cold water on him and they found him the next morning lying on the ice-covered floor, his clothes frozen stiff. After some time in the pen he again feigned insanity and again fooled everyone—including Rudger—even though they knew he'd done it before. Back in the hospital, Smith did himself in this time by writing a very sane letter to one of the cohabs he'd met in the pen to ask for help in getting out! Smith eventually served out his term, but some time after his release apparently carried out the threat he had voiced to Rudger and others that he would get revenge on the judge who had convicted him. One day the judge received a package with a bomb in it—which he wisely dunked in a bucket of water before opening.

The subject most on the minds of the toughs was escape—which they tried as often as they could think up a new method. Almost invariably they failed.

John Biddlecome tried repeatedly and always ended up in the sweat box. One of his cleverest efforts was an attempt to go over the wall during an outdoor religious service. He had noticed some time before that at one point in the service all heads were bowed for quite a long time. Immediately he set about acquiring a rope and making himself a grappling hook. The next Sunday as heads went down, he swung the hook over the ramparts, but for three tries it wouldn't catch. When the guards raised their heads, poor Biddlecome was only halfway up the wall.

In another particularly imaginative attempt, several prisoners concocted a scheme whereby they would begin beating one of their cohorts as a decoy to bring the guards into the cell, at which point the prisoners would overpower them, seize their weapons, and shoot their way out. But the guards, when they arrived, just stood and watched them brutalize their fellow conspirator. When the warden learned of the incident he put *the decoy* into the sweat box for two weeks!

Another common trick was to start a fire in the bunkhouse and then attempt to escape in the confusion when the guards came in to put it out. This little caper stopped when the warden announced that he had instructed the guards not to open the door if it happened again.

Whenever a break was planned, a thrill coursed through the prison community. The inmates discussed and debated it as if it were a sporting event and put bets on the outcome. Not even Rudger could resist. He always sympathized with the convict no matter how low a character. Likewise he shared in the disappointment when the captured escapee was marched back in through the gate.

Mike Sullivan's case was more poignant than most. Convicted of murder in 1884 and sentenced to fifteen years, he had been a quiet, inoffensive man up until the early spring of 1885. Then he began to go insane, drinking scalding hot water, submerging himself in a freezing tub before going to bed, and walking about gesticulating wildly and talking to himself. Finally, he went berserk, stabbing one inmate in the back with a fork and smashing the ribs of another with an iron shovel. One of the small cells in the yard had been built as a mini-insane asylum for Sullivan until they could get him to another institution.

But even among these men whose natures "were very much depraved," Rudger was impressed with the industry and talent some of them displayed and the efforts made to improve themselves. The objects which came out of the prison workshop, for example, "exhibited a beauty of design and completeness of finish deserving of the highest praise." John Biddlecome, who had been convicted of murder at the age of seventeen and was illiterate when given a life sentence, learned to read, taught himself shorthand and French, and obtained a liberal education by reading widely in history, biography, and literature. Joe Miller, a Frenchman sentenced to two years for burglary, also learned shorthand and was tutoring the warden's two children in French. Oliver Acord, in for five years for robbing the U.S. mails, was studying composition, rhetoric, mathematics, penmanship, and French, and (under Rudger's tutelage) also learned shorthand. Fred Moss (seven years for horse-stealing) was learning Spanish.

This was Rudger's education in human nature.

> I was now familiar with the circumstances connected with the charge, trial and conviction of nearly every man in the yard, and often conversed with them, thus getting a good insight into character. I had previously looked upon the pick-pocket, burglar, horse thief, forger, etc., as a kind of monster, whereas, by this time I had found that these men who were convicted of such crimes, degraded though they were, were in possession of many good qualities, such as generosity and sympathy. . . . I could not help thinking that, if proper influences had been thrown around these rough, rude men in their childhood and youth, many of them might have become intelligent and virtuous citizens. . . .
>
> In judging such characters we should place ourselves for the moment in their position, look at matters from their standpoint, and enter into their views and feelings—and not fail to consider the circumstances by which they were surrounded in early life. What an important part therefore should *charity* play in our dealings with the human family! Will these men go down to hell and suffer? Yes, if they do not repent, but, on the

other hand, they will be eventually redeemed, if we may rely upon the
revelations of God, and receive a glory far beyond our finite conceptions.

This was a relatively generous attitude, especially considering that
there was a strong vein of anti-Mormonism running through the
prison community. During those early months Rudger and Joseph
Evans were the only Mormons there to draw its fire—probably Rudger
even more than his friend since it is highly likely that Rudger came
across as more self-righteous. Indeed, Evans won some renown at a
Mormon service one Sunday when he and he alone was applauded by
the convicts for his sermon.

Rudger had experienced this prejudice the night of his arrival, and
it grew stronger as time went on. It was given particularly vehement
voice by Pat Callahan, a big Irishman whose "facility for writing
*mediocre* poetry," Rudger wrote pettishly, "constituted his sole accomplishment." But it won Callahan inordinate respect from the other
prisoners, and it meant that they listened when he "brought all his
influence to bear unfavorably on the 'Mormon' question in general
and upon me in particular." He never missed a chance to take shots at
the Saints and "appeared to take infinite delight in vulgar and filthy
slurs on some of our leading men. . . ." Callahan, on the other hand,
was a favorite with the prison guards. He was one of the more proficient
bridlemakers in the prison, and sometimes sold his bridles for as much
as $80. He had a nice little account with the warden and sometimes
lent or gave money to other prisoners. The guards considered him
kindhearted and passed out one of his poems—a convict's lament—to
visitors curious about prison life. Whatever "kindheartedness" Callahan felt for the other prisoners, it did not extend to Rudger.

"His remarks were never addressed to me, personally, but to someone nearby, and were always spoken in a loud clear tone that every
man in the room might hear. As a result, quite a bitter feeling was
aroused against me. My only weapon of defense was 'silent contempt'
and it did me excellent service."

But silent contempt was not an antidote to all the evils he encountered, particularly those involving prison rules and the pernicious
influence of T. J. Johnson, one of the prison's more devious criminals.
Lydia was visiting. The long table was lined with prisoners talking with
their visitors. Lydia and Rudger were at one end. The guard was at the

other. They were speaking in normal tones, but the guard ordered them to speak up. Later the warden called Rudger in, reprimanded him for whispering, and deprived him of his mail and visiting privileges.

Rudger was now experiencing one of the most arduous aspects of prison life, the absolute control prison officials had over the lives of the prisoners and the arbitrary manner in which they exercised that control. Not only were rules imposed and procedures established to keep the men in a state of submission, they were cancelled, modified, or ignored at the whim of the warden or his superior, the U.S. marshal. The result was not only an atmosphere of repression, but of almost intolerable uncertainty and vulnerability to the capricious use of authority which, while effective in keeping the average prisoner off balance and under control, was bound to be an extreme burden to the self-disciplined, sober-minded Mormons.

William Seifrit, in an article on the prison experience of Abraham H. Cannon, describes vividly the inconsistent enforcement of the rules:

> A source of continuing irritation to all the prisoners were [sic] the frequent and apparently arbitrary changes in prison rules. Facial hair was sometimes allowed and sometimes not. Frequently men were required to have their heads close-cropped and beards removed—often within a week or so of being released. Visiting day was supposed to be the first Thursday of each month, but most of the prisoners seemed to have visitors whenever such presented themselves. Once the men had become accustomed to frequent visits, the marshal would suspend the privilege. Some of the guards intruded themselves into visitors' conversations; others left the prisoners and visitors entirely alone. Newspapers were banned periodically; on a few occasions, however, sympathetic guards (or visitors) would smuggle in newspapers. . . . Still another irritant to the prisoners, toughs and cohabs alike, was the periodic suspension of the privilege of receiving food.

Marshal Ireland's permission for Rudger to visit Lydia at the time of Rudger Remus's birth was an example of this inconsistency. Later, Ireland would refuse John Nicholson permission to visit his dying seventy-five-year-old father.

One of the more arbitrary and painful shifts in the rules occurred in mid-July 1885, and seemed to be aimed primarily at the Mormons, who received visitors and deliveries of packages more frequently. "All at once . . . it was announced . . . that visiting days would be reduced to *one* each month and confined to members of the prisoner's family." Not only that, but the receiving of food, tobacco and other supplies from the outside was also suddenly prohibited. This too was a blow. Because prison fare was so bad, this privilege was "highly esteemed. It was also a source of considerable revenue to the warden, who supplied the men with tobacco, sugar, butter, cheese, canned goods, etc." But no more. "No provisions whatever . . . would be allowed to come into the yard. Thus, in order to annoy and discourage the brethren, early precedents were trampled upon and Warden G. N. Dow was even willing to forego the financial gains he had enjoyed in order to humiliate the brethren."

The change in visiting rules didn't affect Rudger at that point. He would have been happy with just that one day a month. His problem, because of the whispering incident, was no visitors at all, which was a serious deprivation for this sociable, family-oriented man. As usual, however, he refused to take it lying down and immediately set up a clandestine communication system with Lydia.

After describing the "whispering" incident in the first letter smuggled out, he wrote: "You know I did not [whisper], so there must be a lie out somewhere."

Rudger assumed T. J. Johnson was the liar. Johnson, "a man of medium stature with large head, long face, massive jaw, high forehead, big nose and blue eyes," was a Mormon-hater. He was also "an accomplished rogue, combining cunning and shrewdness with a good education." He was serving a twelve-month sentence for forgery, which would have been more (his accomplice got two years) except for the intervention in court of an Episcopal minister who sympathized with him—and whom Johnson later robbed of sixty dollars.

Johnson was serving as tutor to Warden Dow's children and thus had the warden's ear, which, according to Rudger, he filled with a "constant stream of falsehoods and misrepresentations concerning my movements in the yard. . . . He watched me as a beast watches his prey, and magnified the most frivolous acts into an evidence of cunningly devised schemes. . . . As a result it was the consensus of opinion among prison officials that I was secretive, full of subtility [*sic*], and therefore most dangerous."

Rudger was reported for carrying money in the yard, a rule violation, and was called before Warden Dow, a small man with a youthful face who seems to have managed most of the cohabs with a firm but not unkindly hand. Nicholson later called him "a very humane gentleman."

Dow asked Rudger why he was carrying money. Because everyone does it, Rudger replied. Dow didn't believe him.

"Mr. Warden," Rudger insisted, "I have just come from the dining room; there were several games of poker in progress and not less than fifteen to twenty dollars in silver in sight. Please step in or send a guard and satisfy yourself."

Dow still didn't believe him, nor would he send a guard to investigate. He ended by admonishing Rudger once more to observe the rules.

"As the warden took no steps to ascertain the truth of my statement," Rudger muttered in his memoirs, "I very naturally concluded that this rule was intended to apply to me only."

At one point Rudger decided to see if he could earn some money buying and selling the bridles crafted by the convicts. He therefore arranged a system of importing tobacco to trade for the bridles which he then sold outside the penitentiary. But before long he was again in Dow's office. Someone—presumably Johnson—had informed on him. This time he had touched a particularly sensitive nerve, because Dow himself engaged in the tobacco trade. Rudger did confess that in this case he had acted "perhaps a little imprudently" in invading the warden's territory.

Rudger's most serious and overt confrontation with Johnson came in August 1885. Johnson, who was choir leader at Sunday services, was infuriated by the Mormons' refusal to stand and participate at certain points in the non-Mormon services they were required to attend. He threatened to "have them jerked up by the collar," if they didn't stand. Soon thereafter a notice appeared on the bulletin board announcing that in the future they would be required to do so.

Both the toughs and the seven Mormons were angry. The brethren held council. "I was perfectly willing," Rudger said, "to attend divine service no matter what denomination conducted, but I rebelled in my feelings at the thought of being compelled at the signal of the minister to take a responsive part in the service. I had made up my mind, I said, to ignore the rule and take whatever punishment might be inflicted. The brethren took a view similar to mine and we thereupon entered into a solemn compact to stand [or sit!] together and resist the rule.

"The Sabbath day came, the meeting was called at 3:00 p.m. The convicts reluctantly fell into line and slowly entered the dining room. The evidence of suppressed rage was visible on every countenance. Doyle, the guard, was in charge; Johnson, the burglar, presided at the organ; and Rev. Mr. Putnam, an Episcopalian, conducted the service.

"The minister, with a sort of leer in his eyes, opened by announcing a hymn and saying that he would be very glad if all present would *stand upon their feet and take part in the service. . . . The seven cohabs remained seated.*"

Doyle, the guard, his eyes flashing, turned to one of the cohabs, whom Rudger called "Howard" for the sake of anonymity, and yelled, "Stand on your feet."

This was the moment of truth, "a testing time," Rudger called it. "The other six 'cohabs' turned their eyes with fevered anxiety upon Howard, wondering, hoping he would stand by the compact. There was a moment of tense silence. Howard seemed to be in an uncertain state of mind, but upon a second command from the guard his body swayed to and fro and he slowly rose to his feet." The rebellion was broken. The guard turned to the others and demanded that they too stand. Four did so. One, Angus M. Cannon, however, continued to sit and looking up said in a meek voice, "Mr. Doyle, I cannot stand. . . . I'm afflicted with the piles."

"Then, get out of here," Doyle shouted, pointing at the door.

Forgetting his malady, if it really existed, "Brother Cannon reached for his hat, [and] moved with incredible alacrity and passed out of the room. Of the seven 'cohabs' and in fact of the entire congregation I was the only one now who sat while all others rose and stood or knelt in response to the request of the preacher."

Once more Rudger ended up in the warden's office, this time feeling he had been betrayed by his own brethren, although Evans, who had been assigned to do the blacksmithing for the prison, later said that if he had been asked to make chains for Rudger he would have refused. In view of what happened, it was small consolation.

Dow was furious. "Evans," Dow said* (he had had Evans brought in with Rudger) "I have called you out to be a witness to this interview, as I cannot trust Clawson. He is not truthful, and when called out at any time to give an account of himself, misrepresents to the prisoners what passes between us. Clawson, how is it that you did not arise to your feet this afternoon when spoken to by the guard? You knew it was against the rules to remain seated?"

"Yes sir."

"Why then did you violate them?"

"Simply, Mr. Dow, because I did not fancy the idea of being forced into church against my will and there be compelled to take part in the service. You'll understand, Mr. Dow, that I'm not an Episcopalian but a Mormon, and do not accept the doctrines or approve the rites of the Episcopal Church."

"You were not compelled to take part in the service," Dow countered, "but you are expected to show due respect to the minister."

"It looked very much like compulsion for we were requested to stand up and assist in the singing, praying, etc., which I could not conscientiously do."

"It is certainly ridiculous to take that view of the matter," Dow said. "I wish it to be distinctly understood that you are expected to observe every rule of the prison, including the rule respecting attendance at and participation in divine services. . . . You have given me more trouble than any other prisoner in the yard; scarcely a week passes but what you are reported as having been guilty of some misdemeanor. This thing must cease. That will be all."

An hour later Rudger was on his way to solitary confinement. Carrying his cot like a cross, he was marched past the brethren who had betrayed him to

this infernal abode . . . a small [wooden] building containing an inner iron cage that was originally designed for the accommodation of Mike Sullivan, the lunatic. . . . First the outer, then the inner door opened. I passed in and a moment later found myself surrounded by midnight darkness. . . . The iron cage that held me fast was about six feet long by five feet wide by five feet ten inches high. . . . The fierce rays of an August

---

*This conversation, recorded by Rudger under trying circumstances, sounds somewhat more stilted than it probably was.

sun beating down upon the roof created a heat well nigh intolerable, while an almost entire absence of ventilation increased the misery of this inhuman torture ten fold. I felt the necessity of taking immediate steps to guard against being melted into oil, and so I stripped off my clothing. Throwing myself upon the cot and collecting my scattered thoughts, I began to ruminate on the probability of being attacked by vermin. The darkness prevented a satisfactory examination of the place, yet I imagined I could feel their mysterious presence. . . . As the time dragged its slow length along, every hour seemed like an age. . . .

Three days and nights passed away ere I emerged from this place of awful gloom, the intensity of which one cannot comprehend until he has endured it.

In the meantime, his brethren presented Dow with a written appeal for his release—which annoyed the warden no end. What in fact won Rudger's release was the intervention of his father. Hiram, a genial and rather impressive man with polished diplomatic skills, was well known to Warden Dow and was graciously received when he appeared at the prison to inquire about his son.

"May I be permitted to see him?" Hiram asked, once seated comfortably in Dow's office.

"Yes, Mr. Clawson."

Rudger was brought in and Hiram, with a sly wink, which Rudger knew was "intended for me and did not escape my notice," said, in a stern voice:

"My son, I understand you have violated a rule of the prison and for this are undergoing punishment?"

"Yes, father," Rudger replied humbly.

"I am sorry to hear it."

"Yes, father."

"And now my son, I advise you to conform to the regulations of the prison, and give heed to the rules laid down by the warden."

"Yes, father."

The interview ended and as Rudger was being escorted out of the room, Hiram said to Dow: "I don't think, after what I said to the boy, that he will give you any further trouble. I trust you may see your way clear to release him."

The warden was duly impressed and released Rudger from his solitary cell. And the rules concerning religious worship were relaxed;

the cohabs had won a small victory. But Rudger was not pleased. He gathered the brethren together and reprimanded them. "Five of you failed to keep the compact we entered into. . . . The brunt of the warden's displeasure therefore fell on me, and I was made to suffer. Had we stood together, I think the result would have been different." He does not suggest how different, nor does he indicate what his fellow inmates thought of him. He had provoked a confrontation—with characteristic self-certainty—and they would have been justified in considering him somewhat insufferable.

With the summer had come the bedbug scourge. In the hot weather they bred in the straw bedding and crawled along the walls in massive numbers. When Frank Dyer became marshal he announced to a visiting grand jury that in addition to the prisoners, 14,000 bedbugs inhabited the penitentiary.

"A man could write his name," according to Rudger, "with the blood of bugs by pressing his finger against them as they crawled along the wall. . . . Newly whitewashed walls soon told an awful tale of blood and carnage. . . . It was quite amusing to watch the convicts war against their powerful enemies all hours of the night."

During this summer of 1885, Rudger diverted his attention from the bedbugs by carrying on an active sub rosa correspondence with Lydia, writing to her in his neat script on small pieces of paper. Folded and refolded in tight little squares, he would cup them in his palm and pass them in handshakes to acquaintances visiting other prisoners or to his own family and friends, whom he was soon allowed to see again, even while the restrictions on Lydia's visiting remained in force. On the outside fold of the letter, he would write: "Mrs. Lydia Clawson 3 or 4 doors north of Valley House with Mrs. Smith" or "2 doors north Coop. Furn. Store." Lydia would reply by hiding or sewing her letters in various parts of the clothing she washed for him once a week, or in a secret pocket sewn in the valise used for carrying the clothes in and out of prison. One day Rudger could not get his arm into the sleeve of his shirt. On inspection he was delighted to find a picture of the baby blocking the way.

While Lydia was prohibited from face-to-face visits, the warden did allow her on the prison wall. This was a tradition by which family members were able to stand on the wall in view of their loved one—

but no signals between them were permitted. Rudger, of course, immediately devised a way to circumvent the rules.

"If I remove my hat from the head," [he wrote in a letter in August,] "it is a token of my desire to clasp you in my arms, to embrace you passionately and fondly and to impress a dozen warm kisses on your lips. If you place your right hand to your throat as if in the act of buttoning your dress, I shall know that your heart swells with love and that you also greatly desire to be in my *arms* and to be *hugged and kissed fondly and passionately*. If my left hand goes into my left coat pocket you will know that a very strong wish concerning you and myself burns in my heart—but I will not tell it; and if your right hand is carelessly placed on the wall just in front of you I shall know that you have guessed my wish and share it with me. When I wave my handkerchief in the air you will know that I often think of you in the silent hours of the night and wish that you could be with me. And if you transfer the baby from one arm to another it will be an evidence that your thoughts also often turn to me and that my desire is your desire.

This "visiting" from the prison wall became such an event that opera glasses acquired from friends and relatives were passed around among the prisoners so that loved ones could be better viewed.

One day he received an anxious letter from Lydia. She had been denied access to the wall, apparently because she was not considered Rudger's legal wife, even though Florence's divorce was final. Lydia feared this might prevent her from ever visiting him again. Margaret suggested that they remarry in a civil ceremony as a means of solving the problem and later Lydia suggested it too. Rudger refused. "It is a step that would bring reproach upon the priesthood. . . ."

Early in September Lydia wrote that she thought she was pregnant again and was worried about what people would think. But Rudger reassured her in another secret letter. "No matter what people may say or think, so long as I am satisfied, I shall know that this *little darling* belongs to me, for how can I forget the circumstances which brought about such a state of affairs. I was there and you were there and did I not hold you in my arms and did I not press you closely to my heart and did I not kiss you with all the ardor and passion of a pure and vigorous love? You may be sure that if heaven blesses us with a little stranger, I will welcome him or her with open arms and a thankful heart. So do not worry one particle and always remember that we know what we know."*

---

*In a letter believed to have been written in June, Rudger wrote: "Oh! what would I

Rudger was much more worried about her health than about her reputation. To support herself Lydia had been taking in sewing, at least from Spencer and perhaps from others as well. "I am not," he wrote, "at all satisfied with the condition of affairs at home; you work too hard." He included in the letter a note to Spencer asking a credit of $15 per month to be paid to Lydia. "I make this provision for you because I don't want you to use the machine any more. You cannot afford to ruin your health in order to save me some expense."

By early September Rudger was receiving visitors again (at least his father and mother), though apparently not Lydia. In a letter dated September 9, he pointedly assured her that his mother felt kindly toward her, but evidence from later events and reminiscences of Lydia's and Rudger's children, indicate that Lydia and Margaret never wholly repaired the breach which developed during the courtship.

Late September found Lydia back on the wall and perhaps visiting with him face-to-face again. But the passion in his letters did not abate. Rudger's need by this time to express his feelings and desires for Lydia was overpowering. In his letters he dealt with practical matters little more than in passing. For the most part his letters were passionate testimonials to his love, though often they were also wryly humorous: "My darling Lydia, I am going to write you a letter. If you imagine, however, that it will be lengthy, I can only say you are greatly deceived. I do not propose to speak of the weather, my health, my surroundings or other similar topics, but I shall dwell upon a subject which I fancy will interest you more, aye, ten thousand times more, than all those and that is my *love for thee*—a love which is enduring as the Rock of Ages and which blazes forth out of the depth of my soul like a consuming fire. . . ."

And in another: "I love you most tenderly and affectionately, yes, with all my heart, and my mind often turns to you in the silent hours of the night. Be of good cheer, for time rolls slowly but *surely* on and each day that passes brings us nearer to the moment when we shall clasp each other in the fond embraces of mutual love. . . . It is

not give for another such visit as we had when last I was in the city." Other information suggests that this liaison took place some weeks after he visited her at the time Rudger Remus was born. It may be that Rudger was permitted another visit during the spring despite his unpopularity with the prison authorities.

growing dark, and I must come to a close. My one wish is that you might be with me tonight."

*   *   *

In the outside world, the judicial attack on polygamy had proceeded slowly after Rudger's conviction. Although it was vigorous enough to send John Taylor underground in February 1885, the government decided to wait until Rudger's appeals were acted on by the Supreme Court before intensifying its efforts. The courts did, however, develop during this period new interpretations of the law which would be useful when the next attack was mounted. One, which had been used in convicting Angus Cannon, was that proof of having sexual intercourse was not necessary to prove cohabitation. A man could be charged with the "habit and repute of marriage" to more than one wife for which simply being seen with different women at different times was considered evidence. Cannon had argued that he had had sexual intercourse with only one of his wives, but he was convicted all the same.

When the Supreme Court handed down its final ruling against Rudger's appeal in early April 1885, Dickson and Ireland increased the momentum of the crusade. Not only did a rash of indictments follow, but they now started going after bigger game.

As Orson Whitney put it in his *History of Utah:* "Hitherto the cases tried under the Edmunds Act had been those of persons comparatively humble and obscure. . . . Now, it was resolved to assail the head and fount of the Mormon system, and bring such a pressure to bear upon its chiefs that they would succumb to the inevitable and advise their followers to do likewise."

The leading figure caught in the immediate aftermath of the Supreme Court ruling on Rudger's case was his father, Hiram. He was indicted on April 24 1885, tried in the early fall, convicted, and sentenced on September 29. Like his son, Hiram stood up to justify himself.

It was a significant moment. After Rudger's conviction, Judge Zane began offering to drop the charges against any polygamist who would swear to obey the law in the future. A number of Mormons had agreed to do so over the intervening months, though no one of any note.

Then, at the time Hiram Clawson was about to go to jail, John Sharp, bishop of the Twentieth Ward in Salt Lake agreed to take the oath. Sharp was not only a prominent churchman, he was one of the wealthiest men in the territory. He was superintendent of the Utah Central Railroad, a member of the board of directors of the Union Pacific, and was frequently referred to as the "Railroad King of Utah." Church leaders were not only stunned, they were furious and promptly removed Sharp from his bishopric.

Sharp explained himself in a clear, simple statement:

> I acted according to the dictates of my conscience, and just as in all wisdom I should have acted. . . . I do not renounce my religion or any part thereof. I simply give up the practice of polygamy, because the United States law forbids my indulging in it any longer. As long as I am a citizen of the United States I do not see how I can do otherwise.

Sharp eventually returned to the good graces of the church. But for the moment, emotions ran high against him. In his September 23 letter to Lydia, Rudger wrote: "I cannot tell you how much I regretted to learn of the course taken by Bp. Sharp. He was a man I always greatly admired, but it appears to me that he has made a serious blunder. I say this too after having been myself nearly a year in prison, being thereby competent to judge of the matter. Six months behind the bars is not a drop in the bucket compared with the unhappiness that must inevitably follow such a step. Rather than that father should assume a similar position, I would prefer to hear of his death. These are my feelings, and I will not for one moment do father the injustice to think that he will seek by any pretext whatever to evade the issue."

And of course, Hiram did not. When he spoke up in court, Judge Zane listened impatiently. Here was yet another Mormon justifying what he, Zane, thought was simply criminal behavior. Hiram reviewed the "covenant" he had, as part of his faith, undertaken in marrying his wives. The major issue was whether or not he would meet the solemn obligations he had to them. To fail to do so would be dishonorable, "To me there are only two courses," he ended, "one is prison and honor, the other liberty and dishonor."

Zane finally lost his temper. If Hiram, who was perhaps even more prominent than Sharp, had been willing to knuckle under, they might have been able to break the back of the church right there. So Zane lashed out, saying that plural marriages had always been against the law, even before the Morrill Act, and were therefore void. The second wife in the eyes of the law was nothing but a concubine and the children born of these relations nothing more than bastards. He also accused Hiram of cowardice for not being willing to say he would obey the law.

More shock waves went through the Mormon community. Which was more cowardly, the pro-Mormon papers asked, to go to prison for one's belief or to assail a prisoner powerless to protect himself?

It was at this point that Marshal Ireland decided to launch his own little attack on the powerless. It was in response, or at least so Rudger believed, to the equanimity with which the cohabs suffered imprisonment.

"The prison authorities could not well endure the spirit of resignation manifested. It seemed to be galling to them. Something must be done to humiliate these indifferent men. It was thought that the introduction of striped clothing would do the trick. The brethren, however, received the blow with their usual equanimity and smiled complacently as they passed into the warden's office, one by one, to be fitted with the new suits."

The other convicts were not so calm. "Their fury knew no bounds. Pacing the dining room in extreme agitation many of them cursed and swore in a frightful manner. Thunderbolts of wrath were hurled at Marshal Ireland's devoted head for thus seeking to make a display of their degradation. The shot fired at us glanced off, but struck and wounded them deeply."

Many of the cohabs delighted in being photographed in their stripes; it was a badge of honor. Today their pictures abound in the scrapbooks of Mormon families and in Utah archives. But striped suits were not all that the marshal had prepared for them. "To add to the humiliation of the 'Mormon' prisoners, the United States Marshal . . . required that all, without exception, should submit to a clean shave and a close haircut."

If Ireland thought he had found the means of cowing these intractable Mormons, he had obviously not taken into account Bishop Hiram Bradley Clawson. Zane may have been furious with him and Ireland ready to humiliate him, but Warden Dow was clearly somewhat in awe of the bishop.

Rudger and the others had succumbed to the shaving rule (in one of his letters to Lydia, Rudger had sent "all that remains of my moustache"), but not Hiram. "One man of rare diplomatic ability," wrote Rudger years later but still guarding the identity of his father, "approached the prison doctor with a five-dollar gold piece hidden away under his thumb, and said: 'Doctor, I'm afraid that if my moustache is shaved off it will be detrimental to my health.'

"'What is your trouble, Mr——?' inquired the doctor.

"'Why,' replied the man as he took the doctor's hand into which the gold piece slipped, 'there is a weakness in my throat.'

"With a knowing smile the doctor said: 'Mr——, I'm sure your health would be much impaired if your moustache were removed. I shall, therefore, give strict instructions that you be not shaved.' He was the one and only prisoner who moved among his fellows with a fine moustache that was the envy of all." Dow did nothing, and Hiram wore his thick, shaggy moustache during his entire time in prison.

Things changed in other ways with Hiram's arrival at the penitentiary and with the new wave of cohabs who came with him. He gradually undid the damage done by T. J. Johnson, who had been poisoning the warden's mind for months with tales about Mormons. At Hiram's suggestion, a new toilet replaced the horrible "Dunnigan," with its "odor rank as death"; skylights were put in the dining hall; an inside door to keep out the cold was added to the new, more comfortable bunkhouse which had been built in the summer of 1885 to accommodate the anticipated influx of cohabs—and to which Rudger and Hiram were both eventually moved. A calendar clock was installed; older brethren were eventually permitted to keep their beards; more supplies and articles from the prisoners' families were permitted in; and festivities on Thanksgiving and Christmas were expanded, with Hiram able to attract some of Salt Lake's most talented singers, musicians, and actors, including his daughter (Rudger's half-sister) Edith. It was the beginning of a new era in the prison life of Rudger Clawson.

By mid-October there were twenty-four cohabs in the pen. One of the new arrivals, John Nicholson, an editor at the *Deseret News,* became a particularly good friend of Rudger's. Nicholson, in order to spare his family the kind of ordeal the Clawsons had gone through, waived his rights and offered himself as a witness for his own prosecu- ·

tion. He was fascinated by the story of Joseph Standing and spent long hours listening and taking notes as Rudger told his tale. He later published an account of the murder in *The Martyrdom of Joseph Standing.**

By this time, Rudger was also seeing Lydia again face-to-face, possibly through the intervention of Hiram. Rudger nevertheless kept up the secret correspondence. There were no private meetings (though he challenged her to get one so that he could prove how much he loved her). Letters, therefore, remained the only way to get out the frustrated-male feelings that were overwhelming him.

"Just think of it," he wrote in his September 23 letter, "nearly a whole year has dragged its length along [he loved this phrase and used it repeatedly in his letters and memoirs] since I was admitted to this paradise. Ere you realize it, my beloved sweetheart, I shall be a free man, full of life and vigor and all the fire of an ardent and overwhelming lover."

For Rudger, love (and sex), marriage, and time were intertwined inextricably with his religion.

> There is sweet consolation," [he wrote,] in the thought that this separation, so cruel, so hard to bear, cannot last forever; time, inexorable time, defies the power of man and swiftly and noiselessly speeds on, bringing nearer, still nearer, the day when we shall again be reunited in all the tender and fascinating association of married life. . . . This life would present but a dreary aspect without love, the mighty engine which curbs the passions of the human heart and enobles, purifies and exalts the soul of man. . . . The lasting happiness can only be attained by a permanent union of the sexes. The scriptures say: 'The man is not without the woman nor the woman without the man in the Lord.' Exaltation and eternal bliss, [he concludes,] can never be achieved except by marriage in the new and everlasting Covenant.

When Lydia wrote him in November, her sister Millie was living with her. She was a plural wife, and her life was in turmoil as her husband, David James, attempted to evade the law and keep order in his polygamous family.

Still concerned with Lydia's advancing pregnancy, Rudger, in a

---

*The book also included a description of the penitentiary and its Mormon occupants at the time he was there.

letter dated November 30, 1885, once again chastised her for continuing to sew. "You really ought not to use the machine at all." But she ignored him: "I had to pay," she wrote in her short sketch, "8 dollars a month [for rent presumably] and 8 dollars a ton for coal and the baby was so delicate I had to tend to him all day and sew at night. But by the time Rud came out I was out of debt and [had] a Hundred and Fifty in the Bank."

There is no further mention of the new baby in Rudger's letters nor in any other family document or history—nothing about its birth, name, loss, or death. At one point Lydia asked him if he would ever remarry Florence, and once again, Rudger equivocated. He would simply do what is right, he said. But "that is certainly a strange question to ask," all of which reminds one of his response in 1882 to Florence's question about his taking a second wife.

But that did not end it. On December 3 Lydia came to the prison and, like Florence, delivered her own ultimatum. Something, perhaps the difficulties Millie and her husband were having in polygamy, had triggered her worry about Rudger taking other wives after his release. If he did so, Lydia threatened, he would have to choose between them and her.

"It was a matter of great surprise and annoyance to me" he wrote afterward, "that you should take the position you did this morning. . . . Flo came here one day some months ago and asked what I proposed to do in the future. Of course, I could not say. She then continued: if you will not promise to do so and so, you must choose between us. I made my choice and you well know the result. Today, like Flo, you asked what do you propose to do after being released. Of course I could not say. You then said: if you do so and so you must choose between us, almost Flo's exact words." There was no evidence that this issue was resolved in any concrete way.

The year 1886 began auspiciously for Rudger. In January his father arranged for him to replace T. J. Johnson (who had served out his prison term) as tutor of Warden Dow's children. Rudger felt he should decline, considering the warden's earlier hostility and obvious distrust of him. But Hiram insisted, so Rudger took over the tutoring of George (age twelve) and Florence (age five). Even before he assumed his duties, their former tutor was back in prison for committing a burglary in Ogden. Johnson let it be known that he was eager to assume his tutoring job again, but the warden not only refused but rebuked him for his new crime and assigned him to Room One with the toughs.

This was fortunate for Rudger. As he soon learned, tutoring the warden's children brought special privileges, including one he had never dreamed of. Not only could he eat outside the yard with the trusties if he preferred (he declined), he could have visitors at any time without a pass. And there would be no time limit on their visit and no guard present. He could see Lydia in private again.

Rudger found the Dow children bright, interesting, and good students, the boy concentrating on reading, writing, arithmetic, grammar, spelling, history, French, and bookkeeping and the girl on reading, writing, and spelling. Both were taught elocution, with Rudger making a special effort in their voice lessons calculated to ingratiate himself with the warden. Not only was Dow impressed with young George's ability to recite "The Charge of the Light Brigade," which was Rudger's favorite poem, but Mrs. Dow was amazed that little Florence had learned the poem just by listening to George recite it. This resulted in little pieces of cake, pudding, or pie being left in the classroom for Rudger, and when prominent visitors came to see the warden, he would have the children recite for them. The favorable impression "naturally reflected credit and prestige upon the teacher," Rudger noted.

When he needed to punish the boy for not doing a lesson, Rudger made him stay after school and add up long columns of numbers on the blackboard. The boy enjoyed doing this so much that he purposely did things to incur punishment. Ultimately he became so good at adding up columns of figures that he challenged his father to a race and arrived at the answer before his father was two-thirds through. The warden was impressed with George—and Rudger.

March 2, 1886, Rudger recorded as a "day of lights and shadows, of pleasure and sorrow. Father had reached the termination of his imprisonment and upon payment of the fine was released. It was with no small degree of satisfaction that I saw him released from prison bondage, and yet when I remembered the many pleasant moments we had passed together—moments never to be recalled—my soul was filled with gloom and despondency." They had lived together in the same bunkhouse, talked, walked, played chess, and "dined" together. Hiram had brought amelioration to Rudger's life in prison and to the

lives of the other Saints as well. It was under his direction that the
elaborate holiday celebrations were mounted with some of the best
talent and food in Salt Lake. They would miss him.

Ten days later, however, a person second only to Hiram in shaping
Rudger's life entered prison. It was seventy-two-year-old Apostle Lorenzo Snow.

Lorenzo was the first polygamist to be convicted under the doctrine
of "segregation." This was an ingenious idea spawned in the inner
circles of the federal law enforcement agencies. It divided the polygamist's cohabitation with a plural wife into segregated periods of time
and allowed the prosecutors to bring charges against him for each
period separately. It meant that an almost infinite number of charges
could be brought and gave the court the power to jail a polygamist for
the rest of his life and fine him into bankruptcy.

Lorenzo had been convicted on three separate counts of unlawful
cohabitation, one for each of the previous three years, 1883, 1884,
and 1885. He was then sentenced to three consecutive six-month
terms and three $300 fines. For polygamous families, segregation was
a frightening doctrine, but Lorenzo and others who had been convicted under it could only hope that the Supreme Court would hand
down a favorable ruling on the appeal that Richards was arguing in
Washington.

As a young man, Lorenzo had had the appearance of a bulky
Abraham Lincoln. Now at seventy-two, his wavy hair was white and
his face lined with age. He was tall and wore a long, full beard. His
eyes always seemed inordinately wide open, the large, dark pupils alive
and ready to absorb anyone he was looking at into an inner realm.
Some considered him saintly. Frank Cannon, who clashed with Snow
in later years and felt less generous, thought his manners "elegant and
courtly," his voice sauve, and his walk "affected in its gentility."

Born in Ohio, Snow was an early convert, having been impressed
by the intelligence and spirituality of one of Joseph Smith's missionaries and apostles, David Patten. After his baptism, a visitation from
the "spirit of God" in a nearby wood sealed his commitment. As a
young man in 1849, he was ordained an apostle and then served for
many years in England, Italy, and Hawaii as one of the church's most
effective missionaries. In 1854 he was sent by Brigham Young to
preside over Box Elder Stake north of Salt Lake. Here, in Brigham

City in the 1860s, he began to experiment, at Young's urging, with
the cooperative enterprises that would provide the model on which
Young would base the far-reaching cooperative movement he instituted
in later years.

Snow was renowned in the church for having put vividly into words
Joseph Smith's concept of a living God to whose state man could
aspire. "As man is," said Snow, "God once was; and as God is, man
may become." But by the spring of 1886 he was a fugitive like most of
the church's leaders.      *CHRIST — ? Father*

Once again Zane had to sit through a long speech. Lorenzo's
statement was a comprehensive theological and religious justification
of polygamy and defense of the church—a brilliant summary of the
Mormon stand and one that Rudger must have read with delight. But
it did try Zane's patience.

The respect and admiration Rudger already felt for Snow deepened
as they were thrown together in prison. The older man replaced Hiram
as Rudger's mentor and, as an apostle, became the recognized leader
of the cohabs.

Outside, the crusade was beginning to reach its full fury. In 1886
Congress appropriated $5,000 for the hiring of "secret detectives,"
undercover agents assigned to the clandestine gathering of information
about polygamists. Evidence gathered by the first man hired with these
funds, Sam Gilson, was said to have been responsible for the convictions of Snow, Nicholson, and eight others. Eventually, federal agents
and paid informers swarmed the territory invading communities on
"cohab hunts," breaking unannounced into homes, accosting women
in their bedrooms, and shooting at suspected polygamists fleeing in
their underclothes. They asked women "indecent" questions about
their sexual relations and accosted children on the street to question
them about their parents. Neighbors were bribed to give evidence, and
rewards were offered for the top men, especially John Taylor and
George Q. Cannon, who so far had escaped capture. For information
leading to their conviction $300 was offered for Taylor and $500 for
Cannon. They especially wanted Cannon, partly because he had
escaped from their clutches once and partly because he was thought
to be the real holder of power in the underground church. Taylor was
never caught and died in the underground. Cannon was captured in
February 1886, but jumped bail before his case came to trial.

Convicted polygamists arrived at the penitentiary in ever increasing numbers through 1886 and 1887 (there were nearly fifty by the spring of 1886). As this tide of Mormons flooded the prison, Rudger noted the changes:

> The brethren exerted a most powerful restraining influence. Stubborn, rebellious men who were acquainted with every form of vice and lawlessness and who laughed at the 'sweat' box and paid little or no attention to the chains seemed utterly unable to resist the spirit of peace and tranquility and resignation that accompanied the 'Mormon' convicts. The brethren's example was contagious. Profanity did not cease altogether, but it was by no means indulged in to the extent that it had been; the 'sweat' boxes fell into disuse, except at rare intervals, and the chains gradually disappeared from the yard. Jail-breaking was a thing of the past. The heavy responsibility, the anxiety and the fears that constantly harassed the warden's mind, both day and night, were measurably removed.

If he was exaggerating to some extent, it is nonetheless a striking example of how a change in the numbers of one element within a group can influence the overall tone and morale.

Newcomers were called "fresh fish" and, following tradition, were required to put on a performance of some sort, though now it was a congenial exercise and done in good fun to welcome new prisoners into the camaraderie of the prison community.

"The guards felt as much at ease among the prisoners as they possibly could have at home. The marshal abandoned the practice of driving the men into one corner of the yard like so many cattle when visiting the prison. In fact, the change was so marked it astonished every official connected with the penitentiary, although they were slow to give the despised 'Mormons' credit for it."

In the spring of 1886, Caleb West replaced Eli Murray as governor of the Utah Territory. Murray was one of the chief proponents of the political suppression of the Mormons and had been in continuous conflict with them since his appointment in 1880. He was not unpopular in Washington, but in early 1886, in doing battle with the territorial legislature, he recklessly vetoed a routine appropriations bill that threatened to turn turbulence into chaos. It was too much, even for his supporters. President Grover Cleveland, whose election had raised hopes among the Mormons of at least some relief from the

Radical Republican "reign of terror," removed Murray and appointed Caleb West in his place. West, somewhat less abrasive, hoped to bring both the crusade and polygamy to an end through what he felt was an act of generosity.

On May 13, 1886, shortly after his installation, West went to the penitentiary and offered pardons to all the cohabs who would agree in good faith to respect and obey the laws as interpreted by the courts. He spoke first to Snow, but the apostle refused, despite the fact that he had just learned that the appeal of his first conviction had been denied. The governor next addressed the Mormons as a group and then retired to let them consider his offer. The Mormons called a meeting of which Rudger was elected chairman. Lorenzo, Rudger, and fifteen others spoke on the issue, and then under the careful guidance of Lorenzo and Rudger, they drafted a succinctly-worded statement rejecting the offer, which they acknowledged was inspired "by a kind feeling, [but] was not new, for we could all have avoided imprisonment by making the same promise to the courts. . . ."

There were too many questions that the amnesty left unanswered—questions about balancing obedience with their convictions and their responsibilities to the wives and children who depended on them—for it to be acceptable. West gave up and supported more stringent measures.

The months which followed were not bad ones for the Mormons in the pen. There was a great deal of good fellowship. Lorenzo inspired them, while Rudger showed them quiet courage. Warden Dow relaxed prison rules as much as possible. Rudger had become the warden's pet. When Marshal Ireland ordered Dow to dismiss Rudger as a trusty because he, Ireland, had been reliably informed that Rudger was secretly passing out and receiving correspondence, Dow concocted an excuse for his trusted tutor and simply disobeyed the order.

On the Fourth of July, 1886, they had one of the grandest celebrations ever, and once again it was organized by the inveterate showman and ex convict, Hiram Clawson. A long program of songs, speeches, recitations, feasting, and dancing was marred only by the escape of "Nosey" Banks, a burglar who worked in the prison tailor shop. During the festivities he borrowed some boots and a shirt, stole Lorenzo Snow's suit, and escaped by mixing with the crowd when the visiting townspeople left.

It is clear that Rudger Clawson played an important role among the Mormons in the federal penitentiary. "Counselor" is probably the best description, the role of someone who had been there longer than anyone else and could, based on that experience, advise others on how best to deal with the situation.

In a letter to Lydia, he outlined the kind of advice he gave:

> Try and make the most you can of a bad job. Do not waste time that is given you. You are comparatively free from any responsibility and can study and improve your minds. You can become better acquainted with the English language, with history, and I would advise all not to waste the time but to read good books. Do some studying every day and when we leave this place we will be much wiser than when we came here.

Not only did Rudger, at least in his own perception, serve as an advisor to the prison community, he was also one of its most active members. In addition to tutoring the warden's children, he organized a morning physical fitness class, which, he noted, "was replenished with new members twice every year by the activity of the U.S. Prosecuting Attorney." He taught bookkeeping and phonography (shorthand). He learned French from a one-armed burglar in return for bookkeeping lessons. Rudger never became proficient in the language, but he said he derived a great deal of pleasure from reading the entire *Book of Mormon* in French.

At the request of a group of inmates, he organized a formal bookkeeping class, for which he charged twenty-five cents for each of the sixty lessons, earning a total of $500 in the process. Those who completed the class satisfactorily received a diploma written in Rudger's own classic hand. One of his pupils was Bishop William Bromley, who seemed to doubt his ability to master bookkeeping. Rudger replied, that if he believed he could he would, if not he would fail. The bishop did in fact master it, and when he left prison, he returned to the store he managed in Salt Lake, fired his bookkeeper, and initiated the double-entry system he had learned from Rudger. Later, the *Salt Lake Tribune* would comment ill-humoredly on all the Mormons who had gone into prison presumably to suffer for their crimes and had come out with professions.

More significant to Rudger were the frequent visits Apostle Snow made to his class. Snow was obviously impressed with the teaching of the younger man and the scope of his bookkeeping course, which included general merchandising, commissions, jobbing, importing, and farm accounting. This image of Rudger as a kind of master bookkeeper and accountant would stick in Lorenzo's mind and play a role in the future he charted for his young protégé.

Meanwhile, in Washington, Franklin S. Richards, undaunted by the rejection of Snow's first appeal, filed another based on the fact that Snow had received a second conviction and was now serving a second term of imprisonment for a single offense. Finally, in February 1887, the Supreme Court delivered a favorable ruling that struck down the segregation doctrine.

Mormons were jubilant. Lorenzo was escorted from prison with great fanfare. Others convicted under the segregation doctrine were soon released.

But there was Rudger, once again deprived of friend, mentor, and father (or father figure). The prison was crowded with Mormons now, however, and Rudger seems to have taken Lorenzo's departure more or less in stride. Yet his attachment to the older man was deep and abiding. "To know him was to love and admire him," Rudger wrote of the apostle. "A highly cultivated intellect, a sympathetic heart, gentle and winning manners, gave him great influence over all who had the happiness to be numbered among his friends. . . . His views were frequently sought; as we sat around the table during the long hours of the evening, he often discoursed interestingly upon matters pertaining to the past, present and future condition of man. I shall ever look back to those hours—hours passed in prison—as among the most profitable of my life."

But despite Rudger's ability to make the most of his experience, prison was still oppressive. "One day," he wrote midway in his prison term, "so nearly resembles another in every particular as almost to create confusion in the mind . . . one long, tedious never-ending day—a living death."

Three days after Lorenzo was gone, Rudger drafted and sent to President Cleveland an eloquent plea for a pardon based on the irony of his experience at the hands of the law as contrasted with those of *real* criminals.

I am twenty-nine years of age. In November, 1884, I was convicted of Polygamy and Unlawful Cohabitation, and sentenced by Judge Charles S.

Zane to four years imprisonment and to pay a fine of $800.00. I have now
served out two years and three months of this term. That to which I
particularly desire to draw your attention is this: When I entered prison,
*fourteen* of its inmates were undergoing punishment for *murder*, five
having been sentenced to life, and the remainder with two exceptions, to
a long term of years. Of this number, ten have gone out on a full and free
pardon, two have been released and two only remain, one of whom is a
life man.

The immediate outgrowth of my alleged crime is life, of their crime,
death.

A proposition has been made to me, as also to others of my faith, that if
I would promise to obey the law in the future, *as construed by the courts*,
I should receive a pardon; while, on the other hand, no such requirement
whatever was made of the parties mentioned. Why, then, I respectfully
ask, should a promise be required of me and not of them? And what, Mr.
President, will justify a leniency extended to one class of criminals—those
who are guilty of *murder*, as against another class—those who are guilty of
a misdemeanor only?

It was a persuasive argument, but offered the president no *legal* basis
on which to act. He never replied.

In June 1886, Frank H. Dyer replaced Edwin Ireland as U.S.
marshal. There was a general sigh of relief. Dyer was a rather
congenial Southerner who, not suprisingly, was opposed to the kind
of carpetbag government favored by the former governor, Eli Murray,
and radical anti-Mormons. He was against polygamy, but was not an
anti-Mormon. When Apostle Wilford Woodruff counseled Lydia and
Rudger to remarry in a civil ceremony, having overcome Rudger's
objections, the marriage took place in the marshal's office with Dyer
as one of the witnesses. When Lydia had trouble getting a carriage to
take her to visit Rudger, Dyer would send his around for her. He told
Lydia in one of their encounters that "he did not blame Rud a bit
[and] that he would have done the same."

Whatever role Rudger played in prison, he was certainly perceived
by the anti-Mormons as the "leading Mormon," if not the Mormon
leader. He learned this forcefully in October, when Dow resigned and
was replaced by Otis L. Brown. Dow had won the respect and even
the liking of the inmates, Mormons and non-Mormons alike, so that
a "neatly worded paper expressive of our good feelings toward him"
was prepared and presented.

Rudger's tutoring job was clearly at an end, as was his privileged position with the warden. He therefore "surrendered [his] office and gracefully withdrew inside" prior to the new warden's installation. Brown had already tipped his hand by remarking to a guard that "he would send Clawson into the 'yard a flying.' I, with malice afore-thought, robbed him of this exquisite pleasure," Rudger gloated.

The "good life," such as it was, was over for the Mormons in prison. Some were now moved into the tough bunkhouse and toughs were moved in with the Mormons. Whereas Dow had eased up on the regulations concerning beards and moustaches, the shaving rule was again rigorously enforced. The guards knew the Mormons were no longer privileged prisoners and acted accordingly. N. V. Jones was put in the sweat box for talking back to a guard, despite the fact that he had just recovered from a serious cold.

Prison life again became mostly weary repetition of familiar events: escape attempts, conflicts among the non-Mormons, the gathering together of the Saints in mutual support, the various yard activities along with teaching classes, reading, and studying.

One thing that occupied Rudger more and more during this period was his journal keeping. He had begun some time before, writing down an account of his experiences in little notebooks. Each time he finished a notebook he would strip off the cover, roll up the pages, and, tying them with a string, pass them to a visitor. "They were concealed in my trousers at the back just under the suspenders and, as the guard on duty in searching the prisoners simply felt of their side pockets, these rolls escaped notice."

Warden Brown took note of the hours Rudger spent scribbling in his little books and got word to him that he was wasting his time because the manuscript would be confiscated when he was released. Rudger thereupon began making extra copies of every few pages and storing them in his locked trunk. He would have a little surprise for Brown when the time came.

Between December 1885 and April 1886, the exchange of corre-spondence between Rudger and Lydia declined substantially. There were only four letters from Rudger during all of 1886. It is explained in part by the fact that after he became Warden Dow's tutor he had ample opportunity to talk with Lydia in private. But that privilege ended in October 1886 with the advent of the new warden. It may be that letters written between then and the next April did not survive, but that seems unlikely given the care with which Lydia saved the others.

In any event, in April, 1887, Rudger was again smuggling out love letters to Lydia. In May he wrote: "If my wish could be realized at this instant, you would be folded in my arms so close and tight as almost to be hid from view and a shower of warm and passionate kisses would fall upon your lips. . . . You are a woman with a woman's heart and what could be more precious to you or what would thrill you with more genuine pleasure than the fond caresses of him to whom you have given your heart. Ah, you can't deceive me. Don't I know just what it requires to satisfy a woman's love, exacting though it may be? Don't I know how to touch your feelings, draw out your affections, and light the pure flame of love that burns with a bright but steady glow. Yes, I have the secret."

He was taken with the fantasy that Lydia should be ready for him to make good his heated pledges. "Keep this letter and let it be the first thing you place in my hand after I reach home," he wrote in one letter. And in another: "P.S. On the second day after I return home, just after dinner, place this letter in my hands. . . . Do this and you will have no occasion to regret it." In the end, it was in his letters that he found surcease from his confinement.

As the summer of 1887 began to settle on the Great Salt Lake Basin, he wrote, "Today is Sunday. The weather is pleasant. I am sitting out in the yard under the blue canopy of heaven, breathing fresh and invigorating mountain air that comes sweeping down Parley's Canyon. My attention is first attracted by one thing and then an- other—by the convicts who are promenading on the boulevard, by the magpies that hang in cages against the "bunk" houses, by a young deer, an interesting docile animal, that was brought into the prison a few days since, and my thoughts turn to thee, beloved one! I say to myself: 'so near and yet so far.' "

He concludes: "As an evidence that you received this letter, and that you love me with all the intensity and fervor that a woman is capable of feeling for a man, wear a *black velvet bracelet* on your left wrist when you come to see me next Wednesday. I shall be quick to notice."

Later in July he asks her to wear a pink ribbon around her neck, and then in August he writes: "P.S. When you come again and sometime during our visit look me square in the eye and say 'Pineapple,' which will be equivalent to saying: 'Rud, my heart yearns with an intense yearning, for the caresses and endearments which thou hast promised me.' I shall then say 'Peach,' which will be equivalent to this: 'Loved one, they shall yet be thine.' "

But alas, Lydia forgot! Rudger chided her in a delightful letter written a few days later.

"The object of this letter is to call your attention to a matter of some importance. Read and consider attentively the Post Script to my note of August 22nd. In that P.S. I made a simple request of you, asked you to do a certain thing and *you failed to do it.* You may be sure that I looked at you closely several times during our last visit and wondered if you would remember to carry out the request I had made—but you did not. Now, what am I to think? All the little commissions I have given you of late were attended to with the utmost decision and dispatch, but when it comes to a matter of vastly greater importance you actually forget. Ah! Lydia! Lydia! I don't think I should have forgotten; in fact I did not forget, but was ready to make the answer as indicated in the P.S. . . . . Well, well, let it pass! We'll say no more about it; it's a small matter anyway."

But he can't resist. "You remember," he goes on in a subsequent letter, "I said to you a short time ago that I wondered if you would forget the many little suggestions made in my letters. I believe you replied by saying—'Do I ever forget?' At that time, I could not say you did—but now—well, well never mind."

In August, a murderer, Fred Hopt, was finally executed after waiting three years, much of it spent in solitary confinement. At his sentencing he had been asked if he wished to be hanged or shot. "I choose to be shot," he had replied cooly.

A pall hung over the prison when "the fatal day at last arrived. The weather was clear but warm. Death was in the air. "At twelve o'clock the prisoners were remanded to the bunk rooms and locked up, the windows having been previously covered with blankets to shut off the view. It would be difficult to describe the feeling of suspense and gloom that settled down upon those bunk rooms. . . . At about quarter to one o'clock the doomed man was conducted to the fatal chair. He maintained a superb calmness to the last, as evidenced by the fact that he quietly smoked a cigar while proceeding from his cell to his death. A sharp ringing report which fairly startled us indicated that all was over."

Just before the execution, Hopt, who had been attended by a Catholic priest for the last few hours and was no doubt being urged to consider his salvation, told the warden that he would send a hailstorm within forty-eight hours if he found there was a hereafter. The storm came—with two-inch hailstones—but there was no indication whether Hopt had sent it from heaven or hell.

A few days later Rudger spent eighteen hours in the sweat box for making a thoughtless gesture to someone on the wall. Rudger wondered if this might have been the warden's revenge for being deprived earlier of the "exquisite pleasure" he would get from removing Rudger from his tutor's position.

In the fall, construction began on a new penitentiary building, but Rudger's attention was elsewhere. When he had been sentenced to jail in 1885, the deduction of time for good conduct ("in copper") was quite liberal; on a four-year term, a prisoner was given fourteen months copper, meaning he would have to serve only two years, ten months. But later that year, a new interpretation of the law, proposed by U.S. Attorney Dickson and sustained by the court, reduced the copper to nine months on a four-year term. Then, in March, 1886, a new copper law, even more liberal than the one in use when Rudger went to prison, was enacted. In October, 1887, Rudger, on the advice of his attorneys, applied for a discharge from prison based on the new act.

On the twentieth of the month the last legal confrontation over Rudger Clawson the polygamist took place before the Territorial Supreme Court. Rudger lost. "At 4:00 o'clock in the afternoon," the *Herald* reported, "the court refused to grant the application." Rudger was furious and so were his attorneys, who advised him to write Cleveland again requesting a pardon—this time based not on moral indignation but on what they felt was the proper interpretation of the law. He did so on November 10 in a carefully reasoned document written, one suspects, more by the lawyers than by Rudger—accompanied by a certificate of good conduct from Marshal Dyer.

The family now mounted a strong new effort to win Rudger's freedom. Lydia says in her reminiscences: "I went to work to try to get a pardon and in time we did," though it is uncertain just what her role was.

Margaret went to Washington where she met with John W. Young, Franklin S. Richards, and John T. Caine (who was not only Hiram's old theater friend but also a former territorial delegate to Congress). These men had been negotiating off and on for several years with Congress and the White House, trying to find a compromise that would end the crusade and win Utah statehood. They had not succeeded and the Edmunds-Tucker Act of 1887, which disincorporated the church and confiscated its property (among other things), had been passed. Nevertheless, they had the ear of the president and no doubt helped convince him that the granting of a few pardons—especially in such a deserving case as Rudger's—would be both humanitarian and good politics.

The telegram came on December 1 telling him that the pardon had been granted. Twelve days later, Rudger was released. It had been three years, one month and ten days.

But he still had his confrontation with Warden Brown to play out. When the day of Rudger's departure arrived, a guard asked for the key to his trunk. Rudger refused and was taken to the warden, who repeated the request. Again Rudger refused. The warden grew angry and threatened to break the trunk open.

"Mr. Brown," Rudger said with mock indignation, "I know what you want. It is my journal. That is something that belongs to me . . . and is of little value to others. I think it would be unkind and unfair on your part to forcibly take possession of it."

But he finally gave up the key and the warden opened the trunk and rummaged through it. "His eye finally rested upon the journal leaves I had purposely deposited there for him, and he seized them with great avidity."

Pleased with himself, the warden apologized and said it was his duty to confiscate the journal.

"I expostulated with him over this high-handed proceeding," Rudger notes dryly in ending, "and left the prison." He must have been smiling as he did so since the journals on which he would later base his prison memoirs had, of course, been smuggled out and were stored safely at home.*

---

*Some time later, Rudger met Brown on the street and could not resist needling him

At the gate, when Rudger emerged from the prison, the Clawson family, along with other friends and well-wishers, greeted him with a rousing cheer and crowded round to congratulate and welcome him. Lydia felt left out and—according to what she told her daughter in later years—resentful. But it was not important; she had a drawer full of Rudger's passionate I.O.U.s to draw him back from the Clawsons anytime she wished.

---

about the journals.

"You will remember," he said, "my last hour at the 'pen,' when you insisted upon taking forcible possession of my journals? Now, don't you think, Mr. Brown, really, that that was a contemptible thing to do, quite unworthy of the warden of an important prison?"

Brown replied that he regretted it but that he was just doing his duty.

"Well, Mr. Brown," said Rudger, "I wanted particularly to say to you that you didn't get my journals at all. The leaves you did get were prepared for you and you were therefore entitled to them. Furthermore, let me tell you, my journal is at home and if you will call in now or later I shall be delighted to show it to you."

Brown, "chagrined and embarrassed," beat a hasty retreat.

# CHAPTER 5
# STAKE PRESIDENT: BRIGHAM CITY

"Just prior to the happy day of my release from prison," Rudger wrote in the diary he was to keep for the next eighteen years, "I was busily engaged in thought, forming plans for the future." He would settle in Salt Lake amidst family and friends, "engage in some business pursuit and move along in life pretty much the same as before. . . ." But it was not to be. The Lord and the church had different plans for him. Once again Rudger's life was shaped by events over which he, as a devout church member, could not exercise control.

This time the shaper of these events was Lorenzo Snow, who visited Rudger on a cold, wintry day in mid-December 1887. Rudger, he announced, had been appointed by the Council of the Twelve to be  president of Box Elder Stake, the headquarters of which were located in Brigham City some distance north of Salt Lake.

Rudger demurred because of his youth and lack of experience. "I shrank in my feelings from so grave a responsibility . . . nevertheless I had faith to believe that the Lord was abundantly able to qualify me. . . ." And so he accepted despite Snow's statement that Rudger could  be offered no financial inducement "but felt to say that the Lord would provide for me and give me joy in my labors."

For reasons that are not entirely clear, Lorenzo was in a hurry to get Rudger off to Brigham City. This may have been because acting president of the stake, E. A. Box, who had succeeded Lorenzo's son Oliver, was not performing satisfactorily or was resisting Lorenzo's influence. (Box would become Rudger's major antagonist during the young man's early years in Brigham City.) When Rudger asked how soon Snow wished him to leave, the apostle replied, "Right now, this minute, within a day or a week, were it possible. Pack all your household goods and chattels into a freight car, take your wife and child and leave for Brigham City . . . at the earliest possible moment."

In ending, Lorenzo consoled his young protégé for being sent off into the wilderness with little chance of prospering by assuring him that there would be compensations: "You will not enounter such alluring prospects for your bodily comfort, but you will enter into possession of a kingdom, so to speak, of six or seven thousand subjects. Sitting upon your throne, you will reign as a king, yes, with greater authority than is exercised by an earthly king, even divine authority. You will mingle among your subjects, you will be to them as a father, a counselor and a friend, a minister of righteousness, going from ward to ward, each in its turn and from priesthood quorum to priesthood quorum and from auxiliary organization to auxiliary organization. You will be able to look into the hearts of people and judge the motives that govern their actions, enabling you to advise them for their present good and eternal welfare. Earthly riches are not to be compared for a moment with the experience you will get in presiding over the Box Elder Stake of Zion."

This may have been a rather exciting prospect for Rudger, but Lydia and his mother, Margaret, were not as happy. Margaret wanted him nearby, and Lydia wanted to live a normal life among their friends in Salt Lake. In addition, Rudger had a job awaiting him in Salt Lake City that would pay him $100 per-month, an ample salary in those days compared to the uncertainties of a move to a small town fifty-six miles away on the Utah frontier.

It was a cold, wintry day two weeks later, in January 1888, when Rudger, Lydia, and two-year-old Rudger Remus left Salt Lake for Brigham City. A severe snowstorm had settled over northern Utah and blanketed the valley with several feet of snow which blew into high drifts.

At Ogden they discovered that the train tracks north were blockaded with snow, and they would have to lay over a day or two. When Rudger learned that a wrecking train was going to be sent from Ogden to break the blockade, which was some distance beyond Brigham City, he obtained permission to take it to Brigham City and wired ahead his new arrival time. But at Willard, seven miles from Brigham City, they were delayed again. An engine had jumped the track, but failed to clear it. A new track had to be laid around it—in the middle of that bitter cold and stormy night. It was 1:00 a.m. when the Clawson family arrived at the little Brigham City railroad station which stood dark and empty. "It was a bright moonlight night and the weather was as cold as 'Iceland,' as it were. We were doubly cognizant of the fact standing there on the platform with the railroad station door securely locked against us and not a living soul in sight." A freezing wind, called the "Canyon Zephyr" by the locals, blew steadily down from the mountains.

Many years later in writing his memoirs he notes that he and Lydia remarked on having received a "*cold* reception." Whether or not this humorous exchange actually took place, there was no shelter for Lydia and the baby, nor even a bench to sit on ". . . so I was under the stern necessity of going uptown, a distance of about ¾ of a mile in search of a conveyance for Lydia and little Rudger; and after calling at Sister Minnie J. Snow's and arousing her from her morning slumbers, I was under the further necessity, by her permission, of going out into the barn and hitching up the buggy. After an absence of about 45 minutes, I returned to the depot for Lydia, and, a few minutes later, we were comfortably ensconced at Sister Snow's, where we took supper and immediately retired.

"What an odd situation! Here I was, with my family, rather unceremoniously landed in Brigham City, among strangers, my destined future home, with but little means and no resources whatever financially; and yet I felt no particular concern as to that realizing that the Lord was amply able to provide."

Not the least of Rudger's worries was his relationship with the church leaders in Box Elder Stake. Lorenzo Snow's son, Oliver, had taken over the stake presidency when the stakes had been reorganized by Brigham Young in 1877. In recent years he had let it be known that he wanted to resign in order to spend more time on his business (a year and a half later he opened the first locally-owned bank in Brigham

City) and did so in October 1887. Elijah A. Box, his first counselor, was appointed temporary president.

The lack of welcome at Brigham City station was not due entirely to Rudger's delay or what Rudger himself admitted was an "unseemly hour." The leadership in Box Elder was not pleased with Rudger's appointment as their stake president. He was a foreigner in Brigham City with no leadership experience in the church. The church elders—almost certainly included E. A. Box—felt there were a number of people already in Box Elder who were as well, or better, qualified as Rudger for the post. Rudger was also only thirty-five years old while his competitors for the position were all substantially older. (Both of the men he ultimately chose as counselors were forty-eight.) Snow's urgency in getting Rudger launched was almost certainly to put a lid on the pot before it boiled over. Rudger himself felt the sting of the church elders' resentment and might have become discouraged had he not been thoroughly convinced that the call to Box Elder, like the call to go on his mission, had come directly from the Lord.

In any event, Rudger's appointment was the result of Lorenzo Snow's intervention, so that even if the Mormon tradition of accepting higher authority had not been so strong, it is improbable that Snow's choice would have been openly opposed. He was, after all, the patron saint of Brigham City.

Back in 1824, Jim Bridger, in order to settle a wager with trappers gathered at Cache Valley in what is now northern Utah, paddled down the Bear River into what was to be the Brigham City area and "discovered" the Great Salt Lake (which he thought was an inland bay or spur of the Pacific Ocean). As early as 1850 settlers had moved into the area, then called Box Elder Creek, setting up camps and beginning to till the land.

In the fall of 1853 Brigham Young sent his apostle Lorenzo Snow and fifty families to Box Elder Creek—which Snow renamed Brigham City—to preside over the settlement and see to its spiritual, social, and economic growth. With characteristic vigor and imagination, Snow launched into the task. He created a willow-covered bowery in the fort (constructed for protection against a tribe of Shoshones inhabiting the area who were thought to be unfriendly) and organized church meetings. He sponsored socials, theatrical and musical events (offered at first at Snow's home), brought in lecturers, and organized debates.

He established a school system and mediated disputes over land and water, critical issues in this dry county where a few early settlers had laid claim to most of the arable soil. He oversaw the laying out and building of the town, expanding it beyond the rough fort.

He also established, in the 1860s, a series of cooperative enterprises which turned Brigham City into a "hive of industry." They were so successful, in fact, that Brigham City's prosperity continued virtually unhampered by the devastating Panic of 1873. As a result of the Panic and the severe effect it had on other Mormon communities, Brigham Young put into effect the United Order, a cooperative movement designed to realize certain principles of the faith and free the Mormon economy from the effects of gentile-driven economic forces. He used Lorenzo's Brigham City experiment as a model.

When, in 1877, Young decided to release the apostles from their responsibilities as stake presidents (and define stake boundaries according to county boundary lines), it was not surprising that Lorenzo Snow's son Oliver was selected to succeed him. In announcing the selection, Brigham Young emphasized that Oliver's youthfulness (he was twenty-nine years old) was a desirable characteristic since he would be "more likely to follow advice and counsel." His loyalty to Snow would also be unquestioned.

Now, ten years later, Snow once again selected a young man who would seek advice and counsel from the authorities and whose loyalty could not be questioned.

Early in February at a quarterly conference of the stake, Rudger's name was put forward by Snow for approval by the stake membership. Snow spoke of how in the Bible David was called from the shepherd's pasture and made king. He recognized that Rudger might not be "the choice of everyone here . . . but the Lord's ways are not man's." When asked to sustain Rudger, all hands in the congregation were raised but one, which belonged to "a man whose standing in the church was of doubtful character . . . because of a 'spirit of opposition' to the priesthood." But Rudger, as he would prove later on a number of occasions, was a savvy politician. "Having learned the name of the brother who voted against me and accompanied by Sister Clawson, I went to his furniture store and bought a nice bill of furniture. He ever after was quite friendly and gave me his support in the new office conferred upon me."

There was much more, of course, to the settling-in process than mollifying church members and buying furniture. He had to find a place to live and a way to earn a living. His financial situation was indeed precarious. "When I left the penitentiary after three years' confinement," he wrote in his memoirs, "I was stripped" and stood there 'naked and bare,' as it were, financially." He had about $300 when he left Salt Lake and found that being eaten up rapidly, especially by rent, during the first weeks in Brigham. So in March, after extensive inquiries and a survey of Main Street, he identified a house on a corner lot that looked like what he wanted and bought it in April for $980, which he considered a bargain. But it put him seriously in debt.

Fortunately, two other events followed close on the heels of the purchase. One was a letter from the First Presidency announcing that as stake president he would henceforward receive an annual allowance of $600—though it had to be drawn from the Box Elder tithing office "in various kinds of tithing received," i.e., in flour, butter, meat and vegetables, but not in cash.

The other fortuitous event was the offer of a job for three months writing abstracts for the county court. It paid three dollars per day and lasted for three years rather than three months. As was his custom, Rudger later toted up the economic significance of this professional endeavor. "The sum total of my earnings for this task was about $2,400. It enabled me to cancel the indebtedness on my new home, to pay $400 for flour mill stock that in dividends kept my family in flour for twenty years; helped pay for a five-acre piece of hay land that furnished feed for a horse, milch cow and chickens, and if the fruit and vegetables raised on our lot are taken into account, I can truthfully say we were blessed of the Lord and were getting along famously."

To his credit, he did recognize the major contribution made by Lydia as a professional dressmaker and as a "woman of unusual executive ability" who was watchful and thrifty in her habits and who also made all her own dresses and most of the children's clothes as well.

By the fall of 1889, Rudger felt financially secure enough to begin what proved to be the first in a series of renovations and add-ons to his home. The house was increased in size to nine rooms and several ceilings were raised. The renovations dragged on for over a year and were quite inconvenient, but Rudger was characteristically proud of the economy with which he did it: "I, myself, did all the inside painting except the parlor, thus saving about $100 and advancing myself in the art of painting."

Brigham City is located due north of Salt Lake City at the base of the Uintah foothills. It sits on a narrow plateau that rises above the valley floor and affords a broad view of the Great Salt Lake Basin. When the original settlers arrived, the area was grown up in what was called "bunch grass," which soon succumbed to overgrazing and the land reverted to sagebrush until irrigated farms were established. In a region in which dramatic settings are commonplace, Brigham City's is particularly striking because the rugged mountains are so immediate, rising into high rugged ridges and peaks almost out of the backyards of the easternmost houses.

When Rudger moved there, Brigham City consisted of approximately 2,000 people, about 70 percent Latter-day Saints.

The streets were wide and lined with shade trees, box elder, locust, and lombardy poplar. The original lots, ranging from a half-acre to an acre and a quarter, had not yet been subdivided, and most were occupied by single family houses. There was neither much wealth nor much poverty in Brigham so that the houses were uniformly substantial and well-kept. Rudger notes that the Salt Lake and Ogden newspapers called Brigham the "city of homes." It was also noted for its shoe factories "because the people of Brigham City required more shoes 'for the protection of their soles than any other city of similar size in Utah, owing largely to the sharp gravel that cuts the leather and soon uses up a 'pair of understandings.' "

Peach trees grew well in the soil around Brigham and peaches were a principal crop. From the mountainside the area looked like one vast orchard. Strawberries, raspberries, and blackberries were also important commercial crops.

The center of town was dominated by the county courthouse, a large, square, adobe building with a classical portico and an elegant balustrade around a hipped roof. "A clock," Rudger observed, "looks out from the tower high above the city and announces the time of day."

Several blocks to the south stood the tabernacle on a large, green square planted with carefully placed shade trees. It was a striking building, constructed of sandstone and limestone with a heavy white spire dominating the front entrance. Along the exterior of each side, a row of square brick pillars rose from the ground topped by miniature replicas of the principal tower, though more sharply tapered. Inside, the design was of typical Mormon simplicity with the tall, arched windows casting a profusion of light.

Box Elder County, and thus Box Elder Stake, was large, stretching north to the Idaho Territory and west to Nevada. The small towns in the west, such as Snowville, Park Valley, and Grouse Creek were far from Brigham City, isolated by the Great Salt Lake Desert and the Grouse Creek Mountains. The authorities visited these areas only once a year on long arduous treks.

The Union Pacific and Central Pacific railroads had been joined by the Golden Spike at Promintory in Box Elder, thirty or so miles from Brigham City. The advent of the railroad had produced an economic boomlet in Corinne, a little town just west of Brigham, resulting in the influx of non-Mormon laborers and drifters. For a number of years it scandalized the quiet Mormon communities in Box Elder with what the Mormons considered its drunkeness, licentiousness, and generally wild behavior typical of gentile settlements. Then the bubble burst, the population declined, and Corinne became a quieter, more stable community.

In his early diary entries, Rudger offered descriptive and evaluative commentary on each, or at least most, of the towns in the stake. Among the most important were Willard, the second in size and so rich in the productiveness of the soil that it caused a "lack of enterprise" in its citizens; Bear River City, out on the plain and desperately in need of good water to irrigate its fields; Mantua, nestled four miles up in Box Elder Canyon and composed of thrifty, hardworking Scandinavians; Three Mile Creek (which was a ward but not formally a town) was also composed of hardworking farmers; and Honeyville, which was populated entirely by the family of polygamist Abraham Hunsaker and which would be the setting for what, despite his experiences in Georgia and in the penitentiary, was one of the most bizarre episodes and sticky problems Rudger ever had to face.

In his description of the towns in which the faithful now in his charge lived, Rudger, characteristically, judged each according to the degree to which tithes were paid and other requests for support by the church were responded to. Those found wanting, he vowed to reform. Though not yet the kind of issue that Lorenzo Snow would eventually make it, tithing and the financial state of the church were clearly of concern to the authorities in Salt Lake, and in Rudger Clawson they found the responsiveness of a man who was a born accountant and manager of money.

Snow himself was now playing a stronger role in the church. During the years before his imprisonment he spent much of his time on the underground and had been a prime target of polygamy hunts by federal officials who frequently raided his home in Brigham City. He escaped by hiding in a small cellar room under his bedroom. It was equipped with a chair and a bed, ventilated by a small grill in the foundation, and entered through a trapdoor under the rug in his bedroom. Here he would wait out the raid in modest comfort. He was finally discovered by the deputies during a raid in November 1885.

But Snow had served his time, so that while he had to be discreet (he lived in an apartment in Brigham City separate from his wives), he was able to move openly in performing his church duties. This was in contrast to John Taylor, Wilford Woodruff, George Q. Cannon, and other members of the Quorum of the Twelve, the ruling body of the church, who remained underground during this period while the crusade intensified. But the church stood firm on the Principle. President John Taylor and his Apostle Abraham H. Cannon reported having revelations from God affirming the rightness of their stand on polygamy. For many Mormons it was a deeply religious issue. They risked God's wrath if they denied God's revealed word. As a result, in the spring of 1887, the Edmunds-Tucker law was enacted which in addition to providing for a harsher application of the antipolygamy laws and giving more power over elections to the Utah Commission, called for disincorporation of the church and the escheatment (confiscation) of church property to the U.S. government. It was a devastating blow despite the fact that much of the wealth of the church had already been transferred by John Taylor to the private ownership of carefully selected and trusted church members.

As for the Saints, they took two tacks. One was the dispersal of polygamous families, especially to Mexico, where large numbers were resettled. The other was statehood.

Since 1849 the Saints had sought territorial self-government or statehood and had always been rebuffed. Now in 1887 they renewed their efforts, seeing statehood as an answer to federal attacks on the Mormons. Church leaders assumed that even though polygamy would have to be formally outlawed, the dominance of the Mormons and of the church in the new state would be sufficient to mitigate the severity of the antipolygamy crusade and would eventually neutralize the issue. But the issue, of course, was not simply polygamy. The church's control of the politics of the territory was as distasteful to many politicians as plural marriage.

In June 1887 a constitutional convention was called, presided over by Mormon John T. Caine, the territory's delegate to Congress. A constitution outlawing polygamy (though only as a misdemeanor) and prohibiting the union of church and state or the dominance of the state by the church, was drafted and endorsed by the church authorities. But it was rejected by congressional leaders who considered it a ruse to perpetuate church dominion in a state in which its members would constitute an overwhelming majority. The maelstrom of the crusade continued unabated as the church became more and more beleaguered. And into the maelstrom—not uncharacteristically—stepped Rudger Clawson.

In April 1888, only four months after his release from prison, he was invited by Lorenzo Snow to speak at the General Conference in Salt Lake. Wilford Woodruff, who had not been formally ordained but who by seniority was in line for the presidency of the church after John Taylor's death in July 1887, was in hiding. But conscious of the growing crisis, he instructed Lorenzo to keep the lid on discussions of polygamy. ". . . if any one attempted to speak on polygamy," he wrote to a friend, Snow should 'throw his hat at him.' "

The effort to gain statehood had made headway with President Cleveland and other members of the executive branch in Washington, but had run aground in Congress. John W. Young, Rudger's former employer, had directed the church lobbying team in Washington up to this time, but had now been replaced by Joseph F. Smith. None too soon; Young had reached the point where he was asking for money to bribe key antistatehood congressmen.

In the meantime, the church had struck a deal—negotiated principally by Rudger's father, Hiram Bradley Clawson—with California financial and railroad representatives. These interests would throw the weight of their lobby in Washington and their influence with the press behind the Mormon quest for statehood. In return the church would bring its influence to bear upon the territorial judiciary and legislature to the benefit of the Californians.

By the spring of 1888, Hiram and his California associates were making significant progress. The anti-Mormon agitation in the press had subsided—as a result, in part, of payoffs to a number of influential newspapers in San Francisco, New York, Philadelphia, Chicago, and St. Louis—and Congress seemed more malleable. Everyone agreed that it was critical to the statehood cause to restrain Mormon leaders from making statements regarding polygamy.

How or why Snow allowed Rudger—and one or two other lesser-known church officials—to speak on the subject at the conference is not recorded and is hard to understand, but he did. Rudger gave a long, rousing speech in which he reaffirmed the belief that had sent him to prison. "I was convicted of having rendered obedience to the law of God," he said, defiant as ever, "That was my offense." What did he feel now in relation to this matter? "I feel like honoring the Lord." Then in a burst of rhetoric he mentioned each of the major principles of the Mormon faith and asked if "we," the members of the church, believed in it, affirming in each case that they indeed did. Finally came plural marriage. "The Lord has revealed the principle of celestial marriage. Do we believe it is true? We most assuredly do. And will we honor this principle? By the help of the Lord we will not make a promise to do away with this principle any more than we will promise to do away with the principles of faith, baptism, or the laying on of hands for the reception of the Holy Ghost."

"We were considerably annoyed not to say mortified," Woodruff later wrote, "at the want of care which was manifested in cautioning the brethren who spoke not to touch on topics that at the present time, were likely to arouse prejudice."

Woodruff's comments put it mildly. Rudger's speech caused a furor in the national press and reinforced the belief of many people around the country and in Congress in the duplicity of the Mormon position. Further, it seriously undercut the efforts of the California lobbyists, who now pulled away from the Mormons. President Cleveland was angered, and the opposition in Congress stiffened. It could be argued—though not proven—that Rudger's speech was a turning point, making the confrontation which resulted in the full enforcement of the Edmunds-Tucker law and the capitulation of the church in the Woodruff Manifesto inevitable. There is no indication in Rudger's papers what, if anything, Hiram said to him about the matter.

In Utah, of course, the truth was that church leaders were as committed as ever to polygamy and that the church, the First Presidency, and the stake presidencies—if Box Elder was any example— were heavily engaged in managing or influencing the politics of the territory. By August 1889 Rudger himself was deeply involved in local politics and was, in fact, chairman of the central committee of the People's party.

The People's party had been established in the early 1870s as a countermove to the formation of the Liberal party. An alliance of excommunicated and dissident Mormons with non-Mormons, the Liberal party sought a political voice to counter the influence of the church. For the Liberals, Mormon theocracy was the issue, and antipolygamy the cause which rallied them.* The *Salt Lake Tribune* was their voice. The People's party, on the other hand, immediately became the political arm of the church and mobilized the Mormons in the cause of maintaining control over life in the Utah Territory.

By 1889 the People's party in major population centers of Salt Lake and Ogden, where there were significant numbers of non-Mormon residents, was somewhat beleaguered. The Liberals had been joined by many nonpolygamist Mormons who felt their political rights were being sacrificed to a practice in which, whether they accepted it as church doctrine or not, they did not engage.

When John Taylor died in 1887, Wilford Woodruff had been next in line for the presidency. Several apostles—Moses Thatcher, Heber J. Grant, and Francis M. Lyman in particular—wanted a younger man to succeed Taylor. They felt that, at eighty-one, Woodruff was too old to guide the church through the difficult times ahead. The resulting

---

*In 1888, Elliott F. Sanford, chief justice of the territorial courts, stated the issue clearly: "We care nothing for your polygamy. It's a good war cry and serves our purpose by enlisting sympathy for our cause; but it's a mere bagatelle compared with other issues in the irrepressible conflict between your parties. What we most object to is your unity, your political and commercial solidarity; the obedience you render to your spiritual leaders in temporal affairs. We want you to throw off the yoke of the priesthood, to do as we do, and be Americans in deed as well as name."

conflict delayed Woodruff's succession to the presidency for two years while the church floundered. He was finally sustained as president in April 1889.

Whatever the conflict over succession, the quorum was united in its opposition to abandoning polygamy, though they debated at meeting after meeting the possibility of making some kind of public statement that would mollify their critics. But they could not find an acceptable formula.

In November 1889 they were reinforced in their positiion when Woodruff reported a revelation in which God explicitly warned them against promising to give up plural marriage.

The next month they attempted to marshal their ecclesiastical forces, calling on the faithful to observe a special day of fasting on December 23rd, Joseph Smith's birthday. Liberal candidates had been elected to the territorial legislature. In early 1889, Ogden had fallen to the Liberals and in 1890 they would win Salt Lake City as well.

In Brigham City, however, the People's party was still alive and healthy. For one thing, there just weren't very many gentiles. Non-Mormons in Utah tended to congregate in railroad and mining towns and in the major urban centers of Salt Lake and Ogden. The smaller towns and farming areas remained overwhelmingly Mormon.

Until the local elections of 1889, politics in Brigham City had been relatively placid because of the paucity of non-Mormons. Rudger estimated the number of People's party members at about four hundred while the Liberals were no more than forty. But the Liberal supporters in Box Elder County had been increased by an influx of laborers working for the Bear City Canal, and in 1889 the party had high hopes and mounted a vigorous campaign. In part, their hopes were pinned on what was happening elsewhere in the territory.

The political phase of the battle over polygamy and church influence in the Utah Territory was reaching a climax. The church had been disincorporated and its property and wealth escheated under the Edmunds-Tucker Act, though the Supreme Court was hearing a challenge to its constitutionality and there was an expectation among Mormons that the law would be struck down. The Supreme Court was also hearing a case on the constitutionality of an Idaho law that disfranchised Mormons. If upheld, the antipolygamists in Washington would certainly push for a similar bill to disfranchise the Saints in

Utah. This was a crucial development. Given the numbers, disfranchisement was virtually the only way to break Mormon control of politics in Utah, and its advocacy by Mormon opponents demonstrated the extreme to which they were prepared to go.

In local elections, the Utah Commission was attempting to disfranchise Mormons piecemeal by sending registration agents into the communities to hear challenges against Mormon voters. To Brigham City they sent one Alfred Heed, "a man of low instinct and knavish proclivities" who started striking from the registration lists anyone who said he believed in polygamy. Heed had disfranchised about two hundred people before the commission reconsidered and withdrew him.

Under Rudger's leadership, the central committee organized the Mormon voters into companies of ten with a captain in charge to see that they got to the polls. The Liberals were riding high and were so confident of victory that they made plans to move the county seat to Corinne after the election. The People's party triumphed, however, despite the fact that the Liberals spent a great deal of money and, according to Rudger, "resorted to dishonest methods. . . . The defeat was a crushing blow from which they will be slow to recover. In the Collinston precinct where the canal men were located, the registration list was stuffed in a manner that will consign the registrar, one Mr. Standing, to lasting infamy, and ought to have consigned him to the Penitentiary."

But Brigham City politics was a mere sideshow to the events sweeping Mormondom in 1889 and 1890.

Meetings were to be held in all wards where the Saints would be expected to pray for their church and against "the plots and schemes of our civil and political rights." They were also to pray for the Supreme Court—should it not have by then rendered its decision on the Edmunds-Tucker Act that the Lord would "So move upon the hearts of the judges that they will be strengthened and filled with courage as to render a righteous decision."

Meetings were held throughout Box Elder. In Brigham City at the tabernacle Rudger "had the honor to preside," ably abetted by the ubiquitous Lorenzo Snow.

> After singing especially prepared for the occasion, Prest. Lorenzo Snow offered up a powerful petition to the Throne of Grace in behalf of Zion.

. . . The meeting was extremely interesting and was an occasion never to be forgotten. At the conclusion of the services the whole congregation arose to their feet by invitation, each one taking out his or her handkerchief, and the sacred shout led by Prest. Snow was given. The words are as follows 'Hosannah! Hosannah! To God and the Lamb! Amen! Amen! Amen!' The building seemed to tremble upon its very foundations and as each word fell from the lips of the assembled multitude a sea of handkerchiefs was waved in the air. Not often is such a scene witnessed in the world.

A few months later, in February 1890, the Supreme Court confirmed the Idaho law disfranchising the Mormons, whereupon bills were introduced into Congress to do the same in Utah. Then in May, the Supreme Court also upheld the provisions of the Edmunds-Tucker Act under which the church had been dissolved as a corporation and its property confiscated.

In August, another blow fell when it was learned that the government was intending to renege on an earlier assurance by the U.S. Solicitor General that the Logan, Manti, and St. George temples would not be among the properties confiscated.

Backed into a corner now, the church battled ferociously against disfranchisement, embodied ultimately in the Cullom-Strubble bill, and sought help among Republican friends in Washington, especially James G. Blaine who was then secretary of state. According to Frank J. Cannon, George Q. Cannon's son, Blaine thought the enemies of the church could be diverted "*this* time but that the Mormons must get into line." Cannon reported the feeling in Washington that the Mormons *must* give up plural marriage.

By fall, it was clear that further resistance was impossible. On the 24th of September 1890, President Woodruff informed a small group of church leaders that he had been "wrestling with the Lord all night" over the plural marriage issue. The result was a statement which, after significant revisions made by a small group of church leaders, became the Manifesto of 1890, which was released to the press and later sustained at conference. "Woodruff," wrote George Q. Cannon in his diary, "stated that the Lord had made it plain to him that this was his duty, and he felt perfectly clear in his mind that it is the right thing." These statements are important. The degree to which the Manifesto was or was not a revelation from God became a central issue in the conflict over polygamy that continued through the next two decades and had profound implications for Rudger Clawson.

The Manifesto was a somewhat ambiguous document in which Woodruff declared his intention to submit to the laws of the land and advised Latter-day Saints "to refrain from contracting any marriage forbidden by" the law. Interestingly, it was a communication from Wilford Woodruff as president of the church and not from the First Presidency or the quorum as a whole. It also made no comment on the doctrine of plural marriages nor on the fate of those who had already entered into it.

Curiously, Rudger did not comment in his diaries on the Manifesto or on the controversy surrounding it, though he must have had strong reactions to it.

Rudger was, of course, thoroughly occupied by his responsibilities in Box Elder Stake. In the spring of 1891 a maverick group within the People's party, led by one of Lorenzo Snow's sons, A. H. Snow, challenged the regular ticket chosen by Rudger and the stake leadership. They were soundly defeated. A. H. Snow, who had been counseled by his father to give up his divisive efforts, but refused, apologized afterward and offered to mend his ways by "renewing his interest in the cause of God."

But the People's party, as well as the Liberal party, was doomed. After the disfranchisement and disincorporation issues were settled, statehood became the focal point of Mormon political efforts to rid them finally of the heavy hand of the federal government. But the politicians in Washington and the people in Utah, both Mormon and non-Mormon, who opposed the political power of the church, were fully aware that it would maintain its power via control over the People's party. The message came back from Washington loud and clear: the price of statehood would be the dissolution of parties divided along Mormon/non-Mormon lines. The best defense against what the politicans believed was a theocratic political structure in Utah, it was argued, were the Republican and Democratic parties. While the Republicans had taken the lead in the anti-polygamy campaign, they were now, after the Manifesto, ready to support statehood, seeing it as an opportunity to counteract the growing strength of the Democrats in Utah. The church leadership agreed, but the price was the disbanding of the People's party. Whereupon the church leadership—the views of which were most strongly articulated by First Counselor Joseph F. Smith—began to reorient itself to its recent adversary, the Republican party.

In Brigham City, Rudger took the advice of his mentor, Lorenzo Snow, on how to respond to the poltical realignment. Snow "counseled the brethren to move cautiously in the matter of dividing up on national politics. . . . Would say to the brethren 'Keep cool—don't get excited. We may look for surprises. If the Democrats come along, why, listen to them, hear what they have to say but keep cool. If the Republicans come, why, listen to them, hear what they have to say, but keep cool—don't be in a hurry.' "

Rudger wasn't. In his diary he mentions the organization of the Democratic and Republican clubs and describes briefly Democratic and Republican rallies he attended on successive nights in July of 1891. "There is some good in both parties," he concludes, "and much that is bad."

Nevertheless, in the local elections of that year, his sentiments were with the Democrats who, it appeared to him, lied a little less about their opponents than the Republicans. He seemed edgy about sitting on the sidelines, and he noted with dismay the attacks leveled at the priesthood for interfering in politics. The dissolution of the People's party and the splitting of the Saints into Democrats and Republicans was a steep price to pay for statehood. Not only did it loosen the church's grip on the political process, it fostered the kind of contention and divisiveness that Mormon leadership had always preached against. Unity was a bulwark against the enemies who surrounded them. For the time being, however, Rudger still remained the arbiter of local politics.

His leadership was challenged to the utmost in the battle over the proposed city waterworks. The first mention of the waterworks in his diary appears in January 1892 when he notes the exemplary behavior of the mayor and city council of Brigham City in consulting the priesthood, which approved the project. The behavior of those who opposed it was less exemplary. The leaders, R. H. Jones and, more important, E. A. Box, immediately began organizing "indignation" meetings to rally opposition.

The water system to be installed was not extremely complex. It involved a six-mile main from springs in Devil's Canyon into Brigham which would give the city an independent supply of water. This was chosen in preference to a more complicated arrangement whereby a shorter line would be built to the village of Three Mile Creek and exchanged for water from Box Elder Creek leaving Brigham City somewhat at the mercy of the smaller town. The opposition argued that the waterworks would be a costly failure and end up a burden on the taxpayers.

When the engineers working for the city went to survey the line in Devil's Canyon, they found a number of men from Brigham who claimed they had taken possession of the springs. "They were busily engaged in digging trenches, cutting down brush, etc., etc., and when asked what they were doing simply stated that they were developing the water they had just secured."

That the water from the springs belonged to Brigham City had never been disputed, according to Rudger, and to make sure, the city council had obtained formal possession just two days before. These actions, Rudger fumed, were "in strict harmony with the methods adopted by the water 'Kickers,' " those who opposed the waterworks and who were led by Box and Jones. "One is a High Priest and the other is a Seventy,* and it is safe to say neither is worthy of standing in this church." The Kickers, mostly Republicans, formed a "Safety Society" of which Box was the vice president and fought the water system each step of the way.

Rudger was so angry that when Jones, who was chairman of the Brigham Young Memorial Fund Committee, came to him seeking his advice and suport, Rudger said he would not cooperate with the committee while Jones was on it. And when the Box Elder Stake sunday school superintendent wrote requesting that Box—because of his contentiousness and opposition to the church authorities—be removed from his position of superintendent of the First Ward Sunday School, Rudger readily complied. This action backfired, however. Box went to the First Presidency in Salt Lake and argued that he had been dismissed solely because of his opposition to the waterworks. The First Presidency requested that Box's removal be suspended until the matter could be investigated.

---

*A large group of elders who manage certain of the administrative affairs of the church.

Snow, who supported the removal of Box, suggested that Rudger and his counselors go immediately to Salt Lake and argue their case. On May 19, 1892, they did.

While most of those present were sympathetic to Rudger (especially John Winder, Joseph F. Smith and Franklin Richards), John Henry Smith, a strongly partisan Republican, considered Rudger's action "a grand mistake—a serious blunder—an unwise and foolish action, etc." supporting Box's argument that Rudger's action was purely a political matter. This despite Rudger's contention that Box had been stirring up trouble and opposing the stake authorities for several years and that his, Rudger's, action was not merely "political."

But Smith's attack, which was joined by George F. Gibbs, a clerk in the president's office who interjected his "extremely offensive" remarks without invitation, "swayed the others." Rudger was asked to withdraw his letter requesting Box's resignation.

While in Salt Lake, Rudger visited his mother, who apparently relayed the news of his meeting with the apostles to Hiram. Hiram talked with Cannon and then wrote Rudger a short time later advising him to "yield to the judgment and advice of the First Presidency." By then Rudger was able to write back that he had already done so.

This was Rudger's first reprimand by higher authorities and it must have hurt even though he dutifully accepted their counsel. Local politics were a sensitive issue in the Utah Territory at this time, and if church leaders were caught suppressing political dissent, it would hardly further the cause of statehood.

Even so, Rudger would have the last word in his diary. "In view of the general situation of the Saints in Salt Lake the action taken by them was correct and in view of the local situation here our action was proper." He also had the last word on the waterworks.

The water system was completed and turned on in 1892. "July 8 was a red letter day for Brigham City. The water was turned into the mains of our new water system for the first time. The booming of cannon announced the fact. The water came rushing through the pipes with a force that both pleased and astonished people. What a volume of water the fire hydrants send forth! The Reservoir is a solid piece of cement work and will hold 150,000 gal. of water. . . . A great many people are having it put into their houses, and lawn sprinklers are whirling in every direction."

On July 12 the system's fire-fighting potential was demonstrated. The water from the hose shot seventy feet into the air and easily cleared the roof of the courthouse. "It goes without saying that Brigham City has excellent fire protection."

Almost as important, early indications were that the system would be a financial success as well.

At this point a group of Water Kickers filed a lawsuit claiming that the system diverted water from Box Elder Creek on which the plaintiffs depended for their water supply. Rudger was certain Box and Jones were behind the effort, especially since Jones appeared as attorney for the plaintiffs.

The issue was settled politically in the November election of 1892 when the Republican party embraced the antiwaterworks stand and nominated a slate "made up almost exclusively of Water Kickers," who were committed to selling the waterworks to private interests, arguing, apparently, that it would forever be a drain on city finances. The Democrats swept the county offices and captured the mayorship and enough of the city council to keep the Water Kickers at bay.

In January 1893, the fiscal issue was settled when a six months' financial report was submitted by the superintendent of the waterworks. It showed net earnings of $800 which paid the interest on the $24,000 loan for the period and left a balance of $160. "It was the general opinion that for the first 2 or 3 years, the system would be an expense to the city, but with a continuation of the above favorable showing, it will pay its way from the start and in a few years will be a source of revenue to the city. Those who fought the enterprise with a spirit of rancor and bitterness, as many did, trying to persuade the good people of Brigham that it would plunge the city into irretrievable ruin, now begin to see their folly made manifest. While pretending to be friendly to the interests of the people, they were enemies at heart."

The last word on Box came the following May:

A few days ago a most sensational announcement was made in Brigham City, viz: that Elijah A. Box, Secretary of the Box Elder Benefit and Building Society, was a defaulter to the extent of some $4,000. Investigation confirmed the rumor. The company attached some Real Estate and sheep belonging to Box to cover the shortage. The course taken by Elijah to evade the responsibility of his official conduct and mislead the board of directors of said company savors of downright rascality and dishonesty of purpose.

Furthermore, Box himself disappeared, or at least for a few days was nowhere to be found. Seizing the opportunity, Rudger fulfilled his desire to eject Box from his position as superintendent of the First Ward Sunday School by appointing a replacement. Box turned up a week later and attempted to take charge of the Sunday school again. This time Rudger simply fired him, and that ended it. In March 1893 R. H. Jones, Rudger's other nemesis, was sued by his mother for nonpayment of debts to her. Rudger had the privilege of presiding over the church court (High Council) that tried the case and decided against Jones.

\*     \*     \*

By now Rudger was a dedicated Democrat. Even if he had not been naturally inclined toward the Democrats, the Water Kickers would have pushed him there. Later, when he began to move toward the Republican party, he would have trouble reconciling the shift with the fact that it identified him with his enemies in Brigham City.

Despite the concern of church leaders about the divisiveness and disunity resulting from party politics, the Saints divided on political lines during these post-Manifesto years. Snow's advice to keep cool simply did not work.

By the fall of 1892 Rudger was attending Democratic meetings fairly regularly—including one where he heard arguments, which he thought were incontrovertible, against a high protective tariff, a Republican policy. No mention was made of attendance at Republican meetings.

The church too was wrestling with the new politics. A number of leading figures became outspoken supporters of the Republican Party, though others found the Democrats more congenial. President Woodruff, First Counselor Joseph F. Smith, and the latter's cousin, Apostle John Henry Smith, were among the most vocal in expressing their Republican sympathies. In 1892, Frank J. Cannon, Apostle George Q. Cannon's son, was the Republican candidate for delegate to Congress. Frank had been the church's liaison with Congress and the

Republican party during the months prior to the Manifesto. Links had been forged during this period that led the hierarchy to believe that the Republicans offered the best hope for relieving the pressures Washington had been applying for so long, having the church property restored (it was being held in escrow by the federal government at this time), and obtaining statehood.

Further, while the Smiths and other apostles actively supported the Republicans, attempts were made to muzzle leading churchmen such as B. H. Roberts and Apostle Moses Thatcher, who were Democrats. Thus, while the church, on the one hand, claimed that it accepted the principle of separation of church and state, it was heavily engaged, on the other, in attempting to control the political process in Utah— as it had done from the day the Saints trekked into the valley.

This dilemma in all its ramifications was reflected in Box Elder Stake where Rudger and Lorenzo wrestled with it at a priesthood meeting just before the election in November 1892. Since they were both Democrats, they had to be careful not only about being perceived as controlling the politics of the stake, but also about earning the ill will if not the censure of the First Presidency.

Rudger's sentiments on the election were quite well known, given his support of the waterworks, which the Republicans opposed. He had in fact been accused of trying to influence the vote, so he addressed the issue head-on. "The brethren in this stake, many of them, are unneccessarily sensitive. . . . Some have accused me of advising the brethren how to vote. If I have done so, I am not conscious of it. I must have been asleep. Since I have the name of it, I might as well deserve it. I think I will counsel the brethren in this matter—Now when you go to the polls on next Tuesday vote for—the man of your choice, vote just as you please."

But when Snow, whose political sentiments must also have been well known in his hometown, rose to speak, he could not resist. "The mouths of authoritites in Zion are closed," he said, "but the Lord's is not. When you consider the qualifications of the two candidates for Congress, does not the Spirit whisper to you as to how you should vote?" And what about the prohibition against church leaders like Wilford Woodruff ("the Mouthpiece of God") and Rudger Clawson having anything to do with politics or holding public office. "Is that right? No, it is not."

Grover Cleveland and the Democrats won the election while Frank J. Cannon went down to defeat in Utah. The irony is that though President Benjamin Harrison, as a lame duck, rewarded the Saints for their efforts on behalf of Republicanism with an amnesty for polygamists, it was under Grover Cleveland and the Democrats that carpetbag government was ended in Utah (with a law requiring that federal officials be selected from residents of the territory), church property was restored, and the statehood enabling act passed. The inability of the church to swing the territory to the Republicans may have been better proof of the church's declining control over Mormon politics than any disavowal that could be made.

During these early years in Brigham City, Rudger's family increased. The birth of his son, Hiram Bradley, took place on November 6, 1888, and his first daughter, Margaret Gay, was born on September 1, 1890. Gay was followed by Daniel Spencer in July 1892 and by Vera Mary in May 1894.

Daniel may not have been very healthy from birth. In November 1892, Rudger described him as suffering from a large swelling under his left ear, which after three weeks "broke and discharged about a pint of corruption." Then in May 1893, Daniel contracted "La Grippe" and died.

Whether Rudger called a physician for Daniel or administered any medicine is not certain. He did not believe in medical care, feeling that the Saints should depend instead on the "Ordinance of the Lord's House" (or as fully stated: the ordinance of the laying on of hands for the healing of the sick).

At a Relief Society meeting in December 1892, he recorded in his diary, "the nature and importance of the Ordinance of the Lord's House for the healing of the sick was clearly explained. The sisters were exhorted to exercise faith in the Lord when sickness comes into their families, and avoid the folly of resorting to the aid of doctors and trusting to the "arm of the flesh."

When someone was sick, he or she was administered to with prayer, anointment with consecrated oil, the laying on of hands, and an exhortation to faith. If the person died, it demonstrated either an improper administering of the ordinance or a lack of faith. In one instance the dying person "had been a careless and indifferent member of the church."

In his memoirs Rudger cites a case of a child with a severe eye inflammation which a doctor had been unable to treat, though he thought it was of "cancerous origin." But, after having been anointed with consecrated oil and blessed by Rudger, the child was healed. Rudger, of course, recognized that "although this is a day of miracles," not all the sick who are treated by the anointment with oil and the laying on of hands will be healed. "Those who have the gift of faith to heal can heal and those who have the gift of faith to be healed can be healed." But ultimately it is God who holds "the issue of life and death in his hands."

The most striking case, or miracle in Rudger's view, was that of Ella Jensen, a young woman of twenty, who was severely ill with scarlet fever. The day before the miracle, she predicted her death (a long deceased uncle would come and get her) at ten the next morning. On schedule her pulse stopped and she was pronounced dead. Snow was sent for to see to the arrangement of the funeral. Instead, with Rudger along, he went to Ella's home, arriving just before noon. He and Rudger blessed the dead child and then to Rudger's surprise Snow commanded her to come back to life, "Your mission is not ended. You shall yet live to perform a great mission." An hour later Ella came back to life and told a long and complex story of her experience in the spirit world. She had not, in fact, wanted to come back, but she could not resist Snow's call. As for Ella's mission, "She afterwards became president of the Young Ladies Mutual Improvement Association" and later married and had a large family, "and surely a woman can do no greater work in the world than to become a mother of men."

In Daniel's case, "The Ordinance of the Lord's House was employed in his behalf and everything done that love and sympathy could suggest for his restoration, but all to no purpose for heaven had ordained it otherwise, and when I perceived that he was dying I laid my hands upon his head and dedicated him to the Lord." Rudger commented on how much of a loss Daniel's death was, "but if a father feels the blow, with what keenness and poignancy does it strike the mother— she who gave him birth, who nursed him in health and who watched over him in sickness with all tenderness until the messenger from above came and bore his pure spirit away to the realms of eternal bliss."

According to the testimony of one of her daughters, Lydia did

Margaret Gay Judd Clawson     Hiram Bradley Clawson

*Left,* a curious old photograph. The boy is Rudger. The man is Robert Ferris, an English immigrant who lived with the Clawsons, who always called him "Grandpa," although he was not related.

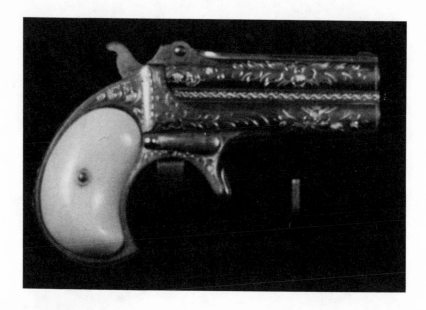

RUDGER'S
THREE
STEPFATHERS

Henry Dinwoodey
Courtesy of the
Utah State
Historical Society

David K. Udall
Courtesy of the
Arizona
Historical Society Library

Daniel Spencer

Dec. 9 1939

Dear Lydia

This pistol has been in the family a long time and is an <u>antique</u>. It came into the possession of your Grandpa Clawson many years ago and was carried by him when he was appointed among others as a guard to protect Brigham Young during the presence of Johnson's Army in Utah in Pioneer days. Your Grandma Clawson gave it to your Mother over 40 years ago. It is made of Silver with Ivory handle.

It is not only an <u>antique</u> but is also a heir loom, and consiquetly very valuable. <u>Do not use it with Violence but Hang On' to it.</u>

With love.
Father - Mother

Utah's historical landmarks are part of Rudger's youth. *Left,* probably the nation's first department store, the Zion Co-operative Mercantile Institution (Z.C.M.I.), where Rudger worked as a young man. Eventually, his father and his father's partner, Horace Eldredge, would merge their dry goods firms with Z.C.M.I.

*Below,* the Salt Lake Theater, sometimes known as the "Cathedral of the Desert." Rudger's father played a key role in urging Brigham Young to build the theater.

The theater's ornate stage, where Rudger's mother, Margaret Judd, known as the "Mother of Drama in Utah," performed often and where Rudger himself appeared several times.

460. Eagle Gate, *Salt Lake City, Utah.*

*Above,* the original Eagle Gate was designed by Rudger's father. The supporting structure was later rebuilt when the street was widened, but the wings of Hiram's Eagle are still spread above State Street, said to be the longest straight street in the world. *Below,* the H.B. Clawson home (originally designed and built by Lorenzo Snow) in which Rudger grew up. The home, on South Temple street near Third East, has since been torn down. Rudger's mother, Margaret Judd Clawson, is one of the women on the porch.

H.B. Clawson and his sons from four wives. H.B. is seated, third from right; Rudger is standing third from right. Rudger's half brother, Will Clawson, the artist is standing on the far right. Seated on the far right is half brother Spencer Clawson, and next to him, half brother Selden Clawson. We cannot be sure of the other brothers and half brothers. Half brother Roy Clawson is not here; he would have been just a baby.

*Right,* John Morgan, President of the Southern States Mission at the time Joseph Standing was murdered.

*Below,* the courthouse in Ellijay, Georgia, a way station on Rudger's foot journey to find his fated missionary companion, Elder Joseph Standing.

Both photographs are from *The Life and Ministry of John Morgan* by Arthur Richardson.

Rudger, *left,* and Joseph Standing, the missionary who was murdered in Georgia in July of 1879.

*Left,* the monument to the martyred Joseph Standing at his gravesite in Salt Lake City.

From *The Life and Ministry of John Morgan* by Arthur Richardson.

*Below,* an artist's rendition of the murder of Joseph Standing.

Courtesy of *The Church News.*

Lydia and Rudger Clawson at about the time of their marriage.

Spencer Clawson's Wholesale Dry Goods store on South Main Street in Salt Lake City (to the right of Clark, Eldredge & Co.) where Rudger was working at the time he was arrested and tried for taking Lydia as his plural wife.

# THE DAILY HERALD

Salt Lake City, - - Utah.

THURSDAY, : : OCTOBER 23, 1884.

## THE MISSING WITNESS.

### The Dastardly Tribune Excoriated by Judge Bennett.

### LYDIA SPENCER IN COURT.

### Deputy Varian's Underground Railway Still Receiving Passengers.

#### A MARSHAL'S WILD GOOSE CHASE

#### Full Report of Bennett's Scathing Speech—An Open Venire for Fifty Names—No Change of Venue—An Eventful Day's Doings.

Yesterday presented a succession of surprises all around. Instead of the Clawson case sinking into the obscurity to which its recent notoriety might seem to entitle it, yesterday's events throw it again before the public gaze, intensified and recolored by the force and interest of the new circumstances which surround it. On Tuesday night at 9 o'clock, about the hour the jury brought in their verdict of disagreement and were discharged by Judge Zane, Deputy Marshal Lindsay Sprague served a subpœna upon a witness more material than any yet brought forward, and one whose presence has reopened the whole matter and again brought the defendant into court—the young lady, Miss Lydia Spencer herself. It appears that she came to the house of Mrs. Smith (where she had rooms) on Monday evening, and remained there that night, and all day on Tuesday. She was expecting a visit from the party or parties who had been keeping her posted as to the progress of affairs, and when a knock came at the back door, supposing that some one had come with the expected news, the door was at once opened, and Mr. Deputy Sprague stepped in with his subpœna. Miss Spencer accepted the service quietly and without comment, but Mr. Sprague says she turned quite pale. The news of her being discovered did not become general that night, but on the streets yesterday morning it was the all-prevailing topic.

Marshal Ireland had apparently directed all his forces for a simultaneous attack. About the same hour that the above occurrences were taking place,

---

# THE DAILY HERALD

Salt Lake City, - - Utah.

SATURDAY, : : OCTOBER 25, 1884.

## THE CLIMAX.

### Lydia Spencer Refuses to Take the Oath.

### AND IS A NIGHT IN PRISON.

### Judge Zane Will Pronounce Judgment To-day.

### A VERY DRAMATIC SITUATION.

### The Prosecution's Browbeating of Mr. Dinwoodey.

#### INTERVIEW WITH MISS SPENCER.

#### The Jury Finally Filled, and the Case Once More Started on Its Slow Course.

Marshal Ireland and his twenty-four refugees were on hand promptly at 10 yesterday morning; a full attendance on the spectators' benches testified to the unabated interest still attendant on the case.

The proceedings were opened by Mr. Bennett's interposing a challenge to the twenty-four names returned, on the same grounds that the challenge was made on the day previous to the fifty; also on the additional ground that the venire on which the twenty-four names had been obtained, had been issued while the second venire for fifty was still out.

Marshal Ireland and Captain Greenman were put on the stand to testify in relation to the two venires. The challenge was overruled.

---

# THE DAILY HERALD

Salt Lake City, - - Utah.

SUNDAY, : : OCTOBER 26, 1884.

#### TWELVE PAGES.

## FOUND GUILTY.

### Lydia Spencer's Testimony.

### SHE OWNS THE MARRIAGE

### The Jury Agree After Twenty Minutes' Consultation.

### AN UNPRECEDENTED MOTION.

#### The Prosecution Thrive with Might and Main to Imprison Mr. Clawson on the Instant—Defeated by the Defense—To be Sentenced November Third.

Long before the hour for calling court to order yesterday morning the room was jammed with a mass of humanity that swayed, struggled and bussed in an effort to obtain a footing from which the witness stand could be viewed to advantage. Marshal Ireland went below to look at the supports to the floor, but was evidently satisfied of

---

Newspaper clippings from the trial of Rudger Clawson.

Courtesy of the Utah State Historical Society.

Mormon prisoners in the Utah Territorial Prison in the summer of 1885. From left to right are Francis A. Brown, Freddy Self, Moroni Brown, Amos Milton Musser, George H. Kellog, Parley Pratt, Jr., Rudger Clawson, and Job Pingree. The Browns and Musser were veterans of the Nauvoo, Illinois, persecution; Pingree was active in public affairs in Ogden, Utah, and Pratt was the son of an apostle.

The Utah Territorial Prison in 1885, as painted by prisoner Frank Treseder and purchased by Rudger for approximately $6.00. *On the opposite page is one of the love letters Rudger smuggled to Lydia from prison.*

My dearest Lydia:

Utah Pen
Oct. 15/85

If I cannot see you at this moment, & iron bars prevent my arms from encircling your waist, and if distance precludes any chance on my part of bestowing upon you all the tender endearments of a warm and ardent love, I can at least write you, and the thought gives me pleasure. Now what do you think is on my mind as I pen this note? Why your last visit of course. It was a great surprise to me, but at the same time extremely gratifying. There was only one thing that marred the pleasure & happiness of that half hour chat. Methinks I see you start up in wonder & ask, Indeed and pray what was it? Cannot you guess? No? Very well, then I will tell you. The visit was not sufficiently private to suit my taste. I am a little peculiar in some respects for when my beloved wife, the companion of my youth, calls to see me, I must confess I prefer to be alone, aye entirely alone, with her. I think you know that statement to be true. You were certainly not as shrewd as usual or you would have ordered the guard to step into the adjoining room or would have prevented to take a stroll with our darling baby, leaving us to ourselves. In failing to do this you missed that manifestation of my love & affection which I had it my heart to bestow upon you. It might be asked what more could I have done (as I certainly did do) through those eyes that often turned with a wistful expression upon me, and read there the love that is mine, what more could I have done than to exhibit by signs & tokens the tender, regard & passionate love I bear you. I will not, I cannot tell you all that you have lost, but you may know this much: I would have embraced & kissed you with a vehemence and at the same time with a tenderness that would thrill with pleasure & fully satisfy the most exacting heart. Your knowledge of me will confirm this assertion, while your soul whispers to you: yes, he would do it, I know he would do it.

(Letter from PRISON)

Grover Cleveland,

President of the United States of America,

To all to whom these Presents shall come, Greeting:

Whereas, at the November term, 1884, of the United States District Court for the District of Utah, Rudger Clawson was convicted of polygamy and unlawful cohabitation, and sentenced for the two offences, to five years imprisonment in the Utah Penitentiary, and to pay fines amounting to eight hundred dollars;

And whereas, the said Rudger Clawson has been in prison more than three years and since his incarceration has conducted himself well;

And whereas, after his conviction, his legal wife obtained a divorce from him, and since the divorce, he has contracted a legal marriage with his plural wife;

And whereas, his pardon is recommended by the Chief Justice of the Territory, by the Governor, the District Attorney and his Assistant, by the late District Attorney and his Assistant and by the U. S. Marshal:

Now, therefore, be it known, that I, Grover Cleveland, President of the United States of America, in consideration of the premises, divers other good and sufficient reasons me thereunto moving, do hereby grant to the said Rudger Clawson, a full and unconditional pardon.

In testimony whereof, I have hereunto signed my name and caused the seal of the United States to be affixed.

Done at the City of Washington, this Fifth day of December, A.D. 1887, and of the Independence of the United States the one hundred and twelfth.

Grover Cleveland

The letter from President Grover Cleveland releasing Rudger from prison.

Lydia stands in the front yard of the house in Brigham City, Utah. The two children in front of the fence are probably Gay and H.B.

A monument to Rudger's years as Brigham City Stake President, the tabernacle in Brigham City, which was totally destroyed by fire in February, 1896, and which Rudger quickly and economically had rebuilt.

*Above,* the completed temple, which took forty years to build. Rudger attended the dedication in April of 1893, which, he said, was "an occasion never to be forgotten and not easily described." *Below,* the ceremony at the laying of the capstone of the Salt Lake Temple on April 6, 1892, which Rudger attended.

From *The Life and Ministry of John Morgan* by Arthur Richardson.

From *The Great Temple*

*Above,* the Council Room of the First Presidency and the Council of the Twelve in the Salt Lake Temple, where Rudger met with the First Presidency and his fellow apostles to conduct the affairs of the church. *Below,* Rudger Clawson's earliest photograph with the First Presidency and the Twelve Apostles of the Church of Jesus Christ of Latter-day Saints, taken October 10, 1898. Seated from left to right are Anthon H. Lund; Brigham Young, Jr.; George Q. Cannon, First Counselor; President Lorenzo Snow; Joseph F. Smith, Second Counselor; and Franklin D. Richards, President of the Quorum of the Twelve. Standing are Marriner H. Merrill, John W. Taylor, Francis M. Lyman, Rudger Clawson, Heber J. Grant, Matthias F. Cowley, George Teasdale, Abraham O. Woodruff, and John Henry Smith.

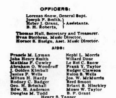

OFFICERS:

Lorenzo Snow, General Supt.
Joseph F. Smith,
Heber J. Grant, } Assistants.
B. H. Roberts,

Thomas Hull, Secretary and Treasurer.
Evan Stephens, Music Director.
Horace S. Ensign, Asst. Music Director.

AIDS:

Francis M. Lyman      Nephi L. Morris
John Henry Smith      Willard Done
Mathias F. Cowley     Le Roi C. Snow
Abraham O. Woodruff   Frank Y. Taylor
J. Golden Kimball     Rudger Clawson
Junius F. Wells       Rulon S. Wells
Milton H. Hardy       Jos. W. McMurrin
Rodney C. Badger      Reed Smoot
Geo. H. Brimhall      Briant S. Hinckley
Edw. H. Anderson      Moses W. Taylor
Douglas M. Todd       B. F. Grant
          Henry S. Tanner

Office of
General Superintendency
Young Men's
Mutual Improvement Associations
of the Latter-day Saints.
214-215 Templeton Building.
Telephone 910.

Salt Lake City, Utah,      Oct. 9, 1901.

TO PRESIDENTS OF STAKES, BISHOPS OF WARDS,

AND STAKE AND WARD OFFICERS OF YOUNG MEN'S

MUTUAL IMPROVEMENT ASSOCIATIONS,

Dear Brethren:

Elder Joseph Facer has been duly called, set apart and appointed as a missionary to labor among the young men of Zion, and is fully
authorized and equipped to engage in that work. We desire that Stake
Presidents and Bishops of Wards will give him their entire and hearty
support and influence in making his mission a perfect success.

He comes to your Stake with full authority in this mission and
we expect the Stake Superintendents to go with him, or send with him one
of their counselors or aids, to visit all the Associations, and also see
that arrangements are made for his entertainment in the various wards and
for his transportation from place to place.

                    Your brethren,

                    Lorenzo Snow
                    Jos. F. Smith
                    Rudger Clawson

                    FIRST PRESIDENCY

Courtesy of *The Improvement Era*

A church magazine, *The Improvement Era*, recorded Rudger's short tenure as a member of the First Presidency by printing a composite photograph of the three members (below, from left to right, Joseph F. Smith, Lorenzo Snow, and Rudger Clawson) and reprinting the only official document to come out of the brief First Presidency, which was dissolved after Snow's death.

Rudger plays his favorite game—chess—with an unidentified opponent.

Lydia and two of her children on the porch of their home at 51 Canyon Road in Salt Lake City, within walking distance of the temple.

## Creation

"God made an awful lot of things—;
Some summers, several thousand springs,—
The morning and the afternoon,
The sky, the mist, the sea, the moon;
The south wind and the new mown hay,
The mountain brook and ocean spray.

And then there are some things, you see,
That God made specially for me;
Red roses, yellow daffodils,—
The shadows on the purple hills,—
A cobweb, pearled with morning dew;
A certain shining star, and you."

*Top,* a love poem by Rudger to his third wife, Pearl Udall, whom Rudger married secretly in 1904. *Above,* the exact size of the small photograph of Pearl Udall attached to the carbon copy of a letter Rudger wrote to her on October 17, 1904. On the back of the photo was written "Dec. 30, 190__." (The last digit was torn off the upper left corner.) *Left,* Rudger Remus Clawson, Rudger and Lydia's first child, whose tragic death at the age of 19, combined with stress over the secret marriage to Pearl, helped produce the most traumatic years in Rudger's life.

Enroute to Europe, the Clawson family visits Mt. Vernon in 1910. The little girl is Lydia, Jr., the mother of the authors. An unidentified L.D.S. missionary stands behind her. The woman to his left is Pearl Bailey, Gay's friend and future wife of H. B. Gay, the elder daughter of Rudger and Lydia, stands to the left of her father and mother.

On board ship for Liverpool are, from left to right, Pearl Bailey, Sam, daughter Lydia, Rudger, Rennie, and Gay. "The ocean breezes were exhilarating ..." said Rudger. "My drooping spirits were revived and health and vigor returned."

*Above,* Durham House, in Liverpool, the Clawson home and headquarters of the European mission while Rudger was in England.
*Below,* the family travelling in England: *(left to right)* Rudger,
daughter Lydia, Lydia, Rennie, and H.B. Rudger is wearing the
top hat which he refused to abandon in order to escape attack
by a Bristol mob.

*Left,* in England the press gave continuing coverage to the activities of the Mormons.

Rudger and participants in a church conference in Norwich, England. Standing from left to right are E.W. Carter, J.A. Wood, J.L. Nelson, A. Williamson, J.R. Pendery, W. Bennion, and E. Weaver. Seated are F.D. Ashdown, A.R. Cook (who officiated at the conference), Rudger Clawson (Mission President), A.T. Johnson, and Byron Mendenhall.

Lydia and her Model T around 1915.

Rudger (*left*) and an unidentified church official at the dedication of the temple in Hawaii, 1919.

Rudger was always willing to pose for photographs with one or more of his grandchildren. He sits here with the authors, grandsons Roy, *left,* and David, at Mt. Vernon in 1929.

He poses with Ronald and Roxanne, the adopted twins of Samuel Clawson, *right*, and *below*, under a portrait of Lydia, with Linda Hoopes, Lydia Jr.'s daughter, in 1941.

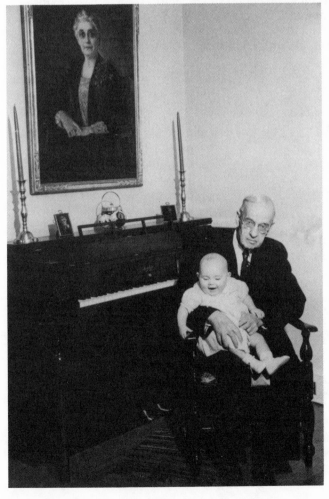

*Above,* Rudger's first photograph as President of the Quorum of the Twelve, taken April, 1921. Seated from left to right are Rudger Clawson, Reed Smoot, George Albert Smith, George F. Richards, Orson F. Whitney, and David O. McKay. Standing are Joseph Fielding Smith, James E. Talmage, Stephen L. Richards, Richard R. Lyman, Melvin J. Ballard, and John A. Widtsoe.

You are invited to hear
President Rudger Clawson, of
The Council of The Twelve
Apostles
Wednesday, July 5, 1933, 8 p.m.
K. of P. Hall
Fourth and Washington Sts.
Portsmouth, Ohio

RUDGER CLAWSON

Rudger was an untiring speaker and traveller for the church. *Left,* a calling card sized invitation to hear Rudger speak in Portsmouth, Ohio. *Below right,* Rudger Clawson, on Lookout Mountain near Chattanooga, Tennessee, and only 30 miles from the woods in Georgia where Joseph Standing was murdered. With Rudger is Charles A. Callis, then President of the Southern States Mission.

Florence Ann Dinwoodey
Courtesy of the Utah State Historical Society

Pearl Udall

The three wives around whom Rudger built his celestial kingdom: Florence Ann Dinwoodey, in her late teens or early twenties; Pearl Udall, at age twenty-three, and Lydia Spencer, pictured here at the age of seventeen.

Lydia Spencer

RUDGER, LYDIA,
AND THEIR
FAMILY

Rudger

Lydia

Rudger Remus

Francis Marion

Daniel Spencer

Vera May

Lydia

Gay

Samuel

Hiram Bradley

Lorenzo

*Above,* Rudger's last picture with the Quorum of the Twelve, taken in 1942 on the steps of the old church administration building in Salt Lake City. From the bottom of the stairs are Rudger Clawson, George F. Richards, Joseph Fielding Smith, Stephen L. Richards, Richard R. Lyman, John A. Widtsoe, Joseph F. Merrill, Charles A. Callis, Albert E. Bowen, Sylvester Q. Cannon, and Harold B. Lee, the newest member. George Albert Smith is absent. *Below,* pictured from left to right: Roy, Jr., with his eyes closed; Lydia; Linda; David; and Roy Hoopes, Sr., under the portrait of Rudger painted by George Henry Taggart in 1901. DAVID O. MISSING

Seated down the right side of the table are Lydia Clawson; Pearl Bailey Clawson; H.B.; H.B.'s adopted daughter, Elizabeth; H.B.'s adopted son, Richard; Marion Bond; Roland Bond, with his face partly hidden; Brent Bond; Gay Clawson Bond; and Horace Bond. Seated on the left are Rudger; Samuel Clawson; Leah Wood Clawson; Stanley Clawson, Lorenzo's son; Lorenzo; Lorenzo Clawson, Jr.; and Viola Smith Clawson. Missing are Lorenzo's daughter Geraldine, who was two at the time, and Samuel's twins, who had not yet been adopted. Lydia Clawson Hoopes, who had married Roy Hoopes, and her family were in Washington, D.C. at the time this photograph was taken.

Rudger and Lydia amid flowers given in celebration of Rudger's eightieth birthday.

indeed feel the blow of her children's deaths, weeping inconsolably for each and having to be literally pulled from them so that the process of burying the dead could go on.

During the Brigham City years, Lydia contributed significantly to the family income with her sewing, including quiltmaking at which she was highly skilled. Even her grandchildren remember her heavy patchwork quilts brilliant with reds, greens, and golds and trimmed in black with fancy stitching. She managed the boarders they took in, and she may also have sold produce from Rudger's small orchard and from her garden.

According to their first-born daughter, Gay, the relationship between her mother and father was relatively stormy. As a child in Brigham City she remembered heated arguments that often ended with Lydia falling to the floor in a rage and losing or pretending to lose consciousness. Once source of conflict was Rudger's relationship with his mother, Margaret, which was that of a dutiful and admiring son. Rudger copied into his memoirs long letters to his mother which are models of filial devotion. When Rudger visited Salt Lake or Margaret came to Brigham City, the two would sometimes lock themselves in a room and have long, private conversations. Margaret was also free with her advice and not hesitant to criticize Lydia or interfere when she felt the need—so Lydia's daughters said. This, of course, is a one-sided perspective. Margaret no doubt saw the relationship quite differently.

Rudger was satisfied with his marriage. "Yesterday was the 9th anniversary of my marriage with Lydia," he wrote in March 1892. "We have lived happily together. Our family consists of two fine boys and a beautiful girl."

He and Lydia appear to have led a fairly active social life. Dinner parties were frequent, and holidays were celebrated with a variety of festivities. They attended concerts and the theater often, both in Brigham City and Salt Lake. They went on outings, rides in the country, and picnics with the children. They attended the fair in Salt Lake City and spent days occasionally at Saltair on the lake. Rudger also appears to have taken one or more of the children with him from time to time when visiting outlying wards on church business.

In September 1893 he and Lydia accompanied the Tabernacle Choir to the Chicago World's Fair (the Columbian Exposition). The choir was participating in a contest of choirs for a $5,000 prize. They placed second, "but it was pretty widely conceded that they fairly won the first prize." He was awed by the fair and could hardly think of what to say about it. He ended up listing "a few things which attracted my attention," and which covered the next seven pages of the diary. They included such things as a 50,250-pound lump of coal, a map of the U.S. in blocks of wood, a dishwasher, a street car with an upstairs on it, a "double-headed" calf, a 36-car ferris wheel able to hold 1,080 people, a 300-year-old piano, a horse and rider made of prunes, and other wonders.

Rudger Clawson's relationship to the rest of his family also appears only briefly in his diaries and then mainly in letters to his mother. He comments on sister Tessie's marriage outside the temple and for "time" only, not for "all eternity." "Those who are married in the Temple enjoy immense advantages over those who are united for time only. Those who will not profit by the experience and advice of others must learn by what they suffer. This is an immutable and unchangeable law."

He was particularly affected by the illness and death of his sister Birdie Wells, wife of the governor of Utah, Heber Wells. A spreading cancer was the cause. Rudger was remorseful at not being more attentive to her: "I may have a poor way of showing it, but in my heart I have ever felt to appreciate Birdie's true worth. I have loved her above others because of her self-sacrificing spirit." In consoling his mother, he stated fully his beliefs regarding the Ordinance of the Lord's House:

> There is power in [it] to heal the sick where they are not appointed unto death, and inasmuch as the ordinance is being used in Birdie's behalf together with the faith and prayers of the whole family, you may rest assured that under these circumstances, if she shall be taken it is the will of the Lord, otherwise she will recover.
>
> "I know sometimes and often the ordinance seems ineffectual and the Saints lose faith in it, but not because there is no virtue in the ordinance, but simply because the Lord has decreed otherwise.
>
> "The Lord had appointed some to live and some to die, and we must bow to his providence.
>
> "The Lord doeth all things well. We know that if Birdie is taken at this time, she is wanted behind the vail [sic]. There is a work there for her to do, and in the resurrection this will be made plain to those who are left

behind. Nevertheless her departure would be a loss immeasurable to us all and I am sure all of your children she would be the most missed, for Birdie has been most thoughtful of her mother.

Rudger saw a great deal of Lorenzo Snow during these years, and it is clear that there was a special affinity between the two men. One of Snow's biographers says:

> These two men, kindred spirits . . . comprised an unusual and unlikely pair—the aged, erudite, and well-traveled apostle who, when he first became closely associated with his young friend (who was forty-three years his junior) had been in the priesthood harness for half a century, and the young, Utah-born polygamist, who once had defied a mob to shoot him after it had killed his missionary companion. But, desptie vast differences in age, education, and experience, this duo worked together like a team of choice thoroughbreds. Having complete confidence in President Snow and loving him like a father, Rudger Clawson was amenable to the direction of his mentor, and apparently would spring into action or refrain from it at the merest hint from the apostle that something ought or ought not to be done.

Snow composed poems to Rudger and counseled him as a father. As "resident apostle" in Box Elder Stake, he was closely involved in church affairs. Rudger would often use casual meetings on the street to solicit Snow's advice. There may, however, have been some criticism of their relationship. Speaking at a priesthood meeting in 1893, Snow emphasized that it was Rudger who was president of the stake, not himself, and that he, Rudger Clawson, was responsible to the First Presidency, not Lorenzo Snow. In mutual admiration Rudger followed up with a brief talk comparing Snow to St. Peter.

Rudger had other close friends, particularly Charles Kelley, his first counselor, and Joseph M. Jensen, who was mayor fom 1891 to 1893 and with whom Rudger was allied in pushing through the water system. Another close friend was Lorenzo Hunsaker. Lorenzo was one of the many sons of Abraham Hunsaker, a polygamist who settled and populated the small outlying community of Honeyville. Lorenzo and his wife, Florida, entertained and were entertained by the Clawsons. Lorenzo was a frequent speaker at conferences and meetings, and Rudger recorded his sermons in some detail. He often accompanied Rudger on his travels to wards outside Brigham City to speak at church

*[handwritten marginalia: "Apostolic responsibility at a minimum / did 1st presidency with all decisions 5 / 12 - input"]*

meetings. It was Lorenzo Hunsaker who later because the vortex of a controversy which would test Rudger's leadership skills to the limit.

Rudger's personal finances remained somewhat precarious during most of his time in Brigham City. In a letter to his mother in December 1892, he writes: ". . . and, as you surmise, I have some difficulty in 'keeping my head above water' as there is nothing much 'doing' and money is as scarce as hens' teeth. If I could get a class in Book Keeping that would relieve the situation somewhat."

He had started an abstracting business in May of that year in partnership with John Burroughs, recorder of Box Elder County, whose position would enable him to feed business to Rudger. Rudger's office was located at First Counselor Kelly's shoe store.

Actually, a month after writing to his mother about the idea, he did organize a bookkeeping class. He offered a course of forty-five to fifty lessons meeting daily and charged $12 a person. Fifteen people enrolled in the first class.

*[handwritten marginalia: "50 | 12.00"]*

Rudger was also on the boards of a number of companies and invested small amounts from time to time in promising stocks. In September 1891 he bought 1,500 shares of stock in a new mining venture for fifteen cents per share, though he had to arrange to pay in monthly installments.

*[handwritten marginalia: "PAPA"]*

Mining and sugar stocks were the perennial favorites among the Saints and led to more than one unwise investment. Later that same year he cautioned his mother against investing more than she could risk in the Ferris Gold and Silver Mining and Milling Company. The First Presidency and the other apostles, including Lorenzo Snow, had been given stock in this company for promotional purposes—to have the church leadership identified with it. A number had made a public statement offering to return the stock because it might expose them to criticism for accepting it. Snow, however, who was president of the company, retained his interest in it. Joseph F. Smith, one of those who did withdraw from Ferris, was the president of another mining company. "It looks a little mysterious," Rudger commented.

There is little evidence that his investments paid off or that his membership on the corporate boards earned him much if any money. In 1892 he was named secretary of the Brigham City Roller Mill Company (Lorenzo Snow, president). The company was capitalized at $120,000 and issued two hundred shares of stock, of which Rudger got two. In this case, however, Rudger kept the books and was closely involved with it long after he left Brigham City for Salt Lake. As an apostle he often worked on Roller Mill books in President Snow's office. But since Snow was then involved with the mill as president of the church, Rudger may not have received any payment beyond his apostle's compensation for keeping the books.

As noted earlier, Rudger Clawson was not able to articulate in writing his deeper emotions or spiritual feelings. He did not elaborate beyond church doctrine on the nature of his relationship to God. His religion appears as a complete, coherent belief system which it was his job to make manifest in the world.

Yet from his writings emerge themes, ideas, and perspectives which he felt were most important in this belief system and which guided him in his everyday affairs. Not surprisingly one of these is the ultimate importance of the church's hierarchical structure. The Church of Jesus Christ of Latter-day Saints is a completely organized institution with official bodies established to meet every spiritual, moral and temporal need of its members. To function effectively it requires a strong chain of command, which is structurally and theologically built in by the gift of revelation believed to be held by the president. This direct contact with God is the focal point for the governance of the church, and each step from the individual member upward gets closer to God's will. Thus accepting the counsel of the person in authority over oneself is of critical importance in the church, and Rudger refers to it over and over again. Even though he had a number of painful encounters with the First Presidency, he never questioned the authority and, indeed, repeatedly emphasized its importance.

Another theme—and this is about as close as he comes to a deeper spirituality—is his belief in the presence of God and the efficacy of prayer. While faith is important, the key is prayer and the laying on of hands, blessing and being blessed. God intervenes in human affairs, heals the sick, guides the faithful, appears or sends messages in dreams, and gives power to the believer. This was an everyday reality for Rudger Clawson.

Also important was his belief in the necessity of good works. "I occupied the balance [of the time at a Sunday stake meeting]," he recounts, "and endeavored to show that faith without works is comparatively useless." Rudger Clawson occupied himself throughout his life in doing good within the context of his religion. He neglected both himself and to some degree his family, but throughout his life he was known as a good and faithful worker in the Lord's vineyard.

He was also a good administrator and ineluctably mundane. Not only must one do good works, said this dedicated bookkeeper and diarist, one must record them. "Keep full and complete records," he admonished his bishops, "as we will be judged from our records." On another occasion he "endeavored to impress upon the minds of the Saints that a record of our lives was kept by the recording angel and that by it we would be judged. We should endeavor so to live that our records, as they appear in the great Celestial Library, would be pleasing to look upon."

In Brigham City Rudger became engaged in good works and immersed himself in what became his life's occupation—serving his church. He was a builder; most descriptions of his reign in Brigham City note that seven chapels were built. He fought secularism, supported the hierarchy, and mediated disputes. He was, indeed, an almost ideal person to fill the role of stake president because of his skills as a mediator. Not only were issues brought to him officially as chairman of the High Council and head of the church court system in the stake, but he had to deal continuously with lesser disputes. In doing so he also manifested the characteristics of a good manager; he was decisive, he evaluated the situation with care, and he listened to the advice of the capable people around him.

In April 1893 the Salt Lake Temple was dedicated. It was a major event in the life of the church and in Rudger Clawson's life as well. The ceremonies lasted for twenty days, and Rudger was there for at least ten of them. On one occasion the apostles and the First Presidency talked about their religious experiences which included an account by George Q. Cannon of his personal encounter with Jesus. Then a larger group of church leaders formed a circle ("the largest prayer circle ever formed in the church") in the Celestial Room and prayed in concert. Afterward they listened to stories of early church history as told by eyewitnesses. "This was one of the most memorable events of my life—an occasion never to be forgotten and not easily described."

Seventy-five thousand people attended the dedicatory services which included tours through the entire building. On the day before the services began, selected nonmembers were allowed to join the tour of the building, most of which has since been closed to non-Mormons. Some of the rooms were simply decorated while others were richly draped and ornate. Great paintings or murals depicted important aspects of the Mormon scriptures. Some of the paintings had been done by native Utah artists trained in Paris. Stained glass "art windows" pictured other events. Many of the rooms were arched and supported by elaborately carved columns, and globed chandeliers ("electroliers") hung from the ceiling.

Lydia accompanied Rudger to many of the meetings and must have been as awed and inspired as he. Just before services commenced one day she twice heard voices singing when there were none. Two days later, Rudger wrote, she "heard a voice which told her some things about myself." Rudger doesn't say what, and perhaps Lydia didn't either!

Shortly after the dedication ceremonies were completed, President Woodruff named Snow president of the temple.

*   *   *

It was in January 1894 that Rudger made the first mention in his diary of the Lorenzo Hunsaker case that was to occupy so much of his time for the next six months. It all started in October of the previous year when Hunsaker came to Rudger for advice on what to do about the stories that were beginning to circulate about him in Honeyville. Honeyville had been settled by Abraham Hunsaker, a hard-driving veteran of the Mormon battalion, who had marched through Mexico during the Mexican war. Hunsaker had acquired land in the area for grazing cattle and dry farming. By the late 1860s he was growing wheat and had built a grist mill. He had come to Honeyville from Brigham City with his five wives and large family, apparently to give them room to grow. As Rudger notes, he seems to have succeeded. "That he had been blessed in this undertaking is shown by the fact that Honeyville is today a prosperous and thriving settlement. The population, consisting principally of Hunsakers, numbers 164 souls."

Abraham was bishop of Honeyville Ward up to the time of his death in 1889, shortly after Rudger's arrival in Box Elder. He was succeeded as bishop by B. H. Tolman, his trusted first counselor. Lorenzo Hunsaker had been the manager of Abraham's grist mill and had taken care of his father's accounts. He was also a school teacher, and, as we have noted, a close friend of Rudger's. Hunsaker told Rudger of the bizarre stories being told about him by two of his half-brothers, Peter and Weldon Hunsaker. During the last several years they said Hunsaker had committed homosexual acts upon them on a number of occasions while they were in bed asleep.

Rudger's reaction, of course, was one of shock and disbelief. Hunsaker was thinking of bringing charges in the church court against the boys (though they were hardly "boys"; Peter was twenty-four and Weldon, nineteen; Hunsaker was thirty-four), but Rudger dissuaded him, recommending that he "treat the whole affair with silent contempt because the stories were so 'monstrous and ridiculous.' "

Later Hunsaker came back with Bishop Tolman, who insisted that the boys' charges be investigated and warned Rudger that failure to do so would look like Rudger was attempting to cover it up. It was clear from the exchange that Tolman was on the side of the boys.

A Bishop's Court was held promptly in mid-October. The boys testified that over a period of years Hunsaker had committed homosexual acts upon each of them on four different occasions while they were asleep. One other man testified that Hunsaker had touched him while they were in bed together but had done no more. Hunsaker denied the stories and suggested that the motive for telling them was that his brother, Peter, had asked Hunsaker's wife, Florida, to run off with him.

That was the testimony. From this point on, the course of events became almost as bizarre as the story itself. The Bishop's Court, presided over by Tolman, concluded that it could not make a decision and referred it to the stake High Council, presided over by Rudger Clawson. The High Council sent it back saying in essence that the Bishop's Court couldn't so easily get out of the responsibility for making a decision. So, Tolman's court decided against Hunsaker, who immediately appealed to the High Council. The High Council heard the testimony again, though at somewhat greater length than the Bishop's Court. What was revealed—aside from the fact that Peter and Welden were somewhat wild and disreputable—was a bitter, festering conflict among the townspeople over Hunsaker's position. Abraham, at his death, had laid upon Hunsaker the mantle of leadership and given him control of the estate. Most of the family, according to one witness, were jealous of Lorenzo Hunsaker, especially Israel Hunsaker, one of Tolman's counselors.

When the High Council decided in favor of Lorenzo Hunsaker and called upon the boys to recant or face being cut off from the church, Rudger was visited by a delegation of sisters from Honeyville—all Hunsakers—to plead the boys' case and ask for a new trial, which Rudger denied. Next he received a written petition, also pleading the boys' case, which he recorded in full in his diary. It included the names of the signers—to which he appended a note:

*41 signers*
*7 children 7 to 14 yrs.*
*2 not in church*
*2 not members of the ward*

The next day Rudger called in Bishop Tolman and instructed him to withdraw the sacrament from the ward. Peter and Welden, who refused to retract their stories, were also formally cut off from the church. Honeyville was stirred up. Though a number of people came forward and withdrew their support for the petition, claiming they did not know what they were signing, Lorenzo wrote Rudger of "a deep bitter feeling brooding among two-thirds of the people. . . ." Nevertheless, after more disclaimers were obtained and some peace-making efforts had calmed the community down, the sacrament was restored. Curious as to where the petition originated, Rudger asked a couple of loyal townspeople to investigate. It did not take them long to determine that though he did not sign it, Tolman himself had originated it.

In a long, somewhat groveling letter, Tolman apologized, excused himself, and offered his resignation, which Rudger declined. Then, a group of Hunsakers, believed to be led by Lorenzo's arch foe, Israel, filed a petition in the county probate court to have Lorenzo Hunsaker removed as guardian of some of his younger brothers and sisters, a guardianship which had been set up by Abraham before his death.

Honeyville became agitated again. "Most of the people of the ward took sides in the controversy and the feelings of jealousy, hatred and animosity, which were confessed, and, we had hoped, repented of, were once more fanned into life." Again the sacrament was removed. In Rudger's book, going outside the church to the courts of the land was virtually sacrilege.

The climax came when, in late January 1894, Tolman suppressed part of a letter Rudger had written to be read to the Honeyville congregation and then acted contrary to its instructions. What had become clear by now was the fact that the real issue in Honeyville was not whether Lorenzo Hunsaker had committed homosexual acts, but who was going to control the town—or at least the family's affairs, which were not all that distinguishable from the town's. Hunsaker was apparently a good but not a very strong person, though he was stalwart in his resistance to the campaign against him. Israel was adamant in his opposition, but apparently more skilled at stirring up trouble than acquiring power.

It is not hard to imagine the kind of chaos that followed the death of Abraham. A polygamous family with five wives and dozens of children could expand a family feud into community warfare. All of which Tolman felt Rudger did not comprehend. In Tolman's opinion, Rudger reported, "the brethren from Brigham City did not understand the condition of the ward or they would certainly take a different view of things." Ironically, this is just the position Rudger took when his decision regarding E. A. Box was overruled by the First Presidency.

On the advice of Lorenzo Snow (but with the warning that he would probably be rebuked by the First Presidency), an angry Rudger Clawson went to Honeyville and at a ward meeting removed Tolman and made Thomas Wheatley, Jr.—Lorenzo Hunsaker's business partner and an outsider—presiding elder until a new bishop could be appointed. It was an irregular step. Proper procedure called for the matter to be referred to the High Council, but Rudger felt the need for swift action. The discontent over the removal of Tolman and the installation of Wheatley was open and strong.

What was wrong with Honeyville? The trouble appears to have all gone back to Abraham Hunsaker who ruled his family with an iron hand, leaving his sons a legacy of authoritarianism, but not preparing them to deal with the cross-currents of emotion that were bound to affect their relationships after their father's death. Amidst the self-pity in which, in his letter to Rudger, Tolman wallows, a clear perception of the problem emerges: "I do not want to make many excuses. I expect to meet the fate that is just. I simply made one of the mistakes that it seems to be my lot [to make], but do you President Clawson understand the pressure that I have had to endure and meet? I am too full for utterance. It has been a constant war [in Honeyville] ever since Bishop Hunsaker died. While he was alive he took away the agency of some of his sons because what he said was law, and yet, I suppose, he had trials of a severe nature."

As for his own problem, Tolman went straight to the First Presidency, pointing out the irregularity of Rudger's action. The First Presidency wrote a letter calling for an explanation, clearly indicating, as Lorenzo Snow had predicted, a rebuke would be forthcoming. Again on Snow's advice, but this time accompanied by him, Rudger went personally to Salt Lake to explain himself to the First Presidency. President Woodruff was ill, so First Counselor George Q. Cannon heard the case. Settling stoutly into his chair, he listened attentively to Rudger's story. Cannon's face had a soft, congenial look to it, and the neat, white beard he carefully restricted to the edge of his chin and jaw seemed curiously decorative. He had inquiring eyes which, combined with the rest of his features, gave him a paradoxical look of both simplicity and shrewdness. After hearing Rudger out, he said that he recognized that the bishop deserved dismissal, and thought the High Council would undoubtedly dismiss him. "It appeared certain," Rudger wrote, "that President Cannon was on the point of rescinding our action and remanding the case to the High Council, which would have been to us a stinging rebuke. At this critical moment President Snow asked for permission to say a few words, which was granted."

Snow told Cannon that he had advised Rudger to act as he did and cited some similarly irregular actions taken by the prophet Joseph. Cannon was a little embarrassed, but "met the situation grandly. He said, 'Brother Rudger Clawson, I want to say to you that Lorenzo Snow is a wise counselor in Israel and if he counseled you to do that which was done in this case, it is all right.' "

In March, 1894, Tolman made a public confession and was publicly forgiven. Finally, the Honeyville embroglio was brought to an end when in June the sacrament was restored to the ward, and later Wheatley was installed as permanent bishop with Tolman as his second counselor.

A crisis of a different kind occurred during Rudger's later years in

Box Elder. When Rudger arrived in Brigham City to take up the stake presidency, the Brigham City Tabernacle was undergoing extensive renovations at a cost of around $5,000. The remodeled building was dedicated in 1890, and in 1891 a hot air furnace was installed— apparently improperly. Five years later, on February 9, 1896, the tabernacle was destroyed by a fire that started in the furnace room. Only the stone walls were left standing.

With characteristic energy and after his usual consultation with Lorenzo Snow, Rudger set about immediately to rebuild the tabernacle and in the process improve and expand its capacity. Raising the $15,000 necessary to cover the costs was the prime obstacle. Especially needed was about $1,400 for cash outlays needed to begin the job. After a sympathetic article about the fire appeared in the *Salt Lake Herald*, Rudger decided to see if he could raise money among the well-to-do in Salt Lake. Lorenzo laughed at the idea when it was presented to him, doubting if more than $100 could be raised in the city. Rudger, slightly miffed, said all he wanted to know was whether Lorenzo objected.

After several days of cajoling prominent church figures, local merchants, and professional men—including Charles Zane, the judge who had presided over his polygamy trial (and who contributed $10)— Rudger raised $1,500 and the project commenced.

Rudger was in his element. He masterfully organized the subsequent phases of fund-raising and managed the rebuilding with efficiency and imagination. By March 1897, it was ready for occupancy. It had been rebulit at a cost of $13,000 (the original building was estimated to have cost $20–25,000) and, with renovations suggested by Rudger Clawson, seated four hundred more people than the previous building. It stands today a striking symbol of Rudger Clawson's tenure as president of Box Elder Stake.

At home, Rudger's family was increasing and his children were growing up. Samuel George had been born in September 1896. But in March, 1897, three-year-old Vera Mary drank from a bottle containing a carbolic acid solution and died soon thereafter.

Rudger did not often write of the children in his diaries, though he was clearly proud of Rudger Remus's ability to recite "The Charge of the Light Brigade," which he mentioned twice.

In July 1897, when he organized Box Elder's participation in the

Great Pioneer Jubilee of that year, he noted in his diary that the Box Elder float in the big parade in Salt Lake depicted a cornucopia spilling out "a wreath of fine fruits of all kinds" (according to the *Brigham Bugler*) and was graced by five fancily dressed little girls, one of whom was his daughter Gay.

Rudger's son by Florence, Rudger Elmo, died in April 1898 of kidney trouble at the age of fourteen. "He was a very promising boy," Rudger noted in his diary.

By 1898, the major events of Rudger's time in Brigham City were well past. The city council, apparently taken over by Rudger's foes, attempted to repudiate the waterworks debt to the Deseret Bank, but Rudger and his associates intervened. Honeyville had settled down under Bishop Wheatley and could even be reported as experiencing more harmonious relationships.

On September 1, 1898, Rudger chaired a meeting to establish an annual Peach Day celebration to promote the fruit industry and attract investors to the area. As he threw himself into this new project with characteristic vigor, another event was taking place in San Francisco that would affect and redirect his life in almost as dramatic a fashion as had the murder of Joseph Standing, his trial and conviction for polygamy, and the call to the stake presidency of Box Elder. Wilford Woodruff was dying.

# CHAPTER 6
# THE
# APOSTLE

*L* orenzo Snow, next in line for the presidency of the church, was eighty-five years old and in fragile health when he heard that President Wilford Woodruff was sick in San Francisco. He immediately went to the temple and prayed for the president, pleading with the Lord not to let Woodruff die before him. He frankly did not think he had the stamina to take on the responsibility of the presidency. Only six months earlier he had told a church conference that "as we advance in years and come nearer to what we generally consider the time of our departure into the other life, we are more inclined to devote our thoughts and reflections upon those things that we may receive in the next life . . . and the proper preparations that we have made, and are making, to reach that which we anticipate. I know that is so with me."

The Lord, however, did not answer Lorenzo's prayers, or if he did, the answer was no; in San Francisco, Woodruff died of a bladder PROSTATE infection on September 2, 1898. That day, Snow was on the street in Brigham City talking with Rudger when a telegram was handed to him informing him of Woodruff's death.

There is no record of what they were talking about, either before or after Snow received the telegram, but between those two intimate friends the implications of Snow's elevation to the presidency of the church must certainly have been discussed.

171

Snow returned immediately to Salt Lake where he spent a great deal of time in prayer looking for guidance and instruction from God. At one point—as he later told his granddaughter—he met the Savior: "He stood right there, about three feet above the floor. It looked as though he stood on a plate of solid gold." Jesus instructed Snow not to wait, as had been the case after the death of past presidents, but to assume the presidency at once and appoint his counselors. The Lord had work for the aging patriarch to do, and he set out to do it with a vigor that belied his years.

After reappointing George Q. Cannon and Joseph F. Smith as counselors, Snow's next responsibility was to fill the vacancy in the Quorum which resulted from his succeeding Woodruff as president. It was hardly surprising that he chose Rudger Clawson. But he needed the concurrence of the Twelve, so he asked them to submit suggestions. The apostles, as Heber J. Grant later told Rudger, presented Snow with suggestions of brethren whom they would like to be chosen. Snow and his counselors then withdrew to consider the names, and when they returned, Snow said, "We are perfectly united." He "was sure we would want the man whom the Lord had approved of and none of us desired that our own judgment shall prevail. The man we have chosen is Rudger Clawson." Snow then extolled his protégé, citing his heroics and accomplishments.

Rudger Clawson, at the age of forty-one, was ordained Apostle of the Church of Jesus Christ of Latter-day Saints on October 10, 1898. It was a solemn occasion as the leaders of the church gathered in the council room of the First Presidency. The room was large and light with a simple altar in the center surrounded by twelve comfortable armchairs in a semicircle. Three chairs stood in a line against one wall for the First Presidency. A table for the sacramental bread and wine was placed in front of them. The floor was covered with Oriental rugs, and on the wall hung large paintings of Joseph and Hyrum Smith and Brigham Young, along with depictions of early church scenes and settings such as the Hill Cumorah, where Joseph Smith discovered the Golden Plates. Gold chandeliers hung from the ceiling.

Rudger knelt at the altar as the hands of the apostles were laid upon his head, and Lorenzo Snow said, "All the blessings, all the qualifications and all that is necessary to make you perfect in this Apostleship in the name of Lord Jesus we seal upon you, and say that these blessings that we have sealed upon you shall continue upon you during your life and also throughout all eternity."

Then Snow and the apostles had a few words of heavenly and earthly counsel concerning his new duties: "You have been appointed by the Lord to a high and holy calling," said Snow. "Do not think of yourself when important duties are to be performed wherein perhaps there might be advantages to youself, but think of what the Lord requires of you; think of the good that will be accomplished to others without reference to yourself at all. You are now, of course, the young tot of the apostles. There are many of this Quorum that have been in this relationship for a great many years. You must not expect that at once you can feel yourself at home and be equal to them in that knowledge which they have obtained. Let those who have had long experience speak when it comes to matters of high importance, you listen."

The second counselor, Joseph F. Smith, rose to speak. Smith was a big man, with a long, thin, grey-streaked beard which hung from his chin in two distinct sections as if it had been parted. He wore thick, rimless glasses which magnified his eyes, adding to the air of strength about him. "One of the great callings," he said in a deep, firm voice, "and special duties of the apostles is to become living witness of the Lord Jesus Christ. Another principal [sic] is that the Apostles must acknowledge the Order and organization of the Priesthood and the united counsels of the leading presiding Quorums of the Priesthood as supreme above his own judgment. All the Apostles must consent and agree before God that we will acknowledge this organization that God has instituted as His supreme authority on earth."

Finally, George Q. Cannon counseled that when an apostle becomes part of the ministry, "It is the first and most important thing that he should not put this [his ministry] aside to attend to anything else. His whole life and all that pertains to his power of life, his talents, and everything should be devoted exclusively to the apostleship."

Once again a major turning point had come in Rudger Clawson's life, and again it had come at the call of Lorenzo Snow. This time, however, Snow was president of the church, whom Latter-day Saints believe to be a prophet of God and in direct communication with the Almighty. Rudger was clearly somewhat awed. "If I could not feel," he said on accepting his appointment, "that this Call had come to me from the Lord, I would shrink from it." Letters of congratulations from family and friends poured in, but he continued to insist, as he did to Brother C. C. Richards of Ogden, that "the Lord has chosen a weak vessel to bear witness of his power and authority on earth."

On the following Sunday when he spoke to his congregation in the tabernacle in Brigham City he said he felt humble and incapable of magnifying the office.

This kind of ritual self-deprecation was common, if not universal, among those faced with advancement within the church. On one occasion Wilford Woodruff had responded, perhaps a little impatiently, to John Winder when the latter was appointed to a temple post and protested his lack of qualification, "Never mind, I will appoint you and the Lord will qualify you."

Rudger in his Brigham City speech also said his appointment had come to him as a great surprise. Almost everything important in his life had come to Rudger as a surprise. If one is to believe him, he was almost totally unaware of what was going on in the world around him—which may indeed explain many of the things he did, his acts of courage and conviction, as well as his acts of naivete and folly.

It was agreed that, for the time being, he would continue as president of the Box Elder Stake, although he was advised to begin looking for a home in Salt Lake. Until he did, it meant arising at dawn every Thursday and taking the train for the three-hour ride to Salt Lake for the regular 11:00 a.m. weekly meeting of the First Presidency and the quorum.

On these mornings, as the train rolled south, Rudger could see the sun as it rose over the Wasatch Front reflecting pink and yellow-brown against the Oquirrh Mountains. It was strikingly beautiful and the sharp promontory at Millstone Point vibrated in the changing light and brought back memories of Pleasant Green where he and Lydia had first met.

The Quorum of the Twelve Apostles had been established in 1835 by Joseph Smith as a result of a revelation. The role of the apostles was to spread the gospel and see to the development and organization of the church across the country and around the world. As defined in the *Doctrine and Covenants*, "The Twelve are a Travelling Presiding High Council, to officiate in the name of the Lord under the direction of the Presidency of the Church, agreeable to the institution of heaven;

to build up the Church, and regulate all the affairs of the same in all nations."

Rudger soon learned the truth of this description. Traveling for the church and the Lord would be (as it was for most—though not all—of the apostles) one of his primary duties and would occupy much of his time for the rest of his life.

In 1898, when Rudger began his apostleship, the church consisted of 229,428 Saints who lived in 315 wards in forty stakes located in the territory surrounding the Great Salt Lake Basin and extending into what is now Arizona, Nevada, and California. There were also twenty missions throughout the country and abroad containing another 37,823 members, for a total church membership of 267,251. Apostles were designated by the president to attend various quarterly stake conferences and monthly ward meetings. They represented the president and therefore the Lord at these meetings. They preached, helped solve administrative and spiritual problems, ordained high priests, set apart* church officers, and generally advised the leadership in the various stakes and wards to which they were assigned.

In addition to their regularly scheduled administrative meetings, there was a special quarterly meeting initiated by Lorenzo Snow when he was president of the Twelve, for the sole purpose of uniting the brothers personally. During these meetings, each apostle was asked to express his deepest and innermost thoughts in matters relating to the church and to his personal beliefs. Snow hoped that through these special meetings, the apostles would purge themselves of any doubts by discussing with other apostles anything that might be disturbing them, thereby achieving complete unity of thought and expression among them. It is quite possible that he also had in mind averting the kind of divisiveness that flared up at the time of Wilford Woodruff's succession. Harmony among the quorum members was highly valued and referred to often in their meetings.

At the regular Thursday morning meetings, Rudger wrote in his memoirs, "The order of business was singing, opening prayer at the

*One is "set apart" when a superior authority confirms one's appointment to a church position in a ceremony involving the laying on of hands. One is "ordained" in similar fashion when one enters an office of the priesthood. To be "sustained" simply means being approved for a church position or office by a vote of the appropriate body.

altar, singing, correspondence considered and disposed of, individual reports by members of the Council—appointments to stake quarterly conferences announced . . . adjournment and benediction."

There were many reasons—in addition to the call of the Lord and the personal bond between Rudger and Lorenzo—that made the younger man a good choice for the quorum. He was also dedicated, spiritual, and popular (as suggested by the fact that the *Salt Lake Tribune* said at the time that his heroic martyrdom had made him "one of the best-known men in Utah." But, perhaps most important, he had a skill which would make him almost the man of the hour in the Mormon hierarchy. He was an honest, careful, and meticulous bookkeeper. Lorenzo remembered that from their time together in the Utah penitentiary.

Church leaders before Snow had been fully aware that the church was in financial trouble. As early as 1896 Wilford Woodruff wrote in his journal, "The Presidency of the church are so overwhelmed in financial matters it seems as though we shall never live to get through with it unless the Lord opens the way in a marvelous manner. It looks as though we shall never pay our debts." Church indebtedness, amounting to about $1,200,000, was scattered about in expensive, short-term notes. Revenues and assets were not clearly accounted for, and poor management kept the church in a precarious and uncertain position should their debts be called in.

In the mid-1890s an informal financial committee had been established in which George Q. Cannon and his son Frank Cannon had played leading roles. The Cannons had proposed that church financial management be reorganized and placed in the hands of committees appointed at church conferences. Woodruff readily accepted the plan, though his second counselor, Joseph F. Smith, thought it dangerous in that it allowed power to pass from the hands of the president. Nevertheless, the Cannons were empowered to go to New York to see if they could convince Eastern financial interests to buy long-term bonds to relieve the church's position. They had not succeeded, and Frank was still there when Woodruff died in September 1898. He hurried back to find Lorenzo Snow hastily taking charge and committed to keeping the control of finances in the hands of the president—

the "trustee-in-trust."* Rudger Clawson fit perfectly into Lorenzo's scheme.

The younger man had only been an apostle for a few months when, one evening, Snow asked him to come to the Beehive House where the president was living with Minnie, his ninth and youngest wife.

As trustee-in-trust, Snow knew he should be in close touch with the financial condition of the church, but did not feel he was. He knew of course of the outstanding notes and liabilities, but he felt uncertain about the church's assets. During the years when church properties were under escheatment by the federal government, their value had suffered from mismanagement and the sale of several valuable pieces. He was particularly concerned with distinguishing between those that had a clear cash or market value and those (church buildings, etc.) that had only a silent value, i.e., could not be used to liquidate liabilities. Then he said (as recorded in Rudger's memoirs), "Now, Brother Clawson, I appoint you with full authority to take charge of the books in the office of the Trustee-in-Trust and from those books ask you to prepare and submit an itemized report showing the exact financial status of the Church."

Actually Snow did not give "full authority" nor did Rudger "take charge" of the books on a permanent basis. The books remained under the control of church treasurer, James Jack, whose deficiencies as a bookkeeper would not become an issue until several years hence.

"Greatly surprised and alarmed (so to speak) I replied, 'President Snow, you have put upon me a great responsibility. Do you think I can measure up to it?'

" 'Yes, Brother Clawson,' he said, 'I think you can. I know you can.'

"In order to justify, if possible, the confidence President Snow had expressed in my ability, I began with all diligence to accomplish my new task that he might be informed as to the exact financial status of the church."

In the meantime, the church was in a perilous situation. As Snow

---

*"Trustee-in-trust" identifies the position in the church which has the responsibility for its financial and administrative affairs. Legally it lies in the president, but has from time to time been delegated to others. Lorenzo Snow held it during his presidency.

told the story later, on the day he was sustained as president at the general conference, "Brother Jack [the treasurer] came to me and said that a certain man, whom the church was owing, wanted $10,000 immediately and the balance due him shortly after. The church actually could not pay it. This was the first intimation I had of the real condition of affairs. . . ."

Without the backing of the Eastern financiers, the church was in jeopardy. "Had the people we were owing at the time come against us," Snow continued, "this church would have been bankrupt. Such was really the case." However, instead of going back to Easterners for the money, he decided to borrow it "among ourselves" in a series of three $500,000 bond issues. Two, totaling a million dollars, were issued in early January 1899 and were bought up during the ensuring year almost entirely by Mormons and Mormon financial institutions. The immediate crisis was over. But it was a short-term solution.

Rudger was put in charge of a newly established auditing committee, which began its work on January 19, 1899. Within a month it had delivered to the president a seventeen-page report of which Rudger was quite proud. In 1935, when he wrote his memoirs, he described the report and noted with some satisfaction that its accuracy had "stood the test of thirty-six years."

What the report showed was that after direct liabilities of approximately $1,798,000 (which did not even include a large obligation of a million and a half dollars on a Pioneer Power Co. bond issue) were deducted from active assets of $1,880,000 (excluding church property that had value but was not marketable) there was a balance of only $82,000. When approximately $306,000 in tithing-on-hand was added, the net assets on February 18, 1899, came to about $388,000.

The report, Rudger concluded, "clearly pointed to the fact that the church, 'if not bankrupt, was surely on the verge of bankruptcy.'" Lorenzo was impressed with the report—and with Rudger.

While, in the council meetings, Rudger had followed the advice of his elders and said very little on substantive issues, he did speak up on the subject of keeping records. He had recommended that a "strict account" be made of all money collected from church members and of how it was spent. This, Rudger implied, was not being faithfully done.

Realizing that in Rudger Clawson he had the key to mastering the church's chaotic finances, Snow assigned his friend new tasks. The first, in March 1899, was to make up a set of books in condensed form for Lorenzo's private use that would show him at a glance the financial condition of the church. Rudger started immediately but less than two weeks later he had a new assignment. Drop everything, Snow ordered, and develop another set of figures—"a statement of the entire receipts and disbursements of the church commencing with the year 1898."

It took three and a half months. The situation in 1898, as Clawson learned, was this: The church's income amounted to approximately $837,000 (including about $22,000 in stock dividends, $2,000 in rents, $800,000 in tithes); expenses were $514,000, leaving a surplus of $323,000. But the church had just arranged to retire the Pioneer Power bond obligation for $225,000 plus a ten-year 5 percent guarantee on $250,000. In other words, there was still little cash to go toward paying off its almost two million dollars in other debts. Even if the total annual surplus, assuming it remained constant, were allocated to debt retirement, it would take years and severely stunt the growth of the church.

They needed a long-term solution and they found it, but not in the coffers of Eastern, nor even Salt Lake, financiers. It came to Lorenzo Snow in a revelation in the dusty, drought-stricken, southern reaches of Utah.

One morning in May 1899 Lorenzo awoke telling of a visitatiion by God instructing him to go south to St. George in southern Utah and  there call a special conference for a purpose the Lord did not reveal. Without delay he prepared to go, taking his son LeRoi as his secretary and asking Rudger to accompany his party. "Owing to certain matters," Rudger noted in his diary, "I could not accept the invitation, much to my regret."

It *was* regrettable because Snow's trip to St. George was a significant event in the history of the Mormon church. At that time southern Utah was in the midst of an eighteen-month drought. Streams had dried up and the cattle were dying on the range. Everything was turning to dust. The people of St. George had hoped Snow would pray for them and invoke the aid of the Lord in coping with the drought. But the Lord had something else in mind. It came on May 17 in the St. George Tabernacle. Leroi Snow described it later in wondrous terms: "I was sitting at a table on the stand, reporting the proceedings, when all at once father paused in his discourse. Complete stillness filled the room. I shall never forget the thrill as long as I live. When he commenced to speak again his voice strengthened and the inspiration of God seemed to come over him, as well as over the entire assembly. . . . Then he revealed to the Latter-day Saints the vision that was before him.

> "God manifested to him there and then the purpose of the call to visit the Saints in the South. . . . He told them that he could see, as he had never realized before how the law of tithing had been neglected by the people, also that the Saints, themselves, were heavily in debt, as well as the church. And now through strict obedience to this law—the paying of a full and honest tithing—not only would the church be relieved of its great indebtedness, but through the blessings of the Lord this would also be the means of freeing the Latter-day Saints from their individual obligations and they would become a prosperous people. The word of the Lord is: 'The time has come for every Latter-day Saint, who calculates to be prepared for the future and to hold his feet strong upon a proper foundation, to do the will of the Lord and to pay his tithing in full!' More specifically he promised the people of southern Utah that if they paid their tithes faithfully the drought would end. And so, not long afterward, it did.

The law of tithing dated back to a revelation Joseph Smith received in 1838 and was associated with the law of consecration. This was a communal doctrine under which individual Saints were to give their property to the church, a portion of which sufficient to maintain them and their families—identified as their "everlasting inheritance"— would be deeded back to them to be held in stewardship. The balance would be used by the church for the benefit of the poor. On this inheritance, however, they were to pay the church a tithing of one-tenth of the annual income it produced. The law of consecration had not been adhered to, but church members were supposed to pay their tithing, whether in kind or in cash. Although the law of tithing was an important doctrine, by the end of the nineteenth century many Saints evaded their obligation. Snow estimated that 50 percent went unpaid.

As soon as he returned from St. George, he launched his campaign, talking at every opportunity about the subject that would preoccupy him until his death—tithing.

At a meeting in Brigham City in June, which Rudger attended with

him, Snow told the priesthood that "we have come here today to tell
you exactly what the Lord expects of you and me with reference to the
law of tithing." He spoke of the Saints in Jackson County, Missouri,
and the hardships they had suffered at the hands of the gentiles. Why
had they suffered so? It was because the Saints in Missouri had not
adhered strictly to the law of consecration. Had they done so, said
Snow, "the Latter-day Saints would be the wealthiest community on
earth today." After the people failed to keep the law of consecration,
"they were placed under another law, namely that of tithing and we
are now under that law."

He then announced a special meeting of church authorities, a
Solemn Assembly, to take place in the temple in July that, he said,
would be one of the most important gatherings in church history.

To understand the significance of what Snow intended to say, one
must understand the meaning of "Jackson County," which at this time
was central both to the Latter-day Saints' experience in American
society and to Mormon millenarian theology. In 1831, the Latter-day
Saints had settled in Independence in Jackson County, Missouri.
Joseph Smith preached that this site was where the Garden of Eden
had been located and was the site of Zion where Jesus would return to
rule over the kingdom of God in the millenium. It was here that the
Mormons, the chosen people, were called upon to establish the true
church. The old settlers soon found themselves being inundated by
Mormons streaming in from the East and they reacted violently. It
was not long before the Mormons were being driven out by hostile
mobs. Through the persecutions and migrations which followed, the
Saints sustained a belief that one day they would return to Jackson
County where the kingdom of God would become a reality on earth.

Over time, however, with a new generation of church members and
vast numbers of immigrants who had not experienced the persecutions
in the East, the return to Missouri—and the advent of the millenium—had been pushed into the future. The practical task of building
their temporary Zion in the Western mountains took all their energy.

On Sunday, July 2, 1899, about seven hundred church leaders from
the First Presidency to Sunday School superintendents, attended the
meeting in the temple. It was truly a "solemn assembly," Rudger
noted in his diary, and it could hardly have been otherwise, since

Snow during the weeks beforehand had announced over and over the importance of the meeting.

Immediately after the prayer, Lorenzo took the rostrum and presented his message: the return to Jackson County was nigh. Anyone at the meeting who lived another ten or twenty years would go back. "The time for returning to Jackson County is much nearer than many suppose. . . ." he told his startled and probably somewhat overawed audience, who believed this was the Lord's prophet speaking. But there was a price: paying their tithes.

"If the people had paid an honest tithing for the past year, we would have received $1 million more than we did receive and if a full tithing had been paid for the last twelve years, we would have received $10 million more than we did receive." Going on at length, Snow blamed virtually all the troubles the Saints had ever experienced on their failure to pay tithes and told them that if they did not observe the law of tithing, not only would they never return to Jackson County, but there was "no promise that we will remain in this land an hour." It was an apocalyptic warning. In sermon after sermon during the ensuing weeks Snow kept up a drumbeat on this subject, with Rudger faithfully recording his words.

"If you will pay your tithing in the full," Snow said he was authorized by the Lord to tell them, "the Lord will forgive you for your disobedience in the past." The message was clear and Snow did not blush at putting a price tag on redemption: "If we ever get possession of the land of Zion, it will be by purchase, not by blood . . . the land of Zion will never be purchased except by the tithing and the consecration of the Saints."

Nor did Snow neglect the practical side. When the apostles took the message into the stakes and wards, he insisted their sermons on tithing should be "followed up with some definite action." They "should call the bishopric together and give them some specific instructions—especially in regard to visiting members of their wards who were slack in the payment of their tithes or who were nontithepayers and seek, in private, ways to convert them to the principle." Rudger and the other apostles did pick up the message and preached it as relentlessly as their leader.

In the midst of all this—during the summer of 1899—Rudger was in the process of moving his family to Salt Lake. The house he found was the original home of a pioneer leader, Lorenzo D. Young. It was the first house completed and occupied after the arrival of the Saints in the Great Salt Lake valley. Located on Canyon Road near the temple and downtown Salt Lake, it was within what had been the original confines of the Brigham Young properties and must have been familiar to Rudger who as a boy had sometimes accompanied his father during his labors for Young.

It was a big, old, adobe structure very much in need of repair. Rudger hired workmen from Brigham City to do the renovations, which included the installation of gas lighting and a new sewage system. They moved in on July 31, 1899.

Rudger liked the convenience of his new house to the temple, and he walked there regularly to meetings and to work in the president's office. It was a pleasant walk. Arsenal Hill and Ensign Peak rose sharply behind him, and as he rounded the first corner, the gray temple stood high above the surrounding buildings, its towers pointing heavenward. Reaching State Street, he could see through Eagle Gate a long view down the sloping avenue which faded into the often misted valley in the distance.

In October 1899, Rudger could report to Snow that the tithing campaign was working. His figures showed that from June through September of the previous year, the church had collected $67,000 in tithes. During the same months in 1899, the tithes had more than doubled.

Snow now felt he could spare his trusted accountant for other tasks. One of the first was to travel to Canada to visit a Mormon community near Lethbridge in Alberta. Snow had negotiated a contract whereby one hundred Mormons and their families would settle in Alberta and work on a canal being built there. In May, Apostle John W. Taylor began the recruitment of the families. By the fall of 1899 they had settled in and were at work, but a problem had arisen between the canal company and the Mormons, a problem which involved the adequacy of the company's bookkeeping. Lorenzo asked Rudger to join Joseph F. Smith and J. Fewsom Smith, a surveyor, in attempting to settle the matter.

At 8:45 p.m. on October 26, they boarded the train for Canada, arriving five days later at the little town of Stirling, twenty miles south of Lethbridge. It did not take them long to find out what the problem was.

About two feet below the surface of the ground in which the Mormons were digging, they had encountered a form of hard earth known as "gumbo." The Mormon workers felt they should be paid more for having to remove such a difficult substance and the contract with the canal company seemed to bear them out. A trip to the canal site convinced Clawson that his brothers had a good case. "This substance," [he wrote] "is very much like India Rubber in texture and appearance . . . and is very difficult to move. The boys could scarcely accomplish it with three span of horses on the plow. . . . I shoved the point of my umbrella into the gumbo and in withdrawing it the point . . . at the end was drawn off."

The mission then settled down for two weeks of negotiations while Rudger examined the books. He wrote Snow that they were "in pretty fair shape," although there were a couple of accounts that did not satisfy him.

He was favorably impressed by Canada, especially with the size of the vegetables grown there. "You may know that it is fine country," he wrote Lydia, "when I tell you that turnips are raised here without irrigation as big as your head, and radishes as big as your double fist and a cabbage was raised by the brother with whom I am stopping that furnished a meal (with other things) for twenty-five people. . . . The cattle on the range are 'butter fat' and will furnish a steak that is sweet and juicy compared to the tasteless stuff we so often get in Salt Lake." His only real complaint with Canada was that it was so far from Salt Lake.

The contractual dispute was finally resolved, with the canal company agreeing that the Mormons should be paid more for digging the gumbo. Rudger wrote Lorenzo assuring him that "the contract entered into by the church will be observed to the letter and that the company books were in satisfactory shape." He returned to Utah in time to attend the second day of the Box Elder quarterly conference where he had been replaced by Charles Kelley as stake president. After the conference he continued on to Salt Lake to find the family had been well during his three weeks' absence. He noted in his diary, "Lydia and myself went down town and had an oyster supper."

During the years immediately following the 1890 Manifesto the issue of polygamy was played down by the Mormons but continued to simmer in the national consciousness. George Q. Cannon and other church leaders (Hiram Bradley Clawson among them) had plied the halls of Congress and reached a *modus vivendi* with the political establishment in Washington. The politicians would wink at the discreet practice of polygamy by those who had taken plural wives before 1890 as long as no new plural marriages took place. This understanding was important. From the outset of the crusade, Mormon polygamists had insisted they had a moral responsibility to wives they already had.

Among the Twelve, however, there were marked differences in their attitudes toward polygamy and its practice. Many, if not most, of the members still believed plural marriage to be a true doctrine and that the Manifesto had been issued as a policy statement designed to placate their enemies. One day in the summer of 1899 Apostle Marriner W. Merrill had predicted "that the time would never be in this church when children from plural marriages will not be born." In his diary he wrote more bluntly that he did not believe the Manifesto was a revelation but had been formulated by Woodruff and the Twelve for the sake of expediency. Francis Lyman disagreed. "Apostle Lyman," Rudger reported on another day, "made some remarks on the Manifesto suspending plural marriage, showing that it was given by inspiration and [that] to his mind made it equivalent of a revelation." This division between the brethren in the council was deep and would have serious consequences later. For the time being, President Snow kept it in check by affirming his own acceptance of the law of the land.

"Many honorable Americans who made sacrifices for their country," he said at a meeting in December 1899, "look upon the United States as the greatest nation on the earth, and feel that its laws are supreme and that when it comes to a question of law, the Latter-day saints should bow. It is necessary sometimes for the saints to make sacrifices for the good of their fellow-men, that the honorable ones of the earth, perchance, may be saved. This is one of those times."

It was about this time that the B. H. Roberts case came to a head. Roberts, a polygamist, had been elected to Congress in 1898 causing a national furor. A petition against his being seated had been circulated around the country and was reportedly signed by seven million people. The Roberts case aggravated the split within the council. Some felt he should not have run even though he had received permission from the First Presidency. Others, Rudger included, supported him. In January 1900 Congress finally voted overwhelmingly to deny him his seat. The Roberts case was an early skirmish in the battle that lay ahead.

By the end of January, Rudger was off on another trip, this time to Arizona to attend the quarterly stake conference in St. Johns and to discuss the serious agricultural and financial problems facing the community.

Situated in the eastern part of Arizona in a stark but sometimes beautiful setting, St. Johns was plagued by a scarcity of water and by a soil containing minerals and alkalai that rendered it poor for agriculture and made the scarce water unfit for drinking or cooking.

The Saints there had spent $65,000 on canals and reservoirs but repeated droughts made them useless. They were discouraged and broke and were suffering the usual persecution from the Arizona gentiles. Even though the St. Johns Saints had not asked for help, the church had decided to send Rudger and Apostle Heber J. Grant to attend the quarterly stake conference to discuss ways in which the church might be of assistance or, if the situation was hopeless, discuss possible new areas for colonization.

During the stake conference, church members expressed their discouragement, but stated over and over that they did not want to leave. Rudger and Grant assured them, nevertheless, that (if necessary) they could do so with the approval of the church. For those who remained, Rudger offered a long prayer invoking the blessings of the Lord and asking Him to heal the waters in St. Johns Stake.

Stake President David K. Udall, was especially discouraged. The Saints had labored hard, been faithful to their religion, paid their tithes, and done everything they could to solve the water problem. But without results. Their principal reservoir was as yet unfinished, leaving them at the mercy of the droughts that had plagued them for the last few years and with no answer to the alkaline soil.

But Udall had other problems as well. He was on the verge of declaring bankruptcy. He could not pay the mortgage on his farm, and the owner, Henry Huning, had foreclosed and taken possession, though Udall had the option to redeem it. What was worse, a grist mill standing on the farm and the water rights that were attached to it, were the key to economic health in his community, Round Valley. These issues were aired in several long meetings in St. Johns on January 31, 1900. The residents were convinced that if Udall's farm went to the "enemy," Henry Huning, they would all have to move away.

In a discussion with the visiting apostles, Udall recounted that President Woodruff had some years ago promised them $5,000 to assist in building the reservoir, but that they had only received $2,500.

He wondered if it would be proper to apply for the balance. Rudger and Grant thought it would be.

To solve the problem of the Udall property in Round Valley, Grant, who was a businessman and had had his own experiences with indebtedness and near insolvency, had a plan. If the people who depended on Udall's mill would be willing to put up their own homes as security, Grant felt he would be able to obtain on favorable terms a loan with which they could redeem the Udall property. Grant had in mind approaching his friend, A. W. McCune, a financial magnate who had made his money in mining and utilities and was owner of the *Salt Lake Herald*. He had also run for the Democratic senatorial nomination in 1898 with Grant's active support.

The next day they went to Eagarville in Round Valley, ten miles away, to look at the Udall farm and conduct an evening meeting at the ward house. Afterward they returned to the Udall home in St. Johns where they met his family, including Udall's attractive and rather forthright twenty-year-old daughter Pearl. Pearl had recently completed the teacher training course at Brigham Young Academy in Provo and was teaching school in St. Johns at the time. Rudger led the family in prayer before they all went to bed.

After leaving Eagarville, they drove to Thatcher, somewhat south of St. Johns and then entrained for Mexico. Rudger and Grant finally returned to Salt Lake, arriving on March 2. On Thursday, March 8th, they reported to the council on the situation in Arizona and strongly recommended that assistance be given to the people of St. Johns. "After some discussion, it was unanimously decided that one-half of the tithing paid in that stake for the year 1900—approximately $4,500—be appropriated to assist them." Rudger and Grant wrote

Udall and his brethren telling them the good news and noting that they were also making progress with the loan on Udall's property. "The question of raising the $10,000 necessary to redeem the Udall farm is under consideration with fair prospects that the money can be raised. Brother Grant expects to make an effort to secure the money from Mr. McCune at a lower rate of interest than it would be possible to obtain it from any other person or persons. We are convinced that if we borrow from a bank or other corporation, that at least 8% will have to be paid for the money, while McCune may let it go for 5 or 6%."

Udall's reply sounded as if he thought the apostles had accomplished a miracle. "We recognize an overruling Providence in the way relief has come to this Stake of Zion, and we know that the Lord has heard and answered the prayers of his servants and Saints. And to you our dear friends and brethren, we will always feel deeply grateful for the great interest you have taken in our welfare. . . . This appropriation of half the tithes of this stake for the year 1900 is more than we could have conscientiously asked for. . . . Your late visit will always be remembered as one of the brightest spots in my life, in fact I feel that at that time a new era dawned upon me and my household. It is really marvelous the way I have been able to make turns and cancel my indebtedness. I still have faith that the way will open so that I will not have to go into bankruptcy."

Udall's friends did acquire the property, which thwarted Huning, much to everyone's satisfaction. But Udall was never able to buy it back and eventually moved to St. Johns.

This story did not really end until the next July when Grant returned from another visit to Arizona. The reservoir had been completed some months before, but the water had remained alkaline. Now, however, Grant said, the Lord had answered Rudger's prayer and "the waters of the reservoir have been healed and the alkalai is disappearing from their fields. Verily, the Lord is good to His people." (In one St. Johns Stake meetings when Rudger was there, they discussed the problem extensively and decided it was probably due to poor drainage. Some work on their drainage systems may have given the Lord an assist in this case.)

The tithing campaign moved on apace. At a meeting of the priesthood in April, Snow held up one of Rudger's books, which he said contained 10,000 names of people who had not paid their tithes. The total number of non-tithepayers, he said, was 30,000. He also announced that the forty-two stakes of the church would be divided up among the twelve apostles and that each apostle would have direct responsibility for seeing that the tithes in their stakes were paid in full.

Rudger was given Box Elder, Malad, and Davis and threw himself energetically into the campaign. He also made a more characteristic contribution. He prepared a form on which each bishop would record the name of the non-tithepayers in his ward and the reasons given for not paying, which were "many and varied and generally of a flimsy character." And at the annual spring conference of the authorities, he stressed the importance of keeping records, not only of those who did *not* pay their tithes, but of those who did, so they would be given their "proper credits" and have their names "enrolled in the Book of the law of God," that they may be worthy of receiving eternal inheritances in the Kingdom of God." If this sounds as much like a bookkeeping transaction as it does a religious exhortation, it was simply Rudger Clawson bringing his own special perspectives to bear on the problem.

✺ ✺ ✺

One day in March 1900 Rudger sat down and calculated his earnings for the previous nine years. They amounted to $10,000, which comes out to about $1,100 a year, or $90 per month. If he had stayed in Salt Lake and taken the $100 per month job, with his brother Spencer, that was awaiting him when he was released from prison, he would have earned more money than he did in Brigham City, even if his salary had not increased during the entire time.

His earnings improved when he took up his apostleship, but not by much. At the time he was ordained, some apostles were receiving salaries and some were not. The salaries of those who did ranged from $150 to $250 per month. Francis Lyman and John Henry Smith were at the high end of that scale, while Rudger was at the low end.

Rudger of course was not without other means during this time. Shortly before taking up his apostleship he had entered the insurance business in partnership with Homer Rich. By the spring of 1900 he was bringing in about $300 a year, though a year later he sold out to

Rich who felt that Rudger was not able to give the business the attention it needed to continue to be successful.

Rudger also invested money in a sheep farming venture with his brother-in-law, Samuel Spencer. The extent of Rudger's total income, however, remains cloudy. He, like most of the other members of the quorum, was extensively involved in the businesses which were owned by the church, in which the church had an interest, or which a member of the quorum owned.

As seen during the Brigham City years, Rudger was always ready to explore an investment opportunity, though he rarely noted any substantial returns from the investments made. He continued investing, after becoming an apostle, in the wide and diverse business activities of the church. They did not appear, however, to be any more profitable for him.

Rudger also kept the books of a number of companies, but again most of them were ones in which the church and/or Lorenzo Snow (and, subsequently, Joseph F. Smith) as trustee-in-trust had an interest. Rudger usually worked on the books "in the president's office" so that it is probable that doing them was considered part of his church responsibilities for which he received his $150 salary. He did, on the other hand, get paid for keeping the books on the Utah Coal Company—at a rate of $10 per month.

Finally, he, like most of the other members of the quorum, served as a director on the boards of a number of companies: Lewiston Sugar, Salt Lake Knitting Works, and Utah Light and Power among them. While in earlier times it had not been usual for church authorities to receive payment for serving on boards of directors, by 1900 it was common, though the salaries were modest for any one directorship. Rudger's income was no doubt supplemented by his membership on corporate boards, both those of church-owned and non church-owned businesses.

Early in 1899, Frank Cannon, who saw his own political career being undermined by Snow and others in the quorum called a public meeting in Salt Lake. Before a large crowd he attacked the "Pharisees" and "Financial Apostles" who were presently in control of the church and accused them of selling their political influence.

But the appellation doesn't really fit Rudger Clawson though he was certainly the financial right-hand man of those who were Cannon's targets (particularly President Snow). He did not engage directly in politics and despite his directorships he rarely became involved in the management of a church-owned industry. The record shows that over the years he demonstrated little aptitude for business, and the financial affairs of his family were left mostly in the capable hands of "Sister Clawson." But he was very much caught up in the business side of the church and often his diaries read more like the minutes of the meetings of a board of directors of a large company than the record of an ecclesiastical body.

The church in fact *was* a large financial institution and had been for many years. Brigham Young had recognized the need for the church to play a major economic role in the development of the Latter-day Saint community in their mountain retreat. Had it not done so, the Saints, as they attempted to build the Kingdom of God, would have been vulnerable to the control of outside commercial interests. By the turn of the century, however, the church was rapidly being forced to give up its goal of becoming an economically independent nation-state and was finding it increasingly difficult to compete in business with the gentiles.

Nevertheless, the church still owned, controlled, or influenced (through apostolic board membership) a vast array of businesses including salt, railroad, sugar, mining, and insurance companies, banks, ranches, utilities, a woolen mill, and a newspaper (the *Deseret News*). The president of the church was nominally president of most of these and, in the case of those owned by the church, ran them more or less as he chose.

The church leaders were not eager to give up the power and revenue accessible to them through their business holdings. From the outset of his presidency, Snow reined in church finances tightly, and, while consolidations and some strategic divestments occurred, there was general agreement that the church should remain commercially engaged.

At a long meeting in April 1899, called to discuss an offer from an Eastern businessman to buy Saltair Beach, a lake resort owned by the church, Snow had asked each of the apostles to express an opinion as to what they should do. Not only were they uniformly opposed to that sale, most made it clear that they were opposed in general to the church disposing of its properties. Rudger said that "he regretted to see enterprises inaugurated by our people go into the hands of the gentiles. We lose prestige and influence." George Q. Cannon put it most bluntly, saying that "he had always been opposed to selling out our enterprises." He mentioned the early railroads, as an example and said "it was a mistaken policy." Joseph F. Smith expressed it particularly vividly at a council meeting in the second year of his presidency. As Rudger recorded it: "President Smith expressed himself strongly to the effect that we must hold on to the enterprises in which the church is interested, otherwise, we will become like the other sects of the day. God does not so design. We must be men of affairs in building Zion." It was a doctrine of profound importance in the history of the church.

They did, however, have to recognize their limitations and to solve pressing problems, which included the consolidation or divestment of enterprises that were a burden to them or which could be better managed within other arrangements. Such was the case with Bullion, Beck, and Champion Mining Company which had once been prosperously managed by Hiram Bradley Clawson. The mine had come upon bad times and was near bankruptcy. The apostles were worried that it would fall into the hands of the gentiles, but Snow refused to bail it out. Instead, he arranged for the church-owned Zion's Savings Bank to meet with Bullion, Beck officials to work out a financial solution.

Sugar was another matter. Sugar production—from the sugar beet— was a major industry in Utah and in the Mormon communities in southern Idaho. The church was the principal owner of one of the major companies, Utah Sugar, and was concerned with sugar production in general because of its importance to the economic welfare of its members. During these years the church's holdings in the sugar industry expanded and contracted, but always ended up substantial and were closely tied to the sugar trust which controlled much of the production and was dominated by Eastern interests.

In 1903 a group of Mormon businessmen started a new company which was viewed as competing with the sugar trust and being in opposition to the church and Joseph F. Smith. In an obvious political maneuver they recruited Rudger and Abraham O. Woodruff—two of the newer, younger, and more naive members of the quorum—for the. company's board of directors. Rudger accepted before he knew what was happening and then had to chart a wary course to avoid being caught between the competing forces, at least until they had worked out their differences and—in keeping with the monopolistic practices common at that time—joined into an even bigger trust than before.

The church remained heavily involved in the sugar industry in the years that followed. When Apostle Reed Smoot took his seat in the U.S. Senate in 1907, protection of the sugar industry was high on his agenda. The Smoot-Hawley Tariff for which he became famous—or infamous—was, according to his critics, designed specifically for that purpose, and his dedication to the industry ultimately won him a second sobriquet (he was already known as the "apostle of protection")—"sugar senator." He made an irresistible target for a Will Rogers lampoon: "Lot's wife (or somebody in the Bible) turned around to look back and turned to Salt. If Reed ever glances back, we are going to have a human sugar bowl on our hands."

In the end, Rudger's role in the financial affairs of the church, as bookkeeper and maintainer of the records, was relatively small but extremely important. There was a mountain of financial paperwork to be done and Rudger, while bearing his full share of responsibility as a "traveling high counselor," applied himself assiduously to doing it.

The life of a Mormon apostle circa 1900 varied, of course, from man to man. None seemed to have been as heavily involved in office work as Rudger. Most spent more time on their personal business affairs. But they all shared the responsibility for overseeing the stakes and wards in the far-flung Mormon kingdom. Their lives consisted, in part, therefore, of long trips of the kind Rudger took to Canada and Mexico. His trip in March 1900 to Arizona covered 4,000 miles and involved him in fifty-six meetings.

But more typical was a week beginning on a Friday morning in May of that year, when he went to Farmington, Utah, to attend the monthly priesthood meeting of the Davis Stake. He arrived in time for a 2:00 p.m. meeting, with Stake President Hess presiding. It opened with singing by everyone and then a prayer by Patriarch John Thornley and a roll call. Attendance was "fair." President Hess spoke on the importance of missionary work and then the stake counselor said the call had been made for missionaries to go abroad; especially needed were experienced Saints who would not have to attend missionary school. Rudger made a few remarks on the sacredness and power of the priesthood and how dangerous and unsafe it was for anyone to speak against the Lord's anointed. He also spoke briefly on the law of tithing. Then there was more singing and a benediction by Elder Ezra T. Clark and the meeting was adjourned. At 4:00 p.m. Rudger attended the meeting of the stake presidency where he spoke on the question of how to deal with nontithepayers. There were approximately 290 in the Davis Stake who did not observe the law of tithing and the responsibility for converting them was on the ward bishops. He suggested a plan whereby the bishops would use the forms he had devised for reporting their labors, which the bishops accepted.

Rudger returned to Salt Lake at 5:00 p.m. that night, where he found Lydia not feeling well. He put the children to bed and read to them from the Bible. At 10:50 p.m. he and Apostle Joseph F. Smith took the train for Montpelier, Idaho, to attend the Bear Lake Stake conference in nearby Paris. They were met by the local bishop at the train at 8:15 a.m. the following morning and, after breakfast at the bishop's house, they arrived in Paris in time for the 10:00 a.m. opening session. Singing, prayers, and opening remarks were made by Stake President William Budge. After reports by various church stake officers, Rudger spoke for thirty minutes on the importance of these quarterly conferences, stressing that all stake officers should attend and outlining the duties of a bishop. There was singing and a benediction before adjourning for lunch.

The attendance was much larger at the afternoon conference, which opened with singing and prayer. Then a number of Saints gave testimony to their faith: Elder James Hart called attention to the many good works of the Saints such as building temples, tabernacles, and academies and said there was no such word as "can't" in the vocabulary of the gospel. Elder John Bagley rejoiced in his membership in the church and bore testimony to the truth; Elder Hyrum Rich said he was thankful he had been born in the church and thankful for the pioneer life and the blessings now enjoyed by the faithful. Elder John Sutton rejoiced in the work of the Lord and said he had great respect for the priesthood. There was singing, followed by Smith giving an account of his recent trip to Houston, Texas, and Mexico. He spoke of the native Mexicans, descendants of the Lamanites who had been conquered by the Spanish and their spirit broken which resulted in their becoming peons or "beasts of burden." But he reminded the brethren that the Lord had promised their forefathers that they would be restored to His favor and pointed out that Porfirio Diaz, the President of Mexico, was a fine man and looked favorably on the church.

After supper, Rudger attended the meeting of the local Young Men's Mutual Improvement Association, where he spoke on the gift of the gospel and loyalty to the cause. The next morning was Sunday and he and Smith called on President Budge and administered to his wife, Lizzie, who was "troubled with heart disease." Clawson anointed her, Smith confirmed the anointment, and they both blessed the Budges' daughter who was "afflicted with an unnatural swelling on her throat." *Thyroid scrofula* At 10:00 a.m. he attended the Second Ward Sunday School and made a few remarks. The conference was continued at 11 a.m. in the Paris Tabernacle, where President Budge spoke about their desires to complete the stake academy now being built and called on the brethren for an additional $7,000 in contributions. He stressed that this money should not interfere with their tithing payments. As Rudger noted, Budge made "something of a considerable exhortation on his subject." Then Smith endorsed what Budge had said, ending with a few comments on the advantages of theological training and the beauty of morality. After the meeting, Rudger anointed Sister Krage for her failing health and eyesight and Smith "sealed" the anointment.

At 2:00 p.m., Sunday, the conference was continued and Rudger gave them the message straight from Salt Lake City, which he recorded in his diary: "Spoke of the authorities present as being watchmen upon the towers of Zion and that it became their duty to lift up a voice of warning against evils existing among the Saints—sins of commission or sins of omission. Said that President Snow was the Chief watchman on the towers of Zion and had lifted up a voice of warning to the Latter-day Saints that were not observing the great law of tithing. He had visited many stakes to deliver this message; he called a Solemn Assembly of the priesthood to deliver it. As a result of his labors and the labors of his apostles, $300,000 more tithing was paid to the Church in 1899 than in 1898. . . . nothwithstanding the good showing, some 10,000 members of the church were reported as nontithe payers. President Snow . . . placed responsibility for correcting the evil on the shoulders of the apostles. We were now endeavoring to discharge that obligation."

Smith had a few more words to say on tithing, urging the bishops to pass among their people after they left and see that the tithe was paid.

Rudger had supper with President Budge and his family and then attended the Mutual meeting that night and spoke on how the gospel had been served by the anti-Mormon crusade, the confiscation of church property, and the B. H. Roberts case. Then Rudger and Smith were driven by horse and buggy to Montpelier, where they stayed with Bishop Clark until they boarded the train for Pocatello at 3:45 a.m. He was back in Salt Lake by Monday night and spent Tuesday working on the church books in the president's office. Wednesday, he and Lydia traveled to Brigham City to attend a program at the Brigham City Tabernacle. He was back in Salt Lake by 8:00 p.m. and ready for the regular Thursday meeting of the Presidency and the Twelve.

It was a typical week and obviously not very exciting. But, except for a three-year interlude which he would spend abroad as the head of the European mission, it would be his life for the next forty years.

In August 1900, Lydia gave birth to her sixth boy, Francis Marion, named after Rudger's close friend, Apostle Francis Lyman. Gay was "somewhat disappointed," according to Rudger. Actually, as the only surviving girl among the children, Gay received special attention from her father. Later she remembered her early years as a happy time when she was "Daddy's pet."

The birth of Francis Marion was not difficult, but several days afterward Rudger stayed home with Lydia because she was "weak and suffering more or less from her heart."

Then in the fall he was off again to Canada, this time with Francis Lyman, and the surveyor, Fewson Smith. They departed in mid-October. The weather was more severe this time as were, apparently, the activities of the devil. At a stop in Butte, Montana, Rudger discovered "great wickedness. I passed as many as twelve houses of ill-fame on one block, at each window was stationed a prostitute, dressed in gaudy colors with her face painted and powdered excessively, beckoning to the passerby in male attire to come in and pass the night with her. There were abundant indications that these fallen women were all patronized." McGrath, in Canada, was not any better. A proliferation of saloons was threatening the work of the Lord, and he advised the Saints "to set their faces as flint against the saloon evil." If they did not, and refused to repent their sins, the Spirit of the Lord would search them out. "The voice of the Lord is unto all men," he warned, quoting the Book of Covenants, "and there is none to escape and there is no eye that shall not see, neither ear that shall not hear, neither heart that shall not be penetrated."

One reason Rudger and his colleagues had to return to Canada was to settle claims the church was making against the canal company. Church leaders charged the company with owing the laborers $9,000 which the church had guaranteed to them. The president of the company arrived in his private railroad car, and after several days of negotiating (with Lyman doing most of the talking, supported by facts and figures supplied by Rudger and surveyor Smith), they reached a settlement in which the company gave the church some land and a check for $2,383.24.

On the return trip they encountered a blizzard so severe that the company had to provide a special train from McGrath to Stirling. In Stirling, where Rudger had to deliver some important letters to the local bishop, it was so cold that on a short walk to the bishop's house he was convinced he would have frozen to death had he not been wearing a "coonskin fur coat." They finally arrived in Salt Lake and presented their report and the check to the president, who "heartily approved" their work.

In later years, Rudger's children frequently commented on the degree to which he had been an absent father. It was true, the life of a Latter-day Saint apostle was by nature an itinerant one. It was the apostles' responsibility to watch over the church wherever it was implanted, at home and abroad. It was to them that lower church officials were expected to turn for counsel and they had to be available to give it. And if the apostles expected to know enough about what was going on in the stakes and wards to minister to them, then they had to be visited. It was a sensible and effective system in a hierarchical church and had a powerful effect on keeping the flock together since the president and prophet was spoken to by God and the apostles brought God's word directly to the faithful. But it did take a fearful toll.

"Dinner at home," Rudger wrote one Sunday. "First time for several weeks."

Being a Mormon apostle was no sinecure, least of all for Rudger Clawson—even when he *was* in town. As he wrote late in the evening of December 26, 1900, punching wearily at the keys of his typewriter: "*Salt Lake City*. Cloudy and cold. I was busily engaged all day on the books of the Utah Coal Co. Besides this work I am keeping the books of the Brigham City Roller Mill Co. and also from time to time am getting up financial statements relating to the condition of the church. These things added to the requirements made of me as an apostle are almost more than I can attend to. As it is, I often work until ten and eleven-o-clock at night."

But despite the degree to which he was absent—even when in town—Rudger was not neglectful of his family. Sprinkled liberally through the pages of the diaries are notations on what he did with them. "In the afternoon took the family for a ride." "Went with Lydia and the children to Saltair [or Calder Park]." "Took Rudger, Lydia, Samuel and Lorenzo on a 'seeing car' to view the city." He also took the children to such entertainments as the county fair and the circus ("The animal show was very good").

He took Lydia on outings and to concerts, operas, and more popular entertainments, but his—and one hopes, Lydia's—first love was the theater. He, with Lydia or alone, attended plays the way a film buff would attend movies in later decades, often several in a week, occasionally even on successive nights, seeing such favorites as *Camille*, *Julius Caesar*, *School for Scandal*, and *The Fall of Santiago*. He would even work a play in amid a long day at the office. "I was engaged all the forenoon on President Snow's private books. At 2:00 p.m. went to a matinee at the theatre. *The Sign of the Cross* was the piece given. The attendance was crowded and the interest manifested by the audience was very great. It is truly a thrilling drama. . . . After leaving the theatre, I went to the President's office and worked from four till seven on President Snow's books."

As for Lydia, there is not a great deal more in Rudger's diaries about her than there was during the Brigham City years. We know she continued to earn money sewing as she had in Brigham City, and she took in boarders. Rudger mentions times they went somewhere together and faithfully reports her accidents and illnesses. At one point she was on the verge of developing pneumonia, and Rudger was "working hard to prevent the threatened evil." Shortly after that she stepped on a nail and her foot swelled up. He came home to find that she had called in a doctor to "draw out the bad blood" and prevent blood poisoning.

Another time, one of the children accidentally kicked her in the breast. A lump appeared and persisted to the extent that Rudger was worried about cancer. They "worked assiduously" to reduce the swelling, applying hot water and linament, and she took "iron and wine for her blood." The swelling abated, but then she contracted "La Grippe." The trouble with her breast continued until May when the pain—accompanied by "weakness and tendency to fainting"—was such that they called in a doctor who predicted the swelling would soon "gather and break." Rudger offered to cancel an impending trip to San Francisco in order to be with her, but she insisted he go. On his return, she indeed was better; the swelling was almost gone.

It is perhaps significant that on two occasions doctors were called in to treat Lydia. It had only been the year before that Rudger wrote of the illness of Elder Elmer Loveland who lived in Loa in Box Elder Stake and who "is suffering from a cancer in his breast and throat, which is growing very fast, and without help would undoubtedly soon kill him. Patriarch Blackburn has the gift of healing in a marked degree, and it was for the purpose of putting himself under his care and ministrations that Brother Loveland had gone to Loa. . . . After a visit of only a few days Brother Elmer was greatly improved with fair prospects for complete recovery to health notwithstanding that, in the opinion of many and especially doctors, he would surely die. I am watching the case with great interest."

Unfortunately, he does not comment subsequently on the fate of Brother Loveland. But his skepticism about doctors appears to have yielded in the face of Lydia's need.

The church as a whole was also yielding. In 1882 the Deseret Hospital had been established by the Relief Society, and in 1893 President Woodruff took steps endorsing medical practice. It created a dilemma that George Q. Cannon expressed straightforwardly in 1893 when writing in the *Juvenile Instructor*; "Children who are taught by their parents to desire the laying on of hands by the Elders when they are sick, receive astonishing benefits therefrom, and their faith becomes exceedingly strong. But, if instead of teaching them that the Lord has placed the ordinance of laying on of hands for the healing of the sick in His Church, a doctor is immediately sent for when anything ails them, they gain confidence in the doctor and his prescriptions and lose faith in the ordinance."

Later Joseph F. Smith would counsel simply that when faith doesn't work, call a doctor—especially as opposed to depending on quacks, fakirs, and peddlers of cure-alls and patent medicines. As time went on, leaders came to thoroughly recognize the value of medicine. During the very time Lydia was experiencing these health problems a debate was raging over smallpox vaccinations, with the *Deseret News* taking the traditional church stand in opposition, especially to compulsory vaccinations. Lorenzo Snow, on the other hand, favored it. While Rudger no doubt continued to believe in the power of faith to heal, he acknowledged the services doctors could provide. After this time, in contrast to the Brigham City days, the Ordinance of the Lord's House is referred to very little in his diaries, and when the great tragedy strikes later, he can only bow in the face of the Lord's will.

Rudger remained close to the Clawson family, visiting his parents often and joining the periodic large family gatherings. On Christmas Day 1900 (squeezed in between days at the office): "We all called in to see Grand-papa and Grand-mama Clawson. All of Mother's children and grand-children were there—some 36 grandchildren in all. We spent a very pleasant evening. The children were much amused by selections from the graphophone and Punch and Judy."

As did many polygamous families, the Clawsons arranged great gatherings, such as the one on his father's seventy-sixth birthday held at the ward meeting hall and including his two living wives, twenty-eight children and a hundred grandchildren. Rudger and his brothers also formed a family organization to arrange family social activities.

Rudger saw his brother Stanley and his half-brother Fred, both of whom were dentists, with some frequency and invested $250 in his half-brother Selden's yeastless bread-making machine. "It is the purpose of the invention to revolutionize bread making . . . if it proves to be of any value at all, [it] will undoubtedly be a 'big thing.' "

He also mentions frequently his sisters, Tessie Grosbeck and Birdie Wells, whose death, as we have seen, affected him deeply.

Among his brothers and sisters, however, the person with whom Rudger had most contact was Spencer Clawson. Spencer had assisted Lydia financially while Rudger was in prison and then had forgiven the debt. There is a nice letter from Spencer written from New York (and copied into the diaries) in which he congratulated Rudger on his appointment to the quorum.

Spencer seems to have been perpetually in financial trouble and during one period was heavily in debt to the church. Several times Rudger intervened with Snow and the council in an effort to help him out, and on one occasion personally asked Reed Smoot to guarantee a debt Spencer had with Eastern creditors which threatened to sink his business.

In the spring of 1901, two deaths occurred which were important to Rudger. On April 12, George Q. Cannon died. Cannon was an experienced, intelligent man who had been a wise leader in the church for many years. He not only applied his wisdom and experience to the affairs of the church, but served as a valuable counselor to the younger apostles as well. His death also left a vacancy in the First Presidency, which, during the months that followed, Rudger and the other apostles waited expectantly for Snow to fill.

Later in the month, baby Francis Marion, teething at the time, came down with a severe cold. He died on April 28 while Rudger was in Logan attending a stake conference. "He was a bright and beautiful boy. Though young, it can be said of him that he had a sweet and lovable disposition."

Despite his heavy load, Rudger enjoyed serving his friend and spiritual mentor. As he told the apostles in one of their quarterly unity conferences, he had "great pleasure in assisting President Snow in keeping posted regarding the financial condition of the church. Through reports furnished by myself, he was familiar with all the obligations of the church, the receipts and disbursements and revenues and expenses of the church for each year. This information relieves his mind of great anxiety for the reason that surprises never confront him."

One day in early May 1901 a surprise did confront him, but it was a pleasant one and had been engineered by Rudger himself. Rudger had drawn a careful projection of the church income and expenses for the next few years and could tell Lorenzo that if he lived until the end of 1904, he would see the church out of debt. Lorenzo asked how this was possible. Rudger explained that the financial statement for 1900, which he had just completed, showed that church indebtedness had been reduced to $1.2 million and that its annual excess of income (mostly from the increased tithes) amounted to $600,000 more than church expenses. By allocating a minimum of $300,000 of that excess to debt retirement each year from 1901 through 1904, the church would be out of debt at the end of that time.

Well, said Lorenzo, "if that is the case and I live that long, there will be a jubilee in the Temple of thanksgiving and praise to the Lord such as has never been seen there."

&ast;    &ast;    &ast;

Rudger Clawson's diaries are not simply a source of information about their author and what he did and the time in which he lived. In the very keeping of them Rudger also tells us a great deal about himself. Whether his meticulous attention to recordkeeping derived from its theological implications (Joseph Smith had had a revelation which called upon the Saints to keep histories of their time on earth) or for other reasons is not certain, but he, like many if not most of his fellow apostles, assigned great importance to it. Early in the journal he began in Brigham City, he wrote of his "deep and abiding regret having neglected this duty and privilege so long, but am now resolved with a fixed determination to rectify the neglect so far as possible, and ever keep a record of my life. Should these words come to the notice of my children, I trust they will seek to avoid the error I have fallen into and be led to appreciate the importance of keeping a journal. Every young man and young woman should begin early in life to keep a journal."

It was clear during his early years on the Council of Twelve that this conviction had not diminished. If anything, keeping a diary was more important than it had been in Brigham City since now he was reporting the work of the church's governing body where, through the president, God's word was revealed directly to them.

The regular Thursday meetings of the Presidency and Quorum of Twelve make up many of the most interesting entries, although in his first years as an apostle he followed Snow's advice and listened more than he spoke. It is clear, however, that he was a devoutly loyal follower and endorsed almost every decision made by his brethren. If he disagreed, he did so in the mildest terms. Even in the privacy of his diary, he virtually never expressed vigorous dissent or disagreement with them. Only on the question of polygamy when the church disavowed it did he refuse to bend with the wind.

In writing up the meetings he noted the substance and tenor of each member's comments and followed debates through to their resolution, or, as was often the case when there was any disagreement, to their referral for decision to the First Presidency.

But there were other records that concerned him as well. The church historical records were in poor condition, and he repeatedly suggested that all the stake presidents and ward bishops be urged to take a personal interest in seeing that their records be preserved. The situation was so serious that he proposed that the church proclaim a "Records Day," on which the president of a stake would visit his wards and examine the ward's records. The apostles approved this idea and Rudger drafted a letter to the stake presidents and prepared the necessary forms.

He had written the diaries in his graceful longhand for eight years when he announced that his father had given him a new "Blichensderfer typewriter"—probably a present on his birthday a month before. He had gone to Stringham's Store for instructions on its use and intended, "as soon as this book in which I am now writing is exhausted, to use the typewriter for writing up my journal. When I shall have written 300 or 400 pages I will then have them bound." And, indeed, he did, though he did not get around to binding them all. The last thousand pages were found in a box, unbound, at his death.

One of the values of switching to a typewriter was that it made it easier for him to keep his brethren who were overseas, especially Heber J. Grant in Japan and Francis M. Lyman in England, informed of what was going on in the council.

It is in sending what Rudger calls "leaves" from his diary (carbon copies of pages describing council meetings) to Lyman that the close personal friendship between the two men is revealed. Lyman was a big, strong man, energetic and good-natured. He was the son of Amasa Lyman, an early apostle and later an excommunicant and member of the Godbeites. Francis had been with the Saints who fled persecution in San Bernadino at the time of the Utah War and the Mountain Meadow Massacre. He had been a businessman, political leader, and president of Toole Stake. He was a polygamist who had taken his third wife in the Endowment House in Salt Lake in October 1884, only a week before Rudger went on trial, and later served eighty-five days in the penitentiary for unlawful cohabitation. He was thirteen years older than Rudger and had been a member of the quorum since 1880. They were both very personable men, and each had a good sense of humor, which may have attracted them to each other.

In May 1901, Lyman had been assigned to the presidency of the Latter-day Saints European Mission in Britain. He and Rudger corresponded frequently during the two and a half years he was there.

Rudger's letters—which usually accompanied the "leaves" from his diaries—were filled with expressions of warmth and praise and always closed with a very personal comment. He ends one long letter: "Hist, my brother it is now 10 p.m. and sleep, 'nature's sweet restorer' claims my attention. I go to dream of thee and thy success. Good night. Affectionately, Rudger."

Rudger also sent "leaves" from his diary to Heber J. Grant who was head of the Japan Mission during approximately the same period Lyman was in England.

Then in October 1901, once again, but for the last time, Lorenzo Snow intervened in Rudger's life in a way that would affect its course—or at least should have. Snow had not filled the vacancy left by the death of his first counselor, George Q. Cannon. In October, at the general conference he decided to act. Between conference sessions, Rudger called on his friend at the Beehive House. The aging president appeared feeble and was wheezing from a bad cold, but he said that he intended to go to the conference that afternoon because he wanted to present Rudger's name as his second counselor.

After citing Rudger's accomplishments, Snow, with a weak smile concluded: "I remembered, when this appointment [to Box Elder] by President Woodruff and the brethren was made known to you and you were greatly agitated and said, 'If I am chosen as president of the stake, what shall I say? I cannot preach.' It was a very great trial to you, but you were blessed and sustained of the Lord and by your labors were pleasing and acceptable to him. I have thought about these things and the Spirit of the Lord whispers to me that I am to select you for one of my counselors."

Rudger was duly impressed and said that he could only accept the position because he knew the Lord would qualify him.

Despite his ill health, a sky outside full of heavy black clouds, and a chill wind that threatened a storm, Snow did go to the conference. Here, speaking softly and with great effort, he delivered a sermon which was so filled with foreboding that it seemed to reflect the darkening heavens outside; then he announced that his second counselor, Joseph F. Smith, would become first counselor and that he had chosen Rudger as his second counselor.

The conference sustained Rudger's appointment unanimously, whereupon he told his brethren what he had told Lorenzo, that he knew this was the work of God, otherwise he could not accept the appointment.

But apparently God changed his mind. Snow's cold turned into pneumonia. Three days after Rudger had been sustained as second counselor (but not set apart), his friend and mentor died. Rudger was one of the principal speakers at the funeral and he took the occasion to remind his brethren that they were "in the midst of great change." He said he was looking at a picture taken a few years ago of sixteen church leaders—Snow among them—who had labored to build the Kingdom in the desert and of the sixteen, "13 of these stalwarts had fallen. The word of God moves on in majesty and power. It is the work of God and not of man, and God would have the Glory." He also noted that at the last meeting at the temple, attended by President Snow, the choir had sung his favorite hymn 'Shall We Meet Beyond the River?' and when it was over, the president rose and said: 'Brethren and sisters, I say to you: We Shall Meet Beyond the River.' "

Until that time, however, things on this side of the river were moving fast. Four days after the funeral, First Counselor Joseph F. Smith arose at the regular Thursday meeting and said he did not want to seem premature but felt it was urgent that the First Presidency be reorganized immediately. Brigham Young, Jr., endorsed the proposal and nominated Smith, who was the senior member of the quorum. His nomination was approved unanimously. Then after suggesting that they sustain Young as president of the quorum, Smith announced that he had picked his two counselors—Bishop John Winder as first counselor and Apostle Anthon Lund as second counselor. Young, Winder, and Lund were all sustained unanimously.

Rudger was obviously stunned by the turn of events. When he wrote that day to Francis Lyman in England, he said, "The death of our much beloved President Snow was indeed sudden and no less sudden was the reorganization of the First Presidency."

A week later, after Smith had appointed his twenty-nine-year-old son, Hyrum, to the vacant apostleship, he wrote Lyman again: "Verily, we live in a fast age, the world moves with celerity, and the Church moves like 'lightning.' "

"Yet all is well," he added.

Despite his obvious and understandable disappointment, Rudger did not record in his diary any sign of bitterness or resentment. Joseph F. Smith, however, was aware of the affront to Rudger. Traditionally the counselors of a president had been retained by his successor. On a number of occasions in the months following his assumption of the presidency, Smith referred to his choice of counselors. "I thought over the matter night and day," he said in December at a gathering in the temple to celebrate John Winder's eightieth birthday "and prayed earnestly to the Lord. I asked him who his choice was and over and over again the names of John R. Winder and Anthon H. Lund came to my mind. I had thought of other brethren. Brother Clawson was here in my mind. I looked upon him as a martyr who had faced death for the cause of truth unflinchingly and bravely . . . President Snow had confidence in him and felt to honor him. I also felt to honor him and desired that he be one of the Three, but the Spirit of the Lord whispered that it should be otherwise."

But Rudger was a loyal soldier. Shortly after the dust had settled he requested authorization from Smith to close the books of the church for the year 1901.

Snow's failure, for whatever reason, to remove from Brother Jack the responsibility for the books had prevented the introduction of orderly accounting methods and seriously hampered the auditing committee in its effort to keep track of the church's financial position. Smith was fully aware of the problem and gave Rudger the authority he requested.

Rudger went to work. By March he could report both that the books were in order and that they showed the church with a surplus of a million and a half dollars at the end of the year. But arriving there had taken a small palace coup. As he described it (in the third person): "During Brother Jack's absence in California, [Rudger] had balanced cash at the President's office, the first time in nine months, and had introduced a simple method of his own by which a daily balance is taken, and weekly reports of the receipts and disbursements are furnished to the Presidency. The title of James Jack, Treasurer, had been abolished and all checks are now signed by Jos. F. Smith, Trustee-in-Trust."

☆ ☆ ☆

In January 1902, Joseph F. Smith made a decision that would lead to one of the most celebrated political controversies in Mormon, if not American, history, and raise a storm that would break over the church like a tidal wave and shake it to its foundations. He decided to allow Apostle Reed Smoot to run for the United States Senate.

When Reed Smoot became an apostle on April 8, 1900, he had already distinguished himself as a businessman and financier in Provo. He had made his money in a variety of industries: retailing, wool manufacturing, contracting, banking, and buying and selling sheep and cattle. He was also active in politics and was considered to be the leading Republican south of Salt Lake. Smoot was a thin, tense-looking young man with firmly set lips. In the questions and remarks addressed to him at the time of his ordination, the First Presidency and the council members clearly reflected their interest in and concern over his political potential.

"Apostle J. H. Smith," Rudger wrote in his diaries, "asked Elder Smoot if he accepted Lorenzo Snow as the leader of the church and as having the right to counsel him in all things. He answered yes, but further remarked that he was of a positive nature, and when he saw and felt a thing to be right, it was hard for him to change and see it differently. Pres. J. F. Smith remarked that the Presidency and apostles were all constituted that way, but sometimes it became necessary to change our views. Pres. Snow said a condition like this has prevailed, namely, that there are men in the church who have stood out against the combined judgment of the [church leadership]. This, he said, was damnable and had in some measure grown out of the spirit of the devil in politics." He was clearly referring to Moses Thatcher and B. H. Roberts.

In 1896, at the penultimate moment in the drive for statehood, when the Enabling Act had been passed but not yet signed by President

Grover Cleveland, Roberts and Thatcher had run for office (Roberts for the House and Thatcher for the Senate), on the Democratic ticket without obtaining permission from the First Presidency. They were criticized, first privately and then publicly, by Joseph R. Smith (a Republican), whereupon church interference in politics became a controversial and pivotal issue in the campaign. Thatcher and Roberts openly defied the church; others charged the hierarchy with partisan Republican motives. Ultimately, they were both defeated. In the aftermath Roberts, a first president in the Seventy, repented and returned to the good graces of the hierarchy. Thatcher, an apostle, did not. A long history of conflict with other members of the council had embittered his relationships with his brethren. When a "political manifesto" was drawn up stating the obligation of church authorities to clear any action to seek or assume political office with the First Presidency, Roberts signed but Thatcher refused and was stripped of his apostleship. Since that time all the apostles had been expected to seek counsel, as far as running for political office was concerned, and Reed Smoot was no exception.

It was not long before Smoot would be put to the test. By fall his political ambitions had surfaced, and he had asked Snow's permission to run for the Senate seat that had been left vacant in 1899 when the legislature, caught in the flux of bizarre forces—Mormon, gentile, Republican, Democrat—failed to elect a senator. Snow put the matter before the council in December. The response of the apostles was for the most part positive since "the gentiles already had two Congressmen from Utah and it is thought that the Mormons are justly entitled to the third." Smoot was sent to Washington to test the waters and confer with Republican leaders. They were impressed with him, but they made it clear they favored Thomas Kearns, the non-Mormon million-aire and owner of the *Salt Lake Tribune*, for the Senate in 1901. They felt it was too soon to nominate a high church official. It had only been the previous January that B. H. Roberts (having run then with official church approval for the House of Representatives and won) had been denied his seat in Congress because he was a polygamist. Even though Reed Smoot was a monogamist, it was too risky. The Republicans did not want a battle in Utah that would weaken the party there, which was just getting back on its feet after being thrashed by William Jennings Bryan and the Democrats in 1898. Despite the fact that the *Tribune* regularly published scurrilous attacks on the church and its leaders, Snow decided to support Kearns in order to forge a link with the Republican leadership in Washington. (There was also speculation that Smoot and Kearns had come to an agreement. Smoot would support Kearns in 1901, and Kearns would return the favor in 1903.)

Snow summed up his feelings about Smoot and Congress in some remarks that probably would have prevented Smoot or any other Mormon from *ever* holding national office if they had been repeated outside the quorum. "His [Smoot's] duty as an apostle is of greater importance and responsibility than that of a senator. It would therefore be far better for him to remain and magnify his present calling than go to Washington. There will be opportunities for Brother Smoot and other Brethren present [probably a reference to John Henry Smith, who also had senatorial ambitions] to go to Congress in the future and also to occupy high and important positions in the government. The president of the United States and those associated with him and the members of Congress are our children. God has given them into our charge and we must plan for their welfare. We will have control among the nations in the due time of the Lord."

Smoot, promised his chance later, dutifully accepted the decision (Snow's "counsel"), and Kearns was elected.

When Joseph F. Smith became president of the church after Lorenzo Snow's death in 1901, there was a substantial change in the image the church presented to the outside world. Smith was outspoken and combative, more in the style of John Taylor than Wilford Woodruff or Lorenzo Snow, both of whom preferred to work more subtly and behind the scenes than Smith (though Smith did mellow as the years wore on).

When, in 1902, Reed Smoot called in Snow's pledge of support for a run at the Senate seat held by Democrat Joseph Rawlins, Smith gave it, despite strong advice to the contrary. His advisors were aware that sending to Congress a member of the highest ruling body of the church risked raising again the whole issue of church dominance over the large body of the American electorate which constitutes its membership. Whether they also perceived the degree to which, in electing an apostle—even a monogamist one—they risked reviving the polygamy issue, is not clear. In any event, what is certain is that Joseph F.

Smith was not afraid to throw down the gauntlet before the United States Senate. It was a decision he would come to regret.

Whatever lay ahead, Rudger Clawson, at this point in time, had more mundane things on his mind. He and Lydia had decided to build a new house on their property, which had been increased in size by the purchase of a contiguous piece of land. It was an ambitious plan which involved turning their old home into a rooming house. "The rooms are of such dimensions we could easily put in 11 beds, all told, which, if rented to lodgers at reasonable rates would bring in a nice revenue."

In February 1902, Rudger and Lydia negotiated a formal financial arrangement of a kind that from this time on would be common between them. "Now, as to the manner in which the means shall be raised," he wrote in his diary, "Lydia has long desired a new home. She has about $2,000 in cash [ from an inheritance from her father] and can raise, she thinks, about $500 more, and this added to $1,000 [to be borrowed] will meet the cost of the new home complete— namely $3,500." Rudger agreed to deed her the land to build the new house on and to pay back the borrowed $1,000 from revenues from the rental of the old home. He also offered to pay for the whole thing—"The husband should provide the home," he said. But Lydia refused.

"The statement concerning the building of our new home, as now under contemplation, and as above set forth, is correct in every particular," he concluded.

Lydia was tired of living in No. 49. It was an old pioneer home without electricity or other modern conveniences. She had lived for too long in old houses constantly under renovation. She wanted something new and constructed to her specifications.

They wasted no time. Three days later their architect called and reviewed the plans with them, adding and changing as required. "He then said he could build the house . . . according to plans and specifications for $3,036," and would complete it within ninety days.

Lydia supervised the construction each step of the way to assure that she got the home of her dreams.

Lydia enjoyed telling her daughter, born a year later, about how she had supervised the building of the house. As the daughter subsequently told the story: "The workmen labored and fumed under her proddings, no doubt exasperated at themselves for getting into such a mess, yet fascinated with the whole business. With the cleverness of a woman who can fix anything with a hairpin, she would tell them how to solve tricky problems of construction, then praise them and bring them hot doughnuts and milk in reward. They all learned to love her and were among those who trailed to the back door for years to sit in the rocker [in her kitchen] and laugh over the building of the new house."

On June 2 the house was finished and they began moving in. In the final accounting, Rudger had contributed the land (worth $1,000) and $562 in furnishings. Lydia paid the rest, and Rudger duly deeded the property to her. "The old home still belongs to me," he noted, "and will be of great value for renting purposes" which turned out to be quite true.

Meanwhile, in the council, the apostles were having their annual debate over Saltair Beach, which was the favorite summer resort of Rudger and his family—along with thousands of others living in the Great Salt Lake valley. *Why ??*

Built in 1892 by the church to provide a wholesome resort and "control in some degree" the amusements pursued by the young, Saltair was billed as the "Coney Island of the West" and was touted as having the largest dance hall in the world. Designed by Richard Kletting, who had been strongly influenced by Middle Eastern architecture, Saltair looked as much like a gaudy mosque as it did a beach resort. It was constructed out over the water on 2,500 wood pilings driven into the lake bed. The central structure was a huge, domed dance hall, similar in design and appearance to the Salt Lake Tabernacle. It was fronted by a great arched entryway and surrounded by ten onion-domed towers over which ensigns blew in the wind. At night the whole structure was outlined in electric lights and stood like a fairyland palace hovering over the waters of the lake. To either side of the main building, two-story wings stretched in long semicircles into the lake.

Saltair offered a variety of amusements but swimming or floating in the Great Salt Lake and dancing in the grand pavilion were the most popular. People rented swimsuits and changed in the bathhouses, which lined the wings, and then descended into the lake down wooden stairs.

The church owned 50 percent of Saltair and controlled its management. But they faced a dilemma. If they allowed the sale of liquor, they violated their professed principles as codified in the Word of Wisdom. If they did not, they lost money. / /

During Lorenzo Snow's tenure, liquor was sold because he could not risk another losing investment. Virtually the entire membership of the quorum disapproved, and, one day when he was absent, voted unanimously to recommend that he stop the sale of liquor "as an experiment." He refused.

But Saltair had other problems too. The stirrings of change that would be the hallmark of the early twentieth century were being felt in Utah as they were elsewhere in the nation. The Mormon church, even with something as attractive as Saltair, could not control the amusement of the young. "The problem was not only drinking," said Apostle George Teasdale. "There is an evil practiced at Saltair almost if not as great as liquor, and that is the indiscriminate association of the sexes in bathing."

Brother Anthon Lund was worried too. "It seems that a wave of immorality sweeps over Zion. In a certain ward in Sanpete Stake, sometime ago, the bishop informed him that out of 12 marriages during a period of six months, 7 were forced."

Reed Smoot also spoke of "almost a total disregard for the Word of Wisdom" in one of the stakes he had recently reorganized, and a "tendency among the young people of that stake . . . to commit themselves before marriage." (At a meeting sometime later Rudger would contribute to the list of evils besetting Zion: disregard of the Sabbath. "The evil in this case has taken the form of Sunday riding in the afternoon and evening.")

By the summer of 1902, Joseph F. Smith had replaced Snow and Saltair went dry—which only drove people to competing amusement parks. Apostle John H. Smith reported that "a strong effort is being made to induce our young people to visit the Lagoon and Calder's Park. The latter place, he said, "is a veritable hell-hole. It is said that some 400 people there upon a recent occasion were intoxicated." Joseph F. Smith added "that there were a class of men among us who sought the destruction of young ladies who visit that resort by getting them intoxicated and then taking them into the bushes."

At Saltair, the change showed at the gate. At a later meeting Joseph

F. Smith reported "a wonderful falling off of patronage." The situation was irremedial. Rudger recommended certain improvements (such as extending the bathhouses out to the water, which had receded from the original structures) as a solution. But these not only failed to improve the situation, they increased the losses. Saltair was eventually sold to the Western Pacific Railroad.

In May, amidst the heated discussions about Saltair, Reed Smoot had announced his candidacy for the Senate. From the outset he encountered strong opposition, especially from Kearns's *Salt Lake Tribune*. If Kearns and Smoot had made any agreement, it became clear as the campaign wore on and Kearns formally came out against him that Smoot had been double-crossed. When the Republicans swept the November election and captured the state legislature, the issues surrounding Smoot's candidacy became more critical since Republican candidates now had the inside track. The campaign heated up and the church leadership threw its weight behind Smoot.

Even Rudger—as apolitical as he was—became involved, supporting Smoot at church meetings in Brigham City and probably elsewhere. Just before the election Rudger had dinner with Smoot in Provo on the latter's forty-first birthday. Kearns was making a last-ditch effort to stop him and marshaling big names to do it, "The legislature is about to convene," wrote Rudger, "and it is expected that Elder Reed Smoot will be elected United States Senator. A strong effort is being made to defeat him, President Roosevelt having sent word to the Utah Legislature through Senator Kearns that he hoped an Apostle would not be sent to Congress. If this be true, and the papers so report the matter, it is an unwarrantable interference on the part of the President, and deserves to be treated with cold indifference (as doubtless it will be)."

Smoot, if not quite indifferent, did treat coldly Roosevelt's effort to untrack him, an effort undoubtedly engineered by Kearns.

Eleven days later, Smoot won handily on the first ballot. Though very different in personality, Rudger and Apostle Smoot were relatively close. This was the result in some degree of working together on the auditing committee that oversaw the church's bookkeeping system. Smoot admired Rudger's skills and the good sense he brought to financial management.

It was Smoot who, ten days after his election to the U.S. Senate, called to the attention of his brethren that Rudger was still being grossly underpaid. Rudger had just completed presenting the report of the auditing committee for 1902, "which was an exhaustive statement of the financial condition of the church." After the council's acceptance of the report,

> Elder Smoot arose and said that he felt that there were some contradictions in reference to the compensation allowed to the clerks in the President's office, as for instance, Brother Jas. Jack is receiving $225 per month, and Brother David McKenzie, assistant book-keeper, is receiving $200 per month, while Bro. Clawson who has been engaged in closing and reopening the books and directing how the work should be done, as well as furnishing complete reports of the financial condition of the Church, is receiving only $150 per month. He did not think this was right, and felt that it should be rectified. Felt that Brother Clawson should receive at least $200 per month.
>
> Elder Teasdale expressed himself similarly to Elder Smoot and moved that the matter be referred to the First Presidency for their action. Carried by unanimous vote.

Rudger does not tell us whether or not he received his raise. One suspects he did.

The Smoot election, as expected, brought out the critics, with the Salt Lake Ministerial Association, which had been the original source of the petition against B. H. Roberts, again taking the lead. The basic charges were (1) that Reed Smoot was a member of the ruling hierarchy of an autocratic church that governed its followers in all matters thus uniting church and state and (2) that the hierarchy of this church encouraged the secret practice of polygamy—both of which charges were close enough to the truth to rekindle the old controversy. (One leading minister went further and accused Smoot himself of being a polygamist—which was not true.)

The storm was soon raging countrywide, stirring anew the anti-Mormonism that had been so disastrous for the church in the years before 1890. In March, Smoot went to Washington where the Senate had been called into special session and at which newly elected senators—including, to the surprise of many, Reed Smoot—were sworn in.

His supporters in Utah were delighted. His opponents, however, in Utah, Washington, and elsewhere around the country were only driven to greater fury, which increased over the ensuing summer months. Battle lines were drawn for the impending conflict.

As August came, Rudger Clawson prepared to go on another trip to Arizona and his own appointment with destiny. This time he traveled with Joseph W. McMurrin, a member of the First Council of the Seventy, who had achieved some renown during the antipolygamy crusade when he was shot by a deputy marshal. Now McMurrin traveled regularly to outlying communities to oversee missionary and priesthood activities. A prominent churchwoman, Aggie Campbell, accompanied them.

They departed on August 14, 1903. The trip lasted two days and three nights, as the train made its way eastward through the Rockies into Colorado and then south to New Mexico and, finally, to Holbrook, Arizona. "The journey was delightful in every respect," noted our inveterate traveler.

After a conference in Snowflake, they went by team to St. Johns. Stake President David K. Udall joined them along the way. It was a warm reunion between Rudger and Udall, who was still grateful for the efforts that had been made on his behalf three years before. He had never been able to buy back his farm, but he had managed slowly to pull himself out of the financial quagmire he'd been in.

That evening Rudger attended a ball sponsored by the Young Men's and Ladies' Mutual Improvement Associations. Here he renewed his acquaintance with Udall's daughter, Pearl, who was now twenty-three and teaching at Thatcher, a town some distance south of St. Johns. "A very select company of young people had gathered," Rudger wrote, "and seemed thoroughly to enjoy themselves. Good order was maintained, and a spirit of sociability rested upon all. To me it was a very pleasant and enjoyable affair." Afterward they visited a wedding in the Mexican quarter of town and then went back to the Udall home for ice cream. Rudger said the evening prayer.

Pearl, who was an officer in the YLMIA, had come to attend the stake conference taking place that weekend. In the morning the men's and women's groups met separately, and Rudger attended the young men's meeting. At noon there was a joint session of men and women and a picnic. Then in the evening there was another joint session. At some point during the day, one of the young women spoke to the group about her belief in plural marriage. Later, on his return to Salt Lake, Rudger would describe it to the council:

> Notwithstanding the fact that many were under the impression that the principle of plural marriage is dying out in the hearts of the people, he [Rudger] could testify that such was not the case in those southern stakes of Zion. The spirit of it seems to be working upon the hearts of the young people. One young woman in the St. Johns Stake of about 18 years of age speaking for herself and a number of companions of the same age, said that they would much prefer to take a married man in the church who had proven his faithfulness and integrity than to marry a single young man who was untried.

It is not certain whether the speaker was Pearl (who was much older than eighteen but who was also the only single woman on the program) or someone else. But it clearly reflected Pearl's feelings.

A close relationship developed rapidly between her and Rudger. Pearl was a lovely young woman, deeply religious and strong-willed, herself a child of a plural marraige. At forty-six, Rudger was handsome and engaging. His heroism in Georgia was by now legendary, and he was an apostle, much admired in St. Johns, who embodied the religion to which they were both devoted. Perhaps as important, his culture and religion allowed him to pursue a relationship with a young woman which in another context would have carried a burden of guilt and social disapproval.

Whatever their feelings for each other, Rudger, as usual, was unable or unwilling to express them in his diaries. Indeed, he never mentioned Pearl by name at all. What he did—here in Arizona and during the next ten months—was note in cryptic, mysterious statements the course of their relationship.

The first such statement appeared in an entry dated Sunday, August 23, two days after the MIA meetings. That evening he wrote: "Note: I will here say that at the close of the morning service I had a very important interview with Pres. Udall upon a subject of vital interest, the nature of which I do not care to mention at this writing."

It was at this meeting that he broached to her father his interest in marrying Pearl.

Given the secrecy with which from the outset Rudger surrounded his courtship of Pearl Udall, it is impossible to thoroughly assess his motives. The fundamental rationale for his action, however, was unquestionably his absolute and unwavering belief in the doctrine of plural marriage. Why he waited nineteen years after Florence Dinwoodey divorced him to reenter it is uncertain. But one thing is clear. As the new tempest over plural marriage was breaking around him, Rudger Clawson, with characteristic unconcern about the consequences, launched himself not only directly into the storm, but ultimately against the church to which he had, over and over again, in public and in private, pledged his total loyalty.

Pearl's father was receptive. He himself was a polygamist and had only the previous April taken a new plural wife in a ceremony performed by Apostle Matthias Cowley.

Three days after his interview with Udall, Rudger and his party went to the railroad station in Holbrook to catch the train south to El Paso and Mexico. The train was four hours late. "However, the time was not altogether lost, for it gave me an opportunity to revise my journal notes and rule up, and also to write an important letter, which was afterwards mailed at El Paso, Texas, a copy of which will be found among my papers [it was not]."

After the visit to Mexico, he returned to Arizona for more church meetings in Thatcher, where he was again able to spend time with Pearl.

Pearl had been born June 20, 1880, to David K. Udall and his first wife, Eliza (Ella) Stewart. It was the same month that Udall was called by President John Taylor to be bishop of the St. Johns Ward in Arizona, a small colony of fifty or so pioneer Mormon families. The site, on the Little Colorado River, was an oasis amid otherwise desolate country. When they first arrived, there had been several years of unusual rainfall and the region around St. Johns was covered with range grass and seemed fertile. But in the years after, alternating droughts and floods, combined with the alkaline soil, made the area one in which survival was an omnipresent issue. In May 1882 Udall married his second wife, Ida, and then in 1885 served a little less than four months of a three-year prison term. As elsewhere in Mormondom, it was a time of conflict between Mormons and gentiles, here complicated by difficulties with the earlier Mexican settlers as well. Ida had gone on the underground for much of the time between 1883 and 1892, which frustrated those who wanted to prosecute Udall for polygamy. They convicted him on an essentially trumped-up charge of perjury instead.

In 1887 Udall was set apart as president of the newly organized St. Johns Stake. In this environment Pearl Udall grew into a lovely young woman with wavy, honey-brown hair, and a sense of dedication both to her church and to other people.

The two families increased in size and during the 1890s lived on a farm in Round Valley. It was remembered as a happy time working together to make a go of a difficult economic situation. Then came the financial problems which were besetting Udall in 1900 when Rudger and Heber arrived.

During Udall's difficult economic times, his family, including Pearl (who was teaching school by 1903) and the other girls (many of whom also became teachers) worked and made contributions from their salaries to the family finances. In 1903 they assumed responsibility for the debt owed on a plot of ground in St. Johns where the Udalls hoped to build a new home. During the summer they started a successful ice cream parlor (the product of which they shared with Rudger on his visit) and were able to pay off the note by September.

Rudger returned to Salt Lake on the 25th of September and reported to the council on the trip at the next regular Thursday meeting. It was then that he told them about the spirit of polygamy being alive and well among the Saints in Arizona.

When the meeting was over, the First Presidency (Joseph F. Smith, John Winder, and Anthon Lund) withdrew, at which point Apostle Marriner Wood Merrill, though he was ill and earlier in the meeting had apologized for not reporting on his work because of "bodily weakness," stood and addressed the group. Around him in their thick comfortable chairs were nine of the apostles, John H. Smith, Hyrum Smith, George Teasdale, Heber J. Grant, John W. Taylor, Matthias F. Cowley, Abraham O. Woodruff, Reed Smoot, and, of course, Rudger Clawson. They all still believed strongly in the doctrine of plural marriage and its continued practice by those whose marriages predated the 1890 Manifesto. A number, George Teasdale, John W. Taylor, Matthias Cowley, and Abraham Woodruff in particular, had supported the taking of new plural wives despite the Manifesto. Even Reed Smoot would not become an opponent of plural marriage until it threatened his Senate seat the following year.

Merrill, who had just turned seventy-one was also strong in his belief in polygamy. He had solemnized plural marriages in the post-Manifesto period and had taken a plural wife in 1901. Merrill was a businessman who had been president of the Logan Temple since its completion in 1884. He was stout and had a friendly face, round and rather soft. He was known as a man of few words, who spoke in a low but firm voice. "He bore testimony," Rudger wrote, "to the truth of the principle of plural marriage and said that the brethren of the Twelve should lay the foundation for their kingdoms in their youth, and not wait until old age comes on. If we have a kingdom, we must ourselves lay the foundation for it; we could not expect to inherit somebody else's kingdom. Brethren, he said, do not neglect your opportunities. Otherwise, you may fail in securing a kingdom. This advice is for Brother Hyrum, and Brother Rudger, and Brother Woodruff. Those who will avail themselves of the opportunity when it opens up, will be crowned with glory and exaltation in the presence of God."

It is not wholly clear why these three were singled out. A. O. Woodruff had a plural wife whom he married in 1901 (after the Manifesto). Rudger had had one in the past and, perhaps more important, was, as we shall see, a confidant of Merrill's, so that it is probable that Merrill already knew about Pearl. The main target appears to have been Hyrum Smith, President Smith's son. Hyrum was a monogamist. If he could be persuaded to become a polygamist, it would provide a certain amount of insurance against Joseph F. Smith ever taking serious action to bring polygamy to an end.

Whatever the rationale, the timing of Merrill's comments was strikingly appropriate for Rudger who now had the blessings of his intended wife, her father, and the church (via Mariner Merrill) for his reentry into celestial marriage. All he needed—according to the protocol of Mormon polygamy—was Lydia's approval. He obtained that ten days later. "On Saturday [October 10], I talked with Lydia in relation to the subject of plural marriage, and she expressed a willingness for me to take another wife provided that I should not take the step without her knowledge. I assured her that in case such a step were taken she would be fully advised."

The air of mystery created by his interest in taking another wife seems to have pervaded his life at this point—or at least it does in his diaries. A few days later, he went to Brigham City to work on the roller mill books. "While there I had an important talk with Justin D. Call in regard to a matter of great concern as affecting his welfare." The next day "a young man called to see me on important business." These statements are utterly uncharacteristic of Rudger, who always expressed himself explicitly no matter what the subject.

But the mystery continued. "I was engaged during the day," he wrote soon after, "mostly, in writing a very important letter, the nature of which, I do not care to mention here."

Then just before Christmas, "I spent the day at the president's office. During the day, I received a very important letter, the contents of which made me very happy. I also sent away to a 'special friend' an important Christmas package."

The mystery, of course, is justified in terms of the resurging debate over polygamy, especially relative to new marriages. But why mention these events at all, especialy getting Lydia's approval?

Perhaps it stemmed from Rudger's instinctive flair for drama, imbibed from his mother and father at the footlights of the Salt Lake theater. He did enjoy the dramatic. His daughter would describe it many years later. "Father was a minister by profession and a thespian by inclination. He would often make a dramatic entrance into a room, throwing the door open with a grand gesture and giving his best quote from Shakespeare. With a lack of appreciation for his performances, Mother had dampened much of his enthusiasm by the time I arrived."

Another question is why at this point in time Rudger decided to take up the practice of plural marriage once again.

During the years in Brigham City when he was under the tutelage of Lorenzo Snow, the issue of Rudger's reentry into polygamy did not—at least in any of his writings—arise. Snow himself was opposed to the continuation of polygamy, though others in the leadership were not.

Wilford Woodruff and his two counselors, George Q. Cannon and Joseph F. Smith, continued to believe in and practice polygamy as did most of the other apostles. They continued to cohabit with their plural  wives, and they authorized new polygamous marriages, especially outside the U.S. Where earlier polygamists had gone to Mexico in large numbers to escape the crusade, now they were advised to go there to take polygamous wives in officially sanctioned ceremonies.

When Lorenzo Snow succeeded to the presidency, church policy changed. Snow believed that God had removed the privilege of plural marriage from the Saints. He himself cohabited only with Minnie now. He announced both privately and publicly that plural marriages would not take place during his administration.

But simple pronouncements, even from someone as venerable as Lorenzo Snow, could not settle this issue. For many of the apostles, polygamy and celestial, or plural, marriage was still both a fundamental religious doctrine and a moral issue. They felt bound not to abandon their wives whether cohabiting with them or not. They believed one's place in heaven depended on the size and nature of one's family on earth. They would not give up that belief easily, nor were they willing to absolutely prohibit their brethren from expanding their families even if they themselves did not wish or need to.

So Joseph F. Smith and George Q. Cannon, apparently for the most part without Snow's knowledge, continued to authorize plural marriages. They countermanded an order from Snow to end the sealings in Mexico, and they also gave permission, most notably to Apostle Matthias Cowley, to have them performed in the United States.

When Joseph F. Smith succeeded to the presidency after Lorenzo's death in 1901, the stage was set for a new burst of plural marriages and for an intensification of the conflict between the Saints and the rest of the world. The gauntlet he had thrown down in supporting Reed Smoot was willingly picked up by the Senate. When the Committee on Privileges and Elections began its hearings on the unseating of Smoot early in March 1904, Joseph F. Smith was the first witness.

At the outset Smith stated unequivocally: "It has been the continuous and conscientious practice and rule of the church ever since the Manifesto to observe that Manifesto with regard to plural marriages; and from that time till today there has never been, to my knowledge, a plural marriage performed with the understanding, instruction, connivance, counsel, or permission of the presiding authorities of the church."

The statement was, of course, false. Not only had church-countenanced plural marriages taken place since the Manifesto in 1890, they had been on the increase since 1901 (the year of Joseph F. Smith's accession) and had reached a peak in 1903. Even more important, they had taken place among members of the church hierarchy.

Later, Rudger would write that Smith's testimony was a "wonderful thing" because appearing before a Senate committee gave him the opportunity to show the gentiles that he was a prophet of God and leader of a church that enjoyed the spirit of revelation, a testimony which became "part of the records of the Senate for all time to come."

It is doubtful that the prophet agreed. His trip East to testify was a more earthly revelation.

He had been questioned intently for three days by a sometimes courteous, sometimes hostile, and sometimes incredulous committee. Smith admitted to breaking the law by cohabiting with his wives, but denied, against all the evidence, that he had anything to do with Smoot's election or had ever engaged as a church official in politics. He described the extent of the church's commercial and financial interests, revealing it as an institution which could hardly be viewed by his audience as other than a substantial center of economic power. Finally he proclaimed that his was the only church that possessed the divine authority of the priesthood and the fullness of the Gospel of Jesus Christ and that he, and only he, received revelations directly from God regarding the true church.

His testimony created a sensation in Washington and in the newspapers, especially when he was followed by a stream of people who testified under oath about church-sanctioned, post-Manifesto marriages and in other ways contradicted Smith's testimony—or reinforced the negative impressions he was generating. From the faces of his interrogators and the response to his testimony, Smith had driven home to him that to the rest of the country "the self-perpetuating body of fifteen men" (the president, his two counselors and the twelve apostles) was an un-American, autocratic dictatorship that totally controlled the economy of Utah and the thoughts and actions of the Latter-day Saints and defied the law of the land, not only in practicing but in officially sanctioning and perpetuating the practice of plural marriage. Smith returned from Washington clearly shaken.

With the spotlight on them and the pressure mounting, it was clear that some definitive statement from the church was called for. The result was another Manifesto, this one issued by Joseph F. Smith at the annual conference early in April 1904. It declared that plural marriages had not been solemnized with the sanction of the church and, more important "that all such marriages are prohibited, and if any officer or member of the church shall assume to solemnize or enter into any such marriage he will be deemed in transgression against the church, and will be liable to be dealt with according to the rules and regulations thereof and excommunicated therefrom."

The day before, in a meeting of the council, Smith's new manifesto was discussed. Anthon H. Lund recorded in his diary that Rudger spoke against it. He "feared that it would do no good but make many hearts ache."

Rudger, perhaps more vulnerable after the passing of Lorenzo Snow, had once again been swept up by forces that were beyond his control.

# CHAPTER 7
# CRISES
# AT MIDLIFE

*I* gnoring what would soon be called the Second Manifesto, Rudger continued his courtship of Pearl Udall, exchanging "very important letters" with her regularly during the winter and spring of 1904. In May she came to Salt Lake to receive her endowments. Returning home early one Monday morning from Lehi, where it had been raining, Rudger noted in his diary (probably clacking away on his typewriter as the train made its way north through the valley) that he had "a very important meeting at 10 a.m." and was "concerned about the weather." It wasn't until several days later that he recounted what happened that day. "I came home from Lehi Monday morning and during the day walked up on Ensign Peak. The weather for a few hours was reasonably fine and I much enjoyed the view." So, one hopes, did Pearl. He saw Pearl again three days later, and five days after that he "made a call on a friend from the south."

Soon thereafter Pearl left for California to visit her sister Louella in Los Angeles.

In mid-May, Rudger traveled north to Smithfield for a conference, stopping off to visit Marriner Merrill who was still ailing. Rudger administered to him, and later noted in his diary, "We had a very interesting conversation. He blessed me and said that the desires of my heart would be realized."

225

The phrase, "the desires of my heart," suddenly casts Rudger's courtship of Pearl in a different light. Polygamy is so often treated as a theological and political issue that the personal relationships involved are sometimes ignored or obscured.

Rudger Clawson was not only attempting to secure his kingdom in the life to come, but he was deeply in love here on earth.

The "very important" letters that took him a whole afternoon or an entire day to write were not long epistles on the celestial glories of plural marriage, they were love letters, and they took so much time to write because they included long, carefully composed love poems to Pearl.

Shortly after her visit to Salt Lake in May he wrote:

### In the Month of May

I do not know what skies there were,
Nor if the wind was high or low;
I think I heard the branches stir
A little when we turned to go;
I think I saw the grasses sway
As if they tried to kiss your feet—
That day to-gether, sweet!

I think it must have been in May;
I think the Sunshine must have shone
I know a scent of Springtime lay
Across the fields, we were alone.
We went together you and I;
How could I look beyond your eyes?
If you were only standing by
I did not miss the skies!

I could not tell if evening glowed,
Or noon-day heat lay white and still
Beyond the shadows of the road;
I only watched your face, until
I knew it was the gladdest day,

The sweetest day that summer knew—
The time when we two stole away
And I saw only you!

The poems are about love, nature, religion, and God—sometimes all together. They are poems of devotion, sentiment, romance, and homey truths, and are companion pieces to his love letters from the penitentiary.

Rudger collected these poems carefully, writing them out in long-hand in a notebook which he dated "September 12, 1906."

After May the references in his diary to the unidentified Pearl end without explanation. This may have been related to the fact that his friend, Francis Lyman, who had returned from England in January, had been given the responsibility by the First Presidency to see that the Second Manifesto was enforced. In July Lyman wrote to one of the more dedicated polygamists, George Teasdale, "Every member of our council, must sustain the stand taken by President Smith and must not talk nor act at cross-purposes with the Prophet. What has already been done is shaking the confidence of the Latter-day Saints. We are considered as two-faced and insincere. We must not stand in that light before the Saints or the world. The Presidency hold me responsible to see to it that the members of our council be thoroughly advised that we will not be tolerated in anything out of harmony with the stand taken by President Joseph F. Smith before the Senate Committee on the subject of Plural marriage. We must uphold his hands and vindicate the Church."

George Teasdale and Rudger Clawson were, of course, not alone in their resistance to the Second Manifesto. Matthias Cowley, in particular, could not be shaken in his belief in the truth of the doctrine of plural marriage, and he continued to solemnize such marriages after the Second Manifesto. Cowley was a short, stocky man, always well-groomed with a dark, neatly trimmed beard and carefully combed hair. He was soft-spoken and rather gentle by nature and was especially well-loved by Rudger.

It was Cowley who was awaiting Rudger and Pearl Udall in Grand Junction, Colorado, on August 3, 1904. Here he married them for time and all eternity.*

---

*It is believed by members of the Udall family that sometime during April or May

Three weeks later Lydia negotiated a formal agreement with Rudger which provided her with the financial security which she may have felt was jeopardized by Rudger's taking a second wife. In it Rudger agrees to give her "from his church appropriation" $135-a-month along with the rents from the "old homestead, No. 49 - Canyon Road, Rear." Lydia for her part agrees to "meet and pay all the household and family expenses whatsoever (including the taxes)" excepting Rudger's personal expenses. A signed carbon copy made on Rudger's typewriter appears in his papers; presumedly Lydia was given the original. The striking thing about the agreement is how formal and legal it is in appearance. But it was quite significant in the history of the Clawson family because it served as the foundation on which Lydia built her financial "empire" which, as we shall see, later played such an important role in the lives of her children. Having now entered a plural marriage not only after the first manifesto, but after the second as well, Rudger was very vulnerable. The risk of excommunication had to be considered. Notations in a diary could, if they fell into the wrong hands, be quite damaging. Rudger probably realized that.

So did the First Presidency. The question of the security of the private journals kept by many of the council members had arisen over the years. Francis Lyman felt it was important to keep a journal ("If we don't write our own history . . . nobody will"), but others were nervous about what would happen if they got into the hands of the wrong people. Since virtually all of them kept some sort of journal, comments in the quorum were generally limited to cautioning each other to make sure they were deposited with the church historian at their deaths.

Then in October 1904, the issue came to a head. The diaries of George Q. Cannon, who had died in 1901, and his son, Abraham H. Cannon, who had died in 1896, had not been left to the church.

<hr />

1904 Rudger and Pearl were married by Los Angeles Stake President Joseph Robinson aboard a ship sailing between Los Angeles and Catalina Island. (Other prominent Mormons had been married in that fashion so as to be able to say they were not married on American soil.) A careful examination of Rudger Clawson's diaries during that period shows no mention of a trip to Los Angeles, and there is no time left blank when such a trip might have occurred. Unless Rudger falsified his diaries, which is highly unlikely, the best inference is that he was married in Colorado in August.

Joseph F. Smith brought the matter up in a council meeting on October 4.

> Pres. Smith said that he wanted to refer to a matter that had given him much concern namely, the private journals of the brethren of the Council. Many things are written in them which if they were to fall into the hands of the enemy might bring trouble upon the church. After the death of the brethren, you cannot tell what may become of their journals, and even now the brethren felt an anxiety in relation to Pres. Geo. Q. Cannon's journal, who made a pretty full account of everything that transpired in the Councils of the brethren; the same with Abram. Cannon.

Other apostles agreed. Then "Pres. [John H.] Winder noted that it be the sense and feeling of the Council that the brethren should not write in their journals that which took place in the Council meetings. Carried by unanimous vote." That evening when Rudger wrote Heber Grant, who had replaced Lyman as the head of the European Mission, there was a note of sadness in his announcement of the council's decision. "You will see by the 'leaves' of to-day that I am debarred from writing in my journal the doings of the Council, which of necessity debars me from sending you any further 'leaves.' I regret this exceedingly, but of course you will see the wisdom of the Council's action in the matter."

Other members of the council did not interpret this ruling strictly, but Rudger did. Thereafter he makes no record of the substance of council meetings.

As we have seen, his references to his new wife had also disappeared. But one more document surfaced in his papers after his death which did shed valuable light on his relationship with Pearl.

It had been folded to a small rectangle like the love letters smuggled out of the pen to Lydia and had been inserted in some tight place, perhaps a wallet, where the creases were pressed sharp and the exposed surface blackened over time. It was a carbon copy, typed on a half sheet of plain paper, and dated "at home October 17, 1904." It said:

> Dearest Z:-
> Did you receive my letter of Sep. 29th, and did you answer it? If so, your letter has miscarried, for it is several days past due.
> Whether it has miscarried or not, I think it would be a good idea to change the name occasionally. Don't you? So when you write me again

address the letter to Alexander Stevens, No.67-East South Temple St. [the church president's office] and I will be sure to get it. Don't forget. . . .

I'm looking for a letter daily, but if it has miscarried, of course, I shall not hear from you until this note reaches its destination.

I trust you are well and happy, and, believe me, I pray for you always— that you may be brave and fearless, yet wise and prudent, in the dark hour of trial. A crown of resplendent glory awaits the soul that has been tried and tested and found not wanting. You are now facing the supreme trial of your life. Be patient, be hopeful, be happy, and glorify the Lord in your heart, however bitter the trial may prove to be. And remember this, there is an eternity before us in which to work out our destiny. Let that thought be bright within you during all your present troubles.

I send you the choice love of one who loves thee and seal it upon thy lips with a kiss.

A

P.S. Remember, Alexander Stevens

The "A" at the end was handwritten in Rudger's careful script. And attached to it was a small photo of an attractive young woman, Pearl Udall.

Though unable to comment on two of the most important parts of his life, Rudger continued to keep his diary faithfully—at least he did for another year.

And even then it was not the restrictions placed on him by the council or his entry into the no-man's-land of plural marriage that brought to an end the journal-keeping of this inveterate diarist. It was caused by a convergence of forces at work in his personal life which came to an explosive head in a tragedy involving his especially beloved son, Rudger Remus.

Rudger Remus was enrolled in the business course at L.D.S. University (which was actually half-high school, half-college). He was an energetic, restless, nineteen-year-old, engaged, as young people his age frequently are, in searching for himself. He had a thin face with relatively sharp features, harking back to Daniel Spencer, his grandfather, more than to the Clawsons. Sporting a wide-brimmed Stetson, he looks in his photos a little wan and mysterious, as if there were some secret about himself he wanted you to guess at.

His personality emerges rather vividly in the diary he kept for the first seven months of 1904. He "bummed" around with his friends, patronized the "bubble shop" (a young people's gathering place), went bowling at Saltair, attended football games, hung around an auto shop where a friend worked, "sluffed" classes, and plied himself with candy and other "junk." He occasionally smoked cigars and drank a great deal of beer with his friends at their homes, though from time to time he would also have one with Lydia at lunch, presumably when his father wasn't there. He chased girls and, like his father, enjoyed dancing, though perhaps for different reasons ("made Rhea hot," he wrote after one episode).

But Rudger Remus also had a pronounced aesthetic sensibility. He played the piano, practicing *often* if not *regularly* and playing the popular pieces of the time, though there seemed to be a slight bias toward operatic arias. During the period covered by his diary, he took up the violin and, after lengthy examination and exploration of what was available, finally bought one. He appears to have mastered it rather quickly since he was soon playing it with a group of friends. He enjoyed plays and worked as an usher at the Salt Lake theater. In the diary he comments on and evaluates the plays he sees. On Ibsen's *Ghosts:* "Nutty—morbid. I like it. . . . Making quite a stir in S.L." He read extensively, wrote verse, composed music, and started a novel called *Horizontal Thumb*, about a young man who decides to run away from home (apparently by hitchhiking to Colorado, though we will never know because Rudger finished only the first paragraph). He also collected and mounted butterflies, for which he built a special display case.

During that summer, young Rudger decided to have his teeth "drawn" by Uncle Fred Clawson, a dentist who did orthodontic work. So all summer he had plugs and wires in his mouth and was most uncomfortable though it was a small sacrifice for the improvement in his looks that would result. (His father had for some years been keeping brother Fred's books for $10 a month in dental work.) But Rudger, Jr.'s, teeth were not his only vanity. His parents thought he needed glasses, but it took the agreement of three different eye doctors to convince him.

Rudger Remus was basically a serious young man. He was a ward teacher in the church and during this period was working on a biblical map with his young charges. He also studied hard, but did poorly on exams and thought of dropping out of school, with which he was clearly bored. Two years earlier he had asked to be allowed to concentrate the four-year curriculum into three so that he could get on more quickly to the University of Utah and more interesting studies. But Rudger, Sr., disapproved. "By doing this he would have to dispense with the study of theology," his father wrote in his own diary, "to which I am opposed." Rudger, Sr., called in a professor from the University of Utah (who agreed with him) to talk to Rudger Remus about this request. "My son has had the very best of counsel in this matter, and I trust he will give heed to it."

Rudger Remus was also an artist. The drawings and paintings, which have survived the years show marked talent. Earlier in 1903, he had asked his father's permission to go to Paris to study art. It was an idea not without precedent. A group of Mormon artists had congregated in Paris in the late 1880s and early 1890s. They were a talented though, not surprisingly, a penurious group. To solve their financial problems there, the idea occurred to them that the church might be willing to help support them. In letters to friends and church officials, they suggested that the temple, which was nearing completion after almost forty years of construction, would need to be decorated and who better to call on than Mormon artists. George Q. Cannon liked the idea and began sending small amounts of money to them. When the temple was dedicated, the church authorities could point with pride to five or six rooms containing the work of Mormon painters. One of the painters in Paris at the time was Rudger's half-brother Will, who was later commissioned to paint the portraits of the apostles, including Rudger.

But there is some question as to whether Rudger Remus was ready to settle down and pursue any concentrated study. During this period, he switched from piano to violin and then dropped both apparently to study Spanish on his own. He spent a good bit of time working on wood-burning projects and then took up the "beadwork fad." He thought of becoming a doctor and began reading on medicine and gathering information on mail order medical books. He thought about a civil service career and during the summer wanted his father to talk to the mayor, Richard Morris (Florence Dinwoodey's husband), to see if he could get a job on a survey crew. At one point he thought of going on a mission. During these seven months the only evidence of his interest in becoming a painter came one day when he sketched some workers on a downtown corner.

But Paris beckoned. On a warm day in June at Saltair, Rudger Remus broached the subject to his father. "I had a long talk with my son Rudger while at the lake, regarding a trip to Paris. He is desirous of going there with Prof. [Avard] Fairbanks of the Latter-day Saints University to study art. While Rudger has some considerable talent in that direction, I showed him why it would be unwise to go to Paris. The reasons briefly set forth were these:—He had not completed his schooling in the common branches of education; he had not progressed to that point in the study of art that would justify a trip to Paris, and last, but not least, he had not decided in his own mind to take up art for a life profession. I did not feel that it would be wise for him to go to Paris, and remain there a year or two to ascertain whether he had a sufficient taste for art to adopt it as a means of securing a livelihood later in life. Another important reason, which I considered fully as important as those mentioned, though I did not call his attention to it, was that he is not sufficiently grounded in the faith of the gospel to go into the world to pursue his studies. Rudger was not altogether pleased with the views I expressed in the matter, but it was due, I think, to an error in his judgement."

Lydia, on the other hand, was in favor of the idea and offered to raise the money to pay for it. But his father remained adamantly opposed, so Rudger Remus stayed home.

There is little other information about the relationship between father and son. Rudger, Sr., as we have seen, only rarely mentioned his children individually in his diaries. Curiously, one of these occasions occurred that October when he noted: "Accompanied by Rudger, I went to the tabernacle to hear Nannie Tout, the young Utah singer from Ogden who has been studying in London. She is very fine." There is no indication that Rudger appreciated the irony of taking his son to the performance of an artist who had been allowed to do what he had been denied.

Three weeks later, on October 29, Rudger Remus came down with a severe fever, which was diagnosed as typhoid. During the ensuing days, his condition fluctuated and Rudger, Sr., stayed home often to help care for him. But then, on November 18, after a period of recovery, he sank rapidly and died.

It was a heavy blow which Rudger was able to soften only by his unshakable faith in the will of God. "He was a good, virtuous boy, and was well prepared to go. The blow falls heavily upon his parents, who feel that they have sustained a great loss in his departure. To raise a boy to his twentieth year and then lose him is indeed a serious trial, and is only exceeded, perhaps, by the loss of a husband or wife. Nevertheless, we feel to say, 'The Lord giveth and the Lord taketh away and blessed be the name of the Lord.' His providences are inscrutable but some day it will all be made plain. Then we can of a truth say, 'The Lord's ways are not as man's ways, but yet, He doeth all things well.' "

To Lydia, her son's death was devastating. Rudger Remus was her firstborn. He had been with her during the hard times when his father was in jail and during the difficult early years in Brigham City. He was artistic, talented, and sensitive, and the sound of his music must have been an integral and important part of her life. His death was devastating not only because it took her beloved son, but because she believed that it would not have happened at all if he had been allowed to go to Paris.

Other things had been happening also to keep Lydia under emotional stress during these early years of the twentieth century. In March 1903, another daughter, named Lydia, had been born. Gay finally had the sister she wanted. "This was very gratifying news to me," Rudger wrote in his diary, "for we were anxiously looking for a girl—we now have living 4 boys and 2 girls, and dead 3 boys and 1 girl." But then a year later, Lydia, Sr., at the age of forty-three, had become pregnant again. This time she miscarried at three months and almost died.

But the death of her son was the principal catalyst for the change that took place in Lydia at this time. In her own reminiscences Lydia's daughter, Lydia Clawson Hoopes (Lydia, Jr.) describes the impact of Rudger Remus's death on her mother. "Mother said he [Rudger Remus] showed no will to recover because of his disappointment at not being able to go to Europe with his friend [Professor Fairbanks]. She seemed to blame father for his death and became grim and a little bitter. I was only three and have no memory of her before then, but my sister said her personality completely changed after Rud's [Rudger Remus's] death. He must have been her favorite son because she took his loss hard. We lived with Rud's ghost ever after and knew him almost as well as if he were alive."

Lydia, Jr., says her mother "almost lost her mind" during this period. "Old Dr. Wilcox [Charles F., who was by now the family doctor and who had delivered Lydia, Jr.] must have been a honey. He told Mother she must get out of the house and have more recreation and he gave her his horse and buggy and bought himself an automobile." Dr. Wilcox prescribed a daily horse-and-buggy ride as the best therapy.

The accumulation of stresses in their lives had taken its toll. Her daughters remembered bitter arguments between their parents. Rudger ultimately moved upstairs to sleep in a different room, though in his diary he gives no specific indication of difficulties between him and Lydia. In March 1905 he came home to find Gay on the table under chloroform with Dr. Wilcox sewing up an arm she had put through a window.

The following August Pearl was in Salt Lake, which must have put added stress on the relationship between Rudger and Lydia. Afterward, Pearl visited her grandfather in Nephi and then went back to her teaching job in Thatcher.

In early November Rudger left with Francis Lyman to attend conferences in Arizona and Mexico. Rudger did not record what, if any, contact he had with Pearl during this trip. His diary reads almost as if she did not exist. He accounts for virtually every minute of his time in his comings and goings on church business, except for one long conversation with David Udall on an unspecified subject. Of course, he was accompanied by Francis Lyman, whom he now faced across the battleline formed over the Second Manifesto.

Meanwhile, back in Salt Lake, Apostles Matthias Cowley and John W. Taylor were under the gun. Both were known to have taken plural wives after the original Woodruff Manifesto in 1890, and Cowley had taken one only months before. Cowley had also in recent years been the apostle most active in performing plural marriages for others. Both were called to testify at the Smoot hearings. While a number of polygamists called by the committee did testify, Cowley and Taylor fled the country, Cowley to Mexico and Taylor to Canada. Smoot's antagonists on the committee were enraged. At the hearings, demands were made that President Smith produce the two men. The credibility of the church had reached bottom and Smoot's Senate seat was at risk. The politicians, even Smoot's supporters, were blunt. Something had to be done about Taylor and Cowley. Finally, the beleaguered apostles were asked to submit their resignations from the council and did so late in October, just before Rudger left for Arizona.

While the resignations were held up, pending Smoot's determination of their necessity in saving his Senate seat, the message, for Rudger at least, was clear: he was now in extreme jeopardy. Whatever contact he had with his wife during this trip had to be clandestine. During the years that followed, the church became more and more strict in its treatment of polygamists in the hierarchy. Cowley and Taylor were dropped from the quorum. Later Cowley was disfellowshipped and Taylor excommunicated, though many years after both were readmitted to membership, Taylor posthumously.

Up to the time Rudger left to take charge of the European Mission, he and Pearl carried on their relationship in secrecy at occasional meetings in Arizona, Salt Lake, and in other cities where adjoining hotel rooms were reserved for them by a friend.

In 1906 when floods had, in Udall's words, "washed away our financial prospects," Ella and her family moved to Holbrook where Pearl and a sister helped Ella operate the Apache Hotel.

Sometime in 1907 Pearl developed an interest in becoming a practitioner of osteopathy. In October she went to Salt Lake to discuss the idea with Rudger who agreed to pay at least part of the tuition for her schooling. By 1908, she was studying osteopathy at a college in Los Angeles and living with her sister Louella. (She had also been elected vice president of the class of 1910) She came to Salt Lake in the summer of 1909 to be near Rudger and to earn money to support herself, returning in the fall for her final year and graduating the following July.

Whether Rudger was seeing Pearl on his 1905 trip to Arizona or not, one can guess what Lydia's feelings were about him going off to where Pearl lived and about her state of mind when their son Lorenzo became seriously ill. Rudger was in Thatcher, Arizona, when he heard: "At 12-noon we received a dispatch from President Jos. F. Smith saying that my little boy Lorenzo, between six and seven years, was dangerously sick and that we must return home immediately. This was very sorrowful news to me."

It was Tuesday, December 5, 1905. Within a half-hour, he was on a train headed home. He arrived early Friday morning.

The next entries in his diary were apparently recorded all in one sitting, since he does not use his normal daily format. In his entry for Friday the 8th to Monday the 18th he says "Being in quarantine, I spent these days mostly at home. Lorenzo gradually improved until he recovered." Actually by Thursday the 14th Rudger was out attending his regular council meeting and, on subsequent days, other meetings. Then he writes: "On Thursday, there was no meeting of the Presidency and Twelve on account of the absence of Presidents Smith and Lund and several of the Apostles, who have gone east to be present at the Joseph Smith Memorial service at Sharon, Vermont."

On December 17, 1905, the Rudger Clawson diaries stop. Was it at this point that Lydia's resentment finally exploded and the conflict between the two became so sharp and stressful that Rudger could no longer find the will or the desire to continue keeping his diaries? In 1935 he did prepare a volume of memoirs, but he never took up writing a diary again. As noted earlier, he also never bound the last years of his diaries into volumes as he did the earlier ones. It appears also that he did not even consult the diaries—or did not consult them closely—when writing the memoirs, since there are a number of instances where the statements appearing in the memoirs vary significantly from those in the diaries and are clearly in error. Did the diaries (packed in boxes and trunks and left undisposed of at the time of his death) represent something too painful in his life for him ever to come back to?

As for Lydia, she followed the doctor's advice. After acquiring the buggy, she took the children out for a ride every day. "It was always the same," wrote Lydia, Jr., "down Main Street to Sixth South, over to Sixth East, down to Liberty Park, around the Park, back to Main Street on Nineth [sic] South, up Main Street, along South Temple, through the Eagle Gate and home. It never varied unless we stopped along the way for mother to make a call."

Lydia was a strong person who had managed to weather many difficult times, and she survived this one, although it left scars and an underlying bitterness that came out in jibes against the church, or religion, or men. "The Lord will provide," she was heard to say from time to time, "if the wife's strength holds out."

Her daughter describes her as she looked then: "Medium-tall and slim, she carried her head high. She had a finely chiseled nose, a rather square chin and heavy dark hair which in later years turned to a wonderful silver grey. But her lashes and eyebrows remained black to frame those bedroomy eyes which flashed and sparkled expressing her every emotion until the day she died."

She reigned over her household with a firm hand and watched the children carefully, always aware of where they were. She held court in the kitchen, which was the center of her domain and through which passed neighbors, friends, and an assortment of tradesmen, salesmen and others. It was a big room, half of it carpeted, where a dining table stood always covered with a clean, white tablecloth. Beside the table was a small white chair where she could be found sitting when she wasn't at the stove cooking for her children. "It was at this table that she conducted all her business with the butcher or grocer, whipping up her long black skirt to reach into a voluminous petticoat pocket for her purse. In one corner of the room was a book shelf that held our school books in the days when the coal stove kept the room cozy for lessons. In the opposite corner was a washstand with a large mirror hanging cornerwise over it. We could see ourselves full-length in this mirror so the kitchen was always the last stop when we prepared to go out."

To Lydia, Jr., her mother always "seemed to have great personal wealth which came only from the fat purse that swung deep in her black petticoat pocket. I never wearied of watching her slip into her chair, swing up her full skirt and dig into that pocket for her purse. It was black and round as an orange. It opened into several compartments and into each was stuffed neatly folded greenbacks or silver. Paying a bill became quite a ritual. She would open each section until she found the one which contained the greenbacks of the correct denomination, unfold it carefully, and lay it on the table. Then the change would be counted out on top of it, down to the right penny. She was never careless about finances. The purse was her budget. Each compartment was tagged for certain expenditures. She had a horror of bills, payed [sic] cash for everything and would have settled each morning with the electric light company if they had let her."

Lydia preserved fruit in great quantities and every Friday baked bread for her family and for the tenants in No. 49. She was also skilled in the practice of folk medicine. She made blackberry poultices to cure a growth under her arm, set a child's collarbone, sewed up wounds, and treated her son Lorenzo's badly burned face with consecrated oil so that no scars were left. It was part of caring for her brood, and when she went to England she adopted the missionary group there and cared for it in the same way—and was greatly loved.

Lydia was also a believer in signs and frequently consulted astrologers. One response, based on her birth date, suggested calcium, almonds, and pine nuts were good for her and that she needed "plenty of Ozeon from the Canyon Streem [sic] ." Her planet was Mars! She should express joy and service to others. "It's the vim and pep Note of your soul. Hundreds need it from you."

Another advisor, a numerologist, based his (or her) analysis on Lydia's "compound" number, which was "(4)." How the number was arrived at is not stated, but the characteristics attributed to "(4s)" were surprisingly consonant with Lydia's: a good manager and organizer, practical, materialistic, showing endurance and faithfulness to duty.

Then there was "Prince Kasimir," who wrote her on stationery from the Semloh Hotel in Salt Lake City giving brief answers to a series of four questions Lydia had posed. There was probably good reason for him to set up shop at hotels, which could be vacated rapidly if necessary.

But more important for Lydia were her dreams. For many years her father, "Pa," had visited her in her dreams, guiding her on what to do and telling her what was going to happen. Later Rudger Remus, "Son," joined Pa in these nocturnal reunions. "They guided her to lost articles, advised her on child-rearing, directed her finances, and kept her generally informed on Father's [Rudger's] activities."

The greatest service her father and son were supposed to have provided to Lydia was guidance in investing her money. There is a tradition in the Rudger Clawson family that Lydia made large amounts of money investing in the stock market. It is true that she somehow acquired significant sums and distributed them generously to her children. Hiram Bradley, her second son (called H.B.), put it into words on a celebratory occasion in the 1920s: "Throughout her life she has been saving and careful and everything of that kind. I will say this much, and I defy contradiction, that she could have thousands in the bank today if it was not for what she has done for her children.

She has done it out of the freedom of her heart because she has been able to do it, and she has helped us liberally to gain experiences in life. She has given us comforts in life that she has been able to do through her savings and her investments. Being a businesswoman she has made and accumulated means to give her children experience and help that many children do not have."

But there is no concrete evidence that she earned her money through stock market investments. Nothing appeared in Rudger's papers, and there is no mention of it in his diaries (where he describes his own investments and even, on at least one occasion, those of his mother). Indeed, at a family meeting after Lydia's death he seemed to go out of his way to put the idea to rest.*

Lydia, Jr., indicates that the stock market speculation began just before Rudger took up his assignment as head of the church mission in Britain in April 1910. "The church would pay only his passage and he said he could not afford to take Mother and the children. . . . Mother wanted to go, so . . . she borrowed a hundred dollars (we never learned from whom) and began to play the stock market. She entered a sort of pool with some businessmen (we never learned their names), and they bought and sold for her. While she was in England she repaid the hundred dollars and cleared another seven hundred. From then until the end of her life, thirty years all together, she continued to make money on the stock market in the same secretive fashion. She built up an estate of some fifty thousand dollars besides financing her kids to all sorts of luxuries, yet it always remained a mystery how she did it."

It is certainly true that over the years she gave her children a great deal of financial assistance. She helped them buy cars and homes and make house repairs, gave them small loans and gifts, and, indeed, in some cases seemed to be simply continuing their allowances from childhood.

But when one thinks of the way Lydia managed her pocketbook (as described by Lydia, Jr.), budgeting and husbanding her money as she did, one might not be unjustified in thinking that Lydia needed the

---

*He was quite explicit: "The great bulk of her money came through me." Lydia's estate did include stocks, but there was no evidence they were part of a systematic investment program that made her rich.

intervention of neither Pa, Son, *nor* help from the stock market to enable her to realize her financial aims in life.

During the years between 1905 and 1910, Rudger continued, along with his other apostolic duties, to oversee the keeping and auditing of the church's books and to monitor the church's financial progress. In the fall of 1905 he was able to stand up in conference and announce that the church was free of debt.

He traveled to the outlying church communities and saw Pearl when he could. But the heavy responsibilities he carried (and his own unstinting commitment to them) combined with the stress at home, finally took their toll. Rudger had once before, in 1902, developed a severe rash, which was diagnosed as psoriasis and which the doctor said was caused by too much uric acid in his blood. "Only those who have been afflicted in a like manner know how almost unbearable it is." Now he suffered again from a similar rash which may well have been stress-related.

The assignment to head the European Mission, which was head-quartered in Liverpool, England, was an important one, and the family responded with excitement when it was settled that they were to go.

As significant as the assignment was, however, getting away from Utah was to Rudger just as important. It struck him sharply the minute he boarded the ship in Montreal bound for Liverpool. "The journey . . . was exceedingly pleasant. Close attention given to the accounting in the Trustee-in-Trust's office for nine years in connection with my apostolic work brought me very nearly to a physical breakdown. This I discovered as soon as the office work was lifted from my shoulders and we entered the ship that took us safely across the 'briny' deep. The ocean breezes were exhilarating to a degree. My drooping spirits were revived and health and vigor returned. The family was likewise benefited."

# CHAPTER 8

# MISSION PRESIDENT: LIVERPOOL

G reat Britain had long been a favorite missionary ground for the church, and their aggressiveness and success had won them the hostility of large numbers of Britons. As elsewhere, much of the overt anti-Mormonism focused on polygamy, and stories about Mormons kidnapping young women and wives and whisking them off to harems in Utah were a staple of the British press. The subject was so popular that when Arthur Conan Doyle turned from practicing medicine to writing mystery stories, the first case of the great Sherlock Holmes—A *Study in Scarlet*—centered on a Mormon wife-stealing incident.

The first missionaries to England were sent in 1837 after the Lord told Joseph Smith in a revelation that it was necessary for the salvation of the church—which was mired in trouble and conflict in Kirtland, Ohio. He chose Apostle Heber C. Kimball to head a small group, including two other apostles.

This little band of missionaries arrived in England on July 20, 1837, and on their first Sunday preached to a small gathering of the curious in Vauxhall Chapel in Preston, about thirty miles north of Liverpool. "I declared that an angel had visited the earth and committed the everlasting Gospel to man," Apostle Kimball later recalled. "They cried 'Glory to God!' and rejoiced that the Lord had sent his servants to them."

A week later, nine persons were baptized, the first of more than 126,000 British who would be baptized by Mormon missionaries in the next hundred years. At that time polygamy had not become a factor in the Mormon religion, but baptism was essential, and it brought opposition from the clergy and fascinated the public. Only the Baptists practiced baptism by immersion, and they performed the ritual privately in chapels. The Mormons, however, baptized in the open, usually in a gentle river, and the first Mormon baptism in England drew a crowd of between seven and nine thousand onlookers on the banks of the River Ribble in Preston. The apostles returned home in April 1838 feeling their work in England was well established.

But in 1839 when the Mormons were on the verge of being driven out of Far West, Missouri, Smith had another revelation. He was told that the nine remaining apostles should, on April 26, 1839, be dispatched "over the great waters and there promulgate my gospel." Smith put the revelation in motion and most of the apostles went to England, despite the hardships it inflicted on some of their families. Although they remained in England only a few months, it was for the Saints a period of intense activity in which sometimes whole villages and entire congregations and their preachers were baptized into the church.

Mormon missionaries preached primarily among the lower classes where poverty and despair were common. Their message was part adventist and part economic, in the sense that the proper Kingdom of Zion to which Christ would soon return had first to be made suitable, a place free of suffering, hardship, and warfare.

But Mormonism also appealed to those who were searching and felt that no religion adequately served them, people who believed the old religions had grown corrupt and had fallen away from the truth. Mormonism offered a simple, literal interpretation of the Bible and a new fascinating scripture of its own. It also had what Arrington and Bitton call a "mythic potency" in its stories and a powerful sense of certainty that transcended the confusion resulting from the warfare among sects in the Christian world at that time.

Later Lorenzo Snow would describe the manner in which the Mormon missionary should properly present himself: "I have come in the name of the Almighty, in obedience to a call from God to deliver you from your present circumstances. Repent your sins and be baptized. . . . Gather out from this nation, for it is ripening in iniquity, there is no salvation here. Flee to a place of safety . . . go to the land that the Lord God has appointed for the gathering of His people"— the land, of course was in America, first in Missouri, then Illinois, then Utah (with a promise of an eventual return to Jackson County, Missouri, when the time was ripe).

But while the principal response by the general public to Mormon baptismal practices had been for the most part curiosity, the reaction to polygamy was stronger. From the time it was openly acknowledged in 1852 until well into the twentieth century, and long after the 1904 Manifesto brought it to its true official end, polygamy kept the Mormons and their missionaries in Britain embroiled in continuous controversy, just as it had in Georgia, Tennessee, and elsewhere. And the principal issue was the recurring charge of spiriting British women off to Utah.

Many young single women were, of course, drawn to Mormonism and emigrated from Britain to Utah. and unquestionably some of them married into polygamy. Mary Jane Cutcliffe, Lydia's mother, was a case in point. But the number was not large and certainly declined rapidly after 1890. In 1911 Rudger could demonstrate with statistics that the number of single women emigrating was modest indeed, and he could argue convincingly that none would marry into polygamy.

These charges had been especially damaging during the period of the Perpetual Emigration Fund (eventually outlawed by the Edmunds-Tucker Act of 1887) which advanced all or part of the money necessary for an immigrant to reach America. By the latter part of the nineteenth century, critics of Mormonism in America were pointing to the "hordes" of European immigrants crossing the country, headed for Zion.

In 1879, Secretary of State, William Evarts, even went so far as to try to enlist Europe's help in closing the gates on this perceived flood of Mormon immigrants, but was rebuffed. As the *London Examiner* put it:

> Their views may be abhorrent to everyone of common sense and decency— yet, so long as they do not transgress the law of the land, there is not injustice enough in England to punish them simply because some of their faith may have 10 wives in another part of the world.

By the time Rudger set sail for England, government policy had been reversed, largely through the efforts of Reed Smoot. He had rallied the support of President Theodore Roosevelt and his Secretary of State, Philander C. Knox, who was protesting to European governments over the harassment and expulsion of Mormon missionaries. Rudger was about to learn more of that firsthand—on the continent *and* in Britain.

After a warm farewell party in Brigham City, where he was given a $150 gold watch as a going-away present, Rudger left Salt Lake for Liverpool, England, on May 17, 1910, accompanied by Lydia and four of their children: Gay, Samuel, Lorenzo, and six-year-old Lydia, Jr. H.B. was already in England on a mission.

On the way, they stopped in Washington to visit Reed Smoot and do some sightseeing, which included a trip to Mt. Vernon where Samuel, who had been given a camera as a going-away present, photographed them in front of the mansion. Lydia didn't feel comfortable with the Smoots, but then they went to New York and stopped to see Ben Rich who was mission president there and with whom Lydia got along famously. "Was this because she liked him," Lydia, Jr., wondered, "or because he was a more gracious personality than Reed Smoot? Of course, Smoot was a Republican and mother was a Democrat and never forgot her politics."

From New York they traveled to Montreal where they set sail for Liverpool, arriving June 4, after an uneventful journey "across the briny deep" which Rudger described in a letter to a friend with his characteristically dry wit:

> Strange as it may seem, your humble servant came through without a qualm. How it must have grieved the ship's company to see me sit down at every meal and take my full portion of the rations. I did it nevertheless. I have to smile when I think of the numberless prescriptions that I gathered to guard against seasickness, and then had no occasion to use them. A case of love's labors lost; however, I am not quite sure even now that I am a good sailor, as we had comparatively smooth sea. With a rough sea, who could tell how it might go with me. Sister Clawson and one of the children, and two or three of the Elders devoted much attention to the fishes for one day, and after that they came up with smiling faces.

Eventually they steamed into the Mersey River estuary, where Liverpool and then the Mersey dockside came into view. As cloudy and damp as it was, it still impressed the little group of Clawsons gathered at the rail to watch the scene emerge from the mist.

At the riverside several large and stately buildings, including the new Mersey Dock and Harbour Building with its impressive dome, bright green against the dull sky, presided over the river traffic. These stood like marble merchant capitalists counting the ships pulling in and out of the Albert Docks and extracting their due—monuments to Edwardian money, taste and enterprise.

Other large ships lay in the docks, many of them "Cunarders." Liverpool was one of the principal embarkation and arrival points for passenger travel between Britain and America, and the Cunard lines dominated the shipping lanes. On the river, little ferry boats plied back and forth between Liverpool and Birkenhead, its sister city on the south bank of the river.

The little group of travelers went directly to Durham House, the headquarters of the European Mission, which was located in a substantial middle class neighborhood on Edge Lane in the Edge Hill District. It was a large brick house with high bay windows on either side of the porticoed entry. Lydia, Jr., recalled Durham House in her reminiscences: "A high wall surrounded the estate and trees and shrubbery lined the inner side. Huge stones lay under the trees in front but as the property neared the house it was cultivated into a smooth lawn. A driveway circled in from the street and up to the front door.

"We entered a large hall with a . . . staircase running up to the second and third floors. To the left was what might once have been a ball room, now converted into a meeting house, with a small dais at one end and rows of seats facing it, with the backs to the front windows. These windows . . . were heavy plate glass and reached from the floor to the ceiling. . . .

"To the right of the hall was the dining room with its huge center table. The entire family ate here beside all the elders who lived at Durham House and carried on the clerical work of the mission."

Edge Lane was not a lane at all, but a wide, busy thoroughfare with a tram line running down one side. Double-decker trolleys passed from time to time clanging their bells.

Across from Durham House were the Botanical Gardens and Wavertree Park, a large, attractive expanse of green lawn, gardens, and trees.

The arrival of the Clawson family in England was somewhat "dampening," wrote Rudger later. "It rained steadily day and night for two weeks, which caused me to wonder if we could possibly get used to the English weather." He hardly had a chance to think about the weather, however. His predecessor, President Charles W. Penrose, left Liverpool within two weeks after Rudger's arrival and "the affairs of the Mission have fallen all at once, as it were, on my shoulders. But I am taking hold with what energy I have and hope soon to get in touch and harmony with the situation."

As president of the European Mission, Rudger presided directly over the British Mission which had offices in thirteen districts scattered throughout the British Isles. He was also responsible for overseeing the Scandinavian, Swiss-German, Netherlands, South African, and, eventually, the French missions. He had to attend conferences at least twice a year in the British districts and at least once a year at missions on the continent. In his three years in Europe, he traveled extensively in England as well as Denmark, Norway, Sweden, Holland, Belgium, Germany, Switzerland, and France—fifty thousand miles and five hundred meetings in all. Of this heavy schedule Rudger often quoted to friends a favorite adage: "Better to work out than rust out."

In addition to his work in Europe, he produced a mountain of correspondence and hundreds of editorials for the *Star*. The *Star* was a small periodical which served as a medium for disseminating news about the church and the work of the mission. It was also the vehicle for presenting the Mormon side of debates over controversial issues, especially during the periods when the British press would not give them equal space with the anti-Mormons.

The foreman or production manager of the *Star* was James Foggo. For thirty-seven years he had remained in this position and was admired for never having missed a deadline. Foggo and his family became close personal friends of the Clawsons.

The Liverpool Mission offices were located downtown and meetings were held in Hope Hall, a large, grey stone building, which the church rented for conferences and other occasions. It had a balcony and would seat 700 people on long wooden benches.

Within three weeks of his arrival in Liverpool, Rudger was off to the continent on a 500-mile trip during which he attended forty-two meetings and met all the presidents of the European missions. He found the most intense activity in Germany, where the opposition was both strong and officially sponsored. In Berlin one of the meetings he was speaking at was broken up by the police, and Rudger and several other elders spent the night in jail. Despite the fact that Mormon missionaries had been banished from the country, Rudger was not discouraged. He wrote home that "the work goes steadily on, the gospel is preached and honest souls are baptized into the fold. . . . We are told that 'there must be opposition in all things.' We do not pray for it, we do not invite it, but where there is opposition we have success, and where there is no opposition there's 'nothing doing.' The nightmare of a travelling Elder is the spirit of indifference."

There also seemed to Rudger a spirit of indifference back in Utah— at least as far as supplying him with missionaries was concerned. As soon as he returned from the continent, he began a campaign, that would continue for his entire three years in Britain, to obtain more elders. He did not want additional missionaries, just enough to replace those headed home. "I hesitate in mentioning this matter again," Rudger wrote the First Presidency at one point, "but the conference presidents are pleading so long and loud for help that I felt that I must mention it."

Another problem was that of British missionaries taking pleasure trips to the Continent, which Rudger felt was detrimental to the mission's work, not only because of the time they took (ten days to three weeks) but because when a missionary returned he seemed to have lost "the spirit of his work" which took him some time to regain. Rudger finally resolved this one by insisting that the missionary add double the time of his pleasure trip to the end of his mission, a rule which he found had a "splendid restraining effect."

As for the family, life had its ups and downs. The children were not put in school and thus had a little more time on their hands than they knew what to do with. It was easy to feel lonely or blue. Mr. Foggo took the boys swimming and other places with his own sons, and converts occasionally brought their young daughters to visit and play with Lydia, Jr. But they were living in a relatively hostile foreign environment and so did not have as many outlets as they would at home.

The Botanical Gardens and Wavertree Park were favorite places to play and to take family walks. There were arbored pathways and grassy knolls where cherry trees and tall sycamores grew. The gardens were surrounded by centuries-old sandstone walls, vine-covered and crumbling with time. In the spring there were jungles of rhododendrons, and in summer roses bloomed in neatly laid-out plots of ground.

Nearby on Picton Road the children were delighted to find a tiny house squeezed in between two stores. It was the width of a single door (with a single window above it) and was advertised as the smallest house in England.

They loved to ride outside on the upper deck of the double-decker trolley and watch the people hurrying along below them. Lydia took them shopping in downtown Liverpool where they gawked at wondrous goods and products from all over the world. Liverpool was a city of large, ponderous buildings and substantial houses, a prosperous commercial city with wide cobblestone streets. In the center, at Lime and William Brown streets, St. George's Hall, a huge, columned Greco-Roman building stood in the midst of a plaza, surrounded by gardens and other buildings of similar design. It was a scene out of ancient times and, in the center, on a high round pillar of stone, General Wellington watched over it just as Lord Nelson watched over Trafalgar Square in London.

They also went on outings to New Brighton Beach where they picnicked and swam in the ocean. They particularly enjoyed going down Dockside to watch the great Cunarders pulling in and out, or simply sitting awesomely at the pier. At one time or another they saw the *Mauritania,* the *Aquitania,* and their doomed sister ship, the *Lusitania.* They also saw the smaller ships on which the Mormon converts who wished to emigrate gathered and began the long journey to Zion.

They were all, of course, involved with life at Durham House and in the mission. Lydia mothered the missionaries. Gay played the organ at the Liverpool meetinghouse. Their oldest son (H.B.) was a missionary in Sheffield, "a kind of general missionary," Rudger wrote, "bearing his testimony and preaching the gospel wherever and whenever he was called to labor." Samuel "did what he could to help the good work along. He is young in years but has a fairly good understanding of the gospel with a good strong testimony"; Lorenzo and Lydia were too young to be of much help, but Rudger felt that they were being given a good education in the ways of the church.

Gay particularly enjoyed herself. "She was nineteen," Lydia, Jr., wrote in her reminiscences, "and as cheerful as her name implied. She loved crowds and the busy life of the mission home. The young missionaries flocked around her and she had a wonderful time. Her sweetheart, Horace Bond, was on a mission there, but it did not deter her from flirting with all the other young men.

"While we were there my cousin, Ivy Spencer, visited us and Gay's school chum, Pearl Bailey came also. Pearl was a tall, pretty girl and very reserved. She later married my brother H. B."

One of the missionaries took Lydia, Jr., for a picnic at the beach on her eighth birthday and earned her undying love. Hazel Dawn, a Mormon singer, who later made her name on Broadway, came to dinner once, and Lydia, Jr., sniffed out the story behind it: "One of the missionaries was madly in love with her and through overheard conversations I learned that he wanted to marry her after his return home, but would not do so unless she gave up her career. There was much talk pro and con and debating of the issue among the family. I believe my sister felt that a woman had a right to her career and mother was all on the side of the young man. Hazel had a very successful career and the missionary married someone else."

They went on trips every few weeks, according to Lydia, Jr. They loved London, and her father was overawed by "the biggest city on earth. We visited the British Museum," he wrote to a friend, "St. Paul's Cathedral, the Wax Works and other places of note, but of all that I saw, the thing that impressed me most was the hustle and bustle and bewildering movement at Picadilly Circus and on the Strand. . . . It was almost as much as one's life was worth to attempt to cross a street without the aid of a policeman." Trips to Ireland and the Continent were to follow.

The days seemed to rush by, as he wrote an ex-British missionary (in the process showing that he had read his Dickens):

> My time is fully occupied with preaching, teaching, expounding the Scriptures, bearing testimony to the Truth, attending conferences, meeting with the elders in Priesthood gatherings, and carrying on the correspondence of the Liverpool office Wilkins Macauber [sic] was always waiting for something to 'turn up.' We do not wait here; the thing naturally 'turns up,' and we have to deal with it. When I get the desk fairly cleared and the ends tied and feel free to sit down and take it easy for a brief spell, the

unexpected happens, and something comes along that requires my immediate attention.

"I trust I shall not wear out and I know that I will not rust out," he wrote his brother Selden. But nonetheless he was homesick. One night late in 1910 he had a dream which he reported to Heber J. Grant: "I dreamt that I was in Salt Lake City with my family; some party met me and said 'What are you doing here?' I answered in a sort of careless way, 'Oh I've simply come over for a little visit.' The party then asked: 'Who gave you permission to come. . . . What do you think President Smith will say when he sees you?' That question was like a dart that had pierced my very soul, and I answered: 'My gracious, I never thought of that.' "

Grant had opened the church mission in Japan in 1901 and had also headed the British mission, replacing Francis M. Lyman early in 1904. He wrote back: "I had the same dream while I was in Japan, and maybe you do not think I did not dodge more than one corner while I was home in that dream for fear that I might accidentally meet President Smith."

In his waking world Rudger was "far distant from home," he wrote in a Christmas letter to Lorenzo Stohl, his old friend from Brigham City, "with the faces of many dear friends shut out from view, and am bereft of their association, and sweet communion with the Saints of God in our Mountain vales; yet, I can say with truth it is a relief for me to be here. I enjoy my labors and am most happy in the work the Lord has given me to do."

At the year's end in a summing-up mood, he appeared satisfied with the progress he had made in taking hold of the mission: "We have introduced some changes here in the past six months which I trust experience will show to be valuable to the Mission, and may be recognized equally with the many important changes that have gone before," he wrote home.

Once again Rudger's devotion to properly kept records emerges. The changes mainly involved improvements in the mission's record-keeping procedures. He was obviously proud of them because he mentioned them in numerous letters to friends. They included establishing a record file for each missionary, developing a book of instructions for conference presidents, creating a repository for materials from each conference, and separating out the record-keeping of the British Mission from that of the Liverpool office.

As the year 1911 began, all seemed tranquil at one of the most important outposts of Mormonism. But there was trouble ahead. The polygamy issue had been revived in Utah during the bitter elections of 1910, in which Mormon Republicans and Democrats scathingly attacked each other (which Rudger deplored). Charges exchanged between B. H. Roberts and Reed Smoot were particularly bitter. In the midst of this on October 8, 1910, the *Salt Lake Tribune*, edited now by Frank J. Cannon, who had been excommunicated some years before, published a list of two hundred men who had taken wives after the 1890 Manifesto. In addition, hostile articles, some so extreme that not even anti-Mormons took them seriously, began to appear in national magazines, climaxed by a series in *Everybody's* written by Frank J. Cannon and Harvey O'Higgins which was later published in book form as *Under the Prophet in Utah*. The Smoot hearings had been widely reported in the British press during the years 1904–1907, and the question of post-Manifesto polygamy had been raised from time to time. Now, as accusations, charges, and counter charges— including one that the *Tribune* had orchestrated the whole campaign— flew between the Mormons and their enemies, it was only a matter of time before they were heard in England as well.

And before they were very far into February 1911, Rudger and the British Mormons were embroiled in a conflict that would last, with varying degrees of intensity, for most of his remaining years in England. The conflict was twofold: part of it was waged in the pulpits and the streets around various Mormon meetinghouses, as often large, and sometimes frighteningly hostile, mobs attacked the elders. At the same time, there was a running battle in the press between anti-Mormons and church officials, with Rudger—who now revealed significant talent as a polemicist—serving as the leading spokesman for the Saints. In the middle of this war of words were the British editors and journalists, most of whom sided with the anti-Mormons. Many, however, tried to give the Mormons a fair hearing, although they usually took pains to stress that they did not agree with Mormon beliefs.

The conflict was foreshadowed in late 1910 by the appearance of Hans Peter Freece in Ireland. Freece had been born in Utah into a polygamous Mormon family. After apostatizing and ultimately obtaining a law degree from Columbia University, he became a professional anti-Mormon, traveling throughout New York state giving "eyewitness accounts" of life in polygamous Utah. He had been sent to Britain by the Interdenominational Council of Women in America to sound the warning against the threat the Mormon missionaries posed to Britain's young women. More specifically, his purpose was to arouse British public opinion against the Mormons and force their missionaries out of England as agitators had done (temporarily at least) in Germany.

Freece was an inflammatory speaker, full of inside information and witty slurs on the Mormons. While he did not arouse much excitement in Ireland, a series of lectures in England attracted large crowds and contributed significantly to the stirring of anti-Mormon sentiment. Rudger believed that Freece may also have influenced members of Parliament to take up the issue.

The year before, Winston Churchill had been appointed the second youngest home secretary since Sir Robert Peel and was at the takeoff point in his brilliant political career. In November 1910, Churchill had been questioned about the Mormons: Was he aware, asked E. A. Fitzroy, a conservative M.P., of Mormon efforts to induce English women and girls to go to America and if so was he taking steps to stop them?

Churchill replied that he had made inquiries and determined there was no ground for action. "It would appear from this," said the *Liverpool Post and Mercury,* "that the Home Secretary has an intelligent understanding of the situation and is friendly to the Church."

Churchill may have been friendly and seemed to have the situation under control, but others were not. The first large anti-Mormon rally took place in Liverpool in January 1911 with Hans Peter Freece as one of the featured speakers. The meeting was presided over by a long-standing British foe of Mormonism, the Reverend Daniel H.C. Bartlett, the Anglican vicar of St. Nathaniel's Church in Liverpool. Earlier Bartlett had carried on a series of heated debates with Rudger's predecessor, Charles Penrose. In Rudger's opinion, it was this meeting which sparked the turmoil that would plague the British mission for the next two and a half years.

Reverend Bartlett started out by calling Mormonism a "travesty of Christianity" and saying that the "numerous cases of homes shattered by the seduction of one or more of their inmates to Mormonism which have been brought to my notice in my own parish in the last three years" had compelled him to take action. He then described three of the cases: the first consisted of two "girls," twenty-one and eighteen, who belonged to "a highly respectable home" and who seemed to be zealous Christians, but whose moral characters were completely altered after a few weeks' acquaintance with the Mormons. With passage money obtained from Mormon sources, they sailed to Utah and when their father made an indignant complaint, President Penrose . . . replied cruelly and defiantly that the girls were eighteen."

Another girl, said Bartlett, was a typist in a Liverpool biscuit factory. After becoming "infatuated" with the Mormon elders she encountered at an open-air meeting, she left her "heartbroken mother and paralyzed brother and departed to Utah." The third case involved the wife of a captain of a ship sailing between Liverpool and Boston. While he was at sea, she was baptized a Mormon, along with her two grown-up children. Later, she left England for America with one of her children, and, said Bartlett, her husband (who was in the audience that night) was "bereft of both his wife and his daughter." ("Shame," cried the audience, according to the *Liverpool Post*.)

Bartlett concluded by pointing out that last year the Mormons had converted a total of 5,500 souls in Europe and that many of them sailed for America through the port of Liverpool, which was, of course, the main embarkation point for all European Mormons heading for Utah. "Let Liverpool, which has been the depot of the sect for the last seventy years stir up the government to a proper investigation of the subject and strike a blow at the nefarious traffic which was going on."

Freece spoke next. He said that despite the church's banning of polygamy, it was still practiced in the American West, many of the elders in the church still believed in it, and President Joseph F. Smith still had five wives, all of which was true enough. He suggested that Home Secretary Winston Churchill was misled by the fact that the Mormon church had banned polygamy when, in fact, it is still practiced, and in some cases its elders "commanded it."

Freece was followed by an Anglican archdeacon who proposed a resolution (quickly passed) that "the attention of the Home Secretary be called to the extensive proselytizing of the agents of Mormonism in the British Isles" and the fact that polygamy is still practiced and taught by Mormon missionaries.

In the months to come, Freece, Bartlett, and others would join rallies organized in communities around the country to stir up resentment and further their aim of ousting the Mormons from Britain. The *Liverpool Daily Post* carried a story on the meeting accompanied by an editorial headed "The Mormon Invasion," which said that "when the mask is thrown off, Mormonism stands revealed as a mockery of religion and morality hidden behind a veneer of good Bible doctrine." The paper endorsed Freece's charge that the Mormons still very much believed in polygamy.

This was Rudger's first significant challenge in England, and he quickly demonstrated that he would be an effective defender of the church. First he wrote an article entitled "A Mormon Defense" and sent it to the editor of the *Liverpool Daily Post*, which published it in full. In this lengthy polemic, Rudger said the church declares "unqualifiedly that since Oct 6, 1890—the date upon which the church by common consent gave up the practice of polygamy—no plural marriages have been solemnized with the sanction of the church either in Utah or any other part of the world" and that no prosecution "on this score" has been made anywhere in the world. *

He also refuted the argument that justice could not be meted out in Utah, because the machinery of law was controlled by the Mormons, by citing (with names) all the non-Mormon judges in Utah and pointing out the number of municipal officers in Utah who were gentiles.

He further set the record straight on the three cases of the Mormons "stealing" young girls and wives: in the first case, the 18-year-old girl was now happily married to Mr. Robert Sutler, one of Rev. Bartlett's former parishioners to whom she was engaged before she went to Utah. They were living in Provo, Utah. The other girl was employed as a domestic in Denver, Colorado, in a "respectable gentile home." The young typist was fired by the biscuit company because she would not renounce her Mormon faith. The wife of the sea captain had his permission to be baptized a Mormon and she and her daughter did

---

*(No where in any of the papers he accumulated during his time in Britain did Rudger take note of the fact that he himself was living proof that this statement was untrue.)

not emigrate to Utah, but did go on a visit to Nova Scotia. He also stressed that no married woman could be baptized without the consent of her husband and no child under the age of eighteen could be baptized without the consent of the parents. "This rule is absolute the world over."

The next day he wrote to Winston Churchill:

Dear Sir:

In view of the numerous petitions recently sent you asking that action be taken looking to the prohibition of 'Mormon' missionary work in Great Britain, we beg leave to say that in case of any investigation we stand ready and willing to render you whatever assistance we can.

We enclose herewith [newspaper clippings about the Mormon question] . It is a rare thing for us to get space in the papers for any kind of a defense. We are usually refused, but we are anxious to be understood and known as we are. Our character is our own, though our reputation may belong to anybody.

With full faith in the fairness of the British Government, I beg leave to subscribe myself,

.            Yours very respectfully
            (Sig.) Rudger Clawson, President
            European Mission, Church of Jesus
            Christ of L. D. S.

Churchill replied, but it is apparent from his biographies that never during his brief tour as home secretary did he consider the "Mormon question" a serious problem. He always acknowledged the letters Rudger wrote him, but other matters not surprisingly captured his attention: prison reform, national health insurance, a major coal miners' strike in Wales, and a battle between the police and anarchists in Whitechapel ("The Siege of Sidney Street").

But with such issues as polygamy, "wife stealing," and "kidnapping young girls for harems in Utah" involved, the more sensational elements of the British press quickly demonstrated that yellow journalism was not confined to America and the newspapers of William Randolph Hearst. They knew a good circulation-building subject when they saw one and had no difficulty picking up and keeping alive the challenges hurled by Freece and Bartlett, which in turn, kept the troublemakers in every town stirred up until eventually some of them went into action. All this meant Rudger was busy around the clock, preaching, writing responses to every "Mormon" item that appeared in a newspaper (which were carefully collected and pasted in "Lydia's Scrapbook," which still exists in the Clawson papers), granting interviews to reporters, and writing long reports to the church officials in Utah describing in detail the attacks on the Mormons and his reactions and defense.

Rudger's responses to newspaper attacks were not always printed in the paper which ran the initial hostile story, but they usually appeared in the weekly *Millennial Star*. Although the head of the mission was not normally the editor of the *Star* (S. Norman Lee and Hugh Ireland were the editors during Rudger's tour of duty), Rudger wrote most of the lead editorials and in many cases corresponded with potential contributors. Early in February, Rudger did manage to have printed in the *London Evening Times* a long explanation of church doctrine signed by the First Presidency—at that time Joseph F. Smith, Anthon H. Lund, and John Henry Smith. Five days later, the *London Daily News* carried a story, "Mormons in England," which reported that Freece was making a vigorous effort to persuade the archbishop of Canterbury to launch an investigation of the Mormons. Rudger wrote the editor of the *News* saying the Mormons would welcome an investigation, asking only that "the patrons of your valuable and widely read paper will reserve judgment until the full facts are brought out."

At the same time, he was continuing a skirmish with the British Weekly, *John Bull*, over a four-part series called "Beware of the Mormons," written by a number of people, including a well-known British novelist, Winifred Graham, and Robert Edmondson, one of the weekly's star contributors. Edmondson visited Liverpool to interview Rudger and although he asked some tough questions, Rudger thought Edmondson would write a balanced story. For one thing, he told Clawson that he had glanced at Freece's book, *Mormonism*, and had "thrown the damned thing in the trash basket."

But when Edmondson's story appeared, it not only consisted of the same kinds of attacks other anti-Mormon writings contained, it misquoted Rudger from the interview. Rudger's first response was a long rebuttal, "The Question of the Hour," which *John Bull* would not print, but which he published in the *Star* and reprinted as a tract, 85,000 copies of which were distributed across England.

He responded to Edmondson on a number of points and then dealt with what he considered the main thrust of all the attacks appearing in the press, the charge that the Mormons still practice polygamy and that "the chief aim of the 'Mormon' missionaries is to convert young women exclusively and ship them off to Utah." He cited a letter printed in the *Liverpool Post* from a non-Mormon who had just returned from Utah who said that he could report authoritatively that polygamy is no longer practiced in Utah, that several other religious sects are thriving there and all are under the watchful eye of the law. Rudger also said that the lengthy investigation of Senator Reed Smoot by the United States Senate bore out the fact that the American government was relentless in stamping out polygamy. He also cited figures documenting that since 1890, the number of Mormon polygamous families had been reduced from 2,451 to 897 and that many of these Mormons had died since the latest figures were compiled. Finally, he wrote:

> The charge that young girls, either from Great Britain or Scandinavia, are being shipped to Utah to furnish wives for members of the 'Mormon' Church is ridiculous in the extreme. The young women of England and other countries are beautiful and attractive, but they are not specially needed in Utah. There are hundreds of beautiful American-born girls growing up in Utah, and the most serious problem in the 'Mormon' Church to-day, and one which worries parents greatly, is to find husbands for these young women. There are 26,000 young 'Mormon' women in Utah and adjoining states, identified with the Young Ladies' Mutual Improvement Associations, the majority of whom are unmarried, and 57,993 female students in the 'Mormon' Sunday Schools.
>
> It might be proper to state that if it can be shown that any one of the 'Mormon' missionaries at present in the field is paying his addresses to a young woman with a view to marriage, he will be at once released and sent home, 'without honor.'

Rudger, of course, reported all this in detail to the First Presidency in Salt Lake but also gave them his assurance that "the Lord almost invariably overrules their [the editors of the attacking papers] intentions and wicked machinations for the good of his great latter-day work." As evidence, he cited a number of letters he had received from conference presidents in England reporting that the agitation was "arousing general interest in the 'Mormon question' and bringing many new faces into their meetings." He quoted one as saying: "The Elders are reporting many strangers in attendance . . . and they are besieged on all sides with questions pertaining to our teachings and practices. . . . Cannot you convey my personal thanks to Rev. Bartlett and his abettor Hans P. Freece."

Subsequently Rudger exchanged letters several times with Edmondson in which each argued his case, neither, obviously, convincing the other.

After the *John Bull* series began, Rudger was visited by another reporter—Alan Lethbridge of the British Associated Press—whom he believed was "fair-minded." In fact Lethbridge conceded that he was prejudiced in Rudger's favor and would enjoy giving *John Bull* a "slap in the face." He also told Rudger, confidentially, that, despite all the pressure on the home secretary to launch an investigation of the Mormons, Churchill had virtually concluded that the evidence did not warrant it. In Lethbridge's opinion, the whole Mormon question had been blown up out of proportion and he said he would like to do something about bursting the bubble.

Rudger must have thought the Lord had sent Lethbridge. He showed the reporter facts and figures on almost every aspect of his work, including one that Lethbridge thought especially significant: the actual number of men and women adults who left Europe from Liverpool in each "company" of Mormon immigrants. (One of the *John Bull* articles said that eight hundred women—mostly from Britain and Scandinavia—had landed in Boston and been sent to Utah.) Lethbridge took two or three sample companies and after deducting children under the age of ten, he found that in one company there were twenty-five males and fourteen females, and in another six males and three females. Lethbridge was surprised at this, but Rudger assured him: "We don't need your English girls in Utah and don't particularly want them there. . . . The question of finding husbands for our girls is greatly worrying parents. . . . We would be glad if you could send us over some young men to marry our daughters." He also showed Lethbridge some photographs of young Mormon girls in Utah, and he and the reporter agreed they could not be surpassed for good looks and a strong healthy appearance.

He also showed Lethbridge his publishing operation, stressing that it was not financed by the church but was self-supporting, which surprised the reporter. Lethbridge, incidentally, was a Catholic, and "the Roman Catholics, like the 'Mormons,' are unpopular in England," Rudger reported home.

Rudger's faith in Lethbridge was more than justified. His article appeared first in *M.A.P.* (*Mainly about People*) and then was made available to *Pearson's Weekly Home Notes, London Daily Express,* the *London Standard,* two papers in Birmingham, and one in Newcastle—most of which printed the two-part article.

Lethbridge refuted the main charges of the anti-Mormons both inside the press and out and concluded that "the 'Mormon scare' is a pure piece of journalistic engineering."

Rudger reprinted the articles as a tract titled a "Truthful and Unbiased Statement"—and 61,000 of them were distributed throughout Great Britain. In appreciation he also wrote Lethbridge, thanking him and sending several Mormon books and a little "enclosure" in the form of a postal money order. Lethbridge declined Rudger's rather naive gesture, saying that he was well paid by his paper and accepting even a small financial gift would lay him open to accusations of being biased in favor of the Mormons. He did say, however, that he was going to America hoping to "establish myself in journalism on the other side," and that he would appreciate letters of introduction to the Utahns in Congress.

Clawson, somewhat chagrined that his gift would be perceived as a payoff, replied that he fully agreed with Lethbridge and promised to write a letter to Senator Reed Smoot, which he did. Three months later, Lethbridge wrote that "After all, I did not go to America, worse luck." He also said that he had been instrumental in persuading some other British journalists—including the prominent William T. Stead, editor of the *Review of Reviews*—to give the Mormons fair play in their publications. "As I told you personally, I don't understand your creed and I have no sympathy with it, but I do love a game called cricket."

Meanwhile, although their meeting halls may have been seeing new faces inside, as the press agitation continued to create interest and curiosity in the Mormons, there were also new faces outside and a lot of them were very angry. One night in early March 1911, while Rudger was away, a rock crashed through the window of Lydia's bedroom and jolted her out of bed. Durham House was under attack. Other windows were broken and the front door pounded and battered as the elders gathered in the hallways to assess what was happening. Then, armed with pokers and other makeshift weapons, they charged out the door—to find only one obsessed anti-Mormon making the ruckus. S. Norman Lee engaged him and in a brief struggle both men were injured. The attacker was then driven off.

Early the following month, in Heywood, a small town in Lancashire north of Liverpool, a mob lead by the town rector, the Reverend J. T. Wilson and the Reverend T. M. Tozer, a local vicar, appeared at a Sunday Mormon meeting being held in Trades Hall. They demanded to make a statement, were denied, and then interrupted the meeting to announce that if the Mormons were not out of town in seven days, they would not be responsible for what might happen. Fortunately, Rudger was at this meeting. Some of the elders refused to agree to the demands, but Rudger, sensing that the anger against them was so intense that someone might be killed if the mob took action, agreed to go. "It was the only thing to do," he said. "We were in dangerous circumstances."

The next day, he consulted a lawyer and although the law was on their side, the counsel agreed it was best to leave peacefully because both the mayor and the chief of police were against them. So the Mormons left. But later that month, one of the townspeople involved in the confrontation wrote Rudger asking his forgiveness, saying he was ashamed of his conduct. And the secretary of Trades Hall wrote, assuring the Mormons that they could come back and hold their meetings in peace.

About the same time, an article appeared in the *Liverpool Evening Express:* "MORMON PERIL—HUSBAND'S PLIGHT IN LIVERPOOL—YOUNG WIFE DISAPPEARS—SAID TO BE CARRIED AWAY BY MORMONS." A gentleman named John Wilde had come down from London, claiming that his wife had been stolen by the Mormons while he was in China. W. P. Monson, president of the London Conference, and *Star* editor, Norman Lee, immediately set out to uncover the facts and they found that Wilde had obtained his information about his missing wife from neighbors who, he said, lived at Reynolds No. 43 Maida Vale; but there was no such address. There was no one named "Wilde" on the lists of Mormon conversions and emigration, and no Mormon missionary had been proselytizing in the Maida Vale area in recent months.

Rudger reported all these facts in a letter to the *Liverpool Express*, which the editor at first refused to print. He also considered a libel suit against Wilde, but after being told by his solicitor that it would cost around $5,000, he decided "libel suits were a luxury intended only for the wealthy." But the solicitor did prevail upon the *Express* to publish Rudger's letter.

Meanwhile Rudger was carrying on an intensive correspondence with Home Secretary Churchill, sending him clippings describing the attacks on the Mormons and the libelous anti-Mormon stories. And on March 7, in the House of Commons, the home secretary was once again asked if there was any truth to the charges that young English girls were being induced to emigrate to Utah and, if so, whether steps were being taken to safeguard English homes. "My attention has been called to the matter," Churchill replied, "and I am making inquiries. I have at present no official information showing that young girls are being induced to emigrate to Utah. . . . The matter is causing a great deal of concern in certain quarters in this country. I am treating it in a very serious spirit [hear, hear] and looking into it very thoroughly."

Rudger assumed from the amount of time the investigation was taking that they wre not unearthing much derogatory information. He also heard that Churchill had asked the British ambassador in Washington for information, so he quickly wrote Reed Smoot urging him to have a talk with the ambassador. The "Mormon question" came up in Parliament again in early May and Churchill said that although he had not completed his investigation, he had found nothing against the Mormons. He also said he had looked into the question of the Mormons in Germany and found that, although local police officers had expelled some of the elders, there had never been any official action. In the meantime, he said he was aware of the attacks on the Mormons and that "anything in the nature of rowdyism and mob action ought to be strictly repressed."

Although mob activity diminished as spring arrived and brought pleasant weather to the British Isles, the attacks in the press intensified. Then Freece appeared at another meeting—this one held in Holborn Hall, London—primarily to urge the British government to take action against the Mormons. But William T. Stead helped defuse the Holborn Hall meeting by writing a long and brilliant letter to the *London Daily Express*. In it he said this "whole so-called Crusade is an outbreak of sectarian savagery worked up by journalists who in their zest for sensation, appear to be quite indifferent to the fact that the only permanent result of their exploit will be to advertise and spread the Mormon faith among the masses, who love fair play and who hate religious persecution, nonetheless because it is based on a lie!"

Despite the unkind cut at the end, Rudger reprinted the letter in the *Star* and as a tract, which was widely distributed throughout the country.

For the May issue of the *Review of Reviews,* his own journal, Stead wrote what must have been the most convincing defense of religious freedom to have appeared during this period. After dealing with a few specifics of the anti-Mormon crusade, Stead launched into an attack on religious intolerance and a defense of the Mormons that is so cogent, penetrating, and well written that it still makes compelling reading:

> That Mormons in their heart of hearts believe that polygamy is a divine ordinance may be as true as it is undoubtedly true that many Roman Catholics hanker after the right to save the souls of men by dealing summarily with the bodies of heretics. But that is no reason for persecuting either of them. There are more so-called Christian Englishmen living in non-legal polygamous relations with women in the United Kingdom than there were Mormons living with plural wives in all the world, before polygamy was abolished in Utah. The Mormon wife is honored. She bears her husband's name; her children are recognized and carefully brought up. The English Christian's mistress is despised; she is not allowed to call herself by the name of the man to whom she bears children; and these children are branded as bastards and disowned by their father. It is probable, nay, absolutely certain, that there are more prostitutes in London to-day than there are plural wives in all Utah. Why, then, this Pecksniffian zeal to save innocent English girls from the horrors of Salt Lake, while not a word is said about the dangers of Picadilly? The Mormons in this country are not polygamists. They do not preach polygamy; they repudiate it. No English girl has yet been proved to have contracted a plural marriage as the result of their teaching. The parsons and priests and bishops who have been befooled by the *Daily Express* and *Daily Mail* ought to be thoroughly ashamed of themselves. . . .

Stead went on to examine the evils of religious intolerance with anti-Mormonism the case in point. It was a classic statement. Though not wholly complimentary to the Latter-day Saints, it was an eloquent defense of their rights. Rudger called the article "a noble defense of a persecuted people" and reprinted it in the *Star*. The following April, Stead went down with the *Titanic* which "overwhelmed" Rudger with grief. He immediately wrote the First Presidency a letter which reflected the importance he attached to Stead's 1911 defense of the Mormons: It "helped to allay prejudice and stem the tide and did much to turn public sentiment in our favor." Rudger obtained the name of Stead's mother, his birthplace, and date of birth, and in 1913, after returning to Salt Lake, he stood proxy for him in receiving temple ordinances. "Those who lift up their voice," Rudger wrote in his report to the First Presidency, "and wield their pens in defense of the Latter-day Saints will in no wise lose their reward."

And, indeed, Stead's pen did seem to turn the tide. In early May, an anti-Mormon demonstration in Manchester sponsored by Bishop Welldon, attracted only three hundred people, and Rudger's inquiries suggested that the primary reason for the poor turnout was that some of the ministers were afraid Stead would deliver another rhetorical blast at the "true moral conditions" in England. A man assigned by the Home Office to investigate the Mormons in Manchester said he found nothing to report; and another man in Hyde, instructed to go into a Mormon meeting and take notes, came out and reported to the agitators that he was "done with this business" and would no longer fight Mormons.

Still, it took one more incident and Churchill's report to Parliament on his investigation of the Mormons to bring about what was at least a temporary peace. In Birkenhead, across the Mersey River from Liverpool, a large mob gathered outside the Mormon chapel. Sixty policemen were there to give protection, but the mob attacked anyway, and several of the unarmed bobbies were seriously hurt during the melee. Two of the agitators broke through the police line and presented the Birkenhead elders with the same ultimatum the Mormons had been given in Heywood—they must be out in seven days or "be willing to take the consequences."

Rudger realized that they were at a critical juncture. If they held the next Sunday meeting in Birkenhead, some of the elders might get hurt, perhaps seriously. But not holding it would also have serious consequences. He gathered the elders at the Liverpool Mission headquarters to discuss what to do. "It became apparent," he wrote later to the First Presidency, "that much depended on the holding of said meeting. Our rights under the law were being invaded. The elders had been driven out of Heywood and all eyes were now on Birkenhead. The papers had published the ultimatum and wondered how the 'Mormons' would meet it. It looked to us as if the towns and cities in the Liverpool Conference were simply waiting to see what Birkenhead would do. Our judgment confirmed the thought that if the Elders walked out of Birkenhead under a law-defying and mobocratic ultimatum, they would be compelled to walk out of other cities in double-quick order. We decided by unanimous vote that the meeting should and must be held. There was great danger connected with it, but we had no choice, only to stand in defense of our rights. In this hour of peril it was decided that word should be sent to the elders throughout the mission requesting them to observe Sunday, April 23, as a day of fasting and prayer for and in behalf of the elders of Birkenhead. I am pleased to report that our prayers were heard and answered and very much to the surprise of the entire non-'Mormon' population in this part of the country and elsewhere."

Although a crowd of five thousand appeared at the next Birkenhead meeting, the bobbies were also out in force and there was no violence. Rudger thought this was a turning point. After the earlier incident, when the bobbies had been injured, public sentiment seemed to have shifted in favor of the Mormons (there had been several arrests and severe fines imposed). In addition, various missions around the country reported that the local police were actively investigating the Mormons for the Home Office and failing to turn up any evidence against them. An elder in the Swan District near Liverpool reported that a chief of detectives had turned in a favorable report on the Mormon Liverpool operation which was sent to the Home Office without change. "The only thing, so far as I know," the detective told the Liverpool chief constable, "that could possibly be brought against the Mormons is that they conduct an Evangelical Emigration agency. As to this outcry against polygamy, it's all rot." Shortly thereafter, Secretary Churchill announced in Parliament that he could find no grounds to take action against the Mormons. For the moment, at least, the public lost interest and turned their attention to the coronation of George V.

*"I don't care what you say but please don't misspell my name."*

Although Rudger was glad to report that the opposition was dying down, it had had its advantages. "When we attempt to advertise, we fail to reach the people," he wrote a brother Mormon in Loa, Utah. "When the devil advertises, we reach the people and go considerably beyond, and out of seeming evil, good comes forth."

Rudger now had a period of relative calm which enabled him to give his attention to the shortage of missionaries in Britain, a subject he constantly wrote about to church officials in Utah. The shortage was aggravated by some missionaries who ran out of money in eight or nine months and had to be sent home. "This is the cry that comes up from all over the mission," Rudger wrote in late 1911. "We are now between sixty and seventy short and the eight who are expected to reach Liverpool next Friday . . . will be swallowed up immediately without relieving the situation."

In the summer of 1911, Rudger planned to join his family on a trip to Scandinavia before going on to visit the German missions. But he had to send them on ahead while he negotiated a change in the steamship companies that were shipping Mormon emigrants to Boston. Then a strike on the line serving Scandinavia forced him to drop that leg of his trip entirely. He went straight to Germany instead.

In the meantime the family, accompanied by the Foggos and Pearl Bailey, were having a grand time. They went north "to the land of the midnight sun and saw it across the water," wrote Lydia, Jr. She also remembered "the ice cave in Norway, which was furnished with chairs and tables carved from ice and the caretaker said they would eat their Christmas dinner there."

They visited Denmark and then went on to Germany where Rudger met them. Belgium, Holland, France, and Switzerland followed. Except for Italy it was the grand tour and they wore themselves out visiting museums, churches, historic sites, and natural wonders. Lydia, Jr., was particularly thrilled by the deep blue color of Zurich Lake and a ride in a cable car across an Alpine gorge.

She remembered, too, the inevitable funny little incidents—her mother and father haggling over saving money, for instance. "I was large for my age but poor little . . . father had to carry me through turnstiles all over Europe because 'children in arms' were free. Once we got stuck, to the embarrassment of both of us.

"There was the time in France when we visited some sort of night club and Mother clung to Sam. He was such a 'pretty' boy and all the women were ogling him. She was sure it was a decadent nation, full of bad women, and one was sure to kidnap Sam if she did not hang on to him."

When they marched onto the ferry back to England they were exhausted, though they were probably standing at the rail when Dover came into view. The white ragged cliffs, grey in the fog, took on the shapes of castles, dim and ominous like those from which, in one's imagination, characters in Shakespearian plays delivered their great orations.

Settled again in Liverpool, Rudger said he found "it just as quiet here in England as if there had never been a moment's agitation. The newspapers are taking absolutely no notice of us and meetings are held throughout the mission without any disturbance or interference."

By this time, the decision had been made that Lydia and the children would return home for the remainder of Rudger's mission. She was generally in good health but had developed rheumatism and a persistent cough, and once her nose bled so badly that she fainted. Her doctor advised her to leave, and she was not difficult to convince. She dreaded the thought of another winter in the damp, foggy climate of Liverpool. She also, no doubt, had been unsettled by the violence occurring in England and by the attack on Durham House and probably feared for the children's safety.

Rudger, too, had come to hate the British weather, compounded by man-made smoke. "A cloud of tobacco smoke seems to have settled over England like a pall. It gets in your eyes, into your ears, into your nose, into your mouth and lungs, and last, but not least, it gets onto your nerves. I saw a man the other day puffing at a pipe nearly as large as a teacup and the smoke came up around him exactly like it issues from a steam engine." All of which made the mixture of fog, rain and dampness worse. "I was in London the other day and the fog was so dense and so intense that it gave me sore eyes. I am bringing a little of Christian Science to bear on the climate, and while I don't like it, and I know that I don't like it, I keep saying to myself that I do like it. It is said that some people tell a lie so frequently that they actually come to believe it. That's Christian Science."

The family sailed for home on September 23, 1911. After a stopover to see Niagara Falls, they arrived safely in Salt Lake at the end of October.

*   *   *

In the fall of 1911, a new form of agitation broke out. Although the balanced, factual stories appearing in the press and in the Home Office report had tended to silence the anti-Mormon newspapers, there suddenly appeared a wave of movies, which, being fiction, were not subject to reasoned refutation. The titles suggest their content—*A Victim of the Mormons* and *Through Death Valley or The Mormon Peril*. Rudger was asked what he was doing to stop these films. He replied frankly that he did not know what he could do except to assign elders to stand outside the picture houses and hand out tracts.

All this, of course, continued to arouse interest in the Mormons, and Rudger spent much of the fall of 1911 promoting a photo story of the Salt Lake Temple and Tabernacle which was published in the *London Illustrated News*.

At the end of the year, Rudger reported home that "Christmas came and went quietly." It was a bleak time for the Clawsons both in Liverpool and Salt Lake, not only because of the distance that separated them but because money was scarce as well. Lydia was strapped and could not provide much of a Christmas for the children. Rudger was no better off. To her inquiries, he said simply that he did not know what to do. "I wish I was in a position to help you beyond what I'm doing but I am not. Means are very 'tight' with me as you now know I'm doing for you the very best I can."

His Christmas was brightened, on the other hand, by a long, warm letter from young Samuel that revealed an emerging literary talent: "I am sitting here of a Sunday evening in our little green dining room," Samuel wrote his father in a beautiful script, "within comfortable radius of a nice, warm fire humming pleasantly in the confines of our little hot-blast; sitting under the softened rays of our benificent study-lamp writing a Christmas letter to you. Without, the crystal flakes of snow are wafting downward from the leaden sky above, and with hushed stillness, replacing themselves with uniform evenness over the whitened ground already inches deep. Oftentimes, through the crisp, clear air, I hear the gleeful shout of some rowdy youngster reveling in the delicious coolness of the new fallen snow and I feel thankful, even as I sit here, that I am at last folded within the boundaries of my home country and my 'home,' complete in every respect, except the one essential, your presence."

The new year had hardly begun when Rudger received a cable from Utah telling him that his mother had died. Rudger knew she had been seriously ill and had repeatedly prayed "that her life might be spared until we should meet again in the flesh." But, as Rudger wrote his father, "In the providences of the Lord, it was ordained otherwise, and I bow to His divine will." But the shock was staggering and he wrote Lydia, "How much, how very much I miss her and shall miss her on my return is beyond my feeble language of expression." Still, he was consoled by the thought of the church work she had done, at his urging, and he shared this thought with the First Presidency:

> The closing years of her mortal pilgrimage were passed in the House of God where she labored for redemption of the dead. She took great pleasure in this work. I often told her it would be the crowning glory of her life. Surely I am not mistaken in this, and while I am confident that she was received with demonstrations of joy by loved ones beyond the grave, none would be happier to . . . make her welcome than those she officiated for in the temple that they might be released from their prison house.

Then, a month and a half later, he was hit again when a cable arrived announcing the death of his father. But he seemed to take this news more in stride: "I had hoped to see him again in the flesh," he wrote President Smith and the counselors, "but of course I realize that his work was done and being full of years and under the strain of bodily ailments common to mortality, he quite naturally passed off this stage of action." He felt that his father's death coming so soon on the heels of his mother's was something of a blessing. "In life they were not divided and in death were hardly separated. He now has three wives and a number of children behind the veil and one wife and numerous children still upon the earth."

Rudger also felt it significant that his father had always honored the principle of plural marriage and stressed that above all else he was a man of integrity and loyalty. "He was true and loyal to President Brigham Young, with whom he was intimately associated in various capacities for many years. He was equally true to his successors,

Presidents Taylor and Woodruff . . . he never gave away a secret or betrayed a sacred trust."

Despite such personal travails, the year 1912 began quietly enough: "The work in this mission is progressing very nicely," Rudger wrote a friend. "The enemy is not so actively engaged against us as during the spring and summer of 1911. He shows his cloven hoof at sundry times and in sundry places in the shape of moving pictures and sensational dramas. Upon such occasions we usually have our Elders at the door to distribute suitable tracts to the retiring audiences. While the devil is doing evil on the one side the Elders are doing good on the other— the results we are of necessity compelled to leave with the Lord."

The Annual Report for the year 1911 was not an especially good one, and he was forced to write the First Presidency an explanation:

> You will notice that there was quite a decrease in the various departments of missionary work in the British Mission during 1911, as compared with 1910. This is accounted for as follows: As between the two years there was an average shortage of missionaries from month to month in 1911 of between 50 and 70. In December, 53 new missionaries came in. This of course reduced the average shortage but we got no benefit whatever from their labors.

Despite the good advertising the anti-Mormons gave them, he had to conclude: "Generally speaking, the widespread and heated agitation of last spring and summer affected the work unfavorably." There had also been a decrease of 855 baptisms in 1911, but Rudger promised to make a better showing.

Pearl and Rudger corresponded during this first year and a half of his time in Europe, though the letters have not survived. They apparently discussed the possibility of her coming over as early as February 1912 when her brother, David King Udall, Jr., went to England on a mission. But they abandoned the idea for fear of exposure.

In March, Rudger visited the missions in Ireland, but came away rather pessimistic about arousing the Irish to an appreciation of the true gospel.

"We have a fine class of elders there," he reported, "earnest workers, who have a good knowledge of the gospel. They are diligently seeking the honest in heart, but it would seem that the blood of Israel does not flow with the fullness and freedom through Irish veins as through the English. We have a splendid branch of the church in Dublin, but it is composed mainly of well-to-do Germans."

In England, doubters and critics were everywhere—"not bearing down upon us with such mighty force as it did last year," but still on the attack in various ways. The anti-Mormon movies continued to circulate, and Winifred Graham, "a writer of the rankest kind of fiction," said Rudger, was writing anti-Mormon fiction again for the *London Tit-Bits*. Graham had a string of anti-Mormon novels in print. The *Tit-Bits* piece was called *Sealed Women*. Earlier she had published *The Sin of Utah* and *Ezra the Mormon*.

One of the issues the missionary authorities had, for obvious reasons, to be careful about was sex among their charges. Rudger was especially concerned about the landladies where missionaries lodged being (suspiciously) too ready to convert. "So strongly am I impressed concerning this important matter that I have counseled the presidents of conferences to have their elders change their lodges as frequently as possible without disrupting affairs."

Despite repeated warnings to the missionaries, infractions of mission rules would occur. One elder was arrested for exposing himself to a young lady on a street corner in London. Another confessed to committing fornication while performing his missionary duties in Scandinavia. He had gone into a store in Copenhagen to purchase some postcards, Rudger reported, and "the woman in charge, being a lewd character, locked the door, made improper advances to him and he yielded." The elder was excommunicated, and the damage to the church was contained. These, of course, were exceptions to the rule. The behavior of the young missionaries was, for the most part, exemplary.

One missionary with an eye for the girls, however, caused so much trouble that it led to a revival of "mobocracy." In 1911, Rudger had to order an elder to leave Nuneaton, a little village near Liverpool, for "paying the girls undue attention." He also told the elder that if he ever returned to Nuneaton, he would be ordered home. In tears, the elder apologized and left, but a year later he was back once more, pursuing the girls. So Rudger again ordered him home, and again the elder left, only to return a second time. Rudger did finally get rid of him, but not before he had made the people of Nuneaton so angry that they formed an anti-Mormon group determined to run the Saints out of town. They attacked a Sunday night meeting early in March 1912, roughed up a couple of the Mormons, and demanded that the mission leave within fourteen days. The agitation continued all week, although a Congregationalist minister wrote a letter to the *Nuneaton Observer* defending the missionaries—who, along with the usual charges, had been accused of being responsible for the disappearance of a Mrs. Wheatley and her family. There was no record of Mrs. Wheatley emigrating or even joining the church. Rudger wrote that "the better class of people in Nuneaton are with us," and the *Nuneaton Chronicle* offered, for five pounds, to publish a *Star* editorial in one of their editions and give them five hundred copies to hand out. Rudger accepted.

But the hostilities continued, making it impossible to hold meetings (though the police seemed to be on their side), and once again Rudger was faced with a dilemma. "If, under the circumstances," he said, "we quietly walk out of Nuneaton it will hurt the cause throughout the mission and would bring the enemy a victory to which they are in no way entitled. If we are forcibly dirven out, why, that is another question." Since they obviously had police support, Rudger was not so concerned, although at one demonstration, where a crowd had disrupted Mormon services, Albert Smith, the frail sixty-four-year-old president of the Nuneaton Conference, was tarred and feathered. At first he was thought to have been seriously burned, but he recovered without harmful effects. The two men responsible for the incident were caught and fined.

The agitation ceased for awhile, then began again, reaching the point where Rudger wrote home: "The devil is raging in staid old England and conditions are quite as bad, if not worse, than they were last year."

The Mormons stood their ground, and after the trial of Smith's attackers the agitation tapered off, although for most of 1912, the Saints at Nuneaton were forced to hold their meetings in various cottages because rented meeting halls were denied them. As the Nuneaton situation was calming down, the devil showed up in Sunderland, where Rudger suggested the problem lay in the fact that they owned their meeting hall. "We have acquired a splendid little property there in a choice locality, and as a consequence, the devil is angry and bent upon driving us out," he wrote the First Presidency.

The "choice locality" was on Dunstall Road in a well-to-do neighborhood of Sunderland, itself a prosperous little shipbuilding town on the east coast of England near Newcastle-on-Tyne. The "splendid little property" was a small stone building built at an angle to the street next to a cobblestone alley. It was longer than it was wide and the roof was hipped at either end. It had been a garage, when Eugene Lichfield, the Sunderland Conference president, acquired it. The neighborhood had more than its share of horseless carriage owners. But there were no pits so that the floor was saturated with years of grease drippings and the bare walls with the distillation of automobile emissions. Lichfield and his missionaries and some of the converts pitched in and scrubbed it out from top to bottom—though it was some time before they were entirely rid of the odors. Lichfield, who was a carpenter, built a speakers' platform and wooden pews. To save room, the baptismal font was built under the platform, part of which could be removed when a baptism was scheduled.

This had been the scene of perhaps the most violent and ugliest persecution the Mormons had experienced in Britain. The mobs attacked the missionaries repeatedly, pummeling them with bricks, rocks, decayed food, horse manure, and worse. One elder was nearly scalped by a potato studded with sharp glass. Another caught a brick in the face. One night a mob attacked the chapel, pulled off the Mormon sign, wrenched out its props, and used them to beat out most of the windows. Representatives of the various churches held anti-Mormon meetings, and after the windows had been repaired, a mob broke them again. Rudger wrote the mayor of Sunderland stating the Mormons did not intend to leave and asking why his people were being persecuted: "It is not for what they are teaching," he wrote, "but what people say they are teaching; not for what they are doing but for what people claim they are doing." They had police protection, but no one was being arrested and Rudger filed a claim for damages against the town. A citizen's meeting was organized for May 21, with the mayor presiding and Reverend Bartlett the main speaker. Rudger wrote the new home secretary, Reginald McKenna (who, as former first lord of the Admiralty, had switched places with Winston Churchill), protesting: "We greatly fear that if the mayor presides at said meeting, the result will be further riotous demonstrations. . . ."

McKenna acknowledged the letter, but did nothing. The meeting was held, Bartlett and others spoke, and the mayor said Sunderland still had the Mormon "evil" and that something must be done. Lichfield was accused of living with two widows and several young ladies (Lichfield's landlady and her sister and nieces—all non-Mormons who, nevertheless, staunchly stood up for the missionaries despite the damage done to their house by the mobs). The police kept the meeting in order, but President Lichfield was not allowed to present the case for the Mormons or defend himself. Later he received a crude, threatening letter signed "anti-Mormons," saying the Mormons must leave Sunderland.

Rudger wrote the mayor another letter of protest, but the hostilities continued. Nevertheless, Rudger refused to give in and wrote the First Presidency explaining his decision: "We fear that if we walk out . . . *willingly,* we will have to walk out of other cities *unwillingly.*"

On Saturday, June 8, 1912, Rudger decided abruptly that he would go to Sunderland for Sunday services the following day. He boarded the train that morning and soon was passing through the industrial centers of Manchester and Huddersfield. Then the train entered the beautiful rolling farmlands of Yorkshire, where the bright green fields rose sharply up the hillsides, divided by fieldstone walls. The walls sometimes veered sharply off course as though the builders of them had spent a few too many hours in the pub before getting to work. Trees, which only sparsely dotted the fields, were allowed to cluster here and there, especially near the compact little villages of brown or grey brick and stone houses. Occasionally, a grey-brown house stood strikingly alone on the top of a hill.

Changing trains in Newcastle, it was late evening when he arrived in Sunderland. He had not sent word ahead, so he had to take a taxi to the house on Azalea Street where President Lichfield and a number of missionaries lodged. Even in the dark he could see that the windows had all been broken out by the mob and were boarded up.

The next day, he walked with Lichfield to the chapel a few blocks away. At the chapel one of the first things Lichfield showed Rudger was a simple padded chair with a slit in the seat. On one occasion when the mob broke in, a man had rushed at one of the elders with a knife. A church member who knew the assailant called out his name and so distracted him that he failed to see the elder move and brought the knife down on the empty seat.

When the evening service began, there was a large angry crowd outside, which spilled over from Tunstall into neighboring streets and increased in size as the evening wore on—reaching 10,000 according to newspaper reports.

They knew the head of the British Mission from Liverpool was at the meeting; he was the one in the silk top hat, which Rudger wore in England. One elder, wearing a derby, offered to change hats so the mob could not identify their leader. "No, thank you," said Rudger. "Let every man wear his own hat. I'll wear mine."

When it was his turn to speak, the Clawson wit surfaced immediately: "I know you have tried to make the building as comfortable as possible, but you will excuse me if I keep my overcoat on, as the room is thoroughly ventilated." The night air, blowing off the North Sea in through the boarded windows, was chill even in June. He went on to give the usual defense of the Mormons and read W. T. Stead's article. After the meeting, the police provided an escort for the Mormons and although the mob was large and unruly, there was no violence. The *Sunderland Daily Echo* reported the meeting accurately, giving considerable space to Rudger's lecture. In fact, during the entire Sunderland agitation, the press treated the Mormons fairly, once again, pointing out that the "Anti-Mormon campaign . . . is more likely to advertise this strange creed to people who otherwise would never have heard of it than it is likely to suppress it."

Gradually the Nuneaton and Sunderland opposition diminished, and most of the agitation leaders were caught and punished—usually with heavy fines. Eventually the Sunderland chapel was dedicated by Rudger, who said the chapel was a monument to bigotry.

With all rental halls denied to them, the Mormons had no alternative but to ask the church to buy their own halls. "Thus do the enemies of truth help the good work along." The enemies of truth had, been routed for the moment, but they would be back. A year later a mob attacked the Sunderland Chapel one evening during a Relief Society meeting. Elder Ralph Hendricks was slammed against the wall when the mob finally forced the door open, and he later died of his injuries.

The winter and early spring agitation at Nuneaton and Sunderland came during the period when Rudger was mourning the death of his mother and father, which made it all the more difficult. But when spring finally arrived, his health and spirits were high and he had a fine case of spring fever. "I can hardly content myself indoors," he wrote a friend, "but being tied down with work have little time for the open air. I am getting what benefit and satisfaction there are in a glance from my open window. I see children by the score romping on the green grass, under the bright and glorious light of a summer sun. I almost feel like a child once more, and it is a good feeling—sweet and pleasant."

He went to a conference in London over Easter and made sure he had time to enjoy himself. Among the events were a concert featuring Hazel Dawn; an airship exhibit in which one ship went up six thousand feet ("It nearly took my breath, I consider it a desperate thing to do and I felt much more comfortable on the ground looking up"); and a visit to Hamstead Heath, where the "slum element" of London traditionally gathers on Easter Monday. There were an estimated 400,000 people there, "a rummy lot. Boys and girls of 14 and 15 were in great numbers and acted like young barbarians and the conduct of many older ones was but little better. . . . How greatly blessed, indeed, are the young people of Zion, who are born in the far mountains of Israel."

With winter over, it was time for his annual trip to the continent, but just before he left, he received a letter from his son, H.B., announcing his marriage to Pearl Bailey, Gay's friend whom H.B. had met in England, and requesting financial assistance. Rudger responded with a long sermon on the sanctity of marriage and a small advance against more financial help when "I return and pull my affairs into shape."

He received another long, amusing, and flowery letter from young Samuel, this one announcing his graduation from grade school and also bringing up, in his manner, the question of money. "I don't wish to send a begging letter to you," young Samuel wrote, "indeed it is not my wont nor want to do so. I merely intend this to be slightly suggestive, verging on the precincts of a hint. For the past few months I know that you have had on your mind the idea of presenting me with some sort of a 'send off,' but as yet nothing definite."

What Samuel had in mind was a new bicycle, for which Rudger should send a $40 money order immediately. Then by way of a little blackmail, Samuel added: "Things are eventful here for mother. A handsome, well-dressed, cultured man of about forty has been extremely kind to her. When we returned, he gave her a beautiful frosted cake with the words 'Welcome Home' on it. Since then he has presented her with four cakes, one pie, several boxes of candy and two large bunches of winter violets. Write for further particulars when you send my money order." He also announced that he was now wearing long trousers regularly.

Rudger sidestepped this threat of extortion by pleading poverty because of his missionary work though he sent Samuel a check for $15. But Samuel's letter did prompt an exchange of correspondence with his son about his flowery prose. Rudger urged him to try to use shorter words whenever possible. Sam did not agree: "In constructing sentences, I always endeavor to choose words fitted to convey exactly the meaning intended, whether they be monosyllables or polysyllables, rather than encumber them with awkward phrases of small words." (Eventually, Samuel won the debate; the following year, after one of his long, literary efforts, Rudger replied: "I took occasion to read it to the brethren here and they appeared to greatly enjoy it. Some of the words were quite *stupendous* in size, but nevertheless conveyed the meaning correctly. It is a fine letter and does you credit.")

As Rudger prepared to leave for his summer tour of the Continent he reported that time was passing "with lightning rapidity. Morning hardly dawns before twilight overshadows us."

Nevertheless, he complained about the upcoming trip to President Smith: "It involves many weary miles of travel and many meetings with the elders and Saints."

It was a strenuous trip, seven thousand miles in two months, but he said he "enjoyed it nonetheless." He felt he had accomplished quite a bit—most important, a recommendation, with supporting documentation, that the Saints organize a French mission, which they did by the end of the year.

*   *   *

In the meantime, back in Arizona, Pearl was in a state of uncertainty and turmoil. She had been married to Rudger now for eight years. During its entire course it had been a clandestine marriage of secret meetings and long absences. It was illegal and increasingly at odds with the church, and it was a marriage the joys and sorrows of which Pearl could share only with her immediate family.

Her mother and father supported her, but her mother was not sympathetic to the marriage. She knew personally the trials a polygamous wife had to suffer.

Life had become particularly difficult for Pearl after Rudger's departure for England. She was a beautiful woman in her early thirties. She was attractive to men whom she could not allow to court her but could not fend off with the truth. She was lonely and unhappy, and during the time after Rudger's departure began to rethink her relationship and sort out her feelings. By mid-1912 she had decided that she had to see him and talk with him, regardless of the dangers. She had consulted extensively with an advisor and confidant in Los Angeles—probably Stake President Joseph Robinson—about her dilemma. Robinson agreed that she should go to England and attempt to resolve the matter.

She left in early October and arrived in England on the 17th. She had thought long and hard on the way over. Her first encounter with Rudger was at a public meeting where she once again had to pretend that their relationship was something other than what it was, and the experience confirmed her feelings.

"The facts are," she wrote to her parents two weeks later, "that Bro. R's blessing in L.A., his talk—my feelings as I came across the sea— as I came hourly nearer—as I shook hands in a hall filled with people, everything makes me feel that I shall someday soon, be released from present conditions."

In the next few months they met secretly from time to time. David Udall, Jr., served as liaison, carrying messages back and forth and providing cover for their trysts. It was a role the young missionary did not enjoy, and it left him with unpleasant memories of his time in England.

It is not certain just how often they met or what the nature of their relationship was during the four months she was there. Pearl appears to have lived most of the time in London. They certainly did not cohabit on any established basis, and they may not have slept together at all. There is evidence that Rudger wanted to have a child but Pearl demurred. "I cannot feel right in assuming the great responsibility which he is willing for me to take. I feel I have made no mistake and I know Mother that you will be glad that I am not taking the risks just now. I am not so sure how Father will feel."

Pearl was a conscientious person and would not simply walk away from the serious commitment she had made to Rudger and to God. "I shall be slow and be careful and I want to know that I shall not be doing wrong—that I shall be worthy of God's blessing and care and of the love and approval of you."

But she was sure of herself and saw clearly that she couldn't go on living a life that had become a torture. "I sleep like a baby and I feel ready to accept whatever the future may bring—only I am not going to have eternal warfare going on in my own soul any more, if I can help it. 'God plans it all.' I have always tried to do right and follow His plans so why shouldn't I yet be happy?"

It is almost certain that by the time Pearl left, setting sail on the *Hesperian* in the latter part of January 1913, the marriage was essentially over.

Meanwhile, Rudger was still under pressure from the anti-Mormons in England. The focus of the trouble shifted to Bristol and Ipswich, where antagonism to the Mormons had heated up for a number of reasons: the aggressive proselytizing by the missionaries (sometimes they would pay three successive visits to a household before they would accept a no); a rumor that the Mormons had twelve young girls in a carriage and were ready to kidnap them; another series of articles by Winifred Graham, "A Spirited Historical Sketch of the Mormons"; and the unfortunate incident of the young man who exposed himself on a street corner in London and who had been tried and sentenced  to jail for six months. This was the first time a Mormon missionary had ever been sent to prison in England, and it contributed significantly to keeping the agitation going for most of the fall of 1912.

The hostilities at Bristol were especially ugly. One Sunday evening in November 1912 during a conference with Rudger in attendance, a mob of about two thousand people appeared outside Wollseley Hall in Eastville. The police were notified, but responded with only two bobbies. As the *Millenial Star* reported:

Unfortunately President Clawson was the only elder wearing a silk hat, and the moment the agitators saw it, they cried out: 'Here's the man; there he goes,' etc. A large number of people thereupon followed him and several elders who walked with him, booing and hooting and calling vile names. Thus they were followed up one street and down another, the noise and confusion increasing every moment, until they managed to slip away and escape without personal injury. Apparently, all that was lacking was a determined, unprincipled leader, and, had such a one turned up, President Clawson and his associates would undoubtedly have suffered violent treatment.

The agitation at Bristol and Ipswich continued during the fall and into the early months of 1813, with the principal cause of the hostility being the story about the Mormons having kidnapped twelve girls. Despite newspaper reviews, tracts, letters to the editor, an appeal to the American Embassy in London, and countless speeches, Rudger could not kill this story. He made special efforts to publicize the fact that V. S. Peet, the non-Mormon editor of the *Utah Independent* had, since 1905, been offering a $1,000 reward for proof of any girls being sent to Utah as white slaves or for the purpose of becoming polygamous wives. Peet's offer had been repeated in England regularly since May 1911. But no one ever applied for the reward.

At the same time, Rudger was hit, one after another, with two libel suits, which were time-consuming and frustrating and would eventually lead to his being recalled to Salt Lake City. One was brought by G. H. Potter, a preacher in Sunderland who had been responsible for much of the unrest there. Potter claimed he had once been a member of the Mormon church and that he had been to Utah.

After Rudger returned from the Continent in August 1912, he had written an editorial in the *Star* titled, "The Truth about Mr. G. H. Potter's Visit to Utah." In it he quoted a long article in the *Deseret News* which was intended to expose Potter as a fraud. The article contained charges that the paper could not substantiate, the most serious being the statement that "he used to be a Baptist minister in Dudley [England], but they turned him out, and when he went back to England he tried to get back in the church and they would not have him." Potter sued Rudger and the *Star*, and the case dragged on all fall before it was finally settled, with Rudger paying 125 pounds and court costs. In addition, Rudger had to issue for publication in the local press a written apology to Potter.

Joseph F. Smith was clearly annoyed: "We very much regret the necessity of our having to defend ourselves in a case of libel, a new thing in our history," the president wrote, although he stressed that the quorum stood ready to do anything it could to assist him.

The second legal action was initiated by Frank F. Farncombe, who had attacked the Mormons in an article in *The People*, a London weekly. It contained the usual charges, but also said that the Mormon headquarters in England had warned its missionaries that it faced a "great falling off of converts" which meant "that there will be a frightful shortage of 'brides' in the Holy City, despite the hustling campaign conducted by 250 exponents of polygamy led by the re-doubtable Rudger Clawson, who is the captain of the Old Guard 'tabernacle-raisers.' "

Rudger responded with a letter to the editor of *The People* saying that Farncombe's entire article was a fabrication, and when the editor refused to publish the letter, Rudger had it printed as a tract and began distributing it. Then Farncombe wrote Rudger saying his integrity as a journalist had been attacked and that if Rudger maintained his atti-tude, he (Farncombe) would like to have the name of Rudger's solicitor. Rudger's defense was simply to ignore this and other letters from Farncombe that soon followed.

When the year ended, Rudger, the record-keeper, was especially pleased with the annual financial report. "I am happy to say," he wrote home, "that the British Mission business and accounts are now fully and completely divorced from those of the Liverpool Office. And I may say in this connection that the financial report for the year 1912 was taken, not from the Liverpool Office books as formerly, but from the British Mission *Year Book*. Or, in other words, the entire business connected with the British Mission accounts was carried in a single book which, of course, is complete and all embracing."

He could also report that "the business transacted by the Liverpool office" showed a net gain of $5,998.25.

But he was now fighting legal battles on two fronts, and, for the first time since he had arrived in England, he seemed to be weary and discouraged. He wrote his predecessor, Charles Penrose: "I only wish I could do it better than I am doing and doubtless I could if I had the talent and ability possessed by some of the brethren, but I am endeavoring to 'muckle' the situation as best I can, leaving the outcome and residue with the Lord."

"The year 1912," he wrote Francis Lyman, "will soon have run its length, a year fraught with many interesting and momentous occurrences. Wars and rumors of wars, pestilences, famines and earthquakes are recorded upon its pages in confirmation of the predictions of the Savior and His prophets, as well as the mighty work accomplished by the people of God in the Mountains of Israel and the preaching of the Gospel to the nations afar off."

In March, while Farncombe was still bombarding him with letters, Peter Freece, who had been involved in the Liverpool meeting in January 1911 which ignited the British anti-Mormon agitation, also threatened a libel suit. Freece objected to a *Millenial Star* editorial in which Rudger had referred to "the redoubtable and infamous Hans Peter Freece."

For several weeks Rudger pretended to be on the Continent in order to avoid letters from the two men. Finally, after consulting his solicitor, he wrote President Smith and the counselors asking for advice: "Shall I continue to evade service [of papers], or shall I accept it and fight these two cases in the court? If you say put up a fight, I shall be perfectly willing to do so, but in view of the decision in the Potter Contempt Case and also in the spirit of prejudice and persecution that is rife in this Mission, I candidly confess that I have but little confidence in the English courts and but small hope of success."

If the counselors wanted him to remain and make a fight, they were to cable him: PROCEED TO BIRMINGHAM. But if they wanted him to evade the service of papers and return home at once, they should cable him: REMAIN IN LIVERPOOL.

Although Rudger offered to stay and fight, he clearly wanted to avoid it and just go home. Ten days later, having not heard from Freece, Farncombe, or Salt Lake City, he wrote Smith: "I've learned by experience that if one goes into the sacred precincts of the courts, even though it be just inside the entrance, or glances his eye at an attorney, it means expense. . . . Farncombe has no case whatever and as to Freece, I do not know just how the matter, if prosecuted, might terminate. In a legal fight with these unconscionable falsifiers there is everything to lose and nothing to gain, and in a case of judgment against them nothing could be collected. It is the old mathematical problem solved anew, 'Take nothing from nothing and nothing remains.' On the other hand, I would be butting up against a wall of prejudice and bigotry, as I said in my former letter, to meet the issue in the courts."

On April 2, Rudger received his reply: REMAIN IN LIVERPOOL. Nine days later he was on the S. S. *Virginian* headed for home.

A major chapter in the life of Rudger Clawson was over. In the three years he was in Europe, he wrote letters constantly, recording his activities in detail. Combined with his articles in the *Millenial Star* and other accounts he wrote of this period, a picture of Rudger Clawson, as mission president, emerges clearly. For one thing, from his diaries we see Rudger as a person so highly focused on his work for the church in Britain and on spreading the gospel, that all else becomes secondary.

Like many religionists, he blamed the devil when things went wrong, and everything he did right was due to the hand of the Lord. How aware he was of the more complex forces at work in England and Europe during this time does not emerge from his writings.

But he certainly never missed a chance to preach the gospel. When a niece wrote, concerned about losing her missionary husband for three years, he replied: "You ought by all means to remain true to him; furthermore you ought to be deeply grateful for the opportunity now presented to show your fidelity and loyalty to the man of your choice, especially if he fills a good and honorable mission. It is a little test which, if you can bear it, will be a source of gratification to you and to him. . . . It must be a source of sincere pleasure to you to know that he has gone upon the Lord's errand, and will be engaged for the coming months in a work that will not only develop his character but will bring salvation to the souls of men." Three years, he reminded her, is but a short time compared to the eternity they would be married.

When young Samuel wrote asking him for a suggested course of study, Rudger said it would "not be in good taste" for him to recommend one subject over another because they are all good. But in the case of a language, be sure to learn German—which will be of "immense" value if Samuel should take a mission to Germany. "Whatever you do," he concluded, "be sure to take lessons in singing.

Learn to sing, my boy, it will help you amazingly in the mission field."

To a man who gave him information which enabled him to recover a grip and umbrella he had lost in Stafford, he replied, after thanking him: "It will perhaps be a matter of some surprise to you that I am one of those 'terrible Mormon missionaries' who have been receiving so much attention from the press of late. I can assure you, however, that the many evil stories in circulation about us are absolutely false. We are here on a peaceful errand and our purpose is simply to deliver a Gospel message to the people of this country. . . . We bear our own expenses . . . and also support our families at home. If you should ask: 'Why do you do this, how can you afford to make so great a sacrifice?' The answer is, 'It is a labor of love; we are seeking the salvation of souls." He then said he was sending the man several Mormon tracts and proceeded for another page or two to give a little sermon on Mormon doctrine.

And the importance Rudger attached to the saving of *one* soul can be seen from his comments on the question of street-corner proselytiz- ing, which some Saints thought was a waste of time: "It is true that in these street gatherings there are many contemptible characters who are wholly unworthy of notice, but on the other hand many intelli- gent, thoughtful and fair-minded people will also be found among them. Much prejudice at times has been allayed on the street corners and honest souls have been converted to the Cause of Christ. Even one honest soul reached in this manner will justify the trouble and inconvenience and persecution which sometimes follow."

Just before he returned to America, Rudger was able to report home: "After two years of almost continuous persecution in which mob violence was often in the ascendant, all is quiet in the British mission." But, of course, it was the Lord's work. He "has never failed to hear and answer my prayers. . . . Truly He has caused the wrath of men to praise Him."

Before leaving, Rudger wrote a "Valedictory" which was published in the *Star* on April 17, while he was on the high seas. In it he recounted his achievements during three years as head of the European Mission—the twice-a-year visits to the thirteen conferences in En- gland, the annual visits to the Continent; the organization of the French Mission; the many properties he had helped acquire in

England; the vast correspondence; the ten million tracts and 212,000 books distributed there; the 1,470 baptisms in England and more than 5,000 baptisms in Europe.

But perhaps his real valedictory came in a *Star* editorial he had written the previous January. It was about the situation in Sunderland, but he could just as well have been speaking of the whole two years of hostility and persecution in England: "Just in proportion to the intensity of the agitation, so is the calm which has followed. . . . Some day curious people may be prompted to say: 'Were the Mormons at one time persecuted in Sunderland, and, if so, why was it?'

"And then we fancy other curious people will arise and answer: 'Yes, they were, but we do not know why; there was no fault found in them.' "

# EPILOGUE:
# PRESIDENT OF
# THE TWELVE

*I*t is not known how the marriage of Rudger Clawson and Pearl Udall was formally ended. It had begun under the ministrations of an apostle who was subsequently cut off from the church, and it had no validity in the eyes of the law. Anthony Ivins, who had officiated in many post-1890 Manifesto marriages and became an apostle in 1907, knew of the marriage (even before 1913) as may have Joseph F. Smith. Smith definitely was aware of it by 1917 when he was asked to approve Pearl's appointment to the general board of the Young Ladies Mutual Improvement Association. It is most likely that President Smith officially dissolved the marriage sometime between 1913 and 1917.

During these years Pearl continued to practice osteopathy in Arizona, traveling to California on at least two occasions to take the California board exams. Then in August 1916, she took the Utah boards in Salt Lake, passed them, and began to practice there.

In 1919 Pearl married a Salt Lake widower, Joseph Nelson, in a temple ceremony. According to family tradition, Nelson asked and received the assurance of Heber J. Grant, who had succeeded Joseph F. Smith in the presidency the year before, that the sealing of Rudger and Pearl had been canceled. Pearl is remembered in the Udall family as an especially well-loved person who devoted much of her life to doing for others.

Rudger, though probably sympathetic to Pearl's distress, had other reasons for allowing the marriage to be dissolved. Antipolygamy forces had for some time been growing stronger within the church itself. Church officials in increasing numbers were being punished or excommunicated for supporting polygamy. Among church leaders, the pendulum, so long the captive of those who refused to give up the Principle, was swinging in the opposite direction. The church crusade against polygamy was underway. Rudger's position as a post-Second Manifesto polygamist *and* member of the highest governing body of the church was untenable.

The secret was relatively safe with Ivins and Joseph F. Smith. Smith was a strong believer in plural marriage, and continued to the end to cohabit with his own wives. He was also sympathetic to those who had been involved in post-Manifesto polygamous activities. But if the marriage had become known to very many others—particularly Francis Lyman, who was actively involved in rooting out polygamy, and Reed Smoot, who was now one of its most vocal opponents—it is unlikely that the marriage could have been kept secret for very long, certainly not seventy years. It would have, at least, been extensively debated within the quorum and been recorded by some of those involved.

Matthias Cowley, the most obvious source of information about the marriage, kept it a secret during the three interrogations by the apostles which he underwent in 1905, 1911, and 1914 as a prelude to being disfellowshipped (and at the first and last of which Rudger Clawson was present). Had Rudger and Pearl attempted, however, to continue to maintain an active polygamous marriage, there is little likelihood the secret could have been kept.

So ended the last of the dramatic events which over the years had determined the course of Rudger's life. From then on, it moved essentially on an even keel. And it is worth noting that when Rudger put together his memoirs in 1935, he concluded them with his "Valedictory," published in the *Millenial Star* in April 1913, at the end of his mission in Europe. Rudger himself almost seems to have considered the rest of his life an epilogue. He settled back into his role in the quorum, carrying out his apostolic duties as diligently as ever. He and Lydia raised their children to adulthood and remained closely in touch with them throughout their lives. The church grew and changed around him, but the one thing—his accession to the presidency of the church—that would have reintroduced into his life the kind of dynamic that characterized his early years did not occur. Heber J. Grant, who became president in 1918, outlived him by two years.

During the months after his return from England, he corresponded extensively with people in Liverpool and at the missions on the continent. He also received a number of gifts from his friends abroad, one of the most prized being a Delftware plate from President Roscoe Eardley and others at the Netherlands Mission. "It completely knocked me off my feet, so to speak," Rudger wrote in his inimitable style. "Believe me, brethren, the noble face of William of Orange, so indelibly stamped upon the Delft Plate, will have a prominent place in my dining room. . . ."

The French Mission gave him a vase, and the other mission presidents joined in giving him a diamond scarf pin. "It is a chaste and beautiful gift," he wrote effusively in his thank-you letter, "dazzling the eye with its lambient [sic] rays of sparkling light, and will be found among my choicest treasures."

On returning home Rudger noted, in a letter to James Foggo, that when she met him at the depot, "Sister Clawson was younger-looking in appearance than when she left Liverpool to return home. Of course, I could offer no objection whatsoever to such a change."

And how did Rudger look after his three years in Europe and the painful ending of his marriage to Pearl? Lydia, in a letter to Brother Foggo's wife, gives us a rather amusing view. "Brother Clawson is constantly on the 'go.' I see less of him here than I did over there. He has just now returned from the Uintah Stake after covering the distance of 800 miles travel. He came home looking sedate and thoughtful, she said, because "at Uintah two members of the Church were discussing his age, and they came to the conclusion, after surveying him critically, that he was 80 years old. Brother immediately had a relapse, and I am nursing him back to health. The fact of the matter is, you know, he is *only* 57 [actually, he was fifty-six]. But since people are taking him to be 80 years of age, it makes me feel like a 'sporty' young girl. Do you wonder that Brother Clawson's moustache slipped off and was irretrievably lost in the ocean? It was a narrow escape because he feels that had he returned with a moustache he would certainly be taken for a centenarian—a hundred-year-old boy."

Many of the more memorable events in Rudger's later years involved trips to distant places. In July 1915 he traveled to Georgia to dedicate a chapel in Atlanta. He also visited the site of the Joseph Standing murder where he talked with the landowner and a friend who was familiar with the details of the event. Then he stopped at the Whitfield County Court in Dalton where the clerk showed him documents related to the trial and acquittal of the murderers. He was pleasantly surprised by the friendliness of the people he met.

In 1919 he accompanied Heber J. Grant, who had become president the year before, to the dedication of the Hawaii Temple (which had been designed in the form of a huge Grecian cross devoid of towers, and stood on a prominence overlooking the Pacific Ocean looking more like an Aztec than a Mormon temple). Rudger returned to Hawaii in May and June of 1921. This time he had more opportunity to explore life on the Islands which he reported on in long letters to the *Deseret News*.

In that year he succeeded Anthon H. Lund as president of the Council of the Twelve.

The year 1923 was an important one for the Church of Jesus Christ of Latter-day Saints. It was the centennial of Joseph Smith's vision in which the Angel Moroni appeared to him and told him of the Golden Plates. In April a great centennial conference was held at which the Mormon priesthood gathered en masse. Rudger, as president of the Twelve, was one of the principal speakers. At one point, President Grant led the assembly in the hosanna shout (always referred to by Rudger as the "sacred shout"). Then the organ boomed and the Tabernacle Choir burst forth with Handel's "Hallelujah Chorus" filling the great domed structure with music. It must have been a moment of intense satisfaction for Rudger, in which the sights and sounds reaffirmed him in his deepest feelings about himself and his church. That night the temple was brilliantly illuminated. One great globe, wrote B. H. Roberts, lighted up the "entire side of the building and its six noble towers."

In the fall he attended another centennial celebration, this one organized by B. H. Roberts, at the Hill Cumorah in Palmyra, New York, where Joseph Smith is believed to have actually found the Golden Plates. It was the first of what would ultimately become an annual event there.

Among his other trips, one of the most enjoyable was the visit to the New England Mission with Lydia in 1938 where they were driven through the rolling green hills of Vermont and given their first opportunity to see Joseph Smith's birthplace in Sharon, where a simple obelisk of Vermont granite stands in commemoration. He also took a number of long trips east to see his son, Sam, in Chicago and Lydia, Jr., in Washington, D.C.

During these years, Lydia devoted herself especially to the economic welfare of her children and grandchildren, Rudger more to their spiritual well-being, though he did not ply them with religious exhortations, nor did he make a great issue of it if they broke the Word of Wisdom or drifted from close attachment to the church. Rather he offered advice and comment informed by the basic beliefs and principles that had guided his own life. He seemed particularly close to Sam, with whom he would engage in long religious discussions whenever they were together. "When you go to him with a problem," Sam wrote in 1937, "you never come away feeling blamed. What has been right or wrong in some particular instance is never condemned but always explained against a background of a long chain of events leading up to and away from the particular problem you may have brought him. Father has never rebuked me nor felt that I was wrong— but he has often felt that I was unenlightened. He has said to me on more than one occasion, 'My son, you are all in darkness.' "

Rudger's basic beliefs were, of course, the fundamental doctrines of Mormonism, faith in the gospel as taught by Joseph Smith, baptism by immersion for the remission of sin, repentance of sinful behavior, the laying on of hands for the gift of the Holy Ghost, and the ordinance of baptism for the dead. As a church official, he preached about them constantly.

At Rudger's death, John Henry Evans characterized him as a thinker and preacher. "President Clawson was a man of ideas, but his ideas centered in religion, salvation. Few men among the leaders of the church have known the doctrines of our faith more accurately and soundly than he. Not a great preacher, he was more easily read than listened to. He never knew where the emotional stops were, and so could not play them. But his sermons were packed with lucid, reasoned, developed thought. And to be able to do that in an age where there is a premium on loose thinking, is a great achievement."

One subject that was central to Rudger's thinking and is important if one is to fully understand some of the major events in his life, was his idea of marriage. Marriage was not simply a bond between man and woman, but was a link in the eternal chain of existence which is at the heart of Mormon theology.

In that theology, spirits existing in a premortal realm await being brought into the world (by "mothers in Israel") in order, among other things, to learn good and evil and to be tested in their obedience to God. At death they pass on to heaven where they attain a level of glory and godhood according to their works in life. Marriage clearly plays a key role in this process. In fact, the highest levels of celestial glory cannot be gained by either man or woman without marriage for time and eternity.

But in the theology of plural marriage there was more. At the peak of this eternal realm would be those men who could gather round them the largest "kingdom" of wives and children. They would be the closest to and most like the true God. "As man is," Lorenzo Snow had proclaimed, "God once was. As God is, man may become." It was a compelling doctrine, and to the end of his life Rudger believed it without reservation.

"I still believe that plural marriage is a true principle," he said in 1927, at a family gathering on his seventieth birthday. "I would like that to be known among my children as my feeling. If I never speak of it again, that is my testimony. I have suffered for it, believed in it, and I believe in it today. And the Lord has blessed me because of my attitude in this matter."

He would repeat the statement many times, the latest on record being in 1941 after Lydia's funeral. There is every reason to believe that, despite the vicissitudes in his relationships with Florence Dinwoodey and Pearl Udall, he expected them (and Rudger Elmo) somehow to be able to join him—along with Lydia and her children—in his Kingdom in the hereafter.

The celestial kingdom was—and, stripped of polygamy, is—for Mormons a clearly delineated, very concrete realm of bodily existence, human relationships, and perpetual exultation. It can thus be seen that the span of eternity from the premortal to the immortal was very real to Rudger Clawson.

Indeed, for his son, Sam, Rudger's sense of eternity was the key to understanding him. In an article about his father which appeared in the *Improvement Era* in 1937, Sam wrote:

He lives and reacts to men and events as if he had lived forever and will live forever. He does not see time as most men see it; he sees it as *Eternity*. He does not live in time as it is measured by all of our various inventions and mathematical formulas. Father actually lives in *Eternity*.

That gives father strength, for it gives him all the ages past and future to measure things by. A crisis of any kind is small when measured against all events that have passed or may happen. He is unhurried. He takes his time and measures and never judges hastily.

All values to him are relative. Circumstances are self-evaluating in time and in its eternal stretch and he can view them impersonally. He sees possible good in apparent bad and virtues in things and people where no virtues seem to belong. He looks on seemingly important occasions and at past events quite unruffled and he can view the most trivial things with quiet dignity.

What that sort of thing can mean, what it can represent, has always been exemplified to me in a certain blend in father of all of his various characteristics, and particularly a blend of mind and character. He will get hold of a principle and hold to it in the face of persecution, hardships, and long suffering. He can endure anything and will endure the most severe suffering indefinitely. Nothing can switch him from a course once he has his mind set on a goal. Father has on more than one occasion faced death for a principle. . . . More than once he has walked directly into a crisis with the conviction that all possible consequences would be of equal importance. Death to him is only an event in his continuous eternal life. This has made him patient and courageous.

To father I think life looks like a long series of obstacles, obstacles put there to be endured or to be overcome by the force of a man's character, a force which may be strengthened by constant prayer. Over a long period of years he has arisen early in the morning to pray and face the eventualities of the day.

Life has left no residue of bitterness in him; impressions and memories have left no scars. He has never indulged in self-pity, never tolerated self-esteem. There is no elation when he wins—he either wins and turns victory into wisdom for the next encounter, else he endures and waits. He never loses. . . .

I think Father has this feeling of living in Eternity because he thinks and feels and lives his religion. He never talks much about it, but you cannot live around him and understand him without coming to know what his religion means, and what it means to him. It is not merely a philosophy and it is not merely a creed. It is not static; it is vital and dynamic. Religion to him is a living eternal thing and he as an integral part of it will live eternally.

From this perspective, one can see that Rudger Clawson's later years were not an epilogue at all, but a prologue. The best was yet to come.

During these later years, Rudger and Lydia were frequently honored on their birthdays and anniversaries. Long newspaper articles were written about them, invariably mentioning or recounting Rudger's role in the Joseph Standing murder. Lydia appeared in photos of the wives of the apostles or of church events, her deep, dark eyes staring directly at the camera.

Heber J. Grant suffered a relatively severe stroke in 1939 and there was a flurry of speculation about the succession if he died. The rumor was that Rudger, because of his age, might, contrary to church tradition, be denied the presidency, an idea which made his son Sam quite angry, but Grant did not die. However, on February 1, 1941, after a short illness, Lydia did. The family gathered at the home on Canyon Road after the funeral. Lydia, Jr., made notes on what occurred and typed them up later, summarizing what was said.

Someone not identified, but probably Sam, opened with a prayer. "Our Father in Heaven, we, a group of thy children, who loved our dear mother, and the father who is here with us, have met to do her honor in a little family circle to listen to the advice and counsel of our father whom in our hearts we do dearly belove."

Rudger then read Lydia's will. In it she made certain specific bequests: a piece of property to Gay; an Oriental rug to Lydia, Jr.; a watch to Lorenzo; some glassware, cutlery, and personal effects to Gay and Lydia; and a portrait of herself painted by J. Willard Clawson to Rudger (or if predeceased by Rudger, to Lydia, Jr.).

All the rest—and it consisted of most of the possessions accumulated during their lives together—was to be divided equally among the children, who were also designated joint executors of the will.

Rudger then spoke of his relationship to Lydia and the bond between them, that they were married for eternity and would be together forever. It is important to understand that whatever their day-to-day relationship, Rudger and Lydia loved each other deeply. Lydia was a faithful Mormon even though something of a "rebel"—according to Lydia, Jr.—and resentful of the patriarchal structure of the church. But she respected Rudger's commitment to it. And whatever Pearl meant to him, Rudger never wavered in his devotion to the woman who had been central to his life for so many years and to whom he was married for eternity.

Rudger reviewed his own life's work and experiences and once again reaffirmed his belief in polygamy. He talked of the love and unity within the family.

Then he turned to practical affairs, especially the money they would inherit. One of the children had done an inventory of Lydia's financial assets. The cash amounted to around $20,000, most of it split up in dozens of joint accounts with her children and grandchildren.

Lydia also owned the 51 Canyon Road house (in which Rudger still had a life interest) and at least one other piece of property. In addition there were stocks in a number of companies; three hundred shares in one, a hundred in a couple of others, five or six in still others.

This constituted a relatively substantial estate in those days, especially for a churchman's wife who had been spending rather heavily on her children for the past twenty-five years. But it did not conform to the visions of wealth that her children expected to find. Lydia's supply of money had always seemed bottomless to them as she doled it out over the years, and the stories about the killings she made in the stock market were still current among them.

The moment of truth came when they opened her strongbox. It was a finely carved wooden box that had been made by the prisoners at the penitentiary while Rudger was there. She had kept it locked and stored in her closet all her life. No one had ever seen the contents, though it was openly assumed now among her children that it must contain the money and/or stocks that seemed to be missing from her estate.

All were gathered expectantly in the parlor when Rudger lifted the lid and then tipped the box forward for the others to see. In it, still tightly folded in small squares, were the love letters Rudger had written Lydia from prison, along with a picture of each of her babies, the living and the dead.

A month after Lydia's death, Rudger flew to Chicago to visit Sam and then to Washington to attend a stake conference where special memorial services for Reed Smoot, who had died a short time before, were to be held.

Then in September, he went with Gay, Lorenzo, and their families to Brigham City to attend the Peach Day celebration. He had chaired the first Peach Day Planning Committee forty-three years before. "The weather was bright and pleasant. The parade was highly successful. The floats were exceptionally attractive, and 12 bands in line with lots of beautiful girls . . . returned to Salt Lake with a couple of bushels of *Peaches.*" As the floats moved down Main Street past the courthouse and the tabernacle and the other familiar landmarks that were left, Rudger and Gay, who had once been a pretty girl on a float herself, reminisced.

But after that his health began to fail. His life interest in the house was honored by his children who had inherited it. But Salt Lake City was less kindly disposed. Improvement plans in the Canyon Road area called for extending a street through Rudger's property which would require the tearing down of his home. Action was taken by the city to acquire the property, though, after some legal exchanges, Rudger was allowed to remain there until his death.

In March 1942, on his eighty-fifth birthday, he received many tributes. Perhaps the keenest insight came from Richard L. Evans of the First Council of the Seventy: "From his birth, March 12, 1857, to the present time, the record fails to show any instance in which this man did not respond with all his gifts and energies to any call that came to him through the channels of the priesthood of God. Nor does the record show any departure, for any reason of personal advantage or expediency, from any conviction, or principle, or right course, or from justice and mercy and long-suffering patience and kindliness, as it was given to him to see and to know these things."

\*   \*   \*

Rudger Clawson was a person to whom things regularly happened which tested his character. Until he married Pearl Udall, his responses were invariably principled and he seemed always to come down on the side of the angels. But his post-Second Manifesto plural marriage trapped him in a dilemma so conflict-ridden and painful that even for a man with his determination, he could not resolve it without compromise. He believed that the doctrine of celestial marriage was the law of God and that his marriage to Pearl was in conformity with it. Government laws and theologically ambiguous manifestos could not contravene it. Secrecy, hypocrisy, and disobedience to the laws of man were justifiable when adhering to the higher law of God. It was the same message he had delivered to Charles S. Zane in a Salt Lake courtroom twenty-five years before.

Even if Pearl had not wished to end the marriage, Rudger would have remained caught on the horns of the dilemma that pitted his beliefs against his church. Would he have considered joining the fundamentalists who dropped out of or were ejected from the church in order to pursue "true Mormonism"—including the practice of plural marriage? It is doubtful. The church as an institution was too much a part of the warp and woof of his existence. He was too identified with it, too committed to it and to the acceptance of its authority to make the final break. He could secretly defy it, but to give it up would have been too much for him to bear. Rudger Clawson was one with his church.

But this mindset characterized most of the church leaders during the first century of its existence. The Saints had been persecuted in Missouri and Illinois and had been hounded by the federal government almost from the day they arrived in the Great Salt Lake valley. During most of Rudger's life, certainly to 1913 when he returned from England at the age of fifty-six, the "enemy" had always been threatening. It was within the church and its doctrines, within the culture of Mormonism, that he and the Mormon people found their security and identity.

But even if it had not been beleaguered, Mormonism as a belief system does not foster the questioning mind. In most of the world's religions, there is a realm of mysticism or avenues of thought where religious beliefs can be adapted to individual needs. Mormonism has few if any such avenues. It is also especially hard to rationalize since its beginning are so historically recent and—in the minds of many— the events leading to its founding and the nature of some of its doctrines so bizarre.

J. Reuben Clark was a statesman and diplomat of note and had been serving as U.S. ambassador to Mexico when he was called by Heber J. Grant to the First Presidency in 1933. Clark had wrestled with this problem in midlife and had concluded that religious faith could not be rationalized. His own inquiries into Joseph Smith's experience and the belief in the progression toward godhood had led him to conclude that if he continued to question, it would destroy his faith. He quoted Abraham Lincoln: "I have learned to read the Bible. I believe all I can and take the rest on faith." So it was for Clark with the Mormon scripture.

There is no evidence that Rudger ever went through this kind of soul-searching about his religion or that he had a meditative side to his personality. His beliefs were embodied in the religious doctrine which he reflected back in carrying out his church responsibilities. There are no passages in the diaries in which he ponders the meaning of God or life, in which he examines himself, in which he doubts or questions. Mormonism has been called a literal-minded religion, one that not only takes the Bible and its own scriptures literally, but that looks at reality in general from a concrete, matter-of-fact perspective that tends to disregard ambiguity. In his literal-mindedness, therefore, Rudger was not untypical of his fellow Mormons.

Perhaps in his long intimate conversations with Sam he explored his beliefs more critically. Sam was known for his intellectual acumen and on occasion argued general semantics with its celebrated originator, Alfred Korzybsky, in Chicago. As we have seen, Sam loved and admired his father and did not break formally with the church, but he very likely challenged Rudger from time to time regarding his beliefs. Whatever Rudger's response he obviously did not lose his son's respect.

A severe blow came in December 1942, when Sam, at forty-six, died of a heart attack.

By the spring of 1943 Rudger, eighty-six years old now, was having trouble with his digestive system, his eyesight, and his hearing. His feet had also begun to ache. He still walked to his office, though he had to use a cane, and he was increasingly stooped. A housekeeper had been hired to care for him, but trying to keep to his old pattern of life finally became too much for him.

At a council session on May 20, 1943, he announced that he would not be able to attend meetings anymore. He spoke for some time, rambling a bit, about his physical infirmities, his life at home, his work, his love and appreciation for his brethren. First Counselor J. Reuben Clark, who was particularly fond of Rudger, responded:

"Brother Clawson: I am sure I speak the sentiments of all the Brethren when I assure you that you have our love, our respect, and that we honor you. . . . As you have blessed us so we wish to bless you and assure you that you have our faith and our prayers and that in the time that the Lord shall yet vouch to you on this earth you may have health and strength and that all your declining years shall be those of joy."

Less than a month later, on June 21, 1943, Rudger Clawson died. By this time, he had few possessions of any value, but among them, carefully preserved, were those he most treasured: the gold watch and chain which had inscribed on it "Presented to Rudger Clawson by Brigham City friends April 20, 1910"; the Delftware plate, given to him by the Netherlands Mission; the graceful vase from the French Mission; and the diamond stickpin from the other mission presidents, which, with a few other things, he had carefully arranged to distribute among his children.

In concluding a laudatory article in the *Improvement Era* in 1937, John A. Widtsoe had captured something of the essence of Rudger Clawson simply by quoting the statistics that Rudger himself had carefully compiled during his years as an apostle. "Perhaps no better statement can be made concerning President Clawson's Apostolic labors than the following list of his Church-wide service from January, 1899, to December 31, 1936. This information has been recorded and preserved by President Clawson with meticulous care during the long period of thirty-seven years:

"Total priesthood ordinations and settings apart, 5,095; total number of meetings attended, 9,054; total number of addresses given, 6,000; total number of miles going and coming, 576,107."

By the time he died, the total number of miles going and coming had passed 600,000. There is no record of the number he has traveled since.

## Addendum

### The Children of Rudger and Lydia Spencer Clawson

Samuel was the family prodigy. He served a mission in the eastern U.S. and then went to the University of Utah and the University of Chicago Law School. As a young lawyer he joined the U.S. attorney's office and was a member of the legal team that successfully prosecuted Al Capone. Then he practiced law in Chicago until his death in 1942. He married Leah Wood and adopted twins, Ronald and Roxanne.

Lydia, Jr., married Roy H. Hoopes and moved to Washington. Lydia published articles and short stories and had two TV scripts produced in the early days of television. For thirteen years she was the Washington social correspondent for the *Deseret News* and then the *Salt Lake Tribune*. She had three children, Roy, Jr., David, and Cara Linda.

Rudger's other three children lived in Salt Lake City all of their lives. After his mission in England Hiram Bradley (H.B.) married Pearl Bailey, Gay's school friend, who had visited the family in England. He was a professional bill collector for most of his working years. Like Sam and Leah, they adopted two children, Richard and Elizabeth.

Gay met her future husband, Horace Bond, in England where Horace was on a mission at the same time she was there. They married several years later and had three children, Roland, Marian, and Brent.

Lorenzo served a mission in Seattle and on his return married Viola Smith. He was the family athlete, becoming one of the leading handball players in the country and competing in national championships in the East. He was employed as a salesman. They also had three children, Lorenzo, Jr., Stanley, and Geraldine.

# Source Notes

Aside from the Rudger Clawson papers (see bibliography), the general resources that were most valuable in writing this book were the following:

Thomas G. Alexander—*Mormonism in Transition*
Leonard J. Arrington—*The Great Basin Kingdom*
Leonard J. Arrington and Davis Bitton—*The Mormon Experience: A History of the Latter-day Saints*
Gustive O. Larson—*The "Americanization" of Utah for Statehood*
Edward Leo Lyman—*Political Deliverance—The Mormon Quest for Utah Statehood*
John Nicholson—*The Martyrdom of Joseph Standing*
D. Michael Quinn—"LDS Church Authority and New Plural Marriages"
Arthur Richardson—*The Life and Ministry of John Morgan*
Samuel W. Taylor—*The Kingdom or Nothing: The Life of John Taylor, Militant Mormon*
Richard S. Van Wagoner—*Mormon Polygamy: A History*
Orson F. Whitney—*A History of Utah*

## Chapter One: The Murder

Much of this chapter is based on Rudger Clawson's description of his Georgia experiences which appears on pages 29–84½ of *Memoirs of the Life of Rudger Clawson Written by Himself* (University of Utah Library; hereafter referred to as Memoirs). Other principal sources are the *Martyrdom of Joseph Standing* by John Nicholson, which was based on the knowledge Nicholson gained of the incident as editor of the *Deseret News* at the time it occurred and on interviews with Rudger when they were in prison together in 1885–86 and *The Life and Ministry of John Morgan* by Arthur Richardson.

The quotation from the *Atlanta Constitution* describing Rudger appeared on 23 October 1879.

For information on northwestern Georgia during these years, see Ward (1965); Stanley (1975), see especially p. 34 for denominational conflict; Watkins and Watkins (1973); and *Official History of Whitfield County, Georgia*. Additional information was derived from a personal interview with Lawrence L. Stanley.

William Young is identified in Ward (1965) as a physician who practiced in Ellijay during the postwar years but finally removed to Texas. While Rudger does not give in his Memoirs the name of the doctor he encountered, the authors believe that he was Dr. Young.

The material on the relationship between and activities of John Morgan and Joseph Standing are covered in Richardson (1965) Chapters 8–13, pages 101–252. Provided also is a great deal of background information on northern Georgia during these years and on the way Joseph and Rudger, as well as John Morgan, went about their missionary work. See also Driggs (forthcoming).

Wilson (1976) includes information on Varnell.

Information in Driggs (forthcoming) does not prove conclusively that it was the Elleges' house at which Rudger and Joseph stopped on the night before the murder; but, weighing the evidence, the authors feel strongly that it was.

Richardson (1965) calls Mary Hamlin "Mollie" while Nicholson (1886) and Driggs (forthcoming) identify her as "Mary." Mollie was apparently her nickname. Her last name sometimes appears as Hamlin and sometimes as Hamline.

The "limber" quote comes from the *Deseret Evening News*, 1 August 1879.

Rudger called the rider on the broken-down horse "Ormsby" in his Memoirs, but the man's correct name was "Owensby."

The "hang you by the neck" quote comes from the *Desert Evening News*, 1 August 1879.

Richardson (1965), pp. 230–31, says that Joseph actually had a gun in his hands (picked up from one of the mob members who had laid it on the ground when kneeling to drink), as did the *Deseret News*, 1 August 1879, and the *Salt Lake Daily Herald*, 5 November 1879. Rudger apparently told the same story to a reporter in Denver on his way back to Salt Lake with Joseph's body (*Denver Tribune*, 31 July 1879, as printed in the *Atlanta Constitution*, 7 August 1879, and referred to by Driggs, forthcoming). The gun faded in Rudger's mind as time passed. His testimony later at the trial was ambiguous, and by the time he wrote his Memoirs it had disappeared—"he was unarmed to my certain knowledge."

All accounts of the critical moment when Rudger defied the mob differ slightly. Our account is a reasonable composite.

The description Rudger gives in his Memoirs of his search for the coroner is somewhat confusing as to sequence and timing. We have put together the most logical sequence using the major sources plus *Official History of Whitfield County, Georgia*.

White (1954) and Watkins and Watkins (1973) provide information on Catoosa Springs about the time Rudger was there.

The text of Rudger's wire to John Morgan about the murder comes from the *Dalton Headlight*, 26 July 1879, as reported in the *Salt Lake City Daily Herald*, 1 August 1879.

### EXCERPTS & QUOTATIONS FROM RUDGER CLAWSON'S WRITINGS
M. = Memoirs

*Page*
2    "I remember it . . ." M. p. 32
2    "So I interpreted . . ." M. p. 32
3    "I was a . . ." M. p. 33
4    "You will readily . . ." M. p. 34
5    "I espied a . . ." M. pp. 34–45
8    ". . . if I quoted . . ." M. pp. 35–38

10   "He was looking . . ." M. pp. 38–42
21   "From what we . . ." M. p. 4


## Chapter Two: Polygamy

For the most scholarly account of Mormon polygamy see Lawrence Foster's *Religion and Sexuality: Three American Communal Experiments of the Nineteenth Century*; other treatments appear in Young (1954), pp. 82–102; Van Wagoner (1986), Chapters 1–8; Brodie (1945), pp. 297–347. For discussions of the Mormon concepts of heaven and marriage, see Arrington and Bitton (1979), pp. 27–40; for an account of the Mormon Reformation, see Gustive O. Larson, "The Mormon Reformation;" for a thorough treatment of the Utah War, see Norman Furniss, *The Mormon Conflict, 1850–1859*.

While polygamy was practiced by people at all economic levels, ultimately only those who were "righteously able" were expected to take plural wives. Estimates of the number of Mormons married in polygamy at any one time vary from 3 to 20 percent, and the vast majority of those were families in which there were only two wives. See Campbell (1988).

For background on Rudger's family and on his early years, see "Hiram B. Clawson" (1881); "Reminiscences of Hiram B. Clawson" (1912); Margaret Gay Judd Clawson (1919), Ellsworth (1974), and the Rudger Clawson Memoirs, pp. 1–29.

See Lester (1979) for information on the Brigham Street home.

For background on the Salt Lake Theater and the Clawson role in it, see Young (1960); Carter (1940); Pyper (1928); and Ellsworth (1974), pp. 51–53. The Utah State Historical Society also has a valuable collection of photos of the theater.

See Papers of Hiram B. Clawson, Box 1, Marriott Library, for correspondence re family matters.

For a discussion of the Mormon endowment ceremony, see Buerger (1987) and, for a more contemporaneous description, Bancroft (1890). The ceremony was from the beginning supposed to be kept secret, but apostates were soon describing it in detail.

See Richardson (1965, pp. 67–71) for background on Morgan Commercial College.

See Walker (1981) for a description of the activities of the Wasatch Literary Association.

See Hilton (1972), pp. 132–33, for a discussion of dancing among the pioneer Saints; also Bitton (1977).

See Arrington and Bitton, (1979), pp. 214 and 228, and Walker (1981) for background on the MIAs.

See Arrington and Bitton (1979), p. 174, for Brigham Young's comments on the railroad.

For background on John W. Young and the railroads, see Hilton (1972), pp. 116–35; Bishop (1980) and Arrington (1966), p. 290.

See the *New York Evening Post* 17 March 1875 for an article on the floundering Utah Western.

A description of Brigham Young's funeral can be found in Arrington (1985), pp. 399–401.

For the story of ZCMI and H.B. Clawson's relationship to it, see Arrington (1966), pp. 248–49 and 298–314; Taylor (1976, pp. 228–30; Tullidge (1866), p. 725; and "Hiram B. Clawson," (1881), pp. 680–82.

For a description of Rudger's return home with Joseph Standing' body, see *Deseret News*, 1 August 1879; *Salt Lake Daily Herald*, 5 August 1879; and Richardson (1965), p. 237.

Rudger's account of the trail appears in Memoirs, pp. 70–80; see also Driggs (forthcoming); Nicholson (1886), pp. 54–75; Richardson (1965), pp. 235–40; *Deseret News*, 3 November 1879, 5 November 1879, and 12 November 1879; and *Atlanta Constitution*, 23 October 1879.

Rudger's experiences in working for Spencer Clawson appear in the Memoirs, pp. 15a–15d. He disposes of his courtship of and marriage to Florence on a single page of his Memoirs (p. 85)!

For background on Henry Dinwoody, see Lester (1979), p. 176; Whitney (1892), Vol. IV, p. 253; Tullidge (1886), p. 151.

Samuel Spencer gives his delightful description of Lydia's tribulations in a letter to Lydia Clawson Hoopes, 1957, (authors' collection).

Information on Daniel Spencer is derived from "Life Sketch of Daniel Spencer, Jr." (n.d.) and "Amelia Spencer," (1931, University of Utah Library); and from Hilton, pp. 62–103.

Lydia Spencer Clawson, "A Small Sketch of Lydia Spencer Clawson," (authors' collection) provides background on Lydia's youth.

EXCERPTS & QUOTATIONS FROM RUDGER CLAWSON'S WRITINGS
M. = Memoirs

*Page*
34   "He wooed her . . ." M. p. 4
39   "I myself made . . ." M. p. 10
41   "He crossed the . . ." M. p. 2
42   "Early in life . . ." M. p. 22
45   "not because of . . ." M. p. 4 and pp. 16–17
47   "In 1869, my . . ." M. pp. 9–10
48   "To reside, temporarily . . ." M. pp. 11–12
49   "I was transfixed . . ." M. p. 27
50   "I rushed down . . ." M. p. 27
54   "It was not long . . ." M. pp. 74–75
54   "The man whom . . ." M. p. 75
55   "The honorable (?) judge . . ." M. p. 7
56   "While acting as . . ." M. p. 84½
56   "The jury in . . ." M. p. 79
58   "One evening . . ." M. p. 84
62   "Removing our engagement . . ." M. p. 85
62   "My words greatly . . ." M. p. 86


## Chapter Three: The Trial

Much of the information on the movements and activities of Rudger and Lydia before the trial is derived from testimony at the trial. That testimony and other information about the trial is taken from reports appearing in the *Deseret News*, 15 April to 3 November 1884, and from a scrapbook of clippings (now at the University of Utah Library) kept by Lydia during a period of time lasting from approximately the date of the indictment to after all the appeals were denied. They cover the period 25 April to 1 June 1885. The large majority came from the *Salt Lake Herald* and consist of exhaustive daily accounts of the progress of the trial and testimony. For background on the politics of the time, see Gustive O. Larson, *The "Americanization" of Utah for Statehood* and Richard S. Van Wagoner, *Mormon Polygamy: A History.* Also see D. Michael Quinn's "LDS Church Authority and New Plural Marriages" and his forthcoming book, *Polygamy among the Mormons: A Social History.*

See Whitney (1892), Vol. III, pp. 278–79 for comments on the Clawson trial.

See Larson (1971), pp. 106–7; Alexander (Fall 1966) and Whitney (1892, Vol. IV) for information on Zane, Dickson, Varian, and Richards.

See Larson, (1971), pp. 96–97, for Taylor's reaction to the Edmunds Law.

See Taylor (1976), pp. 309–10 (including footnotes) for an interesting interpretation of what the implications of Taylor's testimony were. This interpretation—which suggests that in his testimony Taylor was deliberately laying the groundwork for dispersing the authority to perform plural marriages so as to frustrate federal investigation—is disputed by other historians.

During the trial a number of versions of the phrase Rudger used in his reply to Caine were introduced, including "That's what they tell me," "I've heard them say so," and simply "They say so." "So they say" seems to the authors the most likely to be accurate.

See Whitney (1892), Vol. III, p. 21, for information on the women who were imprisoned during the judicial crusade.

## Chapter Four: Prison

This chapter is based primarily on the description of Rudger Clawson's prison experiences as recounted in his Memoirs, pp. 90–266, and on the letters he wrote from prison to Lydia during the period of his confinement (now in the University of Utah Library). Much additional information on life in the penitentiary at that time can be found in an appendix to John Nicholson's *The Martyrdom of Joseph Standing,* pp. 79–160; in M. Hamlin Cannon, "The Prison Diary of a Mormon Apostle;" in William C. Siefrit, "The Prison Experiences of Abraham H. Cannon;" in Melvin L. Bashore, "Life behind Bars: Mormon Cohabs of the 1880s;" and in William Mulder, "Prisoners for Conscience Sake."

See *Salt Lake Herald,* 15 November 1884, for Rudger's reference to *Paradise Lost.*

Rudger's comment on the profanity and depravity he encountered can be found in the *Herald,* 15 November 1884.

Nicholson (1886), pp. 91–98, gives an especially good account of the meals at the pen. See M. Hamlin Cannon (1947) for the relationship between Rudger and Abraham Cannon.

See Siefrit (1985) for the carbolic acid episode.

Siefrit (1985), p. 232, provides information on Tresedor while Nicholson (1886), pp. 100–101, discusses "the dead line."

See Whitney (1899), Vol. III, p. 323, for a mention of Joseph Evans.

Lydia described to her daughter many years later her conflict with Florence.

See Taylor (1976) p. 378, for comments on Florence.

See the *Herald,* 24, May 1885, for the less biased description of Callahan.

See Whitney (1892), Vol. III, p. 339, for mention of Ireland's refusal to let Nicholson visit his father.

See Nicholson (1896), p. 90, for author's assessment of Warden Dow.

See Bashore (1979) for statistics on the bug population of the penitentiary.

Rudger smuggled letters out to Lydia each of his years in prison, though most were written during two principal periods. The first was from July to December 1885 (though there were several undated letters that may have been written earlier than July) and included fifteen letters. The second period ran from 13 May to 6 September 1887 and included ten letters. Only four letters were written in 1886. All the letters are in the Rudger Clawson collection at the University of Utah Library. Also in the collection is a letter to Spencer, sent via Lydia, requesting that he provide financial support for her.

For information on the new interpretations of the Edmunds Law and their effect on Angus Cannon, see Larson (1971), pp. 111–12, 115–16; and Tullidge (1886), p. 138. See Whitney (1892), Vol. III, pp. 330–31, for his comment on the effort the government was making to apprehend Mormon leaders.

See Allen (1980) and Van Wagoner, pp. 123–24, for a discussion of the Bishop Sharp case.

See Whitney (1892), Vol. III, pp. 424–25, for a colorful pro-Mormon account of Hiram's conviction.

Larson (1971), pp. 128–29, has a good account of the segregation doctrine.

Cannon's negative reaction to Snow is recounted in Cannon and O'Higgins (1911), p. 216.

For background on Lorenzo Snow, see biographs by Romney (1955) and Gibbons (1982). These are both more or less faith-promoting biographies and should not be taken as definitive studies.

Background on the intensification of the crusade can be found in Cresswell (1985); Larson (1971), pp. 115–38; Van Wagoner (1986), pp. 119–24.

Background on Caleb West's accession to the governorship can be found in Larson (1971), pp. 81–89, 129–30; Whitney (1892), Vol. III, p. 354.

Background on Frank Dyer appears in Whitney (1890), Vol. III, p. 282.

Lydia's account of Dyer's kindness to her appears in "A Small Sketch of Lydia Spencer Clawson" (authors' collection).

Allen (1980) decribes the efforts that were made in Washington to obtain Rudger's pardon.

### EXCERPTS & QUOTATIONS FROM RUDGER CLAWSON'S WRITINGS
M. = Memoirs

*Page*

| | |
|---|---|
| 94 | ". . . a strange and . . ." M. pp. 92–93 |
| 95 | ". . . wore away very . . ." M. p. 95 |
| 95 | "At 9:00 o'clock . . ." M. pp. 95–96 |
| 102 | "I was now . . ." M. pp. 113–14 |
| 103 | "His remarks were . . ." M. p. 115 |
| 104 | "All at once . . ." M. p. 137 |
| 105 | ". . . constant stream of . . ." M. pp. 121–22 |
| 106 | "Mr. Warden . . ." M. p. 122 |
| 106 | "I was perfectly . . ." M. pp. 144–52 |

110   "A man could . . ." M. p. 13
115   "The prison authorities . . ." M. p. 152
115   "Their fury knew . . ." M. p. 152
116   "One man of . . ." M. p. 153
119   ". . . day of lights . . ." M. p. 11
122   "The brethren exerted . . ." M. p. 176
125   "To know him . . ." M. p. 222
125   "I am twenty-nine . . ." M. pp. 237–38
127   ". . . he would send . . ." M. pp. 222–23
129   ". . . the fatal day . . ." M. pp. 246–48
131   "Mr. Brown . . ." M. pp. 264–66

## Chapter Five: Stake President: Brigham City

Rudger wrote his diaries between 1 May 1891 and 21 December 1905, a period of fourteen years, but at the beginning of the first diary—which is called "Journal" by the University of Utah Library—he summarizes his life from the time he left prison in mid-December 1887 to the time he actually started writing in May 1891. The Journal runs to 2 March 1892, at which time the diaries begin. Most of this chapter is based on the Journal and the Diaries up to October 1898, at which time Rudger became an apostle. The Journal and Diaries are different documents from the Memoirs, which give a great deal of attention to certain events in his life (the Joseph Standing murder, his prison experience, and his term as European mission president) but neglect others. His description of the Brigham City years appears in his Memoirs on pages 276–367, but fail to record many of the most important events.

In the design of the LDS church, wards—where congregations meet for worship in ward meeting houses (a phrase Mormons use as a substitute for "churches")—are presided over by bishops. The wards are grouped together in larger units or "stakes" which are presided over by presidents, who have two counselors; combined, the president and counselors are called the "stake presidency." This structure reflects the arrangement at the pinnacle of church authority where the president of the church and his two counselors are collectively called the "First Presidency." There is also a president of the Quorum of the Twelve Apostles (a position Rudger later filled for many years) separate from the First Presidency and a number of other presidential positions, including a Council of the Seventy (responsible in particular for overseeing missionary activity) with seven presidents. The result is a profusion of church officials who may formally be addressed as "president," which may be confusing to non-Mormons.

An account of Rudger's early days in Brigham City appears in the Memoirs, pp. 276–89 and the Journal, pp. 1–64.

Reference to Rudger's lack of "welcome" in Brigham City appears in a letter to Rudger Clawson from Lorenzo Stohl dated 10 November 1938 (authors' collection) and the *Improvement Era*, March 1937, "When Box Elder Imported Rudger Clawson." Clearly it did not simply refer to the failure to meet the train.

For background on Box Elder and Brigham City see *History of Box Elder County* and *Through the Years*. See also Arrington, Fox, and May (1976) for an excellent discussion of the economic development of Brigham City. See Arrington (1966), pp.

324–25, for the context of the Mormon economy in which Snow's Brigham City experiment played an important part.

See Gibbons (1982), p. 160, for Brigham Young's perception that Oliver Snow would be receptive to counsel.

The $600 allowance Rudger began receiving shortly after his arrival in Brigham City was provided under a new general church policy which not only authorized payments to stake authorities but shifted control over tithing and the allocation of tithing funds to them from the ward bishops (see *Messages of the First Presidency*, Vol. III, p. 163). Apparently some bishops were keeping more of the tithing funds for their wards than was authorized.

See *History of Box Elder County*, p. 46, for information on the shoe factories in Brigham City and how the gravel uses up a "pair of understandings."

There are many accounts of the Mormon confrontation with the federal government during the late 1880s. See Arrington and Bitton (1979), pp. 181–84; Larson (1971), pp. 115–63 and 207–51; Poll, et al. (1978), pp. 243–74; Taylor (1976) pp. 354–85.

For a description of the statehood efforts by the Mormons and the effect Rudger's speech had on them, see Edward Leo Lyman (1986), especially, pp. 61–92; see also Van Wagoner (1986), p. 137.

Elliott F. Sanford is quoted in Arrington and Bitton pp. 182–83.

There are many accounts of the events leading up to the issuance of the Manifesto. See Quinn (1982), pp. 32–49; Larson (1971), pp. 251–59; Van Wagoner (1986), pp. 132–33; Poll, et al. (1978), pp. 257–74; Edward Leo Lyman (1986), pp. 168–69; Alexander (1986), pp. 6–9; and Taylor (1978), pp. 41–48.

The story of the waterworks is seen here wholly through Rudger's eyes as he recorded it in his diaries during the period from April 1892 to May 1893.

See N. Lee Smith (1979) for background on the "Ordinance of the Lord's House" and the personal attitude of Mormons toward sickness, faith, and medicine. In his Memoirs, pp. 331–32, Rudger refers to Section 42 of the *Doctrine and Covenants*, verses 48–51, as the source of his belief in the ordinance.

Ellan Jensen's story is taken from an article by LeRoi C. Snow in the *Improvement Era* which is copied verbatim into Rudger's Memoirs, pp. 310–30.

References to developments in Rudger's family and his relationships to family members appear in his diaries, especially during the period from November 1892 to September 1893.

The identification of Snow and Clawson as kindred spirits appears in Gibbons, pp. 190–91.

For background on the Hunsaker family, see Hunsaker and Haws (1957).

The Honeyville story is told in the diaries from January to June 1894 and in the Memoirs from pages 335–44, though in the latter he fails to identify the nature of the issue (the accusations against Lorenzo Hunsaker) and withholds the names of those involved (Bishop Tolman is referred to as Bishop Brown). The interview with George Q. Cannon regarding the matter appears in the Memoirs rather than the diaries.

A description of Rudger's rebuilding of the Brigham City Tabernacle appears in his diaries from February 1896 to March 1897 and in the Memoirs, pp. 289–309. See also *Through the Years* (1953).

The article from the *Brigham Bugler*, describing the Box Elder float is dated 25 July 1888 and is clipped and pasted to a page of the diaries.

EXCERPTS & QUOTATIONS FROM RUDGER CLAWSON'S WRITINGS

M. = Memoirs
J. = Journal
D. = Diaries

*Page*
133 "Just prior to . . ." J. p. 1
134 "Right now, this . . ." M. p. 276
135 "It was a bright . . ." M. p. 277
135 "So I was . . ." J. p. 4
137 ". . . the choice of . . ." J. p. 6
137 "Having learned the . . ." M. p. 278
138 "The sum total . . ." M. p. 288
139 "I, myself, did . . ." J. p. 41
143 "I was convicted . . ." J. p. 23
146 ". . . resorted to dishonest . . ." J. p. 58
147 ". . . had the honor . . ." J. p. 56
149 ". . . counseled the brethren . . ." D. 6/6/91
150 "They were busily . . ." D. 4/16/92
151 ". . . a grand mistake . . ." 5/19/92
152 "In view of . . ." D. 5/29/92
152 "It was the . . ." D. 1/10/93
152 "A few days . . ." D. 5/2/93
154 "The brethren in . . ." D. 11/5/92
155 "The nature and . . ." D. 12/13/92
156 "Those who have . . ." M. p. 331
156 "The ordinance of . . ." D. 5/3–4/93
158 "Those who are . . ." D. 12/10/92
158 "There is power . . ." D. 6/30/97
160 ". . . and as you surmise . . ." D. 12/10/92
162 "Keep full and . . ." D. 12/13/96
166 "I do not want . . ." D. 1/30/94
167 "It appeared certain . . ." M. p. 340

## Chapter Six: The Apostle

Much of Chapter Six is based on Rudger's diaries dated from October 1898 to January 1901.

See Gibbon (1982), pp. 211–12, for Snow's comments on his advancing age.

See *History of Box Elder Stake*, p. 51, for Lorenzo's receipt of the telegram announcing Woodruff's death.

For Snow's encounter with Jesus see quote from LeRoi Snow in Emerson Roy West (1980), p. 140.

Definition of the Twelve comes from *Doctrine and Covenants* 107:33.

The *Salt Lake Tribune* called Rudger one of the best-known men in Utah on 10 October 1898 (clipping pasted into Rudger's diary at that date).

Woodruff's lamentations about church finances is quoted in Arrington and Bitton

(1976), p. 250, who also, on p. 249, refer to the mismanagement by the government of the escheated property of the church.

See Cannon and O'Higgins (1911), pp. 205–15, for an account of what happened to the proposal Frank and his father had made regarding church finances; see also Arrington (1966), p. 30 and footnote Chapter One, n. 103, for a clear and succinct discussion of the trustee-in-trust concept and function.

Rudger deals with his years of responsibility for the church books in a brief eight pages in his Memoirs, pp. 381–3. He records the same events off and on in his diaries over a period of a number of years.

For an account of Lorenzo's trip to St. George where he inaugurated his tithing campaign, see LeRoi Snow, as quoted in Doxey (1976), p. 13. See also Allen and Leonard (1976), p. 450.

For background on the law of consecration, see Doctrine and Covenants: 42, 85, 119, 120: also Arrington and Bitton (1979), p. 250, and Arrington (1966), p. 9.

For clarification of the significance of Jackson County, see Allen and Leonard (1976), pp. 87–88.

The conflicting statements on polygamy made by Merrill and Lyman are recorded in Rudger's diaries (see also Van Wagoner (1986), p. 149, for a quote from Merrill's diary) as having occurred during meetings on 11–12 July 1899. Lorenzo Snow's statement on the subject was made at a meeting on 4 December 1899.

For background on the B. H. Roberts' case see Bitton (1957); Madsen (1980), p. 266; and Arrington (1979), p. 245.

See Arrington (1966), p. 399, and Cannon and O'Higgins (1911), p. 223, for information on E. W. McCune, Heber J. Grant, and the Democratic senatorial nomination in 1899.

Background on salaries received by and the economic status of the apostles may be found in Alexander (1986), p. 100; and Quinn (1976), p. 128–32.

The occasion on which Frank Cannon called the church leaders "Financial Apostles" is described in Cannon and O'Higgins (1911), p. 224.

For background on Reed Smoot and the sugar trust see Alexander (1986), p. 79, and Arrington (1966), pp. 407–8. The Will Rogers quote is from the Salt Lake Tribune 5 August 1929 as quoted in M. R. Merrill (1950), p. 383.

See N. Lee Smith (1979) for G. Q. Cannon's quotation from Juvenile Instructor.

Rudger's account of the pleasure he had in reporting in May 1901 to Snow that the debt would be retired by 1904 appears in Memoris, pp. 385–86.

For background on Francis Lyman, see Albert R. Lyman (1958) and Anderson (1901).

See Alexander (1986), p. 99, for an indication of the problems that still existed in the administration of church finances in 1901.

Much of the information concerning Rudger Clawson that appears in the latter part of this chapter is drawn from his diaries dated January 1902 to December 1905. Another valuable source is "In a Vacumn" [sic] the reminiscences of Lydia Spencer Clawson's daughter, Lydia Clawson Hoopes (authors' collection). Information about the marriage between Rudger and Pearl Udall was provided in letters by historian D. Michael Quinn and verbally confirmed by members of the Udall family. See also the Pearl Udall letters in the Udall Collection, University of Arizona Library. Valuable background informatin on David K. Udall and his family was also obtained from Arizona Pioneer Mormon: David King Udall by David King Udall with Pearl Nelson Udall.

For background on Reed Smooth see M. R. Merrill (1950), p. IV–VIII, 7–93.

For background on the drive for statehood and the political conflict involving B. H. Roberts, Moses Thatcher, and other church leaders, see Edward Leo Lyman (1985), pp. 78–88 and Madsen (1980), p. 221–27.

Snow's comments on the president and Congress being "our children" appears in Rudger's diary, 17 January 1901.

See Pusey (1981), p. 187, for an indication of the advice Smith received against approving Smoot's senatorial candidacy.

See McCormick and McCormick (1985), pp. 19–54, for background on Saltair.

It is uncertain whether or not it was Pearl whom Rudger, after his second trip to Arizona, cited as having expressed herself in favor of plural marriage. She was twenty-three at the time rather than eighteen. Rudger may have been a very bad judge of age in women or Pearl may have looked younger than she was (which her photo indicates may well have been true). The speaker may also have been one of the other members of the group he mentions, who was expressing feelings with which Pearl agreed—or Rudger may have deliberately given the wrong age to obscure what was taking place (his effort to marry her polygamously) in case anyone was curious enough to inquire.

The information on the post-Second Manifesto marriage of David K. Udall was provided in a letter from D. Michael Quinn.

Evidence that Reed Smoot only slowly moved toward opposition to polygamy is indicated by an entry appearing in Rudger's journal of January 1902. When several of the apostles felt called upon at a council meeting to affirm their belief in plural marriage, Rudger wrote that Smoot spoke of his father's successful plural marriage and said that he [Smoot] felt that "this order of marriage, if universally practiced, would save the world much sorrow and distress [and he] looked for its restoration."

For background on the apostles involved in post-Manifesto marriages see Quinn (1982), Jorgensen and Hardy (1980), Van Wagoner (1986) pp. 157–90, Melvin Clarence Merrill (1937), pp. 362–93.

It is not known whether Rudger's request for Lydia's approval of taking a new plural wife was presented to Lydia in abstract terms or if he told her he was actually planning to take another wife. If the latter, then her quiet acquiescence seems to belie almost everything we know about Lydia.

Joseph F. Smith's statement before the Senate committee appears as quoted in Kenneth L. Cannon II (1983).

See M. R. Merrill (1950), pp. 41–120, for a description of the Smoot hearings.

The quotation from the Second Manifesto appears in Roberts (1965), p. 401.

The statement from Anthon Lund's journal of 6 April 1904 is quoted in Van Wagoner, p. 173.

EXCERPTS & QUOTATIONS FROM RUDGER CLAWSON'S WRITINGS

M. = Memoirs
J. = Journal
D. = Diaries

*Page*
172   "All the blessings . . ." D. 10/10/98
173   "If I could . . ." D. 10/10–11/98
175   "The order of . . ." M. p. 379
177   "Greatly surprised and . . ." M. p. 381

178    "Brother Jack came . . ." D. 10/14/1900
181    ". . . we have come . . ." D. 6/12/99
182    "The time for . . ." D. 7/2/99
182    "If you will . . ." D. 8/20/99, 10/7/99, and 10/19/99
184    "This substance is . . ." D. 11/3/99
185    ". . . that the time . . ." D. 7/11/99
185    "Apostle Lyman made . . ." D. 7/11–12/99
185    "Many honorable Americans . . ." D. 12/4/99
187    "After some discussion . . ." D. 3/8/1900
188    "We recognize an . . ." D. 3/21/1900
189    ". . . enrolled in the . . ." D. 4/8/1900
191    ". . . he regretted to . . ." D. 4/21/99
192    "President Smith expressed . . ." D. 7/2/03
196    ". . . great wickedness. I . . ." D. 10/16/1900
198    "*Salt Lake City* . . ." D. 12/26/1900
198    "I was engaged . . ." D. 3/22/99
199    ". . . is suffering from . . ." D. 6/2/1900
200    "It is the purpose . . ." D. 9/24/02
201    ". . . great pleasure in . . ." D. 4/4/1900
202    ". . . if that is . . ." M. pp. 385–86
202    ". . . deep and abiding . . ." J. p. 7
203    "as soon as . . ." D. 4/14/99
204    "Hist, my brother . . ." D. 11/9/88
204    "I remembered that . . ." D. 10/9/01
205    ". . . 13 of these . . ." D. 10/13/01
206    "Verily, we live . . ." D. 10/25/01
206    "I thought over . . ." D. 12/10/01
206    "During Brother Jack's . . ." D. 3/31/02
207    "Apostle J. H. Smith . . ." D. 4/8/1900
209    "His [Smoot's] duty . . ." D. 1/17/01
210    "The rooms are . . ." D. 2/8/02
212    "The problem was . . ." D. 7/10/01
212    "almost a total . . ." D. 6/25/03
212    ". . . a strong effort . . ." D. 6/11/03
213    "The legislature is . . ." D. 1/10/03
214    "Elder Smoot arose . . ." D. 1/29/03
215    "A very select . . ." D. 8/20/03
216    "Notwithstanding the fact . . ." D. 8/21/03
219    "He bore testimony . . ." D. 10/1/03
220    "While there I . . ." 10/30–31/03
220    "I was engaged . . ." D. 11/6/03
220    "I spent the . . ." D. 12/19/03

## Chapter Seven: Crises at Midlife

Information on Rudger Clawson between May 1904 and December 1905 comes mainly from his diaries encompassing those dates. Events surrounding the crises that occurred between him and Lydia and information on Lydia's life during the years

1903 to 1910 are illuminated by "In a Vacumn [sic]," reminiscences of Lydia Clawson Hoopes (authors' collection) and by personal recollections she recounted to her sons (the authors) during her lifetime. Some details on Rudger Remus Clawson's life during 1904 come from his diary (University of Utah Library). Information on Pearl Udall comes from *Arizona Pioneer: David King Udall* by David King Udall and Pearl Udall Nelson and from the Pearl Udall Letters (University of Arizona Library). Matthew Cowley's diary, which might confirm the date and place of the marriage of Rudger and Pearl, is held by the Mormon church and is not available to researchers.

For comments on Cowley's personality see Taylor (1978), p. 83.

The agreement Rudger and Lydia drew up regarding their finances begins, "An agreement entered into this 23rd [number handwritten in] day of Aug. 1904 between Rudger Clawson, the party of the first part, and Lydia S. Clawson, party of the second part. Witness: that the party of the first part . . ." and so on. It was to continue in force for three years and longer if mutually agreeable, with a six-month notification period of any change. It ends "Witness our hands this 23rd day of August 1904."

For background on the Mormon painters who studied in Paris during this period see Siefrit (1986).

After 4 October 1904 most of Rudger's diary entries on council meetings read, "I attended a meeting of the Presidency and the Twelve to consider some matters of importance"—occasionally they were of "vital importance."

For background on John Taylor and Matthew Cowley see Jorgensen and Hardy (1980); Quinn (1982); Van Wagoner (1986), pp. 129–31 and 188–89; and Samuel Taylor (1978) pp. 129–31.

Information on Pearl's movements from 1905 to 1910 come from Udall and Nelson (1959), Pearl's letters (University of Arizona Library), and Udall family members.

One of the errors appearing in Rudger's Memoirs (because he, apparently, did not consult his diaries when composing them) dates the burning of the Brigham City Tabernacle as "one day early in 1888." The fire actually occurred on 9 February 1896.

Lydia's contact with astrologers, numerologists, and others who offered her dubious advice is documented in miscellaneous typescripts in the papers of Lydia Clawson Hoopes (authors' collection).

H.B.'s comments at the 1920s celebration (the purpose of which is not entirely clear, though it had to be either a birthday or an anniversary) appear in a typescript in the papers of Lydia Clawson Hoopes.

## EXCERPTS & QUOTATIONS FROM RUDGER CLAWSON'S WRITINGS

M. = Memoirs
D. = Diaries

*Page*
225   "I came home . . ." D. 5/2/04
225   "We had a . . ." D. 5/16/04
229   "Pres. Smith said . . ." D. 10/5/04
233   "I had a . . ." D. 6/23/03
233   ". . . accompanied by Rudger . . ." D. 10/6/04
234   "He was a . . ." D. 11/18/04
241   "The journey . . . was . . ." M. p. 396

## Chapter Eight: Mission President: Liverpool

Most of the information about Rudger Clawson's activities as head of the European Mission are derived from the "European Mission Report made by Elder Rudger Clawson—June 10, 1910 to May 1913" and from the voluminous correspondence he carried on during that time (University of Utah Library).

For background on the British Mission see Richard L. Evans's *A Century of Mormons in Great Britain*. See Whitney (1888) for information on Heber C. Kimball and the opening of the mission. For British anti-Mormonism during the time Rudger was there, see Malcolm R. Thorpe's excellent articles "The Mormon Peril: The Crusade against the Saints in Britain, 1910–1914" (1975) and "Winifred Graham and the Mormon Image in England" (1979). Clawson's mission report includes extensive excerpts from the *Millennial Star* and a number of British newspapers as well as both personal and business correspondence. See *Doctrine and Covenants*, Section 118, for Joseph Smith's revelation regarding sending his apostles on missions abroad.

See Arrington and Bitton (1979) for information on the appeal of Mormonism and its "Mythic potency" (pp. 127–40); for Lorenzo Snow's description of how a missionary should present himself (pp. 37–38); and for the quotation from the *London Examiner* on Evarts's attempt to enlist the support for Europeans to cut off the flood of immigrants (p. 137).

For background on Hans Peter Freece and his activities in Britain, see Thorp (1975).

For information on Winston Churchill's actions relative to the Mormons, see Manchester (1983) pp. 414ff.

See Thorp (1975 and 1979) for more on Winifred Graham.

Information about the renovation of the Sunderland Chapel and the incident with the knife was obtained from interviews with LDS church officials in Sunderland in May 1986.

Pearl Udall's poignant concerns about her marriage to Rudger are expressed in a letter from London to her parents dated 19 October 1912 (Udall family papers).

EXCERPTS & QUOTATIONS FROM RUDGER CLAWSON'S WRITINGS
M. = Memoirs
RC = Rudger Clawson
Report = European Mission Report

*Page*
246    "Strange as is . . ." RC to Arthur Winter 6/20/10
248    "It rained steadily . . ." M. p. 396
248    ". . . the affairs of . . ." RC to J. F. Smith 6/15/10
249    ". . . the work goes . . ." RC to Francis Lyman 9/20/10
249    "I hesitate in . . ." RC to J. F. Smith 10/4/10
250    ". . . a kind of . . ." RC to Heber J. Grant 10/3/11
250    ". . . did what he . . ." RC to J. F. Smith and counselors 8/8/11
251    ". . . the biggest city . . ." RC to E. J. Wood 10/14/10
251    "My time is . . ." RC to J. McMurrin 1/12/11
252    "We have introduced . . ." RC to Adolph Madson 1/11/11
257    "Dear Sir: In . . ." RC Report p. 42
259    "The charge that . . ." RC in *Milennial Star* 2/9/11

259    ". . . the Lord almost . . ." RC to First Presidency 1/26/11
260    "We don't need . . ." RC to First Presidency 2/2/11
265    "Those who lift . . ." Report pp. 82–82½
266    "It became apparent . . ." M. p. 427
266    "The only thing . . ." RC to First Presidency 6/1/11
267    "When we attempt . . ." RC to Joseph Eckersley 1/13/11
267    "This is the cry . . ." RC to J. F. Smith and counselors 8/3/11
268    ". . . it just as . . ." RC to J. F. Smith and counselors 8/3/11
268    "A cloud of . . ." RC to Charles W. Penrose 11/10/11
268    "I was in London . . ." RC to Peter F. Madson 2/4/11
269    "I wish I . . ." RC to Lydia Clawson 10/27/11
270    "The closing years . . ." RC to J. F. Smith and counselors 2/12/12
270    "I had hoped . . ." RC to J. F. Smith and counselors 4/2/12
271    "The work in . . ." RC to Charles Hurt 1/31/12
271    "You will notice . . ." RC to J. F. Smith and counselors 3/5/12
271    "We have a . . ." RC to J. F. Smith and counselors 3/26/12
272    "So strongly am . . ." RC to F. Lyman and Council of the Twelve 12/20/10
272    ". . . and the woman . . ." Minutes of meeting at Durham House 9/1/10
273    "If, under the . . ." RC to George Albert Smith 3/15/12
273    "The devil is . . ." RC to First Presidency 5/20/12 and Report p. 101ff
273    "We have acquired . . ." RC to First Presidency 4/19/12 and Report p. 110
274    "It is not . . ." RC to E. Brown 5/29/12
274    "We fear that . . ." M. pp. 405–06
276    "No, thank you . . ." M. p. 409
276    "The anti-Mormon . . ." RC to First Presidency 6/7/12
277    "I can hardly . . ." RC to Seymour Young 4/24/12
277    "It nearly took/a rummy lot . . ." RC to Lydia Clawson 4/12/12
278    "I took occasion . . ." RC to Samuel Clawson 8/23/12
281    "Unfortunately, President Clawson . . ." M. p. 460
281    ". . . he used to . . ." RC to Charles Primrose 1/27/13
282    ". . . a great falling . . ." Report p. 156
282    "I am happy . . ." RC to Charles Nibley 1/16/13
        "Shall I continue . . ." RC to J. F. Smith and counselors 3/18/13
283    "I've learned by . . ." RC to J. F. Smith and counselors 3/28/13 and M. p. 488
284    "You ought by . . ." RC to "My Dear Niece" 5/1/12
284    ". . . not be in . . ." RC to Samuel Clawson 3/22/13
285    "It will perhaps . . ." RC to George Albert Smith 12/17/12
285    "It is true . . ." RC to J. F. Smith and counselors 8/13/11
286    "Just in proportion . . . RC in *Millenial Star* 1/23/13 and Report p. 129½

## Epilogue: President of the Twelve

As indicated earlier, some of the information on the marriage of Pearl and Rudger is derived from research the results of which will appear in D. Michael Quinn's forthcoming book on Mormon plural marriage. At this writing, the University of Arizona is establishing a repository for Udall family papers. Among these papers is an extensive collection of correspondence between Pearl and her parents.

See D. Michael Quinn's forthcoming book on Mormon plural marriage for background on the actions and attitudes of Anthony Ivins and Joseph F. Smith regarding post-Second Manifesto plural marriages. See the same source for background on Heber S. Grant's management of the cancellation of post-Second Manifesto plural marriages. In a letter to the authors, Professor Quinn suggested that when President Grant assured Joseph Nelson that Rudger and Pearl's marriage had been cancelled he may not have been aware that it had occurred after the Second Manifesto. He cancelled a number of plural marriages during these years and did not always determine the precise date on which they had taken place.

See Roberts (1965) pp. 538–40, for a description of the 1923 centennial conference.

See the *Deseret News*, 17 July 1915, for a report on Rudger's visit to Georgia in 1915; and the *Deseret News*, 13 December 1919, and 30 May and 16 June 1921, for reports of his trips to Hawaii.

For the commentary by Samuel Clawson on his father, see Samuel Clawson (1937).

See John Henry Evans (1943), p. 411, for Evans's comments on Rudger.

See *President Rudger Clawson's Seventieth Birthday Celebration*, for Rudger's latter-day testimony to the truth of the doctrine of plural marriage.

Information about the events which took place after the funeral of Lydia Clawson comes from notes taken by Lydia Clawson Hoopes at the time (authors' collection) and personal recollections of Lydia Clawson Hoopes recounted to her children.

See Richard L. Evans (1942) for Evans's comments at the time of Rudger's eighty-fifth birthday.

For background on Mormon literal-mindedness see Cummings (1982) and Arrington and Bitton (1979), p. 30.

J. Reuben Clark's inquiries into his faith are recounted in Quinn (1983), pp. 24–25.

Rudger's comment to the council that he would no longer be able to attend meetings and the response by J. Reuben Clark 20 May 1943, appear in typescript dated 20 May 1943 (authors' collection).

See Widtsoe (1937) for John A. Widtsoe's tribute to Rudger.

### EXCERPTS & QUOTATIONS FROM RUDGER CLAWSON'S WRITINGS
RC = Rudger Clawson

*Page*
289    "It completely knocked . . ." RC to R. W. Eardley 6/30/13
289    "It is a chaste . . ." RC to elders of British Mission 11/6/13
289    "Sister Clawson was . . ." RC to James Foggo 5/13/13
292    "I still believe . . ." *President Rudger Clawson's Seventieth Birthday Celebration* (1927)
296    "The weather was . . ." RC to Lydia Clawson Hoopes 9/4/41

# BIBLIOGRAPHY

Alexander, Thomas G. "Charles S. Zane, Apostle of a New Era." *Utah Historical Quarterly* 34 (Fall 1966): 290–314.

————. "Federal Authority versus Polygamic Theocracy: James B. McKean and the Mormons 1870–1875." *Dialogue* 1 (Autumn 1966): 85–100.

————. "To Maintain Harmony: Adjusting to External and Internal Stress, 1890–1930." *Dialogue* 15 (Winter 1982): 44–58.

————. *Mormonism in Transition: A History of the Latter-day Saints, 1890–1930.* Urbana and Chicago: University of Illinois Press, 1986.

Allen, James B. " 'Good Guys' vs. 'Good Guys': Rudger Clawson, John Sharp, and Civil Disobedience in Nineteenth-century Utah." *Utah Historical Quarterly* 48 (Spring 1980): 148–74.

Allen, James B. and Glen M. Leonard. *The Story of the Latter-day Saints.* Salt Lake City: Deseret Book Co., 1976.

Andersen, Nels. *Desert Saints: The Mormon Frontier in Utah.* Chicago: University of Chicago Press, 1942.

Anderson, Edward H. "Apostle Francis M. Lyman." In *Lives of our Leaders,* 107–24. Salt Lake City: Deseret News, 1901.

Arrington, Leonard J. *Great Basin Kingdom: Economic History of the Latter-day Saints, 1830–1900.* Lincoln and London: University of Nebraska Press, 1966.

————. *Brigham Young: American Moses.* New York: Alfred A. Knopf, 1985.

————, ed. *The Presidents of the Church.* Salt Lake City: Desert Book Co., 1986.

Arrington, Leonard J., and Davis Bitton. *The Mormon Experience: A History of the Latter-day Saints.* New York: Random House, 1979.

Arrington, Leonard J., Feramorz Fox, and Dean L. May. *Building the City of God: Community and Cooperation among the Mormons.* Salt Lake City: Deseret Book Co., 1976.

Bancroft, Hubert Howe. *History of Utah.* San Francisco: The History Company, Publishers, 1890.

Bashore, Melvin L. "Life behind Bars: Mormon Cohabs of the 1880s." *Utah Historical Quarterly* 47 (Winter 1979): 22–41.

"Biographical Sketch of Rudger Clawson." *Browne's Photographic Monthly and Reporters' Journal* 1 (June 1884): 1.

Bishop, M. Guy. "Building Railroads for the Kingdom: The Career of John W. Young, 1867–91." *Utah Historical Quarterly* 48 (Winter 1980): 66–80.

Bitton, Davis. "The B. H. Roberts Case of 1898–1900," *Utah Historical Quarterly* 25 (January 1957): 27–46.

———. "These Licentious Days: Dancing among the Mormons," *Sunstone* 2 (Spring 1977): 16–27.

Box Elder Chapter of the Sons of Utah Pioneers. *Box Elder Lore of the Nineteenth Century.* Brigham City, UT: Box Elder Chapter of the Sons of Utah Pioneers, 1951.

Box Elder County Daughters of the Pioneers. *History of Box Elder County 1851–1937.* Brigham City, UT: Box Elder County Daughters of the Pioneers, 1937.

Brodie, Fawn M. *No Man Knows My History: The Life of Joseph Smith the Mormon Prophet.* New York: Alfred A. Knopf, 1945.

Buerger, David John. "The Development of the Mormon Temple Endowment Ceremony." *Dialogue* 20 (Winter 1987): 33–76.

Campbell, Eugene E. *Establishing Zion: The Mormon Church in the American West, 1847–1869.* Salt Lake City: Signature Books, 1988.

Cannon, Frank J. and Harvey J. O'Higgins. *Under the Prophet in Utah: The National Menace of a Political Priestcraft.* Boston: C. M. Clark Publishing Co., 1911.

Cannon II, Kenneth L. "After the Manifesto: Mormon Polygamy 1890–1906." *Sunstone* 8 (January–April 1983): 27–35.

Cannon, M. Hamlin, ed. "The Prison Diary of a Mormon Apostle." *Pacific Historical Review* 16 (November 1947): 393–409.

Carter, Kate B., ed. *Heart Throbs of the West.* Salt Lake City: Daughters of Utah Pioneers, 1940.

———. *History of Drama in the West.* Daughters of Utah Pioneers Historical Pamphlet, November 1941.

Chamberlin, Ralph V. *The University of Utah: A History of Its First Hundred Years, 1850–1950.* Salt Lake City: University of Utah Press, 1960.

Clark, James R., comp. *Messages of the First Presidency*, Vols. 3 and 4. Salt Lake City: Bookcraft, Inc., 1966, 1970.

Clawson, Margaret Gay Judd. "Rambling Reminiscences of Margaret Gay Judd Clawson." Parts 1–4. *Relief Society Magazine* 6 (1919): 257–62; 317–27; 391–400; 474–9.

Clawson, Rudger. "In My Youthful Days." *Children's Friend* 41 (April 1942): 148–9.

Clawson, Samuel G. "Some Impressions of My Father." *Improvement Era* 40 (March 1937): 142–3, 168.

Cresswell, Stephen. "The U.S. Department of Justice in the Utah Territory, 1870–90." *Utah Historical Quarterly* 53 (Summer 1985): 205–22.

Cummings, Richard J. "Quintessential Mormonism: Literal-Mindedness As a Way of Life." *Dialogue* 15 (Winter 1982): 92–101.

Daughters of Utah Pioneers of Salt Lake County. *Tales of a Triumphant People: A*

*History of Salt Lake County, Utah, 1847–1900.* Salt Lake City: Daughters of Utah Pioneers of Salt Lake County, 1947.

*Doctrine and Covenants of the Church of Jesus Christ of Latter-day Saints.* Salt Lake City: Church of Jesus Christ of Latter-day Saints, 1971.

Doxey, Roy W. *Tithing: The Lord's Law.* Salt Lake City: Deseret Book Co., 1976.

Driggs, Ken. " '. . . There Is No Law in Georgia for Mormons': The 1879 Murder of Joseph Standing and the Trial of His Killers." *Georgia Historical Quarterly* (Forthcoming, 1989).

Edmonds, George F. "Political Aspects of Mormonism." *Harper's Magazine* 64 (January 1882): 285–286.

Ellsworth, S. George. *Dear Ellen: Two Mormon Women and Their Letters.* Salt Lake City: Tanner Trust Fund, University of Utah Library, 1974.

Embry, Jessie L. *Mormon Polygamous Families.* Salt Lake City: University of Utah Press, 1987.

Evans, John Henry. "Rudger Clawson." *Instructor* 78 (August 1943): 411.

Evans, Richard L. *A Century of "Mormonism" in Great Britain.* Salt Lake City: Publishers Press, 1984.

———. "President Rudger Clawson: Who Has Continued Long in Good Works." *Improvement Era* 45 (March 1942): 138, 189.

Firmage, Edwin Brown, and Richard Collin Mangrum. *Zion in the Courts: A Legal History of the Church of Jesus Christ of Latter-day Saints, 1830–1900.* Urbana and Chicago: University of Illinois Press, 1988.

Foster, Lawrence. *Religion and Sexuality: Three American Communal Experiments of the Nineteenth Century.* New York: Oxford University Press, 1981.

Furniss, Norman F. *The Mormon Conflict 1850–1859.* New Haven: Yale University Press, 1960.

Gibbons, Francis M. *Heber J. Grant: Man of Steel, Prophet of God.* Salt Lake City: Deseret Book Co., 1979.

———. *Joseph F. Smith: Patriarch and Preacher, Prophet of God.* Salt Lake City: Deseret Book Co., 1984.

———. *Lorenzo Snow: Spiritual Giant, Prophet of God.* Salt Lake City: Deseret Book Co., 1982.

Hansen, Klaus J. *Mormonism and the American Experience.* Chicago and London: University of Chicago Press, 1981.

Hill, Donna. *Joseph Smith: The First Mormon.* Garden City, NY: Doubleday, 1977.

Hilton, Lynn M., ed. *The Story of Salt Lake Stake, 1847–1972.* Salt Lake City: Salt Lake Stake, 1972.

Hinckley, Bryant S. "The Youth and Early Manhood of Rudger Clawson." *Improvement Era* 40 (March 1937): 134–7.

"Hiram B. Clawson." *Tullidge's Quarterly Magazine* 4 (1881): 678–84.

*History of Box Elder County: 1851–1937.* Brigham City, UT: Box Elder County Daughters of the Pioneers, 1937.

Hulse, Irene. *From Rags to Riches*. Toole, UT: Toole Transept Co., 1964.

Hunsaker, Q. Maurice, and Given Hunsaker Haws, eds. *History of Abraham Hunsaker and His Family*. Salt Lake City: Hunsaker Family Organization, 1957.

Ireland, Hugh. "With President Clawson in Europe." *Improvement Era* 40 (March 1937): 152–3, 167.

Ivins, Stanley S. "Notes on Mormon Polygamy." *Western Humanities Review* 10 (Summer 1956): 229–39.

Jackson, Richard H. "Great Salt Lake and Great Salt Lake City: American Curiosities." *Utah Historical Quarterly* 56 (Spring 1988): 128–47.

Jensen, Lucinda P. *History of Bear River City*. Brigham City, UT: Box Elder News-Journal, 1947.

Jorgensen, Victor W., and B. Carmon Hardy. "The Taylor-Cowley Affair and the Watershed of Mormon History." *Utah Historical Quarterly* 48 (Winter 1980): 4–36.

*Journal of Discourses*. 26 vols. Liverpool. Published by various presidents of the LDS British Mission, 1854–86.

Keller, Charles L. "Promoting the Railroads and Statehood: John W. Young." *Utah Historical Quarterly* 45 (Summer 1977): 308.

Larson, Gustive O. *The "Americanization" of Utah for Statehood*. San Marino, CA: The Huntington Library, 1971.

———. "The Mormon Reformation," *Utah Historical Quarterly* 26 (January 1958): 45–63.

Lee, S. Norman. "When Box Elder 'Imported' Rudger Clawson." *Improvement Era* 40 (March 1937): 146–7, 166.

Lester, Margaret D. *Brigham Street*. Salt Lake City: Utah State Historical Society, 1979.

Linford, Orma. "The Mormons and the Law: The Polygamy Cases." *Utah Law Review* 9 (Winter 1964/Summer 1965): 308–70, 543–91.

Lyman, Albert R. *Francis Marion Lyman: Apostle*. Delta, UT: Melvin A. Lyman, 1958.

Lyman, Edward Leo. "The Alienation of an Apostle from His Quorum: The Moses Thatcher Case." *Dialogue* 18 (Summer 1985): 67–91.

———. *Political Deliverance: The Mormon Quest for Utah Statehood*. Urbana and Chicago: University of Illinois Press, 1986.

Madsen, Truman G. *Defender of the Faith: The B. H. Roberts Story*. Salt Lake City: Bookcraft, 1980.

Manchester, William. *The Last Lion*. Boston: Little, Brown, 1983.

McAllister, D. M. *The Great Temple*. Salt Lake City: Bureau of Information, 1914.

McCormick, Nancy D., and John S. McCormick. *Saltair*. Salt Lake City: University of Utah Press, 1985.

Merrill, Melvin Clarence, ed. *Utah Pioneer and Apostle, Mariner Wood Merrill and His Family*. n.c.; n.p., 1937.

Merrill, M. R. "Reed Smoot, Apostle in Politics." Ph.D. diss. Columbia University, 1950.

Mulder, William. "Prisoners for Conscience Sake," in Thomas E. Cheney, ed., *Lore of Faith and Folly*. Salt Lake City: University of Utah Press, 1971.

Newell, Linda K. and Valeen T. Avery. *Mormon Enigma: Emma Hale Smith*. Garden City, NY: Doubleday, 1984.

Nicholson, John. *The Martyrdom of Joseph Standing*. Salt Lake City: Deseret News, 1886.

Nielsen, Vaughn J., and Centennial Committee, comps. *The History of Box Elder Stake*. Brigham City, UT: Church of Jesus Christ of Latter-day Saints, 1977.

Poll, Richard D., Thomas G. Alexander, Eugene E. Campbell, and David E. Miller, eds. *Utah's History*. Provo, UT: Brigham Young University Press, 1978.

Pusey, Merlo J. *Builders of the Kingdom*. Provo, UT: Brigham Young University Press, 1981.

Pyper, George D. *The Romance of An Old Playhouse*. Salt Lake City: Seagull Press, 1928.

Quinn, D. Michael. *The Mormon Hierarchy, 1832–1932: An American Elite*. Ph.D. diss. Yale University, 1976.

———. "LDS Church Authority and New Plural Marriages, 1890–1904." *Dialogue* 15 (Winter 1982): 9–105.

———. *J. Reuben Clark: The Church Years*. Provo, UT: Brigham Young University Press, 1983.

———. "From Sacred Grove to Sacral Power." *Dialogue* 17 (Spring 1984): 9–34.

———. *The Mormon Hierarchy: A Group Biography of Middle-Class Power*. (Tentative title; forthcoming).

———. *Polygamy among the Mormons: A Social History*. (Tentative title; forthcoming).

Richards, LeGrand. *A Marvelous Work and a Wonder*. Salt Lake City: Deseret Book Co., 1979.

Richardson, Arthur. *The Life and Ministry of John Morgan*. n.c.: Nicholas G. Morgan, Sr., 1965.

Roberts, B. H. *A Comprehensive History of the Church of Jesus Christ of Latter-day Saints, Century I*. 6 vols. Provo, UT: Brigham Young University Press, 1965.

Romney, Thomas C. *The Life of Lorenzo Snow*. Salt Lake City: Sugarhouse Press, 1955.

"Salt Lake Illustrated." Salt Lake City: S. W. Drake and Co., circa 1887.

Shipps, Jan. "Utah Comes of Age: Politics in the Early Twentieth Century." *Utah Historical Quarterly* 35 (Spring 1967): 91–111.

Siefrit, William C. "The Prison Experience of Abraham H. Cannon." *Utah Historical Quarterly* 53 (Summer 1985): 223–36.

———. "Letters from Paris." *Utah Historical Quarterly* 54 (Spring 1986): 179–202.

Smith, N. Lee. "Herbal Remedies: God's Medicine." *Dialogue* 12 (Fall 1979): 37–60.

Smith, Ruby K. *One Hundred Years in the Heart of Zion: A Narrative History of the Eighteenth Ward.* Salt Lake City: Deseret News Press, 1961.

Snow, LeRoi C. "A Matter of History." *Improvement Era* 40 (March 1937): 149.

Spencer, Clarissa Young, and Mabel Harmer. *Brigham Young at Home.* Salt Lake City: Deseret Book Co., 1972.

Sperry, Sidney B. *Doctrine and Covenants Compendium.* Salt Lake City: Bookcraft, 1960.

Stanley, Lawrence L. *Little History of Gilmer County.* Ellijay, GA, 1975.

Talmadge, James E. *The House of the Lord: A Study of Holy Sanctuaries, Ancient and Modern.* Salt Lake City: Deseret Book Co., 1968.

Taylor, Samuel W. *The Kingdom or Nothing: The Life of John Taylor, Militant Mormon.* New York: Macmillan, 1976.

——. *Rocky Mountain Empire: The Latter-day Saints Today.* New York: Macmillan, 1978.

Thorp, Malcolm R. " 'The Mormon Peril': The Crusade against the Saints in Britain, 1910–1914." *Journal of Mormon History* 2 (1975): 69–88.

——. "Winifred Graham and the Mormon Image in England," *Journal of Mormon History* 6 (1979): 107–21.

*Through the Years: Eighth Ward.* Booklet. Brigham City, UT: Members of Eighth Ward Building Committee, 1953.

"Tributes to President Rudger Clawson." Presiding Councils of the Church. *Improvement Era* 45 (March 1942): 139.

Tullidge, Edward W. *The History of Salt Lake City and Its Founders.* Salt Lake City: Edward W. Tullidge, (circa 1886).

Udall, David King, with Pearl Udall Nelson. *Arizona Pioneer Mormon: David King Udall, His Story and His Family, 1851–1938.* Tucson, AZ: Arizona Silhouettes, 1959.

Van Wagoner, Richard S. *Mormon Polygamy: A History.* Salt Lake City: Signature Books, 1986.

Walker, Ronald W. "Growing Up in Early Utah: The Wasatch Literary Association 1874–1878." *Sunstone* 6 (November/December 1981): 44–51.

Ward, George Gordon. *The Annals of Upper Georgia Centered in Gilmer County.* Nashville: Parthenon Press, 1965.

Watkins, Floyd, and Charles Hubert Watkins. *Yesterday in the Hills.* Athens, GA: University of Georgia Press, 1973.

West, Emerson Roy. *Profiles of the Presidents,* rev. ed. Salt Lake City: Deseret Book Co., 1980.

West, Ray B., Jr. *Kingdom of the Saints: The Story of Brigham Young and the Mormons.* New York: Viking Press, 1957.

White, George. *Historical Collections of Georgia.* Atlanta: n.p., 1954.

Whitfield County Historical Commission. *Official History of Whitfield County, Georgia*. Dalton, GA: A. J. Showalter Co., 1936.

Whitney, Orson F. *Life of Heber C. Kimball*. Salt Lake City: Kimball family, 1888.

———. *A History of Utah*. 4 vols. Salt Lake City: George Q. Cannon & Sons, 1892.

Widtsoe, John A. "Rudger Clawson's Service in the Council of the Twelve." *Improvement Era* 40 (March 1937): 140–1.

Wilson, George O. *Today and Tomorrow Become Yesterday*. Official souvenir book. Dalton, GA: Dalton-Whitfield County Commission, 1976.

Young, Kimball. *Isn't One Wife Enough?* Westport, CT: Greenwood Press, 1954.

Young, Levi Edgar. "Theater in the Wilderness." *Salt Lake Tribune Home Magazine* 26 June 1960.

———. "Drama in the Desert." *Salt Lake Tribune Home Magazine* 3 July 1960.

———. "On the Stage and in the Pit." *Salt Lake Tribune Home Magazine* 10 July 1960.

# MANUSCRIPTS

Authors' collection, Vershire, Vermont. Hoopes Family Papers.

Clawson, Lydia Spencer. "A Small Sketch of Lydia Spencer Clawson." n.d. Handwritten.

Hoopes, Lydia Clawson. "In a Vacumn [sic] "—Reminiscences, n.d. Typewritten.

———. Letters.

Marriott Library, University of Utah, Salt Lake City, Utah. Papers of Hiram B. Clawson.

Clawson, Hiram B. Letters.

Marriott Library, University of Utah, Salt Lake City, Utah. Papers of Rudger Clawson.

Clawson, Rudger. "Memoirs of the Life of Rudger Clawson Written by Himself." Salt Lake City, 1926. Photocopied typescript.

———. Diaries. Brigham City and Salt Lake City, April 3, 1892 to December 21, 1905. Handwritten/typewritten.

———. "European Mission Report Made by Elder Rudger Clawson—June 10, 1910 to May 1913." Typewritten.

———. Journal. December 13, 1887 to March 28, 1892. Brigham City. Handwritten.

———. Letters.

———. President Rudger Clawson's Seventieth Birthday Celebration. Typescript.

———. September 12, 1906 (Poems). Handwritten.

Clawson, Rudger Remus. Diary, 1904. Handwritten.

"Life Sketch of Daniel Spencer, Jr." n.d. Mimeographed.

"Reminiscences of Hiram B. Clawson." Notes taken by Fred Barker, March 1912. Photocopied typescript.

Spencer, Amelia. "Sketch of the Lives of Daniel Spencer and His Wife Mary Jane Cutcliffe." Salt Lake County, 1931. Mimeographed.

Spencer, Daniel. "Biography of Daniel Spencer." n.d. Mimeographed.

University of Arizona Library, Tucson, Arizona. Udall Family Papers.

Udall, Pearl. Letters.

## NEWSPAPERS

*Atlanta Constitution*, Atlanta, Georgia

*Brigham Bugler*, Brigham City, Utah

*Dalton Headlight*, Dalton, Georgia

*Deseret News*, Salt Lake City, Utah

*New York Evening Post*, New York, New York

*Salt Lake Daily Herald*, Salt Lake City, Utah

*Salt Lake Tribune*, Salt Lake City, Utah

# INDEX

anti-Mormonism
  in England, 265, 269, 272–276, 280–286
  in Georgia, 17–19
  in prison, 103, 104–105, 106–108, 126–127
  in United States, 36, 65–66, 70, 99, 121–126, 131
  in Utah, 141–148
anti-polygamy movement, 63, 65–66, 69, 70, 99–100, 113, 121, 141–148
Arthur, Chester A., 63
Articles of Faith, 16
Auer, Mary Jane Cutcliffe Spencer, 59–60, 76, 80
Auer, Ulrich, 59

Bailey, Pearl, 251, 277, 300
Bailey, Queen, 22
Banks, "Nosey," 123
baptism, 17
Bartlett, Rev. Daniel H. C., 254–256, 274
Battle of Chickamauga, 5, 16
Beehive House, 42
Bennett, C. W., 71, 75, 76
Biddlecome, John, 101, 102
Blaine, James G., 147
Blair, Hugh, 29, 55, 56
Book of Mormon, 14, 16
Box, E. A., 134, 136, 149–153, 166
Box Elder Stake, 120, 133, 140, 146, 148, 204
Bradley, Andrew, 25, 26, 29, 55
Bridger, Jim, 136
Brigham City, 133, 134–137, 139, 162

Brigham City Roller Mill Company, 160–161, 198
Brown, Otis L., 126–127
Bryant, Jack, 100

Caine, James E., 68, 73, 80, 82, 87
Caine, John T., 33, 68, 131, 142
Callahan, Pat, 103
Cannon, Abraham, 104, 228–229
Cannon, Angus, 45, 100, 107
Cannon, Frank J., 153, 155, 176, 190, 253
Cannon, George Q., 2, 53, 79–80, 121, 141, 147, 153, 162, 167, 172, 173, 176, 192, 199–200, 201, 204, 220–221, 228–229, 232
Catoosa Springs Resort, 28–29
celestial marriage, 35, 292
Chicago World's Fair, 157–158
Church of Jesus Christ of Latter-day Saints: at time of Rudger's apostleship, 175; and business, 51, 137, 191–193; concept of heaven, 34–35; on dancing, 45; defiance of Congress, 81, 82; and Edmunds Act, 71; and Edmunds-Tucker Act, 141, 145; finances, 176, 177–179, 201–202; General Conference, 2; journals of leaders, 229; missionaries of, 2, 244–245; on polygamy, 9, 11, 34–35, 81, 121, 141–148, 218, 220–223, 227; and Reed Smoot, 207–209; Reformation, 35–36; and Saltair Beach, 211–212; Salt Lake Temple dedicated, 162–163;

325